Quim Monzó and
Contemporary Catalan Culture (1975–2018)
Cultural Normalization, Postmodernism and
National Politics

LEGENDA

LEGENDA is the Modern Humanities Research Association's book imprint for new research in the Humanities. Founded in 1995 by Malcolm Bowie and others within the University of Oxford, Legenda has always been a collaborative publishing enterprise, directly governed by scholars. The Modern Humanities Research Association (MHRA) joined this collaboration in 1998, became half-owner in 2004, in partnership with Maney Publishing and then Routledge, and has since 2016 been sole owner. Titles range from medieval texts to contemporary cinema and form a widely comparative view of the modern humanities, including works on Arabic, Catalan, English, French, German, Greek, Italian, Portuguese, Russian, Spanish, and Yiddish literature. Editorial boards and committees of more than 60 leading academic specialists work in collaboration with bodies such as the Society for French Studies, the British Comparative Literature Association and the Association of Hispanists of Great Britain & Ireland.

The MHRA encourages and promotes advanced study and research in the field of the modern humanities, especially modern European languages and literature, including English, and also cinema. It aims to break down the barriers between scholars working in different disciplines and to maintain the unity of humanistic scholarship. The Association fulfils this purpose through the publication of journals, bibliographies, monographs, critical editions, and the MHRA Style Guide, and by making grants in support of research. Membership is open to all who work in the Humanities, whether independent or in a University post, and the participation of younger colleagues entering the field is especially welcomed.

ALSO PUBLISHED BY THE ASSOCIATION

Critical Texts
Tudor and Stuart Translations • *New Translations* • *European Translations*
MHRA Library of Medieval Welsh Literature

MHRA Bibliographies
Publications of the Modern Humanities Research Association

The Annual Bibliography of English Language & Literature
Austrian Studies
Modern Language Review
Portuguese Studies
The Slavonic and East European Review
Working Papers in the Humanities
The Yearbook of English Studies

www.mhra.org.uk
www.legendabooks.com

STUDIES IN HISPANIC AND LUSOPHONE CULTURES

Studies in Hispanic and Lusophone Cultures are selected and edited by the Association of Hispanists of Great Britain & Ireland. The series seeks to publish the best new research in all areas of the literature, thought, history, culture, film, and languages of Spain, Spanish America, and the Portuguese-speaking world.

The Association of Hispanists of Great Britain & Ireland is a professional association which represents a very diverse discipline, in terms of both geographical coverage and objects of study. Its website showcases new work by members, and publicises jobs, conferences and grants in the field.

Founding Editor
Trevor Dadson

Editorial Committee
Chair: Professor Catherine Davies (University of London)
Professor Stephanie Dennison (University of Leeds)
Professor Sally Faulkner (University of Exeter)
Professor Andrew Ginger
(New College of Humanities at Northeastern University)
Professor James Mandrell (Brandeis University, USA)
Professor Hilary Owen (University of Manchester/University of Oxford)
Professor Philip Swanson (University of Sheffield)
Professor Jonathan Thacker (Exeter College, University of Oxford)

Managing Editor
Dr Graham Nelson
41 Wellington Square, Oxford OX1 2JF, UK

www.legendabooks.com/series/shlc

STUDIES IN HISPANIC AND LUSOPHONE CULTURES

Quim Monzó and
Contemporary Catalan Culture
1975–2018

*Cultural Normalization, Postmodernism
and National Politics*

❖

GUILLEM COLOM-MONTERO

l

LEGENDA

Studies in Hispanic and Lusophone Cultures 45
Modern Humanities Research Association
2021

Published by Legenda
an imprint of the Modern Humanities Research Association
Salisbury House, Station Road, Cambridge CB1 2LA

ISBN 978-1-78188-392-1 (HB)
ISBN 978-1-78188-395-2 (PB)

First published 2021

Copy-Editor: Dr Ellen Jones

CONTENTS

❖

To Helena

Vila de Gràcia, Barcelona, 20 d'agost de 2011

ACKNOWLEDGEMENTS

❖

Writing this book has been a journey of personal and intellectual transformation shared by many friends and colleagues who have played a very important role. The book is partly based on my doctoral thesis, and I would like to thank my supervisor Jordi Cornellà-Detrell and co-supervisor Eva Bru-Domínguez for their guidance and support during my PhD study. I am extremely grateful to the colleagues who have read and commented on earlier drafts: Helena Buffery, Rebecca Butler, Billy Grove, Danielle Hipkins, Louise Johnson and John London. My heartfelt thanks to Sally Faulkner for her encouragement with this project, to Margalida Pons for her intellectual generosity and to my late editor Trevor Dadson for his unstinting kindness in supporting early career scholars. For their academic mentorship, I wish to thank Barbara Burns, Dominic Keown, Bernadette O'Rourke and Ulrike Zitzlsperger.

I am grateful to Quim Monzó for responding so generously to my queries, for granting me the rights to reproduce figures of Chapters 1 and 2 and for choosing the book's cover painting and granting me the rights to reproduce it – thanks are also due to its author, Ramon Enrich. An earlier version of Chapter 5 was published in the *Bulletin of Hispanic Studies* and I would like to thank them for granting me permission to reproduce the material in this book ('Men in Crisis: Pornographic Images in Quim Monzó's Fiction', *Bulletin of Hispanic Studies* 93.5 (2016): 549–65).

I consider my academic research as an integral part of my life and, for this reason, I wish to thank several friends across different geographies who have been a hugely inspiring force. A big, heartfelt thanks to David Pujol, Nando Sabaté and Antoni Trobat for their life-long friendship, fierce intelligence and stimulating political conversations with me, which have been pivotal to my personal and intellectual development over the years – gràcies per ser-hi sempre, bergants! For all the time spent together cooking good food, drinking nice wine and discovering Goggled Cymru, I thank Paolo Basetti, Phil Davies, Hugh Jones, Maureen McCue, Alexander Sedlmaier and Lorena Souto. Many thanks to Silvia Espelt and Tomi Bartole, my Exeter family, whom I miss so much, and to Rick Lechowick for our political discussions in various Devon pubs and for having read this manuscript with his characteristic intellectual curiosity. I am also grateful to Ana Antic, Carl-Henrik Bjerström, Nuria Capdevila-Argüelles, Danielle Hipkins, Ina Linge and Muireann Maguire for welcoming me into their lives with kindness and generosity when I arrived in Exeter. Thank you very much to my *Glaswegian* friends Rhys Machold, Toni Marzal, Antonio García-Muñoz, Vera Pavlou, Meha Priyadarshini, Ana Santamarina and Vladimir Unkovski-Korica, with whom I shared so many walks in Glasgow's West End during the May-July 2020 post-lockdown period, when I was finalizing the book.

El meu agraïment més gran per als meus pares Ofèlia i Guillem pel seu suport constant, la seva infinita generositat i, sobretot, per ensenyar-me que la vida o és comunitària o no val la pena ser viscuda, i també per al meu germà Francesc per la seva energia i positivitat, i per ajudar-me sempre a considerar la realitat des d'una perspectiva diferent.

Finalment, aquest llibre està dedicat, com no podia ser d'altra manera, a n'Helena, qui és part integral d'allò que sóc avui dia.

Guillem Colom-Montero, January 2021

LIST OF FIGURES

❖

INTRODUCTION

❖

Quim Monzó, 1975–2018:
From Counterculture to the Catalan Canon

'— Xisca Ensenyat: Quina és la nostra mancança més castrant?
— Quim Monzó: La mancança d'Estat.'
[— Xisca Ensenyat: What is our most castrating deficiency?
— Quim Monzó: The lack of a State.]
Interview in *Los Cuadernos de Baleares*, 15 July 1984 (Ensenyat 1984: 11).

'No sóc gens nacionalista, però no sóc espanyol.'
[I'm not a nationalist at all, but I'm not Spanish.]
Interview in *Avui*, 31 March 1985 (Guillamon 1985: 5).

On 4 June 2018, Quim Monzó received the *Premi d'Honor de les Lletres Catalanes*, Catalan literature's most prestigious award. Instituted by the association Òmnium Cultural in 1969, the annual prize is granted to recognize the career of literary authors and scientists whose work in the Catalan language has made a significant contribution to the cultural and intellectual life of the Catalan Countries. In contrast to the forty-nine previous editions, in which the award had been bestowed by the President of Òmnium Cultural, in 2018 Monzó did not receive the prize from the cultural organization's president, Jordi Cuixart. Cuixart could not attend the ceremony because he was jailed in Madrid's Soto del Real prison, awaiting trial on charges of sedition owing to his role in orchestrating pro-independence protests on 20 September 2017. In his speech at Barcelona's Palau de la Música, Quim Monzó, himself a lifelong supporter of Catalonia's independence, denounced Cuixart's imprisonment in his characteristically non-weighty, deadpan manner. Monzó recounted his early-teenage years in Francoist Barcelona, when he used to read and write in order to evade himself from 'el món que m'envoltava, el règim claustrofòbic que regia el país i els meus pares' [the world that surrounded me, the claustrophobic regime that ruled the country and my parents] (*Vilaweb* 2018). In his youth, he used to borrow books from the mobile library service *Bibliobús* managed by the Provincial Deputation of Barcelona and which stopped at Plaça de Sants. Monzó continued to say that, at the time, he did not know that the first Catalan *Bibliobús* was established by the Mancomunitat de Catalunya in the 1910s, or that the Catalan Government consolidated the service during the Republican years. Nor did he know that the final journey of one of these *Bibliobuses* took place on 23 January 1939, when the Francoist troops were closing in on the city of Barcelona.

The *Bibliobús*'s last days were spent transporting Catalan authors Mercè Rodoreda, Joan Oliver, Francesc Trabal and Armand Obiols to exile in France. The fact that a bus meant to offer books to the population was driving writers to exile 'és un retrat nítid del que hem viscut al llarg de la història, i del que vivim encara ara' [offers a clear picture of what we have experienced throughout our history, and we still experience today], Monzó added, establishing a connection between Catalonia's past and present (*Vilaweb* 2018). He concluded his speech wondering whether Catalans would soon need another *Bibliobús* 'perquè les persones (siguin o no escriptors) puguin escapar de la injustícia, de l'opressió, de la tirania' [so that people (whether they're writers or not) can escape from injustice, oppression, tirany] (*Vilaweb* 2018). Monzó's lecture is not only testimony to the turbulent times that the relationship between Catalonia and Spain is going through at the moment, but also of the central impact of national politics on twentieth- and twenty-first century Catalan culture. This emerges crystal-clear when such words are delivered by the author who has been credited with having detached Catalan literature from the realm of the politico-symbolic after the death of the dictator, General Francisco Franco, in 1975.

The relations between Catalonia and Spain were significantly different eleven years earlier, in 2007, when Catalan Culture was the Guest of Honour at the Frankfurt Book Fair and Quim Monzó delivered the opening speech, in what is considered as one of the peaks of his career. The tone and content of Monzó's lecture were also remarkably different. Conceived as a short story, Monzó's speech condensed his authorial trademarks of humour, irony and parody as well as intertextuality and metafiction. Specifically avoiding patriotic or sentimental exaltation, Monzó's lecture stood in stark contrast to the address given by the prominent Catalan cellist and composer Pau Casals at the United Nations New York headquarters in 1971, which is still considered a paramount example of an international public speech by a Catalan personality. Exiled throughout the Francoist period, Casals delivered a solemn nationalist speech in which he asserted that Catalonia 'has been the greatest nation in the world' and that it 'had the first parliament, much before England' (Casals 1971). While in both instances Casals and Monzó were presenting Catalonia to an international audience, the political and sociocultural contexts were entirely different. Casals delivered his speech during Francoism, when the very existence of Catalan culture was under threat. By contrast, Monzó's address took place in 2007, when the link between Catalan culture and national identity was not so prevalent as a result of the consolidation of Catalonia's autonomy and the rise of postmodern and market values in the Catalan cultural field. This partly explains why Casals and Monzó addressed the audience from two radically different perspectives. Casals's address is a fine example of the traditional narratives of resistant cultures, whereas Monzó ostensibly parodied the conventions of discourses of national self-aggrandisement and even engaged in an exercise of parodic intertextual playfulness with Casals's address: 'Va ser un discurs que va emocionar els catalans amb la mateixa intensitat que va deixar indiferents la resta d'habitants del planeta' [It was a speech that moved Catalans with the same intensity that left the rest of the planet's inhabitants unmoved] (Monzó 2007). Received with high praise in Catalonia, Monzó's speech, and by extension his career, came to symbolize a new, postmodern Catalan culture, which had unquestionably left behind the dark times of Francoism and the associated discourses of cultural resistance (Bargalló 2008: 48; Cònsul 2008: 130; Galves 2008: 81; Puigdevall 2008: 101). Few could imagine at the time that ten years later the Spanish Government would take direct control of Catalonia's political institutions after the Generalitat de Catalunya organized an outlawed referendum of self-determination on 1 October 2017 and the Catalan Parliament declared independence from Spain by a narrow majority twenty-six days later.

This book analyses Quim Monzó's trajectory as a literary writer, artist and public intellectual in order to explore how his cultural production reveals and responds to the transformations experienced by contemporary Catalan culture since the early 1970s until the present day. The main objective of this monograph is to analyse the dynamic and contradictory interrelations between Quim Monzó's work and the discourses of Catalan cultural normalization. It argues that Monzó's literary and intellectual programme both accelerated and critically responded to the decline of the *resistentialist* cultural model and the advent of the discourses of Catalan cultural normalization under postmodernism and its associated framework of cultural marketization. This study analyses Quim Monzó's public trajectory, from countercultural artist in the mid-1970s to celebrity author and intellectual in the present day, as a phenomenon that has brought to the fore some of the contradictions in the discourses of Catalan cultural normalization vis-à-vis postmodernist attitudes towards the symbolic role of culture and the public intellectual in post-Francoist Catalonia. My book is founded on an interdisciplinary, cultural studies approach to the multiple interactions between one of Catalonia's most celebrated and influential living authors and the shifting cultural and socio-political context.

In the influential work *El malestar en la cultura catalana* (2008), Josep-Anton Fernàndez analyses how cultural normalization attempted to combine discourses and practices from two conflicting cultural paradigms: the modern and the postmodern. On the one hand, cultural normalization is defined by a nationalist programme based on the strong link between language, culture and identity. On the other, cultural normalization also embraces the postmodern tendency of cultural industrialization and marketization. Departing from Fernàndez's analysis, my book argues that, while Quim Monzó's cultural project has benefited from the opportunities for publication, promotion and dissemination offered by the cultural infrastructures developed under the aegis of cultural normalization, it has also moved beyond the parameters of cultural normalization, namely, by engaging with its main values, symbols and metanarratives through a postmodernist critical awareness thereof focused on (self-)parody and the challenging of the traditional link between Catalan culture and high cultural production. In other words, Quim Monzó's work has been exceptionally successful among the public and therefore has been received as a normalizing agent by the cultural field precisely because it has transcended, through a postmodernist cultural programme, the ideological boundaries established by the discourses of cultural normalization.

Quim Monzó's work is widely considered to have been a catalyst in the normalization process of Catalan culture after the fall of Francoism, at a time when there was a need to bring *resistencialisme* to an end and adapt literary projects to the new sociocultural and political situation. Critical studies of Monzó's work have generally remained within the parameters of cultural normalization, often focusing on the ways in which his literary production modernized the field in terms of expression and subject matter in line with changing sociocultural mores. They have also discussed postmodernist aesthetics in his fiction and contextualized his work predominantly within the Catalan literary tradition, while tending to avoid engaging with the political ideas underpinning it. Moreover, Monzó's critical reception has shown a tendency to concentrate on his post-1978 written outputs.

This monograph seeks to extend these critical perspectives through a focus on four key routes of inquiry. Firstly, it aims to emphasize the connections between Quim Monzó's work pre- and post-1978 with a view to showing the strong impact of the sociocultural and political debates of the 1970s in his trajectory. Secondly, I argue that any understanding of Monzó's oeuvre has much to gain from placing it within a transnational framework, particularly in relation to the impact of American cultural trends and political ideologies. Thirdly, this study takes up the often sidelined question of political ideologies informing Monzó's work by addressing the unremitting presence of a series of political themes and debates in it. More specifically, it explores the interrelations between Monzó's cultural production and national politics, gender and sexuality debates, as well as the American political philosophy of libertarianism. Finally, my book examines Quim Monzó's popular and influential profile as a public intellectual through the analysis of his work in mass and social media outlets, which this study analyses as mainstay material to shed light on how the author's trajectory has brought to the fore some of the main anxieties experienced by contemporary Catalan culture. Through a focus on these four main routes, I analyse some of the most compelling and least understood characteristics of Quim Monzó's literary and cultural project. Overall, this study proposes that the dynamic relation between author and context makes Quim Monzó's work an inexhaustibly rich perspective from which to chart the paradigmatic cultural shifts from Pau Casals's speech in 1971 to Monzó's lectures in 2007 and 2018, that is, the transitions from late Francoist to autonomous and post-referendum Catalonia.

The 1970s and 1980s: *Resistencialisme*, Counterculture/*Textualisme* and Cultural Normalization

Born in 1952 to a Catalan father and Andalusian mother in the working-class neighbourhood of Sants (Barcelona), Monzó experienced the effervescent social and cultural atmosphere of the port city during the early 1970s. Taking his first steps as an artist and literary writer, Monzó paid the rent by working as a graphic designer. Monzó's sociocultural and professional background is rather alien to the Catalan cultural and literary tradition (Ripoll 2010: 47), and he has capitalized on this marginal position throughout his career to profile himself as an outsider to a cultural field resistant to change. Monzó's debut publications, a series of travel chronicles, appeared in the newspaper *Tele/eXprés* and the magazines *Flashmen* and *Oriflama* in 1972 and 1973. Western cultural trends from the late 1960s and the relaxation of Francoist censorship, as well as an increased tolerance towards Catalan language publications, allowed for the emergence of innovative projects and discourses at the margins of official culture. *Resistencialisme*, the oppositional cultural model in place during Francoism, was based on the premise that Catalan language and nationalism were inextricable and that literary production was perhaps the vital weapon to wield against dictatorial oppression (Cornellà-Detrell 2011: 26). In Fernàndez's succinct formulation, at the time, 'el que estava en joc no era la reproducció, sinó la simple supervivència de la cultura catalana com a ordre institucional' [what was at stake was not the reproduction but the mere survival of Catalan culture as an institutional order] (2008: 110). However, during the late 1960s, *resistentialist* discourses and cultural practices began to be questioned by a generation of young authors and artists who proposed new, creative models and who divorced culture from the mission of nation-building (Picornell 2013: 34). In Kathryn Crameri's words, 'the authors of the 1970s lived in a postmodern age and an era of multiple possibilities, which stimulated the questioning of "absolutes"' (2000a: 9).

In Barcelona, the 1970s saw the rise of the countercultural movement, a blend of local anarchist influences and the American hippie movement championed by María José Ragué's *California Trip* (1971) and Luis Racionero's articles in *Ajoblanco* (1974–1980). In opposition to classical Marxist proposals, countercultural artists sought to transform society through individual changes by engaging in parallel with new forms of progressive politics (environmentalism, pacifism, anti-authoritarianism), whilst encouraging drug consumption and free sexuality through their lifestyles. Monzó's contributions to countercultural projects included experimental texts and comics that appeared in publications such as *El Viejo Topo, Qwert Poiuy: Revista de Literatura, Tecstual* and the emblematic *Ajoblanco*, to which he also contributed in 1974 by designing its first logo, inspired by Coca-Cola's iconic marketing style. In these artistic creations, Monzó reacted against 'l'estètica realista i l'academicisme i el pensament burgès reaccionari' [realist aesthetics, academicism and reactionary bourgeois thinking] (Maestre 2010: 237). If counterculture modernized social and cultural customs in Catalonia, *textualisme* challenged Catalan literary conventions through radical formal and ideological inspirations geared towards problematizing realist conventions of representation. *Textualisme* advocated new writing techniques in line with the poststructuralist and deconstructionist theories of Julia Kristeva, Roland Barthes and the magazine *Tel Quel* (Cònsul 1997; Pons 2007). In 1970s Catalonia, experimentalist authors attacked Marxist-inspired social realism, known as *realisme històric* in Catalan, the main literary paradigm in Catalan narrative during the 1950s and 1960s (Simbor 2005: 9–14). Margalida Pons remarks the central role played by experimental literature in the modernization of Catalan literature during the 1970s; it 'marca un punt d'inflexió en la literatura catalana per la incorporació de nous models culturals i ideològics, per la investigació de noves tècniques d'escriptura i per la problematització del mateix concepte de ficció' [marks a turning point in Catalan literature for the incorporation of new cultural and ideological models, the experimentation in new writings techniques and the problematization of the concept of fiction] (2007: 7). Quim Monzó's early literary texts are part of the Catalan experimentalist movement, specifically his debut novel *L'udol del griso al caire de les clavegueres* (1976) and the short story collection *Self-service* (1977). The latter featured eight short stories by Monzó and ten by Majorcan author Biel Mesquida, while the former won the *Premi Prudenci Bertrana de Novel·la* the year it was released. Monzó's sense of politico-cultural commitment at the time also materialized in the sixty-one political cartoons and collages that he published in the weekly cultural magazine *Canigó* between September 1976 and April 1978. These works strongly criticized the Spanish Transition to democracy as it was unfolding. By taking part in counterculture and *textualisme*, Quim Monzó started to build an authorial presence whilst opposing the previous tradition and experimenting with innovative cultural and literary creations. As Antoni Maestre aptly puts it:

> Monzó lidera una nova fornada d'autors que, en la dècada dels setanta, van abandonar el camí heretat de les generacions anteriors i en van emprendre d'altres, més conformes als nous temps i que recollien els canvis socials en la societat occidental originats a partir de la revolució sexual, l'alliberament de la droga, el laïcisme, les ideologies llibertàries, el flirteig amb les drogues i el consum de nous productes culturals de masses com la música pop i *rock* o el cinema. (Maestre 2006: 35–36. Italics in original)

> [Monzó led a new generation of authors who, in the 1970s, abandoned the path inherited from previous generations and set out on new ones, adapted to the new times and which incorporated the societal changes unfolding in the West: the sexual revolution, the normalization of drugs, secularism, libertarian ideologies, flirtation with drugs and the consumption of new mass cultural products such as pop, rock and cinema]

Monzó quickly dissociated himself from this experimental period. In an interview in April 1979, Monzó pointed to his disappointment with the sense of socio-political commitment and a belief in the transformative power of literature that his two earliest books displayed. When asked about *L'udol*, Monzó indicated that 'ara n'estic una mica allunyat, potser perquè me la creia força' [I feel quite detached from the novel now, probably because I strongly believed in it] (Figueres 1979: 19). Only four months after the Spanish Constitution was sanctioned by King Juan Carlos I, Monzó already circulated narratives of *desencanto* to justify his detachment from a series of works strongly connected to the tumultuous period of the Spanish Transition to democracy. For this reason, in his subsequent book, the short story collection *Uf, va dir ell* (1978), Monzó declared that, 'he tractat d'aplegar contes i narracions que fossin ben lluny de cap mena de compromís transcendent' [I have tried to collect short stories detached from any type of transcendent commitment] (Figueres 1979: 19). Monzó's disengagement from experimental literary and cultural creations reveals him as an author who wants to work on a project that incorporates certain characteristics from both counterculture and *textualisme*, while ultimately attempting to produce a different type of fiction, detached from the extreme experimentalism of previous works and aiming at a wider readership.

Quim Monzó's work was quickly adapting to the changing socio-political climate in Spain, characterized by the declining influence of radical political movements. For this reason, *Uf, va dir ell* has been considered an early example of cultural normalization.

Normalization is the cultural paradigm that was to become more prominent in Catalonia after the end of Francoism. One of the clearest and most succinct definitions of cultural normalization has been given by Sharon G. Feldman: 'the process of recuperation, revival, relegitimization, and institutionalization of Catalan cultural and intellectual life that began during the period of the Transition to democracy' (2015: 42).[1] The politics of cultural normalization were the new set of cultural discourses and institutional practices developed in Catalonia as soon as political autonomy was recovered in 1980. Normalization was based on the inextricable link between national identity, cultural nationalism and the Catalan language. For this reason, the politics of cultural normalization focused on increasing and consolidating the use of the Catalan language in all social, cultural and political areas, a process known as linguistic normalization. Analysing public policy in the period from 1980 to 2003, Crameri observes that normalization was the government cultural programme implemented by Convergència i Unió's governments (CiU). She regards CiU's cultural policy as a nation-building tool where language was a key factor of social inclusion in Jordi Pujol's modern, inclusive and civic form of nationalism (2008: 7–20). Analysing normalization as a cultural and ideological paradigm, Fernàndez remarks that the discourses of cultural normalization were initially defined as early as 1976 during the Congrés de Cultura Catalana (2008: 20). For him, cultural normalization had a triple dimension: first, it was a political project that carried on with the historical enterprise of institutionalizing Catalan culture; second, it was a process of sociocultural transformation aiming at neutralizing the detrimental impact of Francoist policies on Catalan language and culture; finally, it was the set of discourses that attempted to define Catalan identity as 'legítima i discursivament neutra' [legitimate and discursively neutral] in the Catalan context (2008: 25). In the early 1980s, this cultural programme faced a number of challenges, including: the institutionalization and legitimation of Catalan culture at the symbolic and material levels; the redefinition of Catalan culture in industrial terms through the incorporation of market values to the cultural field; the development of a book industry for Catalan culture by invigorating both the supply and demand of cultural products; the establishment of mass media in Catalan, with particular emphasis on audio-visual media; and the democratization of Catalan culture by reducing the elitist spirit of Catalan cultural works (Bru de Sala 1987: 97–105; Guifreu 1987: 30; Molas 1983: 146–47; Rubert de Ventós 1983: 157–77).

Quim Monzó's literary project is considered a key modernizing force in post-Francoist Catalan literature. His fictional texts have been widely considered exemplars of postmodernist fiction in Catalan literature (Guillamon 2004: 13; Illas 2007: 84–90; Maestre 2012c: 169). In *Narrativa Catalana de la postmodernitat* (2014) Jordi Marrugat describes Monzó as the 'narrador català postmodern més complet, popular i influent' [most popular, accomplished and influential Catalan postmodern author] (12). In Monzó's works, this surfaces in his depiction of alienated characters in late-capitalist urban settings, entangled in fictional plots that often revolve around material objects owing to the rise of consumerism in post-Francoist Spain (Balaguer 1997: 87; Bou 1988: 409; Calafat 1992: 76–79). These storylines are represented through a fragmented and hyperrealist literary style marked with metafictional, intertextual and often (self-)ironic references.

Monzó's literary and cultural work is credited with having led the transition from late Francoism to the democratic period, from *resistencialisme* to cultural normalization. These critical manoeuvres are summed up in Christian Camps and Jordi Gàlvez's assertion: 'Quim Monzó representa una nova i positiva imatge de la cultura catalana, lluny del resistencialisme del passat, plenament instal·lada en la normalitat d'avui' [Quim Monzó represents a new and positive image of Catalan culture, far from the *resistentialism* of the past and fully integrated in today's normality] (1998: 8). Informed by the discourses of cultural normalization, the reception of Monzó's fiction has tended to focus on how his literary project from *Uf, va dir ell* onwards modernized Catalan literary language and introduced themes adapted to the new sociocultural trends. Quim Monzó is depicted as a young author, who, in his quest for a personal literary voice, defied the preceding literary tradition and paradigms, which were no longer effective. As early as 1979, Dolors Oller observed that Monzó's colloquial language represented 'una realitat actual i convincent' [a contemporary and convincing reality] (1979: 93). In the seminal work *Història de la literatura catalana* (1988), edited by Martí de Riquer, Antoni Comas and Joaquim Molas, Enric Bou points out that Monzó's literary style was 'en lluita constant amb els purismes normatius i el corrector d'estil' [in a constant battle against linguistic purism and copy-editors] (1988: 407) and concludes that Monzó's work was already a model for other authors. A new sociocultural reality not only required an original literary style but also innovative topics, which Monzó's early 1980s fiction displayed superbly. Born in 1967, Jordi Puntí remarks that, thanks to Monzó's literary fiction during the 1980s, a new generation of authors realized that they could narrate their own experience in the Catalan language (2010: 72). Together with *Uf, va dir ell*, works such as the novel *Benzina* (1983) and the short story collections *Olivetti, Moulinex, Chaffoteaux et Maury* (1980) — awarded the *Premi de la Crítica Serra d'Or* in 1981 — and *L'illa de Maians* (1985) spoke to a young generation whose lifestyles and interests were completely different from that of their parents. For instance, *Benzina*, revolving around the vicissitudes of two Catalan painters, resident in New York, was a highly innovative work which transcended the traditional borders of Catalan literature.

The narrative of *desencanto*, circulated by Monzó in 1979, is at the core of the mainstream critical reception of the author's career. Previous scholarship has emphasized that Quim Monzó's trajectory exemplifies the cultural shift from the collectivist and utopian 1960s and 1970s to the individualism and scepticism of the 1980s (Gentic 2013: 143; Guillamon 2004: 14; Ollé 2007: 32; Pons 2011: 53). By virtue of this, the division of Monzó's career into two different and well-defined stages has become something of a critical commonplace, according to which

Monzó's pre-1978 cultural production is part of a radical and experimental epoch, whereas his opus after 1978 is seen to represent his artistic maturity (Bou 1988: 408; Maestre 2010: 239; Oller 1979: 91–97). This interpretation has been fuelled by Monzó's public detachment from literary and cultural experimentalism from the 1970s onwards as well as by his refusal to re-publish *L'udol* and *Self-service*. The division of Monzó's trajectory into two mutually exclusive periods is so pervasive that most literary critics tend to refer to *Uf, va dir* ell as the author's first book. However, other scholars such as Isidor Cònsul (1995), Monserrat Lunati (2008) and Margalida Pons (2011) have challenged this division, emphasizing instead the stylistic connections and thematic similarities between the author's pre- and post-1978 literary production. Similarly, this book takes the view that any attempt to divide Monzó's work into clear-cut stages potentially falls short of understanding the complexities of his production. This study builds on these foundations by offering an original genealogy of the largely neglected significance of Monzó's work pre-1978, both literary and cultural, as well as on the impact of the 1970s cultural mores on his cultural project. More specifically, I will show how *L'udol del griso al caire de les clavegueres*, released in December 1976, already prefigures the Transition's *desencanto* and, in so doing, reveals the limits and contradictions of the countercultural and *textualist* movements. Furthermore, by analysing the political cartoons and collages published by Monzó during the Spanish Transition, this monograph will examine the specific configuration and characteristics of the national politics of the author's work, which has consistently shown his support of Catalonia's right to independence from Spain; it is precisely for this reason that Monzó's satirical work strongly criticized the Transition's notion of consensus. Hence, examining his critical stance at the time is also key to any understanding of Monzó's later criticism of the consensual ethos of cultural normalization. Furthermore, my analysis of Monzó's cartoons throws new light on a recent period of Spanish and Catalan history that is undergoing a severe crisis of legitimacy and important revisions from academia (Davis 2015; Delgado 2014; Martínez 2012).

Monzó's literary style and cultural project would be shaped by his 1982 stay in New York, where he acquainted himself with contemporary American literature, in particular with authors such as John Barth, Donald Barthelme, Robert Coover and Tom Wolfe. In fact, foreign authors were Monzó's main literary influences in his youth, as Monzó himself has pointed out in several interviews (Castillo 1989: 71; Miralles 2004; Nadal 1990: 15). Along with the aforementioned American authors, Monzó's key literary influences were the Austrian novelist Peter Handke, French writers Raymond Queneau and Boris Vian, the German language author Franz Kafka, the Italian writer Italo Calvino and Latin-American authors Adolfo Bioy Casares, Julio Cortázar, Guillermo Cabrera Infante, Gabriel García Márquez and Augusto Monterroso (Blake 1997; Guillamon 1985: 6; Miralles 2004; Nadal 1990: 15). During the 1980s Monzó translated a number of American authors from English into Catalan, including Donald Barthelme, Ray Bradbury, Truman Capote, Robert Coover and J. D. Salinger, among others. The most significant translations carried out by Monzó during the decade were of John Barth's highly influential essays, 'The Literature of Exhaustion' (1967) and 'The Literature of Replenishment — Postmodernist Fiction' (1980), published in the journal *Els Marges* in 1983. Monzó's high translation activity in the 1980s is symptomatic of his desire to disseminate American literature and cultural ideas at a time when the Catalan cultural system was in a process of redefinition and thus, ripe for the incorporation of new literary models.

Although several scholars have acknowledged the connections between Monzó's work and American authors Barth, Barthelme and Coover (Bou 1988: 409; Cònsul 1995: 174; Lunati 2008: 218; Marrugat 2014b: 33–35; Nogués 1998: 37–38; Ollé 1998: 50), the connection has not been critically elaborated upon. This line of enquiry has coexisted with critical manoeuvres, in particular from literary critics, which focus on Monzó's text purely in relation to the Catalan literary tradition, linking his fiction to authors such as Francesc Trabal (1899–1957) and Pere Calders (1912–1994), as well as the Grup de Sabadell[2] and the satirical magazine *El Be Negre* (1931–1936) (Alonso 2003: 417; Bou 2009: 570; Cònsul 1995: 174; Dasca 2008: 133; Maestre 2006: 10, 39). Although the connections between Monzó's work and these Catalan authors can be explored in productive ways, the critical trends that frame his literary influences within a nationally defined literary tradition could be seen as another symptom of the discourses of cultural normalization and its promotion of an uninterrupted and internally cohesive Catalan literary canon. As Caragh Wells has observed, Monzó has urged literary critics 'to cease pigeon-holding Catalan literature with what he believes to be the narrow parameters of a national culture' (2008: 312). This book aims to extend the critical analysis of Monzó's trajectory by placing the emphasis on the transnational scope of his literary, intellectual and political influences through a focus on the impact of American culture. For this reason, I examine Monzó's translations of John Barth's texts as well as his joint translation with Maria Roura of James Finn Garner's *Politically Correct Bedtime Stories: Modern Tales for Our Life and Times* (1994) — released in 1995 as *Contes per a nens i nenes políticament correctes* — with a view to analysing Monzó's role as an authoritative mediator in contemporary Catalan culture. Further, drawing upon theories of translation studies, I show how, in his translational activity, Monzó deploys a number of translation strategies in order to bring to the fore the national difference between Catalonia and Spain.

In the 1980s, Monzó took his first steps as a public commentator through his opinion articles in newspapers such as *El Món*, *El Correo Catalán*, *Diari de Barcelona* and *Avui*, compiled in the anthologies *El dia del senyor* (1984) and *Zzzzzzzz* (1987). Transgressing the boundaries between opinion and fiction à la New Journalism, Monzó's articles did not shy away from controversial themes including, but not limited to, Catalan and Spanish nationalisms, CiU's consensual nationalist policies, the representation of Barcelona as a provincial city governed by Catalan nationalism, the still-continuing subordination of the Catalan language, the institutionalization of Catalan culture, the politics of cultural normalization and literary prizes in Catalonia. Over the decade Monzó's work transgressed the borders of written culture through his radio appearances on the newly established *Catalunya*

Ràdio in 1983. Alongside Ramon Barnils and Jordi Vendrell, he presented the radio programmes *El lloro, el moro, el mico i el senyor de Puerto Rico* (1983–1985) and *El mínim esforç* (1985–1987). Much like his fiction, Monzó's radio participation was received as bold, modern and innovative, in tune with the new times that Catalan society was going through. By the end of the 1980s, various negative critiques notwithstanding, Quim Monzó was perceived as a consolidated and influential short story writer who had managed to carve out a professional career in Catalan language writing for himself (Amargant 1991: 207; Cònsul 1989b: 154; Pladevall i Arumí 1990: 145; Orja 1989: 72, 79). In 1988, Enric Bou observed that Monzó 'és un dels narradors amb més ofici, i que ha escrit alguns dels textos més originals dels darrers anys' [is one of our most gifted authors and has written some of the most original texts in recent years] (1988: 410). Published in 1989, Quim Monzó's second novel, *La magnitud de la tragèdia*, was awarded the *Premi de Novel·la El Temps* in 1989 and achieved significant success during Sant Jordi's Day (Merino 1989: 3; Pujol i Coll 1989: 94). Nevertheless, like *Benzina*, the novel was criticized for being a long short story instead of a *proper* novel (Campillo 1983: 57; Cònsul 1989a: 59; Pujol i Coll 1989: 94). Certain literary critics were establishing a hierarchy within which the short story was a minor genre, whereas the novel was a major one. This would be another of the hierarchies within the Catalan literary system challenged by Monzó's literary project.

The 1990s: Postmodernism, or the Contradictions of Cultural Normalization

Although the politics of cultural normalization received criticism from the very beginning, it was in the 1990s when the contradictions of its discourses became more apparent. In 1992, Oriol Izquierdo observed that cultural normalization was based on the dubious premise that, with continued political and cultural interventions, Catalan culture will at some point in the future become *normal*. However, he remarked that what being *normal* meant had not been defined, therefore identifying the lack of clear and defined objectives as a main flaw in the programmes for cultural normalization (1992: 93–95). In *El malestar en la cultura catalana*, Josep-Anton Fernàndez indicates that cultural normalization is defined by a founding contradiction: on the one hand, it intends to maintain the long-established link between Catalan culture and national identity; on the other, it endeavours that the link be received as politically neutral and impartial by the cultural agents and Catalan society (2008: 42). Fernàndez detects three main areas of instability in the malaise experienced by contemporary Catalan culture owing to the partial failure of cultural normalization. Firstly, the 'crisi de discursos de legitimació' [crisis of legitimating discourses] results from the obstacles to developing a strong Catalan cultural market, in part due to the Catalan government's weak capacity for legitimating Catalan cultural products. Secondly, 'the crisi de la producció de valor' [crisis of the production of value] is triggered by the feeble capacity that Catalan culture (as a social institution) has to bestow symbolic capital and prestige on Catalan cultural products. Finally, the 'crisi d'identificació' [crisis of identification] is provoked by the problems to define Catalan identity as well as the invisibility still affecting Catalan cultural products within the realm of mass culture. Fernàndez situates this set of difficulties experienced by contemporary Catalan culture in the wider context of a global crisis of cultural models in the Western world resulting from the sociocultural transformations brought about by postmodernity, namely: the industrialization of culture and subsequent redefinition of literary fields as markets; the shifts on the relations between high and mass culture; and the disentanglement of culture from identity issues and the real of the symbolic (2008: 100–03). During the 1990s in Spain, these transformations became more visible owing to the gradual consolidation of sociocultural postmodern trends from the early 1980s onwards (Balibrea 1999: 17–26). In the 1990s, concerns about the effectiveness of cultural normalization policies were also intensified by the rising impact of globalization and immigration. CiU's nationalist programme intended to tackle the influence of these processes by fighting homogenization and cultural hybridization (Crameri 2008: 175–92).

Most innovative about Fernàndez's work is that he pinpoints the subordinate relationship of the Catalan government to the Spanish state as perhaps the main determining factor in the failure of the project of cultural normalization (2008: 82–83). In other words, the notion of *normalitat* implicitly aimed to emulate the culture of nation states, but this was unattainable because of Catalonia's status within Spain, a status that was never challenged by the consensual politics of cultural normalization, which did not confront the institutional framework that maintained the subordinate position of the Catalan Generalitat. For this reason, Catalan cultural normalization was based on a fallacy. In order to counter this, the vocabularies of cultural normalization unremittingly referred to notions of cultural plenitude, therefore intensifying the nationalistic elements already present in the discourses of normalization. Crameri points out that 'the parameters of the Catalan literary field are quite narrow' because of the strong links between literature and Catalan nationalism, further adding that authors such as Monzó achieved 'a level of popularity that was partly founded in their ability to write for a wide sector of the public' (2008: 89), thus hinting at the possibility that he was successful in trespassing such narrow parameters. Similarly, Edgar Illas observes that the internationally transferable characters and cosmopolitan urban spaces depicted in Monzó's fiction attempt 'to avoid provincialism and the association of Catalan culture with tradition, folklore or the countryside' (2007: 89). My book extends these critical analyses by exploring the national politics of Quim Monzó's cultural production with a view to showing that he moved beyond such narrow limits through a tense and demythologizing cultural programme that embraced the postmodernist tendencies indicated by Fernàndez. I put forward the idea that this is one of the main reasons behind the success of Quim Monzó's cultural project with Catalan audiences. Criticizing the ambiguous vocabularies and objectives of cultural normalization through iconoclastic and (self-)ironic works already in the mid-1980s, Monzó's oeuvre reveals the founding contradictions and flaws of normalizing discourses as well as the fallacy upon which this cultural programme rested. Monzó's critique thereof cannot be detached from his life-long support of Catalonia's secession from Spain, conspicuous in his cultural production during the 1970s and beyond. As my study shows, what connects Monzó's criticism of *resistencialisme*, cultural normalization and the *Cultura de la Transición* is a rejection of their consensual nature regarding the relationship between Catalan culture and the Spanish state.

In spite of its flaws, the policies of cultural normalization also achieved relevant successes from the 1980s onwards, such as an increase in the number of Catalan language speakers, the development of a book industry in the Catalan language, the gradual consolidation of a young readership used to reading in Catalan and the establishment of audio-visual media in Catalan (Crameri 2008: 4, 108; Fernàndez 2008: 44; Cònsul 1997: 14). There is little doubt that the rise of Monzó's career during the 1980s and 1990s is connected to the positive impacts of the politics of cultural normalization in Catalonia, which created the context in which he could reach a wider readership and nurture a more sustained media presence. This is why my study argues that Quim Monzó's successful trajectory interrelates with cultural normalization in a complex and ambivalent manner.

The 1990s saw the consolidation of Quim Monzó as a key figure in contemporary Catalan culture. 1993 was a prodigious year for the author. In February, he released the highly successful and popular short story volume *El perquè de tot plegat* which won the *Premi Ciutat de Barcelona* and, in 1994, the *Premi de la Crítica Serra d'Or*. The following year, Catalan film-maker Ventura Pons brought Monzó's book to the big screen. Two months after the initial release of *El perquè de tot plegat*, Monzó began to appear regularly in the late-night television show *Persones Humanes*, broadcast by the Catalan public television channel TV3. At a time when Catalan language television was reaching a mass audience that Catalan literature found unable to reach (Crameri 2008: 72), Monzó's TV contribution significantly increased his public visibility and fame among a non-specialist audience. Monzó's TV participation can be seen as a turning point in his career; from then onwards, his public events and appearances, along with his media contributions, would be immensely popular. In May 1996, for instance, Monzó was invited by Margarida Casacuberta to give the closing lecture in her course on twentieth-century Catalan literature at the University of Girona. What was initially a small, in-class event morphed into a public reading in the university's foyer when more than four hundred students turned up (Castillón 1996: 19). Monzó read a few short stories from his forthcoming book, *Guadalajara*, which was published in November and which included popular postmodern re-writings of traditional Western mythology and canonical literary texts, including Robin Hood, William Tell and Franz Kafka's *The Metamorphosis*. *Guadalajara* was awarded the *Premi de la Crítica Serra d'Or* in 1997 and, like Monzó's previous books, was top of the list of Catalan-language bestsellers for months.

Throughout the 1990s, Monzó continued to publish regular opinion pieces in Catalan newspapers such as *El Periódico de Catalunya* and *La Vanguardia*. Monzó's personal voice and distinct style as a columnist was particularly appreciated by Catalan audiences and, once he started to contribute to *La Vanguardia* in 1997, by readers from the rest of Spain, boosting his profile across the country. His journalism was compiled in four volumes: *La maleta turca* (1990), *Hotel Intercontinental* (1991), *No plantaré cap arbre* (1994) and *Del tot indefens davant dels hostils imperis alienígenes* (1998). In his articles during the 1990s, Monzó continued to reflect on the politico-cultural relationship between Catalonia and Spain, this time criticizing, for instance, the efforts of Catalan nationalism to promote Catalan in the European Union when the vernacular language was still in a subordinate position at home. Among other topics, Monzó's journalistic texts discussed the impact that the independence processes of the Baltic states of Estonia, Latvia and Lithuania had on Catalan politics, as well as harshly criticizing the urban and sociocultural transformations that his native city of Barcelona was undergoing as a result of the Olympic Games of 1992. Several of his pieces also revealed an incipient criticism of feminist politics, as well as of new education pedagogies, environmentalism and vegetarianism. By the end of the decade, Monzó was regarded as the best author of his generation by the literary field; in Eva Piquer's words, he was the 'punt de referència de la narrativa catalana actual' [reference point for contemporary Catalan fiction] (1998: 168). Monzó was also the bestselling Catalan-language author at the time, as well as a household name thanks to his mass-media participation (Camps and Gàlvez 1998: 8; Fernàndez 1998: 263; Piquer 1998: 168).

Monzó's literary and cultural project, however, has also been met with disapproval in the Catalan cultural field. These critical manoeuvres argue that his literary and intellectual programme are defined by banality as well as by an unremitting and acritical ironic perspective. During the 1980s, the idea that many Catalan literary texts penned by young authors were banal was already present. In *Farenheit 212* (1989), Joan Orja[3] analyses the work of Catalan authors who started publishing in the 1980s, namely, Ofèlia Dracs, Josep Maria Fonalleras, Josep Bras, Sergi Pàmies, Rafael Vallbona, Jaume Capó, Toni Cucarella, Màrius Serra and Maria Jaén. The notion of banality crops up regularly, linked by Orja to the specific spirit of contemporary Catalan society and culture, defined by the rise of individualism, hedonism, consumerism and mass culture, as well as the decline of political activism and the collapse of ideologies (1989: 13–19). For Orja, most up-and-coming authors of the period did not attempt to 'explicar grans històries, sinó fets quotidians, anecdòtics, en ocasions mínims, situats en mons petits i fragmentaris; és una literatura escrita majoritàriament en gèneres narratius breus' [tell big stories, but daily and random events, in some cases minimal, set in small and fragmentary worlds: it is a type of literature mostly written as short narrative fiction] (1989: 41–42). Not only is Orja describing this type of literature with the typical vocabularies used to talk about Monzó's fiction, but later in the book he explicitly considers Monzó as precursor to some of these authors, particularly Sergi Pàmies and Josep Maria Fonalleras (1989: 43, 61, 72). In his study of Catalan literature during the 1980s, Francesc Calafat also highlights banality as a literary feature shared by certain emerging authors, with Quim Monzó functioning very much as their role model (1992: 73–78).

Throughout the 1990s, Monzó's work is more frequently and specifically connected with banality, to enforce both positive and negative readings of his texts.

For instance, reviewing *El perquè de tot plegat* for the *Revista de Catalunya*, Antoni Pladevall i Arumí receives Monzó's book as one of the best literary publications of the year, using the qualifier of 'banal' in the positive sense of light-hearted entertainment (1993: 121). In 1997, Jordi Malés review of *Guadalajara* builds on similar arguments, yet this time from a slightly more negative perspective (1997: 162). Nevertheless, one of the harshest criticisms of Monzó's cultural project came out in 1993 when Jordi Ibàñez, literary critic of *El País Catalunya*, strongly disapproved of the main features of his authorial persona in *Persones Humanes*. For Ibàñez, Monzó's monologues and by extension literary oeuvre were both excessively comical and superficial as well as lacking in intellectual complexity (1994: xi). Ibàñez's piece is illustrative of how Monzó's public profile and mass media engagement in the 1990s were triggering anxieties among certain literary critics and authors. This is not only exemplified by Ibàñez's article, but also by reviewers who challenged the representation of Monzó's work as banal. Emphasizing the 'implacable capacitat analítica' [implacable analytical capacity] of Monzó's fiction (1998: 49), Manel Ollé argued that those who criticized the author's work for its apparent superficiality were disoriented by the author's audio-visual work and, for this reason, failed to grasp the complexity of the author's literary and cultural project:

> confós per la simpatia mediàtica del Monzó radiofònic i televisiu i per l'aparent transparència d'uns contes sempre accessibles, impecables i contundents, algú podria arribar a pensar-se que Quim Monzó és un narrador humorístic, anecdòtic, banal i merament entretingut. (1998: 53)

> [disoriented by the success of Monzó's radio and TV persona and by the apparent transparency of his accessible, impeccable and powerful short stories, one might even think that Monzó is a humoristic, anecdotal, banal and merely entertaining narrator]

The critique of Monzó's work as banal is representative of two opposing attitudes vis-à-vis the rising postmodernization of Catalan culture from the 1980s onwards. It could be suggested that those who endorsed Monzó's cultural project welcomed the cultural transformations brought about by the marketization of Catalan culture, the gradual distancing of Catalan literature from the realm of the symbolic, the growing presence of humour and irony in Catalan cultural products and the blurring of boundaries between high and mass culture. By contrast, those who described Monzó's project as banal in a negative sense can be linked to what Fernàndez terms the 'crítica culturalista' [culturalist critique] of cultural normalization. Owing to the growing malaise in Catalan culture during the 1990s, certain critical manoeuvres claimed that 'el procés de normalització havia mercantilitzat i banalitzat la cultura catalana' [the process of normalization had marketized and trivialized Catalan culture] (Fernàndez 2008: 45). These literary critics and authors, therefore, perceived mass culture and marketization as threats to Catalan culture during the autonomous period. However, Fernàndez argues that this particular trend could not succeed because it resisted in vain, from an elitist perspective, the main cultural trends in Western societies (2008: 61). The criticism of Monzó's work as banal from an elitist understanding of literary creation can also be connected to the critical trends emphasizing that Monzó is a great short story writer but has not yet succeeded in penning true novels, which rely on a hierarchical division of literary genres typical of Western modernity (Campillo 1983: 57; Calafat 1992: 77; Cònsul 1989: 15, 1995: 82–83; Pladevall i Arumí 1993: 122; Pujol i Coll 1989: 94).

It is not by chance that these authors and literary critics attacked Monzó's public profile. As this monograph shows, Quim Monzó's public authorial persona, carefully constructed through mass and social media participation, epitomizes the main traits of his cultural project. While a number of scholars have pointed out the central impact of mass media on Monzó's career and have even suggested that media participation is a key constituent of his cultural programme (Maestre 2011: 64; Marrugat 2014a: 41; Nogués 1998: 35; Piquer 1998: 169), Monzó's authorial persona still remains largely understudied. This book puts forward the idea that Quim Monzó's mass and social media participation has generated a public profile for the author that falls into the categories of postmodern intellectual and of celebrity author. Monzó's authorial persona is therefore distanced from the two main models of intellectual participation in contemporary Catalonia, that is, the resistant and the normalizing intellectual. Both models share the notion of engagement, or *compromís*, at their core, a notion that Monzó's cultural project has dissociated from and criticized.

Quim Monzó's public intellectual profile is in tune with contemporary trans-formations in the model of intellectual engagement, as theorized by Michel Foucault and Zygmunt Bauman. In opposition to the traditional status of the intellectual, who was regarded as 'the spokesman of the universal' and 'the consciousness/conscience of' the people, the postmodern thinker is no longer perceived to be the carrier of truth or the voice of the collective (Foucault 1980: 126). Similarly, Bauman explores the transition of the public intellectual from the 'legislator' in modern times (one whose opinions were received as a guiding force) to the 'interpreter' in postmodern times (one who carries only relative authority) (1987: 110–48). In this postmodern context, intellectuals express their ideas in a completely different public arena, in which 'connectivity is stronger in relation to the media and the public than to the state and civil society' (Davis 2009: 268). Although criticized by participants in the literary and cultural field, Monzó's authorial persona has connected exceptionally well with the Catalan public through mass media participation, a connection which has been a key element in his successful career. For this reason, Monzó's public profile exemplifies how two worlds that traditionally remained separate have merged: literature and celebrity culture. This association has caused concerns in the literary field of several Western countries because it transforms the notion of literary authorship, from the isolated and extraordinary genius to the celebrity writer who enjoys fame and visibility, thus consciously courting the public gaze (Franssen 2010: 92). Celebrity authors encapsulate the tensions between literature and the marketplace, and between high and low culture, whilst simultaneously challenging the view that the consumption of literature is a mark of social distinction (Moran 2000: 3–9; Ommundsen 2007: 245). Drawing upon studies of postmodern intellectuals and celebrity authorship, my book offers an innovative analysis of Quim Monzó's public authorial persona. In so doing, not only does this monograph explore the tensions that Monzó's interdisciplinary media participation has triggered in the Catalan literary field, but it also connects such anxieties to broader cultural debates taking place in contemporary Western literary systems.

The Twenty-First Century: The Literary and Cultural Canonization of Quim Monzó

Despite a steady stream of critical appraisals associating banality with Monzó's work and public persona (Adelli 2007: 24; Ballart 2008: 219; Biel 2011: 5; Bofill 2009: 20; Palol 2007: 24; *Vilaweb* 2004), the author's popularity and recognition continued to rise in the new millennium. The majority of his short stories that came out between 1978 and 1996 were collected in the volume *Vuitanta-sis contes* (1999), awarded the prestigious *Premi Nacional de Literatura* and the *Premi Lletra d'Or* in 2000 and described by the influential literary critic Ponç Puigdevall as 'un dels llibres més imprescindibles de les últimes temporades' [one of the most essential books of recent years] (1999: 30) and by poet and author Josep Navarro Santaeulàlia as a 'clàssic d'ara' [a modern day classic] (qtd. in Vila i Delclós 1999: xxviii). In 2001, Monzó published the short story collection *El millor dels mons*, depicting darker and more mature topics as if the youthful energy and optimism of previous works had faded away. It was received as a book of lost innocence heralding a new stage in the author's work (Castells 2001: 38; Gàlvez 2001: 80; Roig 2001: 2). *El millor dels mons*, spending months at the top of the Catalan-language bestsellers list, includes the novella 'Davant del rei de Suècia', in which Monzó sarcastically represents the Catalan literary and cultural world and which I analyse in Chapter 5. Released in November 2003, *Tres Nadals* exemplifies how Monzó's work blurs the boundaries between journalism and fiction, as it is formed by three unconventional Christmas tales previously published in his column in *Magazine*, *La Vanguardia*'s weekend supplement. Following the attacks on 11 September 2001, Monzó travelled to New York and wrote a series of chronicles for the Catalan press, later compiled alongside some of his earlier travel writings in the volume *Catorze ciutats comptant-hi Brooklyn* (2004). In 2004, journalist and author Xavier Moret published a profile of Monzó in *Babelia*, *El País*'s cultural supplement, emphasizing the author's fame and literary significance: 'Monzó es un escritor de largo recorrido al que ya nadie discute su liderazgo. Multipremiado y multiventas, [...] ha conseguido con los años situarse entre los favoritos del público y de la crítica' [Monzó is a writer with a long career and whose authority and leadership are not questioned by anyone. Multi-awarded and with blockbuster sales, [...] over the years he has managed to become a favourite for readers and critics] (2004: 8). Between the years 2000 and 2010, Monzó, already a famous and exceptionally well-regarded columnist in Catalonia and across the rest of Spain thanks to his regular pieces in *La Vanguardia*, released three anthologies of polemical articles: *Tot és mentida* (2000), *El tema del tema* (2003) and *Esplendor i glòria de la Internacional Papanates* (2010).

Volumes such as *Tres Nadals* and *Esplendor i glòria de la Internacional Papanates* illustrate Monzó's response to the culture wars. Much like contemporary European male authors such as Michel Houellebecq and Javier Marías, Monzó's texts are strongly critical of the main tenets of political correctness as well as ostensibly progressive movements such as feminism, anti-war protests, trade unionism and the movements for pedagogical renovation. While Monzó had already shown his disagreement with these socio-political ideologies in earlier opinion pieces — and even in fictional texts such as 'Fam i set de justícia', Monzó's version of the myth of Robin Hood included in *Guadalajara* — *Esplendor* particularly focuses on criticizing these political movements through a parodic, and at times harsh and even insulting, tone. The anthology includes articles published between 2001 and 2004, including pieces on José María Aznar's convoluted second term of office, determined by Spain's involvement in the American-led invasion of Iraq in 2003, the formation of the first Tripartite government in Catalonia in November 2003, presided by Pasqual Maragall, and the beginning of José Luis Rodríguez Zapatero's government in 2004. At a time in which the newly elected Catalan and Spanish governments embraced the vocabularies of political correctness and, to a certain extent, implemented more progressive policies, Monzó's articles concentrated on challenging and deconstructing some of their proposals. In spite of this criticism, Monzó's public discourse is certainly detached from traditional Spanish and Catalan conservative commentators for a number of reasons. Firstly, owing to his participation in 1970s counterculture, his work has always been linked to moral transgression and anti-bourgeois positions. Secondly, his criticism of Spanish institutions, particularly unionist politicians and the Royal Family, has prevented the public from linking him to either Spanish or Catalan conservative ideologies. Thirdly, a vaguely anti-establishment stance detaches him from mainstream right-wing positions. Finally, during the 1980s and 1990s Monzó was an ardent critique of CiU's policies, in particular owing to his forthright public support for Catalan independence and bolder policies in favour of the Catalan language; furthermore, until the 2010s this was a political stance traditionally associated with the left.

There is little doubt that Monzó's fluid, highly ironical and anti-utopian view-points make it difficult to trace the ideological influences on his writings. Perhaps for this reason, critical studies of Monzó's work have tended to skirt the question of the political ideologies informing his work, either discussing the absence of political topics in his fiction after 1978 (Guillamon 2004: 11; Illas 2013: 19; Martí-Olivella 1982: 253–54) or describing his opinion pieces as examples of neutrality and thus profiling him as an eminently independent intellectual (Maestre 2008: 6; Puigdevall 2003: 4; Reixach 1990: 24). By contrast to these critical analyses, my book aims to shed light on the socio-political ideologies informing Quim Monzó's work with a view to showing that beneath the author's relativism and humour are anxieties about cultural and political change that result in the criticism of progressive ideals. In this monograph, I wish to suggest that the American political ideology of libertarianism provides a suitable framework for examining the political subtext of a number of writings by Monzó published in the 1990s and 2000s. Throwing light upon a largely ignored aspect of Monzó's work, my book explores how his oeuvre has interacted with libertarian and neoconservative ideologies associated with the

New Right, which rose in the Western world from the 1980s and Spain from the 1990s (Balibrea 1999: 195–96; Carmona et al 2012; Curran 2005; 27; Dowling 2013: 112–13; Gabilondo 2002: 238, 252; Hall 1994: 169; Robertson 2004: 328; Tusell 2011: 438–39). By tracing the connections between Monzó's texts and American libertarianism, my study reveals once again the relevance of the transnational framework for examining Monzó's cultural project.

Alongside the study of socio-political ideologies, I also explore the sexual politics of Quim Monzó's work, an area that has merited more critical attention. In general, however, critical studies have avoided discussing the power relations underlying the treatment of sexuality in Monzó's texts, instead stressing that sexual representations in the author's fiction are to be interpreted primarily as a means by which characters can evade the oppressive social structures they inhabit (Cònsul 1995: 184; Gàlvez 1998: 120; Illas 2007: 92; Maestre 2012b: 112; Oller 1979: 94). By contrast, Josep-Anton Fernàndez and Montserrat Lunati have provided wide-ranging analyses of the representation of hegemonic masculinity in crisis in Monzó's literary output (Fernàndez 1998; Lunati 1999). This monograph takes Fernàndez's and Lunati's line of inquiry one step further and analyses the pornographic imagery that permeates Monzó's fiction from the critical prisms afforded by feminisms, masculinities and porn studies. Monzó's pornographic descriptions represent the crisis of hegemonic masculinity as a consequence of changes in interpersonal relationships unfolding from the early 1960s onwards in the Western world (Barker 1992; MacInnes 1998) and from the 1970s in Spain, where the gender relations have drastically changed between the death of the dictator in 1975 and the turn of the century (Brooksbank Jones 1997; Fernàndez and Chavarría 2003; Montero 1995). In contrast to scholars who read sexual images in Monzó's writings only as a means of gratifying recreation, therefore eluding its political implications and problematic dialogue with the sociocultural changes outlined above, I explore how Monzó's male characters become anxious about their own selves and exert sexual violence over women as a consequence of these anxieties. Acknowledging the idea that the Catalan literary establishment of the autonomous period has been 'largely male dominated and resistant to discussion of sexual political issues' (Fernàndez 1998: 262), this book analyses the political implications of Monzó's characteristically dysfunctional male characters vis-à-vis the values of hegemonic masculinity. Monzó's male characters can also be read in relation to the author's strong criticism in his public discourse of some of the main principles of contemporary feminism, a reaction that can be situated in the wider context of the sociocultural transformations brought about by the advent and development of feminist politics in post-Francoist Spain.

2007 was a fabulous year in Quim Monzó's career. On 9 October, he delivered the opening speech at the Frankfurt Book Fair, which was widely shared and circulated in social media and praised as a great accomplishment within the Catalan cultural and political field. Josep Bargalló, director of the Institut Ramon Llull at the time, described the Catalan participation in Frankfurt with vocabulary that is often used to describe Monzó's work: in its presentation to the world, Catalan culture was, like Monzó's own literary texts, 'moderna, desacomplexada, formal i amena a la vegada' [modern, self-confident, formal and engaging at the same time] (2008: 48). After his speech, Monzó's fame and acclaim grew even further. The Catalan participation at Frankfurt, however, had been the subject of a deep and divisive politico-cultural controversy since its inception. Should Catalan authors who write in Spanish represent Catalan culture too? The selection process, designed and organized by the Conselleria de Cultura of the Catalan Government, triggered a flurry of acrimonious articles and public debates not just in Catalonia but also across all Spain. The national dispute was again impacting (and tainting) Catalan cultural debates. To a certain extent, Monzó's successful performance helped overshadow these bitter and oppositional controversies. A couple of weeks later, he published *Mil cretins*, awarded the *Premi de Narrativa Maria Àngels Anglada* in 2008 and adapted for the cinema in 2011 by Ventura Pons. The timing could not have been better and the first three editions were sold out before the volume arrived to the bookshops. *Mil cretins*, which remains Monzó's last fictional book, was received as a continuation of the themes already represented in *El millors dels mons*: illness, pain, death and decrepitude, all viewed from a bitter and heart-breaking perspective (Castells 2007: 45; Cortadellas 2007: 26; Riera 2007: 5). During the book's promotion, Monzó continued to exploit his self-conscious positioning as a transgressive and provocative public intellectual in tune with his times: on 21 November he featured on the front page of *La Vanguardia Cultura/s*'s supplement with transgender make-up inspired by Senyor Beneset, the protagonist of the short story opening *Mil cretins*; the picture remains one of the most famous images of Monzó.

Two years later, in December 2009, a retrospective about Quim Monzó's life and work was organized at the Centre d'Arts Santa Mònica in Barcelona by the Institució de les Lletres Catalanes and the Departament de Cultura i Mitjans de Comunicació of the Catalan Generalitat, an event which can be seen as representing Monzó's definitive canonization within the Catalan cultural field. Once again, the exhibition revealed Monzó's fame and popularity with Catalan audiences, as the numbers of visitors outnumbered those attracted to equivalent retrospectives on canonical authors such as Mercè Rodoreda, Josep Palau i Fabre and Joan Perucho. In early 2010, with the exhibition still running, the three main Catalan cultural magazines, *L'Avenç*, *Caràcters* and *Serra d'Or*, dedicated their front-covers and lengthy special articles to Quim Monzó's career. At the beginning of the 2010s, Monzó was recognized as the creator of a literary style, proving to be a literary forefather to present day authors such as Empar Moliner, Sergi Pàmies, Jordi Puntí and Màrius Serra (Camps 2008: 102; Dasca 2008: 133–34; Guillamon 2008: 5; Maestre 2012a: 17–25; Marrugat 2014: 55; Puntí 2010: 72).

While Monzó has not published any fictional book since 2007, in the 2010s he has remained a highly relevant and influential public voice through his opinion pieces, mass media participation and also a lively and engaging Twitter profile since joining the social networking site in February 2011. A few months later, in September 2011, Monzó opened the second season of the popular TV3 show *El convidat*, with 820,000 viewers tuning in, breaking the programme's previous audience record

(*La Vanguardia* 2011). Monzó's impersonation in the popular and multi-awarded TV3 show *Polònia* has also remained a feature during the decade since he first appeared in 2008. 2017 saw the publication of Monzó's last book, the collection of opinion pieces *Taula i barra. Diccionari de menjar i beure*, which brings together articles on food and drink — the book evidently dodges the term 'gastronomy' — published between 1999 and 2016. Published by Libros de Vanguardia, *La Vanguardia*'s publishing house, this is the first book authored by Monzó since 1978 which is not published by the emblematic independent publishing house Quaderns Crema, founded by the late editor Jaume Vallcorba (1949–2014), closing a collaboration that has undeniably had a deep impact on the post-Francoist Catalan literary field. Moreover, the opinion pieces were not selected by Monzó himself, as was the case with all of his previous compilations, but by Julià Guillamon.

On 4 June 2018, as we have seen, Monzó was awarded the *Premi de Honor de les Lletres Catalanes* in a ceremony at the impressive *modernista* style Palau de la Música Catalana broadcast live by El 33, Catalonia's second public television channel. Attended by a myriad of political and cultural personalities — including the President of the Catalan Generalitat, Quim Torra, the President of Catalonia's Parliament, Roger Torrent, the Minister of Culture of Catalonia, Laura Borràs, and the former President of the Generalitat, José Montilla — the gala celebrated and praised Monzó's literary and intellectual contribution to Catalan culture. Since the award had been made public on 7 March 2018, between early March and mid-June Monzó enjoyed another period of high media exposure, featuring in numerous articles, radio and television news and in lengthy interviews in numerous printed, digital and mass media outlets, including Catalunya Radio's *El Matí* and the TV3 shows *Al cotxe* and *Tot el temps del món*. In his article on the award, the author and literary critic Julià Guillamon remarked that 'en Monzó va obrir tots els camins pels quals, més o menys còmodament, hem circulat tots els altres: els contes, les columnes, la ràdio, la tele' [Monzó opened all the pathways through which the rest of us have more or less comfortably travelled: short stories, opinion columns, radio, television] (2018), while the writer and translator Adrià Pujol defined Monzó as 'un gegant de les lletres catalanes' [a giant of Catalan literature] (2018). Both statements epitomize the reception of Monzó's career by the end of the 2010s, almost fifty years after he published his first travel chronicles in fringe magazines in the late years of Francoism. Quim Monzó being the awarded author, the ceremony departed from the formality of previous occasions to become a lively and entertaining gala night à la Monzó's idiosyncratic style. Hosted by the famous and eccentric TV presenter Òscar Dalmau and with the stage turned into a café and night bar, the ceremony combined on-screen and live performances together with speeches representative of Monzó's work and life. At the beginning, Monzó's Twitter profile was shown on-screen and two songs recently tweeted by the author were played: Sam Cooke's 'A Change is Gonna Come' and 'Eres un enfermo', a song by the cheesy pop band Las Supremas de Móstoles about a women becoming tired of her husband's addiction to cybersex. Two fully nude actors, a man and a woman, did a short performance inspired by Monzó's fiction. Albert Pla, the *enfant terrible* of Catalan music, offered a live musical performance with lyrics describing a fictional drug and alcohol bender enjoyed by Monzó and himself. The scholar Manel Ollé talked about Monzó's characteristic literary features and the journalists Mònica Terribas and Jordi Basté highlighted how Monzó's interdisciplinary profile combines literary creation and opinion articles with outstanding and high-quality TV and radio contributions. A video in which a number of Monzó's translators reflected on his literary fiction in their native languages was also screened with Catalan subtitles, and a few of Monzó's articles in *La Vanguardia* were read in between the performances. As Magí Camps put it in his chronicle in *La Vanguardia*, 'como Monzó es un personaje singular, con un carácter singular y una obra singular, el acto de entrega del premio también tenía que serlo' [given that Monzó is a singular character, with a singular personality and oeuvre, the ceremony had to be singular too] (2018). The bohemian, transgressive and cosmopolitan nature of the event celebrated and commemorated the master lines of Monzó's modernizing literary and cultural programme.

In spite of the event's playful and light-hearted tone, however, the ceremony also denounced political repression in Catalonia and the imprisonments of pro-independence leaders after the events of October 2017. A few 'Llibertat presos polítics' [Freedom for Political Prisoners] flags were hanging on the stage and theatre stands, and when Monzó entered the stalls the public chanted for the freedom of political prisoners. The event was opened by an emotive message from Jordi Cuixart read by a masculine voice-off celebrating the value of culture to bridge divisions. In his welcome to the authorities, host Òscar Dalmau listed the names of all the political prisoners and exiles. Marcel Mauri, vice-president of Òmnium, spoke on behalf of Cuixart and, in his address, described Quim Monzó as 'el nostre autor contemporani més universal' [our most universal contemporary author] and demanded dialogue, justice and freedom. Mauri's speech also emphasized and celebrated the plural and multicultural nature of Catalonia and its culture, and illustrated this by reading a section of José Agustín Goytisolo's poem 'Más que una palabra' ('la libertad hay que inventarla siempre | la libertad puede ser del esclavo y fallarle al señor | la libertad es gritar frente a la boca gris de los fusiles' [freedom must always be created | freedom can belong to the slave and fail the master | freedom is screaming at the rifle's grey barrel]) and listing emblematic Catalan authors and artists in pairs, in most instances one writing/performing in Catalan and the other in Spanish: Goytisolo and Pedrolo, Mishima and Estopa, Raimon and Serrat, Carulla and Pou, Marsé, Pessadorrona and Gil de Biedma (in this instance, Mauri listed three names), Monserrat Roig and Vázquez Montalbán, Najat el Hachmi and Candel. As he stated, 'reivindiquem un nosaltres que és el fruit d'una cultura mestissa [...] perquè només ens val un nosaltres si aquest inclou a tothom' [we reclaim a community with a mestizo culture [...] because we can only build a cohesive community if everyone is included] (*Premi d'Honor*).

The political elements of the event attest to the complex and fraught nature of the relations between Catalonia and Spain by the end of the 2010s, after a convoluted decade defined by the birth of the modern Catalan independence movement and the pro-independence unilateral push of October 2017. Cuixart's and Mauri's speeches at the *Premi d'Honor* ceremony offer two excellent examples of the discourses that have characterised the post-2010 Catalan separatist movement, which has tended to transition towards a notion of sovereignty that does not put so much emphasis on language and cultural identity, instead focusing on democracy and the right to decide (Amat 2017: 28; Dowling 2018: 105–10). Through the analysis of the national and cultural politics in Quim Monzó's work, my monograph illustrates that the author's cultural project has consistently denounced Catalonia's politico-cultural subordination to Spain while at the same time disrupting and problematizing the nationalistic excesses of *resistencialisme* and cultural normalization through iconoclastic discourses. In light of this, it could be suggested that, in the last few years, the public narratives of Catalan nationalism have become closer to Monzó's life-long stance and project. Quim Monzó's national role as a literary author and public intellectual is far from new in the history of Catalonia. In his recently-published study of the interrelations between writers, literature and identity in the region from 1859 to the present day, Jaume Subirana remarks the 'protagonismo de los escritores y de la literatura en la creación y la reelaboración de la identidad nacional' [key role played by authors and literature in the creation and re-elaboration of the national identity] (2018: 28). Montserrat Guibernau notes that nationalist movements in nations without states require 'the existence of some intellectuals prepared to build up a nationalist discourse different from, and often opposed to, that of the state' (2004: 22). This book argues that Quim Monzó has contributed to building a politico-cultural sphere different from and opposed to that of the Spanish state through a transgressive and demythologizing oeuvre that has furthered the gradual detachment of Catalan culture from the realm of the symbolic from the mid-1970s up to the present day. Overall, *Quim Monzó and Contemporary Catalan Culture* casts new light on Monzó's contributions to the (still) ongoing dialogue about writers, literature, language and national identity in Catalonia.

The opening chapter explores how Monzó's work in the mid-1970s can already be read as a postmodernist critique of the politics of *resistencialisme*. I argue that Monzó's first novel, *L'udol del griso al caire de les clavegueres* (1976), not only portrays the complexities and ambivalences of the countercultural and *textualist* challenge to the previous dominant tradition, it also encapsulates the multifaceted and sometimes contradictory sociocultural transformations unfolding in Catalonia since the late 1960s, which defined the authors of the Generation of the 1970s. As such, *L'udol* becomes an exceptional depiction of the sociocultural spirit of the early 1970s in Catalonia. The chapter continues by analysing a political cartoon published in October 1976 in *Canigó* in which Monzó caricatured the foremost national poet and symbol of *resistencialisme*, Salvador Espriu, who had expressed his support for the co-officiality of Catalan and Spanish in post-Francoist Catalonia. Monzó's cartoon turned out to be quite controversial, prompting a flurry of reactions in Catalan culture. I contend this controversy to be a prime example of the conflict between two opposing visions in the debate over the configuration of a proto-institutional, autonomous Catalan cultural field in the mid-1970s, with *resistentialist* practices on one side (a hierarchical model in which respect for major cultural figures is essential), and postmodernist, self-referential and self-ironic modes on the other (a model that favours provocation and disrespect for authority).

Chapter 2 offers an integral assessment of Quim Monzó's satirical work in *Canigó* during the Spanish Transition. At a historical moment in which the 'Régimen del 78' and its associated economic, political and territorial pacts are undergoing a major crisis, particularly in the Catalan region, this chapter explores the ways in which Monzó's early artistic work was producing an integral critique of the Transition as it unfolded. As I show, Monzó's artistic production in *Canigó* depicts, first and foremost, a staunch support of Catalonia's right to independence from Spain. His work therefore portrays a sharp criticism of the principles informing the Transition, which are depicted as in a line of continuity with the Francoist regime, especially in regard to the national debate over the autonomy of Spain's historical regions. For this reason, Monzó's satirical work can be analysed as a denunciation of the consensual politics at the core of the emerging configuration of the Catalan cultural and political fields. A particularly innovative aspect of this chapter is to analyse a series of works by Monzó that, unlike most of his fiction, display an overt political commitment. In so doing, the chapter not only brings little-known material to critical attention and broadens the understanding of Monzó's early years in print at a turning point in Catalan and Spanish history; it also contributes to the understanding of the recent rise of pro-independence positions in Catalonia by revisiting the critical stance demonstrated by Quim Monzó's work as the Transition developed. Furthermore, returning to Monzó's cartoons sheds additional light on how he introduced elements such as humour, irony and self-parody into his works of cultural and political commentary, but also into the field of post-1975 Catalan culture more generally, thus setting the foundation of a postmodernist critique of the process of institutionalization of an autonomous Catalan cultural field.

Chapter 3 explores the links between Monzó's work and American sociocultural trends in order to shed new light on the transnational and translational dimension of the author's cultural programme. I argue that through his translational activity Monzó has acted as a mediator to facilitate the transfer and mobility of American cultural and ideological trends into the Catalan cultural and political fields. The first part of the chapter analyses Monzó's translation in 1983 for the Catalan cultural magazine *Els Marges* of two highly influential essays on postmodern literature by American author John Barth, namely, 'The Literature of Exhaustion' (1967) and 'The Literature of Replenishment — Postmodernist Fiction' (1980). My reading of Monzó's novel *Benzina* (1983) vis-à-vis his dialogue with John Barth's essays helps towards a better understanding, on the one hand, of the ways in which Monzó's postmodernist literary programme modernized Catalan fiction in the early 1980s and, on the other, of Monzó's gradual detachment from literary experimentalism. As I show, the interplay with the postmodern zeitgeist of early 1980s New York is pivotal to *Benzina*'s ground-breaking impact in Catalan literature. The second part of the chapter offers a reading of *Contes per a nens i nenes políticament correctes* (1995), that is, Quim Monzó and Maria Roura's translation of James Finn Garner's *Politically Correct Bedtime Stories* (1994). Through the analysis of Monzó's and

Roura's translation and its reception, I argue that Monzó imported the American conservative criticism of political correctness to the Catalan context at a time in which this was a little-known debate in Catalonia. Further, I examine how *Contes* incorporates references to nationalism as identity politics and echoes the particular terminology of Catalan resistant nationalism, therefore making the question of nationalism more visible for a Catalan readership. *Contes* has continued to be a highly influential text and it has shaped more recent criticism against the discourses of political correctness by high profile commentators in Catalan culture such as Salvador Cardús and Empar Moliner, who in the 2000s recognized Monzó's role as an authoritative mediator in this debate (Cardús 2007: 29; Moliner 2008).

Chapter 4 analyses the politics of Quim Monzó's work with a focus on how his textual production from the mid-1990s has responded to the socio-political transformations unfolding in relation to the rise of the neoliberal agenda and decline of left narratives in the West. I argue that the American political philosophy of libertarianism provides a suitable overall framework for examining the political subtext of a number of Monzó's texts. My analysis of Monzó's re-writing of the myth of Robin Hood ('Fam i set de justícia', *Guadalajara*, 1996) foregrounds the interrelations between Monzó's version and the highly critical depiction of the character's philanthropic actions by the Russian-American libertarian thinker and author Ayn Rand in her seminal novel *Atlas Shrugged* (1957). The second part of the chapter analyses a number of opinion pieces from *Esplendor i glòria de la Internacional Papanates* (2010) with a view to showing how Monzó's work interrelated with certain elements of the American-inspired neoconservative backlash gaining force in Spain in the early years of the twenty-first century. As I illustrate, Monzó's articles — published between 2001 and 2004 — focus on debunking and parodying the progressive discourses, vocabularies and policies that characterized the opposition to José María Aznar's second-term of office (2000–2004), the first years of the Catalan Tripartite coalition (2003–2010) and of José Luís Rodríguez Zapatero's administration in the Spanish government (2004–2011). Monzó's growing disaffection with progressive politics reveals a distaste of certain elements of the legacy of counterculture, the cultural movement which he had championed in the 1970s. As I show, the ideological evolution from counterculture to libertarianism has not been unusual, given how at the core of both politico-cultural philosophies is a focus on the primacy of individual choice.

Chapter 5 explores the presence of pornographic imagery in Quim Monzó's fictional texts drawing upon the critical tools provided by feminisms, masculinities and sexuality studies. Through the analysis of *Benzina* (1983) and five of Monzó's short stories — El regne vegetal' (*Olivetti, Moulinex, Chaffoteaux et Maury*, 1980), 'Pigmalió' (*El perquè de tot plegat*, 1993), 'La mamà' and 'Dos rams de roses' (*El millor dels mons*, 2001) and 'Una nit' (*Mil cretins*, 2007) — I argue that the recurrent depiction of pornographic images in Monzó's texts betrays one of the fundamental tensions of his literary and cultural production, namely, the representation of Western hegemonic masculinity in crisis. Exploring the role of pornography in Monzó's fiction also throws light on the ways in which his work challenged the slow-changing Catalan literary field of the early 1980s, still characterized by a strict division between high and mass culture. By analysing Monzó's text from the perspective of masculinities and sexualities, this chapter takes the often avoided topic of Monzó's public criticism of the feminist movement in post-Francoist Spain. I put forward the idea that Monzó's dysfunctional male characters, some of which repeatedly fail to abide by the principles of hegemonic masculinity, can be seen as the literary depictions of the tensions and anxieties about the contemporary feminist movement expressed in some of his opinion articles and public statements. A key contribution of Chapters 4 and 5 is to offer an innovative analysis of the ironic element in Monzó's postmodern texts, including his re-writings of fairy tales and traditional Western narratives. While most readings have focused on the subversive uses of Monzó's irony, my analyses in both chapters favour less transgressive, more literal readings, since by virtue of their ambiguity, Monzó's ironic strategies neither confirm nor deny the values and principles they portray and parody. To illustrate this, I draw upon Linda Hutcheon's writings on postmodern parodies in *The Politics of Postmodernism* (2002).

The final chapter, divided into two main blocs, explores Quim Monzó as a public intellectual in post-Francoist Catalonia. Through the analysis of the opinion piece 'L'intel·lectual' (*Zzzzzzzz*, 1987) and the novella 'Davant del rei de Suècia' (*El millor dels mons*, 2001), the first part examines the ways in which Monzó's work has sarcastically represented the founding contradictions and limits of cultural normalization, with a focus on discourses about Catalan public intellectuals. I show that Monzó's critique of cultural normalization is strongly linked to his rejection of the authoritarian, elitist and allegedly disinterested public intellectual characteristic of modernity, as analysed by Zygmunt Bauman (1987) and Pierre Bourdieu (1993). The second part traces the practices and discourses at the core of Monzó's media participation over four decades, from the 1980s radio programme *El lloro, el moro, el mico i el senyor de Puerto Rico* and his monologues in *Persones humanes* in the 1990s, to his participation in the sitcom *Plats bruts* in 2001 and in *El convidat* in 2011, as well as his profile on the social media network Twitter. Monzó's authorial image is characterized by a postmodern model of public engagement which celebrates the commodification of literature and the blending of high and mass culture. Monzó's carefully constructed public image has turned out to be incredibly popular among Catalan audiences and, drawing upon theories of celebrity authorship, I suggest that he has acquired a celebrity status in contemporary Catalan culture

After charting the ways in which Monzó's cultural and artistic project has deftly navigated the shifting values and possibilities offered by the Catalan cultural field in post-Francoist Catalonia, I dedicate my Afterword to discussing how Quim Monzó's work has interacted with the transformations emerging in the 2010s as a result of the Catalan pro-independence push and the 15 May 2011 anti-austerity protests. As in previous decades, Monzó's work provides an excellent platform from which to explore the interplay between the national and the social in Catalonia. On the one hand, Monzó has publicly supported the Catalan independence movement, though, in his distinctive stiff and phlegmatic style, he has done so through pessimistic and unenthusiastic discourses rather different from those of mainstream separatism. On the other, Monzó has criticized the *Indignados* movement and publicly attacked the political space of the Comuns in Catalonia, in particular some of its leaders such as the Mayor of Barcelona Ada Colau and the writer, feminist activist and regional MP for Catalunya Sí que es Pot, Gemma Lienas. As I show, during the 2010s, as in previous decades, Monzó emerges as an author and public intellectual who aims to build a sense of national difference between Catalonia and Spain.

Notes to the Introduction

1. Historians generally agree that the Transition to democracy concluded after the landslide victory of the PSOE in the 1982 elections, which brought the first progressive government to the country since the end of the Civil War in 1939 (Aróstegui 2000; Preston 1987; Romero-Salvadó 1999; Soto 1998; Tusell 2007). For the Catalan context, however, Helena Buffery and Elisenda Marcer propose an alternative time frame, where the Transition would have been complete with the celebration of the first autonomous elections of 1980 and the formation of the first government led by Convergència i Unió (2011: 321–23). With them, this monograph favours 1980 as the date in which the Transition can be seen as completed in Catalonia, thus giving way to the autonomous period.

2. Formed in 1918, the Grup de Sabadell, also known as the Colla de Sabadell, was a literary group connected to the European avant-gardes, particularly Dadaism. It aimed to move beyond the model of *Noucentisme* by deploying a humorous perspective and a transgressive irony. Francesc Trabal, Armand Obiols and Joan Oliver were its main exponents (Marrugat 2008).

3. Created in 1985, Joan Orja was a collective formed by Josep-Anton Fernàndez, Oriol Izquierdo and Jaume Subirana.

CHAPTER 1

❖

Moving Beyond *Resistencialisme*

'Nosaltres no sols sortíem d'una dictadura sinó que intentàvem desfer-nos també del *Diktat* de la pana, els dogmes i les barbes dels progres.'

[We were not only leaving behind a dictatorship, but we were also trying to get rid of the leftist *Diktat* of corduroy, dogmas and beards.]

Interview in *Paper de Vidre*, 20 June 2011 (Miralles 2004).

Quim Monzó was born in 1952, during a period of American cultural, ideological and economic expansion in Western Europe. Americanization can be understood as 'the propagation of American ideas, customs, social patterns, language, industry and capital around the world' (Williams qtd. in Ritzer and Ryan 2010: 47), which, in the European continent, intensified dramatically after the Second World War (Duignan and Gann 1994; Pells 1997; Stephan 2006). The Americanization of Europe is a complex and multifaceted process that has been subject to different interpretations by scholars, ranging from those which regard the process as a unidirectional force to those which emphasize the social and cultural interrelations between the US and European countries. Francisco Rodríguez, for instance, parallels post–Second World War American cultural influx to the 1944 Normandy landings (2010: 80), while Alexander Stephan resorts to vocabularies reminiscent of colonial dynamics: having already established a foothold in Europe during the Golden Twenties, American popular culture 'invaded Europe with new intensity in the second half of the twentieth century' (2006: 1). By contrast, authors such as Rob Kroes and Richard Pells criticize this perspective because, from their point of view, it fails to account for the mutual and bi-directional exchanges between the US and Europe. Kroes sees the term Americanization as 'unduly alarmist' because it 'reduces the complex processes of cultural influence, of borrowing, imitation, and reception, to the stark binary form of a zero-sum game' (1996: xi). Similarly, Pells observes how Americans and Europeans have engaged in a process of reciprocal influence, resulting in 'a complex interaction between different and increasingly heterogeneous cultures and societies' (1997: xv). To overcome this critical end, Antonio Niño switches the perspective to focus on analysing the ways in which European societies have experienced American sociocultural influences. This is, from his point of view, the best barometer to understand the tensions and anxieties at the core of Americanization (2012: 14–15).

While Americanization may be a complex and multidirectional process, there is little doubt that US administrations set out to influence cultural and political ideas in Western Europe after the end of the Second World War. The main programmes developed by the US were the Marshall Plan and the North Atlantic Treaty Organization (NATO) in the politico-economic field, and the Congress for Cultural Freedom (CCF) and Fulbright grants in the cultural arena (Pells 1997: 58–63; Stephan 2006: 2). If the Marshall Plan was designed to bring its European beneficiaries closer to US policies in the Cold War period (Duignan and Gann 1994: 40), 'the Fulbright program became a sort of cultural Marshall Plan helping to revive and defend the intellectual vitality of America's closest allies' (Pells 1997: 61). At a time in which Marxism was strong and influential among the European intelligentsia, US policies had three main objectives at their core: first, to counteract the cultural and political impact of Soviet Russia and Marxism; second, to challenge the widespread critique of American policies and cultural impact circulated by Western artists and intellectuals; and third, to surpass France as the leading culture in the Western world (Epitropoulos and Roudometof 1998: 8; Duignan and Gann 1994: 31; Niño 2012: 94–95; Pells 1997: 61, 155; Stephan 2006: 2).

Francoist Spain was no exception to American influence. The US administration played a key role to progressively integrate Spain in the Western geopolitical sphere from 1953 onwards, when the Pact of Madrid was signed by both governments, an agreement which put an end to the international isolation of the Francoist regime (Martín and Martín 2013; Niño 2012; Ñíguez 1987). After the Second World War, the Western international community remained hostile to the Francoist regime due its former sympathies with the Third Reich and Fascist Italy. The US, however, saw Francoist Spain as a potential ally in their cause against the spread of Marxism in Western Europe. The Pact of Madrid determined that the American government would provide Spain with economic and military aid and, in turn, the US would establish military bases on Spanish soil. The relations between both countries strengthened through the decade, paving the way for the growing influx of American culture in Spain through public and private initiatives, one of the most salient being the Fulbright Program, which Spain joined in 1959 (Martín and Martín 2013: 309; Noyes 2006: 318). In 2008, Sergio Vila-Sanjuán, a former recipient of the Fulbright grant, published a long piece in *La Vanguardia* entitled 'La americanización de la cultura española', in which he argued that the Fulbright Program was a crucial element in the transformations unfolding in Francoist Spain from the 1960s onwards (2008: 14). In the early 1960s, foremost cultural figures such as the philologist Fernando Lázaro Carreter and the authors Miguel Delibes and Ramón Carnicer had been fellows at US universities thanks to Fulbright funding. On their return, they published popular and highly-influential books, essays and press articles discussing their experiences (Vila-Sanjuán 2008: 14). These travel accounts reveal a fascination with the quick transformations unfolding in the country, namely, the rapid technological developments, the burgeoning mass culture, the spread of consumerist habits and the associated change in social customs (Vila-Sanjuán 2008: 14–15). These shifts quickly reached Spain and profoundly transformed its society, the youth in particular. This caused a generational gap in morals and habits of cultural consumption that is fundamental to understanding the final years of the Francoist regime.

These were not, however, the only transformations reaching Spain from the other side of the Atlantic. The US did not exclusively disseminate mass production, mass culture and consumerism, but also countercultural discourses and practices of a radically different ethos, such as anti-consumerism, pacifism and alternative lifestyles hostile to capitalist development. Luís Racionero, who spent the year 1968 at the University of California, Berkeley thanks to a Fulbright Grant, became fascinated with American counterculture and, on his return, published a series of essays and articles which helped to ignite the countercultural movement in Barcelona. María José Ragué also lived in California between 1968 and 1970 and, when back in Barcelona, published the successful *California Trip* (1971), which quickly acquired a cult status. At the time, Pepe Ribas, founder of the mythical countercultural magazine *Ajoblanco* in 1974, read Ragué's book and became fascinated with the lifestyle and underpinning ideologies of the American hippie movement: pacifism, anti-authoritarianism, environmentalism, the anti-bourgeois philosophy, sexual liberation, and drug consumption. These sociocultural practices, Ribas tells us, were transforming his generation: 'Lo que más me impactó del libro fue atar cabos y darme cuenta de que aquellas pautas también estaban cimentando un cambio de imaginario cultural entre nosotros' [What impacted me the most about the book was putting two and two together and realizing that those trends were consolidating a change of cultural imaginary among us] (2007: 25). His words illustrate how, from the late 1960s, a new array of signs and symbols of American origin opposed to the values of consumerist culture reached European societies (Niño 2012: 219).

In his article, Vila-Sanjuán also discusses how, prior to the 1950s, Spanish and Catalan intellectuals generally chose France and Germany for their tours abroad. The Fulbright grants, however, contributed to changing this tendency, heralding 'el giro de la mirada española hacia las universidades estadounidenses' [the turn of the Spanish gaze towards US universities] (2008: 14). This illustrates one of the most salient outcomes of the growing American influence in Western Europe, namely, the progressive replacement from the mid-1950s onwards of French by English as the global lingua franca (Martín and Martín 2013: 306; Pells 1997: 205–06). This major cultural shift is encapsulated in the substitution of Paris by New York as the Western capital for cultural creation and impact, a change which emerges as fundamental when analysing the American influence on Quim Monzó's trajectory. In Spain, for those artists born from the 1940s onwards, 'la ciudad del Empire State representó el mito de la modernidad, como para la quinta de Tàpies o Saura lo había representado París' [the Empire State city represented the myth of modernity in the same way as Paris had represented it for the generation of Tàpies and Saura] (Vila-Sanjuán 2008: 15). The gradual nature of the shift and the temporary co-existence of both French and American culture as leading Western influences are exemplified in the transformations taking place in Catalan culture at the time. During the 1950s and early 1960s, the local intelligentsia was strongly influenced by French culture and the Marxist-inspired model of the committed intellectual (Carbó et al 2000: 5–6). However, Damià Pons argues that by the early 1960s, 'el món anglosaxó ja els havia sobrepassat de llarg tant en l'àmbit de la cultura de masses com en el de la proposta de noves idees i de nous costums socials i morals' [the Anglo-Saxon world had already far surpassed them, both regarding mass culture and the development of ideas and new social and moral customs] (2008: 172). In spite of this, Pons adds, thanks to the ideological revolution heralded by the events of May 1968, French culture was able to recover positions as a nucleus of cultural and ideological production (2008: 172). The French May 1968 combined Marxist-inspired discourses against capitalism, consumerism and American imperialism with a support of workers' rights and strikes, this last feature being less prominent in American counterculture.

Counterculture and May 1968 had a profound impact on Catalan culture by the end of the 1960s, when a young generation of authors and artists who had not experienced the Spanish Civil War came of age. Known as the 'Generació dels setanta', they radically transformed Catalan literature in the convoluted 1970s. Born in the late 1940s and 1950s, the authors emerging in the 1970s — Quim Monzó, Jordi Coca, Amadeu Fabregat, Biel Mesquida, Oriol Pi de Cabanyes and Isa Tròlec, among others — shared the common experience of the turn-of-the-1970s zeitgeist and, as such, constitute both a literary and a social generation (Broch 1980: 79; Graells 1996: 11–13; Izquierdo 1996: 65–67; Pons 2007: 14–25). The Generation of the 1970s was articulated around the literary experimentalist trend en vogue in Europe at the time, which in Catalonia took the name of *textualisme*. Conceiving literary creation as cultural activism, these up-and-coming authors aimed to destabilize, from a poststructuralist perspective, social realism and its techniques of literary representation. Their work also problematized the strong link between literature and national identity that had prevailed all through the Francoist period, therefore inaugurating a fresh conception of Catalan literature. The emergence of the 1970s Generation and the popularity of their experimentalist artistic creations contributed to throwing into crisis the *resistentialist* model operative within Catalan culture since the end of the Civil War (Picornell 2013: 9). In this rapidly shifting milieu, a young and promising Quim Monzó took his first steps as artist and author, experimenting with a variety of creative practices that combined graphic design, comic art and literary creation.

1.1 Quim Monzó's Countercultural and Experimentalist Work

In the mid-1970s, besides working as a graphic designer in the car accessories company Harry Walker Automoción, Monzó was publishing artistic and creative work in a variety of fringe, experimentalist and politically radical outlets: film scripts and anonymous pornographic stories, travel writings in the newspaper *Tele/eXprés* and the magazines *Flashmen* and *Oriflama*, comics and creative writing in publications such as *Ajoblanco*, *Qwert Poiuy: Revista de literatura*, *Tecstual*, *El Viejo Topo* and the fanzine *Pol·len d'Entrecuix*. Between September 1976 and April 1978, Monzó was also the main political cartoonist of the Catalan weekly *Canigó*, where he published almost sixty political cartoons and collages, as well as a number of unsigned front-cover drawings. Monzó's eclectic work during the decade attests to his varied interests and immense creativity. In his memoirs, Pepe Ribas describes how he socialized regularly with Monzó in Barcelona's night-life in the period 1974–1975 and recalls that Monzó was determined to follow the path of artistic creation. However, Monzó was unsure about which path of artistic creation he should pursue: 'Quim no estaba seguro de casi nada' and, for this reason, 'se debatía en un mar de contradicciones' [Quim was not really sure about anything [...] was swimming in a sea of contradictions] (Ribas 2007: 271, 289). While Monzó's path as a literary author may not have appeared crystal clear at the time, this chapter illustrates how these multidisciplinary creations already encapsulate some of the key features of his oeuvre, namely, a criticism of the politics of *resistencialisme* from a detached, (self-)ironic postmodernist perspective, a stiff and provocative relation with the Catalan literary tradition, a fruitful dialogue with the multifaceted cultural impact coming from the US and an unequivocal support for the Catalan language and Catalonia's right to independence from Spain.

Monzó's contributions to *Ajoblanco* in 1974 and 1975 were occasionally co-authored with his friend and journalist Albert Abril, with whom Monzó had travelled to Vietnam, Northern Ireland and Kenya in the early 1970s (Cara 1989: 1; Nadal 1990: 12). Ribas recounts how Monzó and Abril were close friends and saw eye to eye politically and culturally. Emphasising their political radicalism and shared pro-independence stance, Ribas describes Monzó as 'un disparate explosivo devoto de la gamberrada experimental y de todos los ismos, especialmente de los prochinos' [a crazy bugger who loved experimental pranks and all isms, in particular the pro-Chinese ones] (2007: 170). At the time, Albert Abril was a member of the pro-independence and socialist revolutionary party Partit Socialista d'Alliberament Nacional (PSAN), which campaigned for the unity of the Països Catalans. While not a member of the party, as a rising author and public intellectual, Quim Monzó was close to its milieu. On 18 December 1976, for instance, together with other artists and intellectuals he signed a letter in *Canigó* against the decision taken by the Physics Faculty of the University of Barcelona not to authorize the use of Catalan in their classes. The letter used radical pro-independence and Marxist vocabularies. Entitled 'Els botiflers de la Universitat Catalana', the eight signatories, Abril and Monzó amongst them, present themselves as 'treballadors de la cultura' [workers of culture], denounce the resolution, which they define as 'impròpia de tota persona que viu i treballa als Països Catalans' [a text which anyone who lives and works in the Catalan Countries shouldn't have supported], and demand that the name of those who took the decision be made public (Àngels 1976: 4). Similarly, in 1978, around sixty intellectuals, Quim Monzó amongst them, sent a public letter of support for the first conference of the PSAN, in which they expressed their 'reconeixement al PSAN pels seus deu anys de lluita per l'alliberament nacional, pel socialisme i la unitat dels Països Catalans' [recognition of the PSAN for ten years of struggle in favour of national liberation, socialism and the unity of the Catalan Countries] (Buch 2012: 127).

Monzó contributed to *Ajoblanco*'s first, second and fourth issues through four works (two authored individually and two co-authored with Albert Abril) that bring together the textual and the visual, a characteristic feature of Monzó's early work, with comic art, collages and calligrams occupying a central position at this stage in his career. In the second issue of *Ajoblanco*, for instance, Monzó published a two-page comic that juxtaposed references to Richard Nixon, the Vietnam War, political violence and corruption, and the allegedly peaceful situation of Franco's Spain. This was combined with images and drawings alluding to different features of countercultural lifestyles (the sexual revolution, drugs, nightlife) and revolutionary politics, including images of workers' protests in Spain and a drawing of the Paris Commune, together with a newspaper clip about the Basque armed separatist organization ETA (1974: 24–25). In line with the times, Monzó's comic conveys a criticism of the United States' interventionist policies whilst ironically highlighting Spanish internal conflicts and the deceptive view that war and conflict must always happen elsewhere. One year later, in 1976, Monzó contributed to the cultural and intellectual journal *Qwert Poiuy: Revista de Literatura*, founded and directed by Federico Jiménez Losantos, who in the 1970s was very active in Barcelona's leftist and countercultural circles (1976–1977: 135–36). Monzó published a highly experimental text entitled 'Lorem Ipsum Dolor Sit Amet', which is the conventional text filler used in graphic design and publishing-industry templates to allow text designers to concentrate on questions of form, typography and layout without being distracted by the content. Monzó stretches this idea further to create a two-page textual block of Latin nonsense, thus extending the relation between text and image to absurdity and problematizing notions of textual meaning à la Derrida — Losantos and his journal were highly influenced by French post-structuralism and intellectuals such as Jacques Derrida, Julia Kristeva and Roland Barthes (Jiménez Losantos 2007: 166).

In December 1976, Monzó edited, together with Carles Hac Mor, Biel Mesquida, Josep Albertí, Pere Comas, Carles Camps, Santi Pau and Rosa M. Rabasa the interdisciplinary magazine *Tecstual*, which featured literary, artistic and cultural creations by this group of authors. Introducing the magazine as an intervention in Catalan culture from the margins of the cultural system, the editorial proclaims their aim to disrupt the oppositional cultural paradigm still operative in Catalan culture, even though they admit recognizing its value and effectiveness up to that moment. In their own words, the magazine is 'un dels intents i realitzacions que s'han fet per tal de trencar — almenys mínimament — la crosta d'inèrcia que la ideologia de (necessària) defensa de la cultura catalana ha format sobre els aparells culturals nostrats' [one of the projects that have been developed in order to break — even if slightly — some of the habits that the (necessary) ideology of defence for Catalan culture has formed on our cultural apparatuses] (Pau et al 1976: 7). Monzó's contribution is entitled 'Capítol de novel·la', a fourteen-page ironic rewriting of a chapter from the novel *El pistolero de Carson City* into Catalan, the original written by Marcial Lafuente Estefanía, the popular Spanish author of Western fiction (1976c: 84–90). The text is interspersed with illustrations influenced by mass culture and comic art, including comic onomatopoeias, alcoholic cocktails, revolvers and an American dollar bill; alongside them, a well-known image of the writer Franz

Kafka is included. By challenging the notion of literary authorship through a postmodern re-writing/translation of a low-brow Spanish author and celebrating the combination of mass and high culture, Monzó's creation aims to destabilize a literary and cultural system which was slowly responding to the sociocultural changes unfolding since the late 1960s. In February 1977, Monzó joined forces with the poet and artist Narcís Comadira and the editor Jaume Vallcorba to create the fanzine *Pol·len d'Entrecuix*, of which only two issues were published. The publication, intended as a collectors' item, combined written pieces, visual poetry and graphic art and had the leading visual poet and artist Joan Brossa among their contributors. Monzó's two contributions are yet another example of his engagement with the experimentalist and sexually transgressive atmosphere of Barcelona in the 1970s. The first is a short story formatted visually in the shape of a penis describing an extremely violent sadomasochistic sexual encounter (1977d), and the second one is a text-less comic strip entitled 'Amor quotidià' representing a sexual penetration (1977a). Both works are clearly influenced by pornographic imagery, particularly the latter, wherein the drawing exclusively depicts the male and female sexual organs in a way that echoes the close-up shots of pornographic films.

Alongside these artistic creations, in the mid-1970s, Quim Monzó also took his first steps as a literary author through the publication of two experimental books associated with the *textualist* movement: the novel *L'udol del griso al caire de las clavegueres* (1976) and the short story collection *Self-service* (1977), which was co-published with Biel Mesquida. In *Literatura catalana dels anys setanta* (1980), Àlex Broch analyses the thematic lines of four of the most relevant Catalan experimentalist novels, namely, Oriol Pi de Cabanyes' *Oferiu flors als rebels que fracassaren* (1973) and *També les formigues, Dylan, algun dia ploraran de solitud* (1974), Jordi Coca's *Alta comèdia* (1973) and Quim Monzó's *L'udol*. In a section entitled 'Fugida i retorn. El mite del "nord enllà"' [Escape and return. The myth of the 'distant north'], Broch explores how their plots revolve around young characters who feel frustrated and at odds with their social, intellectual and political atmosphere, one which impedes their personal development and growth. In light of this, they leave up north to countries such as France and the United Kingdom. For Broch, the experiences of these novels' main characters are representative of the hopes, desires and ultimately disappointments of the authors of the Generation of the 1970s (1980: 77). Their foreign stint will eventually be unsuccessful and thus, will not resolve the personal, social and political contradictions of the protagonists. In light of this, Broch concludes that the novels debunk the myth of the 'nord enllà' [distant north] (1980: 79) — a expression borrowed from Salvador Espriu's seminal *resistentialist* poem 'Assaig de càntic en el temple', published in 1954. According to Broch, Monzó's *L'udol* stands out because it manifests a deeper engagement with its historical context; as such, the novel manages to represent 'el fracàs de les perspectives de tota una generació' [the failure of the dreams of a whole generation] (1980: 79). Drawing upon Broch, my analysis of Quim Monzó's first novel illustrates how *L'udol* offers an excellent platform to explore, on the one hand, the transnational nature of the sociocultural shifts which transformed a generation of up-and-coming Catalan authors and, on the other, the limits and contradictions of the countercultural and literary experimentalist movements. As I argue, *L'udol* already deploys a sense of disillusionment with the transformative potential of counterculture and *textualisme*.

1.2. *L'udol del griso al caire de les clavegueres*, or the Sociocultural Spirit of the Generation of the 1970s

L'udol del griso al caire de les clavegueres revolves around the lifestyle, relations, hopes and frustrations of Andreu, Llorenç and Octavi, three Catalan teenagers who experience the London, Paris and Barcelona of the late 1960s and early 1970s. They illustrate the strong links between political commitment and cultural activism in Catalonia in the post-1968 period. Llorenç wants to become a film-maker and Andreu and Octavi play in a music band. Andreu dedicates more and more of his time and energy to clandestine political activism. They flee Barcelona to escape the monotony of life under Franco's authoritarian regime, and spend spells in London and Paris. In London, Andreu and Octavi learn English, work as waiters, play in a band and indulge in alcohol and drugs, while in Paris, Llorenç takes part in the May 1968 demonstrations, meetings and political events. The novel is narrated from the present, after Llorenç and Octavi return to Barcelona and Andreu is killed during a Guardia Civil raid against anti-Francoist activists. The narrative voices combines the first and third person and, in true experimentalist style, the voices of the three protagonists are at times fused in a way that somewhat clouds their individuality within the plot and which Hilari de Cara interprets as 'dissolució del personatge' [dissolution of the literary character] typical of *textualisme* (1989: 69). Their experiences and adventures in London and Paris are told in interspersed sequences that do not follow a chronological order and in which the past and present tenses are blended together. Moreover, *L'udol* amalgamates fictional characters with real-life Anglo-American and French artists, such as Bob Dylan, Jean-Luc Godard, Jimmy Hendrix, Janis Joplin, John Lennon, Jim Morrison, as well as politicians like Valéry Giscard d'Estaing and Georges Pompidou, among other (non-)fictional characters.

The novel's contemporary reception illustrates the debates, clashes and contradictions of Catalan literary experimentalism vis-à-vis realist conventions of literary representation. Magdalena Maurici, for instance, sees *L'udol* as a highly experimentalist text, so much so that it cannot be considered a novel because 'no hi ha història, ni personatges ficticis' [there is neither a plot, nor fictional characters] (1977: 35). By contrast, Enric Sullà and Carles Hac Mor contend that, although the text gets close to fully disrupting the realist techniques of representation, these are still present. For Sullà, the novel 'no ha resolt la tensió entre la convenció pròpia al génere narratiu i les instàncies actuals de treball del text' [has not resolved the tension between the conventional characteristics of the narrative genre and the current textual trends] (1977: 129). Hac Mor is a bit more critical, expressing his disappointment at the fact that Monzó 'no ha sabido — no ha podido, ni siquiera lo ha intentado, ni le ha interesado — dar un paso más y diluir del todo, o suprimirlas, las técnicas de representación de la realidad, las técnicas de la novela naturalistarealista' [has not been able to — neither has he wanted or tried, nor has he been interested in — go one step further and completely dilute, or supress, the realist techniques of representation typical of the naturalist-realist novel] (1977: 52). Sullà's and Hac Mor's interpretation is more convincing than Maurici's: the novel does indeed have a discernible plot and, although certain characters break the fictional pact in the sense that they represent a real-life individual, they interact with the protagonists and end up being part of the fictional storyline. Despite the fact that the voices of the three protagonists are blended at times, it is still possible to grasp elements of their distinct individual characteristics, experiences and opinions. *L'udol* was awarded the *Premi de Novel·la Prudenci Bertrana* in 1976, which attests not only to the book's significance and perceived originality at the time, but also to the relevance and impact of the experimentalist literary trend during the 1970s. In fact, two *textualist* novels had been awarded the prize in previous years: Oriol Pi de Cabanyes's *Oferiu flors als rebels que fracassaren* in 1972 and *L'adolescent de sal*, by Biel Mesquida, in 1973.

By (re-)locating most of its plot to Paris and London, *L'udol del griso al caire de les clavegueres* becomes a chronicle of the countercultural spirit of the late 1960s and early 1970s. Opening with a lengthy epigraph from Jean-Luc Godard's emblematic film *La Chinoise* (1968), the ubiquitous interspersion of, and interactions with, countercultural references is key to the novel's plot. When Llorenç is in Paris, numerous graffiti characteristic of the era are inserted in Catalan, between brackets and bolded, such as '(oblideu-vos de tot el que heu après, comenceu a somniar/ *La Sorbona)*' [forget everything you've been taught, start by dreaming], '(decreto l'estat de joia permanent/ *fac de Ciències Polítiques)*' [I declare a permanent state of happiness] and the mythical '(sigueu realistes: demaneu l'impossible/ *fac de Lletres)*' [be realistic, demand the impossible] (1976d: 105, 128–30. Italics in original). Some of the destinations which Monzó visited in the early 1970s travels are also integrated into the plot. Before travelling to Paris, Llorenç visits Dar es Salaam, the capital of Tanzania at the time, where he socializes with leading members of the Mozambique Liberation Front–FRELIMO, the People's Movement for the Liberation of Angola–MPLA, the Zimbabwe African People's Union–ZAPU and the African National Congress–ANC (25), thus bringing the anti-colonial African movements of the 1960s into the novel. Graffiti linking television and fascism from the University of Nairobi in Kenya is also integrated: '(televisors pertot arreu = estat feixista/ *universitat de Nairobi)*' [televisions everywhere = fascist state] (1976d: 58. Italics in original). When narrating Andreu's and Octavi's spell in London, the novel is rife with references to and phrases from famous Anglo-American cultural products representative of the age: bands and musicians such as The Beatles, Cat Stevens, Leonard Cohen, Elton John & Bernie Taupin, Jefferson Airplane, Glenn Miller, Otis Redding, the Rolling Stones, Paul Simon and The Who; the artist Andy Warhol; the authors F. Scott Fitzgerald, Henry Miller, Anthony Burgess and his mythical novel *A Clockwork Orange* (1962), brought to the big screen by Stanley Kubrick in 1971; the American film *Strangers When We Meet* (1960), adapted by Evan Hunter from his novel of the same name and directed by Richard Quine. As this diverse set of references illustrates, Paris is associated primarily with politics and London with counterculture. In fact, while Llorenç's time in Paris revolves around political activism, London is described as a location 'orfe de lluites' [void of politics] (1976d: 163). English language counterculture, therefore, is represented as less ideologically-guided than the French events of May 1968, a difference which will emerge as key in relation to Monzó's own evolution from counterculture to American-inspired libertarianism, as analysed in Chapter 4.

Although the characters do not visit the US, the country is represented in *L'udol* as a mythical, dream-like place, both (physically) distant and (culturally) close. Andreu and Octavi fantasize about a tour through the US with their music band, The Goldfingers, inspired by the James Bond film, stating that, 'somiàvem triomfals gires pel món, pels USA tan lluents, tan allunyats' [we dreamt of triumphant tours through the world and through the shinning and distant US] (1976d: 20–21). Quotations from musical and literary creations by American countercultural icons such as The Doors, the folk band Crosby, Stills, Nash & Young and the poet Allen Ginsberg are also integrated in *L'udol*: '(volem el món i el volem ara/ *The Doors: When the music's over*)' [we want the world and we want it now], '(ningú més no pot prendre el teu lloc, podem canviar el món/ *Crosby, Stills, Nash & Young: Chicago*)' [no one else can take your place, we can change the world] and '(el món és una muntanya de merda: si volem moure-la, hem d'agafar-la a grapades/ *Allen Ginsberg*)' [the world is a mountain of shit: if it's going to be moved at all, it's got to be taken by handfuls] (1976d: 122–23, 212). These American references hint at the fact that, across the European continent, subversive youth cultures were enthused by the countercultural ideas and lifestyles arriving from the US. They welcomed its discourses of newness and modernity, as well as its anti-bourgeois and anti-authoritarian discourses which challenged established social hierarchies (Campbell, Davies and McKay 2010: 12–14; Pells 1997: 239–49). Although cultural and societal transformations reached Spain a little later than the rest of Europe due to Francoism, the beginning of the 1970s saw politicized youngsters seduced by values such as hedonism, pacifism, environmentalism and rebelliousness; they questioned the absolutes received from their parents and broke away from the established Francoist social and moral rules (Niño 2012: 219; Pons 2008: 168–69; Townson 2009: xi–ii). This is depicted in the novel, for instance, through Andreu's and Octavi's excursions to The Cavern in Liverpool, the legendary club associated with the Beatles. Defining their trips as '[p]eregrinacions Religioses a Liverpool', one of them says that 'ens han canviat Lurdes [sic] pel Lancashire, te n'adones?' [Religious pilgrimages to Liverpool [...] the Lancashire has substituted Lurdes, don't you see?] (1976d: 40). This sentence can be seen as encapsulating the radically different set of values and life-experiences that the protagonists had vis-à-vis their forebearers, a theme which permeates the novel. When discussing the lifestyles and expectations of his father and grandfather, Andreu points out that each's dream in life was to get a permanent job, self-employed if possible, a family and a house (1976d: 164). Andreu and Octavi revel in the present moment, socialising in London with dreams entirely different from those of their forefathers, as Octavi's recounts: 'Els acòlits d'Elvis Presley somiaven ser cantants famosos, voltats de nenes boniques, de mans que els aferressin demanant-los-ho tot' [The acolytes of Elvis Presley dreamt of being famous singers, surrounded by beautiful girls and by hands that desired and embraced them] (1976d: 209). By focusing on their generation and emphasising the gap, *L'udol* also portrays how the 1960s were 'marked by the emergence of "youth" and young people's popular culture as a new social construction' (Dowling 2013: 77). The generational transformation of principles and moral standards unfolding during the decade is further exemplified by the novel's insertion of an excerpt from Bob Dylan's song 'The Times They Are a-Changin': '(veniu pares i mares de tot el país i no critiqueu allò que no podeu comprendre/ els vostres fills i filles estan fora del vostre control, el vostre vell sistema envelleix ràpidament' [come mothers and fathers throughout the land and don't criticize what you can't understand/ your sons and your daughters are beyond your command, your old road is rapidly agin'] (1976d: 207).

As Dylan's song suggests, his generation's aims triggered mutual incomprehension and clashes with their parents' generation. The topic of leaving the parental nest is discussed at various instances by the protagonists. At one point, one of them states that 'el dia que me'n vagi de casa hi haurà un daltabaix fenomenal' [there will be a great scandal the day I leave home] and subsequently, the text reproduces a line from The Beatle's popular song 'She's Leaving Home', based on the real case of a 17-year old girl who left with her boyfriend: '(se'n va de casa després d'haver viscut sola durant anys/ *John Lenon & Paul McCartney: She's leaving home*)' [She's leaving home, after living alone, for so many years] (1976d: 84. Italics in original). More mundane yet perhaps more revealing generational differences are also portrayed in the novel. Parental involvement in clothing style, for instance, is strongly rejected by Andreu and Octavi. However, the text skilfully represents how, in most cases, teenagers rebelled against their parents for the sake of generational revolt, even when they knew their ancestors had a point. Talking about the summer sandals worn by middle-aged people, Octavi notes how their reaction was strange and logical at the same time: while they understood that sandals were incredibly practical to battle high temperatures, they also knew that wearing them may mean that you were 'un adolescent sense gustos propis [...] que les duies per imposició paterna' [a teenager without personal tastes [...] who wore them due to parental imposition] (1976d: 20). Octavi's words illustrate the complexities and ambivalences of this generational challenge, which seems to be more aesthetico-cultural than political.

While also representing the relevant impact of the French May 1968, *L'udol* also engages with the progressive decrease of French cultural influence as discussed by Damià Pons (2008). Highlighting that the Beatles and the Rolling Stones are their favourite bands, the narrator observes that the protagonists are, with the exception of select French *chansonniers*, mostly familiar with English-language music: 'desconeixedors de qualsevol música que no fos anglosaxona, potser algun Ferré, algun rock bretó que el Georges Pompidou havia dut, gravat en cassette, del París de la França' [they were unfamiliar with any music that wasn't Anglo-Saxon, perhaps they knew a Ferré and some Breton rock songs which Georges Pompidou had brought, recorded in a cassette, from the Paris of la France] (Monzó 1976d: 119).

Beyond the representation of French culture's fading impact, this sentence provides a good example of the (limits of the) experimentalist nature of the novel. President of France from 1969 until 1974, Georges Pompidou's introduction of illegal music to Francoist Spain exemplifies how *L'udol* problematizes the fictional pact characteristic of realist literature. At the same time, however, the novel engages with its specific historical context, as travelling to France to watch films and purchase books that were later taken into Catalonia was a relatively common activity amongst artists and political activists during the final years of Francoism. This phrase, therefore, illustrates how the novel combines the disruption of traditional techniques of literary representation together with certain realist elements. Moreover, this excerpt also encapsulates the historical role of France as a haven and inspiration for Catalan culture, a role which would cease to be operative with the end of the Francoist regime. The gradual substitution of French by English as the leading centre for cultural production in the West is literally portrayed in the following passage, which reproduces the progressive replacement of the French national anthem by the well-known pacifist song 'All You Need Is Love' by The Beatles:

> L'orquestra arrenca amb força: les primeres notes de la Marsellesa que, lentament, es deformen, es desfullen fins que en neix una nova cançó. Als peus de l'amfiteatre, els Beatles i un grapat ample d'amics comencen a cantar *All you need is love*. (1976d: 67. Italics in original)

> [The orchestra starts with great energy: after the first notes, however, the lyrics of La Marseillaise start to dissipate and gradually lose their form until a new song is born. At the foot of the amphitheatre, the Beatles and a large bunch of friends start singing *All You Need Is Love*]

This passage substitutes an epitomic symbol of revolution and national convention with a global cultural product associated with 1960s pacifism. The contrast between the narratives of global peace encapsulated in 'All You Need Is Love' and the nationalist and revolutionary politics at the core of La Marseillaise can also be seen as hinting at a countercultural-led transformation of the notion of political activism. The celebration of spontaneity and hedonism characteristic of counterculture stood in stark contrast to militant Marxist politics, which had been the main and almost-sole opposition to the Francoist regime until the late 1960s. In their memoirs, Federico Jiménez Losantos and Pepe Ribas discuss how, inspired by American counterculture, young activists from Barcelona progressively distanced themselves from Marxism and the political structures and practices of the Partit Socialista Unificat de Catalunya (PSUC) (Jiménez Losantos 2007: 15; Ribas 2007: 70–72). As Jiménez Losantos recounts, 'me había zambullido en la California Dreamin' de los primeros setenta, pasada, naturalmente, por Barcelona' [I had immersed myself in the California Dreamin' of the early 1970s, arriving through Barcelona, of course] (15). At the time he was no longer interested in Karl Marx's writings, instead devouring *El nacimiento de una contracultura* (1969) by the American author Theodor Roszak, translated into Spanish by the Barcelona-based publishing house Kairós, María José Ragué's *California Trip* (1971), also published by Kairós, and the 'antología bilingüe de Serge Faucherau *Nueva Poesía norteamericana*, en Barral. Nada de Marx' [Serge

Faucherau's bilingual anthology *Nueva Poesía norteamericana*, published by Barral. Nothing by Marx] (15). Similarly, Ribas emphasizes how the PSUC leaders grew suspicious towards the countercultural imaginary of the young generations, which was 'más atento a la creación artística que al materialismo dialectico; más cerca del rock visionario y el amor libre que de las doctrinas del socialismo científico' [more attentive to artistic creation than to dialectical materialism, and closer to visionary rock music and free love than to the doctrines of scientific socialism] (2007: 52). This is portrayed in *L'udol* through the several May 1968 graffiti reproduced in the text and also through the characters' own experiences. The slogan '(com més faig l'amor, més ganes tenc de fer la revolució / com més faig la revolució, més ganes tinc de fer l'amor/ *la Sorbona*)' [the more I make love, the more I want to make the revolution/ the more I make revolution, the more I want to make love] (1976d: 128–29. Italics in original) is an example of the conception of free sexuality as political activism, while the following examples illustrate the countercultural critique of traditional Marxist parties and their cultural aesthetics: '(fora el realisme socialista, visca el surrealisme/ *liceu Condorcet*)' [down with socialist realism, long live surrealism] and '(tenim una esquerra prehistòrica/ *fac de Ciències Polítiques*)' [we have a prehistoric left] (1976d: 132, 144. Italics in original). Experiencing this sociocultural spirit first hand, Llorenç has sexual intercourse behind a barricade during the Paris riots. Similarly, one of his friends, Catherine, disappears for a number of days in the midst of the protests. Her friends worry about her safety but, on returning, she relates that she had met a group of anarchists and decided to stay with them, 'al·legant que n'hi havia un que estava boníssim, somrient, disculpant-se per no haver donat senyals de vida durant tant de temps' [claiming that one of them was very hot, and apologizing for having disappeared for so long] (1976d: 128–31). Through the representation of free sexuality as a political act, the novel hints at the changing sociocultural values that characterized the politicized sections of the Catalan youth and also to their distancing from established Marxist parties, which heralds a new conception of political commitment that is key to understanding Monzó's criticism of the PSUC during the Transition, as discussed in the next section.

Alongside counterculture, European youth were also attracted to the consumerist trends arriving from the US, represented in *L'udol* through the several instances in which the main characters drink *Coca-Cola* and *7up*. The references to *Coca-Cola* are not fortuitous, as the soft drink was seen as one of the most potent symbols of the American consumerist lifestyle and, for this reason, very guardedly received in Europe by intellectuals and socialist activists (Pells 1997: 199). Despite this, mass consumption of US products was gradually embraced by European youth 'not as a move to Americanize their societies but as a liberation from rules and customs they grew up with' (Stephan 2006: 14). Monzó's *L'udol* portrays how a young generation welcomed and embraced mass consumption as a sign of modernity and rebellion in line with the new times. Relatedly, the earlier example on the substitution of Lourdes for the Beatles encapsulates how, in Spain, the development of mass consumerism signalled a shift from a society of sacrifice to a society of enjoyment (Crumbaugh 2009: 90–93; Townson 2009: xxvii). However, despite enjoying

Coca-cola, the symbol of American consumerism par excellence, the protagonists of *L'udol* are also critical of American cultural imperialism and Western capitalist propaganda (1976d: 20, 62–63) and other trends arriving from the US such as food industrialization (71) and television. Llorenç, the most politicized character, rhetorically asks Octavi, '¿Saps que un infant nord-americà ha vist, pel cap baix, quatre-centes hores de tele el primer dia que fot els peus a l'escola?' [Do you know that, according to conservative estimates, a North-American kid has watched four hundred hours of television before starting school?] (1976d: 50). Llorenç sees TV as the antithesis of intellectual activity and reasoning and, for this reason, celebrates that his generation grew up without it, an absence which helped them to develop a critical outlook. The main characters' enjoyment of American countercultural lifestyles and consumerism, whilst at the same time deploying a shallow and timid critique of the country's geopolitics and cultural influence, exemplifies the polyvalent and contradictory nature of the American impact. By representing both the fascination with, and critique of, the US, the novel hints at how Americanization was not a simple unilateral force but a fluid and multifaceted interaction involving borrowing, imitation and critique. In this sense, Monzó's first novel portrays how cultural and political activists in the late 1960s 'could act — at least for a time — both as the leaders of a revolution and as the agents of "Americanization"' (Pells 1997: 243).

Through the narration of the characters' adventures in London and Paris, the novel recounts moments of joy and excitement, even of hope. In spite of this, however, *L'udol*'s perspective is not engaged but rather detached. A sense of disillusionment pervades the novel, beginning in the first chapter when Andreu's death at the hands of the Guardia Civil is narrated by Andreu himself in the first person. Antoni Maestre interprets this death as a signal of the loss of idealism that permeates the novel (2010: 214). Hence, the narration of their exciting and transformative experiences abroad is combined with moments, in particular when they are back in Barcelona, in which the young protagonists talk about their generational revolt as a failure, which is (self-)presented as a (generational) debacle:

> i deies cony, aquesta gent, aquesta generació, hòstia, fotrem alguna cosa, vet aquí el detonador, tots encara amb el dubte de si podríem fer alguna cosa, però pensant que la joventut podria esdevenir una nova classe, vull dir un nou element d'unió, heus aquí la primera generació trobada, no corromputs pel sistema i les peles, totes aquestes coses que es deien aleshores. (1976d: 98)

> [and you said, fuck, these guys, this generation, damn it, we will do something serious, here's the spark, everyone was still considering whether we would be able to achieve something or not, but we thought that the youth could become a new class, I mean a new element of unity, here's the first generation not corrupted by money and the system, all the things that were said those days]

This excerpt can be seen as encapsulating the overall sense of disappointment with the political transformative power of the 1960s movements and uprisings. The text seems to portray their generation's failure through a focus on three American countercultural icons who passed away in tragic circumstances in the early 1970s before reaching thirty years of age: Jimi Hendrix, Janis Joplin and Jim Morrison, whose deaths were associated with overuse of alcohol and drugs. Hendrix and Joplin died in September and October 1970, respectively, and Morrison passed away approximately nine months later, in July 1971. The three deaths are represented in the novel in a detached, matter-of-fact manner. Conflating different narrative moments, Jim Morrison is first represented playing the guitar with friends at a Californian beach and, right afterwards, the narrative voice announces his death: 'Una porta de cambra de bany, amb el mirall que no ens reflecteix i les rajoles i la banyera, esquitxada de sang. Un braç que penja: el cadàver de Jim Morrison, ulls closos com la nit' [A bathroom's door and a mirror that doesn't reflect us, the bath and floor tiles splashed with blood. An arm hanging: Jim Morrison's corpse, his eyes closed like the night] (1976d: 141–42). Only a few pages later, the novel describes Janis Joplin's death. The American singer-songwriter is represented having sexual intercourse with an unnamed lover. After describing her orgasm, the narrator tells that 'Janis s'adorm, els ulls vers l'infinit' [Janis falls asleep, her eyes towards the infinite] (1976d: 158). In the next paragraph, Joplin is dead. As the narrative voice tells us, her lover wakes up and 'el llit és buit i, en una butaca propera, hi ha el cadàver nu de Janis Joplin — blues, whisky i amor — amb una volguda sobredosi' [the bed is empty and, in a nearby armchair, is Janis Joplin's nude corpse — blues, whisky and love — with a desired overdose] (1976d: 158). Finally, Jimi Hendrix is depicted taking a hit of heroin after a concert at a venue packed with posters of Malcolm X and the Black Panther leader Stockely Carmichael. Hendrix lies down on the floor cushions to enjoy the heroin high and, afterwards, the narrator coldly announces his imminent death, bringing the chapter to an abrupt end: 'Jimi Hendrix veu colors. D'aquí a una estona, Jimi Hendrix també serà mort' [Jimi Hendrix is seeing colours. In a little while, Jimi Hendrix will be dead too] (204). In the novel, the tragic and unexpected deaths of these three American countercultural icons appears strongly connected to the outcome of Andreu's and Octavis's (failed) countercultural hopes. When leaving London to return to Barcelona, they reflect on these deaths in a chapter which opens with the phrase '[a]ixò s'acaba, nois, l'Andreu i jo tornem cap a Barcelona' [this is about to be over, guys, Andreu and myself are returning to Barcelona] (1976d: 175–76). They get on a train to Gatwick airport and, while staring through the train's window, Andreu muses about their failed London experience, noting that,

> que ens havien donat uns herois i que de cop i volta ens els havien tret/ ja no tenim herois insistia, ens han deixat sols, sols amb els problemes de cada dia/ Jimi Hendrix, Janis Joplin, Jim Morrison ens han abandonat, no han volgut continuar amb la mentida (1976d: 175–76)

> [we had been given heroes and, all of a sudden, they had been taken from us/ we don't have heroes, he insisted, they've left us alone, alone with our everyday problems/ Jimi Hendrix, Janis Joplin, Jim Morrison have abandoned us, they've not wanted to continue with the lie]

The novel's depiction of their deaths can be interpreted as a metaphor for the culmination of the countercultural movement, grimly described by Andreu as a lie which has now come to an end. Andreu and Octavi's feeling of dissatisfaction suggests a displaced criticism of Barcelona's own countercultural scene, which is, in essence, the local version of this movement. This sense of failure was also shared by leading figures of Barcelona's counterculture, such as María José Ragué and Luis Racionero, who pointed out its short-lived nature and hastened closure. As early as 1973, Ragué stated that counterculture was being co-opted by consumerism: 'la contracultura ha atacado desde fuera el sistema de consumo y está siendo o ha sido ya asimilada por el mismo' [counterculture has challenged the consumerist system from the outside and it is now being co-opted, or has already been, by that very same system] (1973: 139). Five years later, in 1979, Racionero noted that, while myths and hopes flourished in the 1960s, disenchantment had indeed taken over by the mid-1970s (1979: 93). His assessment was particularly critical: 'a nivel de cambio social no ha quedado nada; a nivel de cambio personal han quedado algunas vidas cambiadas' [not a single social change has been consolidated; regarding individual changes, some lives have been transformed] (1979: 95). Monzó's appraisal of counterculture in the mid-1970s was already quite aloof. As recounted by Ribas in his memoirs, Monzó's design reproducing the *Coca-cola*'s iconic marketing style for *Ajoblanco* in October 1974 was already a parody of how American counterculture had been co-opted by commercialization. In Ribas's own words, Monzó said that he aimed to 'ridiculizar la comercialización en la que había caido la contracultura norteamericana y el rock combativo. "Parodiaré las letras de la multinacional por excelencia: Coca-cola", dijo' [ridicule the commercialization of American counterculture and combative rock bands. 'I will parody the letters of the multinational *par excellence*: Coca-Cola'] (2007: 206).

These interpretations of counterculture, however, are defined by an overly simplistic dichotomous perspective which fails to grasp the continuum of socio-cultural changes that transformed a generation of young Catalan authors and artists, some of which, such as Monzó, would become key cultural figures in post-Transition Catalonia. As my analysis has shown, *L'udol del griso al caire de les clavegueres* is an exceptional account of such transformations precisely because it does not easily lend itself to binary readings with regards to the nature of the protagonists' revolt. As such, *L'udol* becomes a generational chronicle, even an archive, of the lifestyles and cultural narratives that furthered social change in early 1970s Catalonia. While perhaps not experiencing it first hand as Monzó and other artists and activists did, these new discourses and behaviours would eventually also transform a whole generation of Catalan young adults. Broch points out the novel's strong engagement with its historical context, and, seen under this light, I wish to highlight *L'udol*'s nuanced representation of the main cultural, political and personal narratives at the core of the protagonists' experiences. Maestre's reading of *L'udol* locates it in the socio-political context of the Spanish Transition to democracy, arguing that 'es tracta d'una novel·la compromesa, plena d'il·lusió davant la fi de la dictadura i l'obertura de la societat' [it is a committed novel, full of hopes after the end of the dictatorship and the associated social transformations] (2010: 236). Although it is possible to read Monzó's first novel in connection with the sense of political and ideological momentum associated with the early stages of the Transition, I would suggest that the novel's positioning vis-à-vis such discourses places greater emphasis on how it denies its overall transformative political potential. Reflecting on the outcome of the May 1968 protests, Llorenç states that there was a true sense of hope 'fins que es van fer eleccions i tot tornà a ser com sempre havia estat: una merda, un altre cop' [until there was a general election and everything went back to how it had always been: shit, once again] (1976d: 160). By transmitting that the possibilities for socio-political transformation collapsed due to the limited framework of parliamentary politics, the novel's overall feeling of defeat can be read as a harbinger for the sense of *desencanto* that was to follow shortly due to the outcome of the Transition and which would be key to Monzó's trajectory from the late 1970s. Relatedly, *L'udol del griso al caire de les clavegueres* also illustrates the flaws and limits of the *textualist* challenge to the Catalan literary tradition. On the one hand, despite its experimentalism, the novel does not fully disrupt the realist techniques of representation. On the other, the fact that experimentalist works — Monzó's *L'udol* among them — were awarded relevant prizes within Catalan culture exemplifies how the Catalan literary system did aim to integrate *textualisme* in order to progressively adapt to the new sociocultural ethos. In view of its themes, aesthetics, literary style and impact within the Catalan cultural field of its time, *L'udol* emerges as a text emblematic of the influences and experiences of the literary and social Generation of the 1970s — in other words, a novel which depicts Barcelona's sociocultural zeitgeist of the late 1960s and beginning of the 1970s.

1.3. Monzó versus Espriu, or Counterculture versus *Resistencialisme*

Monzó's longest-standing contribution during the 1970s was his political cartooning work in *Canigó* from 11 September 1976 until 1 April 1978, which I analyse at length in the next chapter through a focus on national politics during the Transition. In the final section of this chapter, however, I would like to offer a reading of one of Monzó's cartoons with a view to analysing how his (countercultural) disruption of the politics of *resistencialisme* triggered a public controversy within Catalan literature, a case study which throws light on the clashes surrounding the configuration of the (proto-)institutional Catalan cultural field during the Transition. This dispute reveals that the provocative and whimsical attitude that has become a staple of Monzó's work and public persona was already a constituent element of his cultural programme during the early years of his career. The sociocultural transformations analysed in *L'udol* are key to understanding this controversy and the characteristics of Monzó's playful public persona.

On 30 October 1976, Monzó published a political cartoon caricaturising the foremost poet and novelist Salvador Espriu, a symbol of Catalonia's literary and national resistance under the Francoist regime. With big, bold text on top of the vignette proclaiming 'Espriu està per la cooficialitat!' [Espriu is in favour of co-officiality], the drawing shows the caricature of the back of an old man passionately reciting a poem, with his arm raised, pointing with his finger towards the front. The text in the speech balloon reads '¡Ens mantendremos fidels por siempre més al servicio d'aquest pueblo' [We shall remain forever loyal at the service of our people] (Figure 1.1). By turning one of Espriu's best-known lines on the intellectual's duty of national and cultural resistance into a hybrid mix of Catalan and Spanish, Monzó's cartoon is not only irreverently mocking the most prominent Catalan poet of his time, but also the notions of language purism and the national literary canon. Monzó's drawing came as a response to Salvador Espriu's public support for the co-officiality of Catalan and Spanish, which the national poet had expressed in the book *PSUC: per Catalunya, la democràcia i el socialisme* (1976), edited by the PSUC. The book opens with an introductory text on the history of the party by Gregori López Raimundo and its core consists of interviews conducted by Antoni Batista with twelve Catalan cultural and political personalities — Raimon, Antoni Tàpies, Lluis Maria Xirinacs and Salvador Espriu, among others — who comment on the most pressing issues and debates surrounding the Transition in Catalonia. The front-cover is the well-known poster that Antoni Tàpies designed for the party in 1976 with the title 'PSUC: per Catalunya, la Democràcia i el Socialisme', which shows the party's initials at the top with the four stripes of the Catalan flag at the bottom, both in red on a yellow background.

This interview with Espriu offers an excellent example of the discourses around the figure of the public intellectual in the oppositional model in place during Francoism. In response to the very first question, Espriu observes that his activism has been mostly cultural and, as such, he has not participated in clandestine activities: 'S'ha cregut, i ho agreixo, que no era un home polític sinó un literat que ha estat al servei del País' [I have not been considered a political activist but a man

FIG. 1.1. *Canigó* 473. 30 October 1976, p. 7

of letters at the service of the Nation, and I am thankful for that] (Batista and López Raimundo 1976: 167). Espriu defines himself as a solitary intellectual and remarks on his devotion and service to the Catalan nation and language from the early years of the Francoist period (1976: 168). In spite of this, Espriu deems it necessary to point out that, 'jo no em considero important i no és falsa modèstia. Només he intentat ser coherent' [I don't consider myself important and this isn't false modesty. I've only tried to be coherent] (1976: 168). The debate over the legal status of the Catalan language was one of the most heated and long-lasting controversies in Catalan and Spanish politics during the Transition and Espriu expressed himself clearly and extensively in the interview. To Batista's question on the matter, Espriu answers that, from his point of view, aspiring to co-officiality is already a success, defines the potential relegation of Spanish as a mistake or stupidity and subsequently adds: 'Bandegem una llengua: l'error que hem criticat tant!' [We block a language: the mistake that we've criticised so strongly!] (1976: 168–69). In this final sentence, Espriu suggests a parallel between making Catalan the only official language of Catalonia and the Francoist policies to suppress the region's vernacular language. Espriu offers more arguments to support his reasoning. First, he links the 'oficialitat exclusivista del català' [exclusivist officiality of Catalan] to the project aiming for Catalonia's separation from Spain, a demand which he sees as unrealistic (1976: 169). Second, he argues that relegating a universal language like Spanish is counterproductive because it severs the culture of the younger generations (1976: 170). Finally, he contends that such a move would mean adopting 'una actitud antipàtica a l'inrevés' [an unpleasant attitude turned around], thus once again associating Catalan's sole officiality with a kind of retaliation (1976: 179). In view of all these arguments, he sees co-officiality as the only rational and prudent move.

On 15 November 1976, two weeks after the cartoon was published, the novelist and journalist Montserrat Roig, member of the PSUC at the time, published an article entitled 'Salvador Espriu, vexat' in *Arreu*, a weekly magazine within the sphere of influence of the PSUC. Although Roig does not directly mention Monzó, it is obvious that she is criticising his cartoon, and all the more in the final paragraph, where she states that Espriu does not deserve the same treatment and caricatures aimed at Adolfo Suárez, the Spanish Prime Minister at the time, and Joaquín Viola, mayor of Barcelona, two typical targets of Monzó's biting drawings in *Canigó*. Accompanied by a close-up photo of Espriu's serious and dignified face, Roig's article makes a strong case for Espriu as a key figure for the survival of Catalan language and literature during Francoism and, as such, a canonical national author who should not be the target of mordant irony. Roig's article reveals how in the mid-1970s *resistentialist* discourses were still operative and seen as compelling and effective. She asserts that, while she would prefer the officiality of Catalan, the debate is too complex and convoluted to allow for a prudent and constructive discussion. Furthermore, she adds, '[m]entre discutim sobre coses que encara no ens passen, n'hi ha que es rifen de nosaltres, com a catalans i com a ciutadans' [while we're arguing about things we're not experiencing yet, others are conning us, both as Catalans and as citizens] (1976: 25). Subsequently, Roig vindicates Espriu's loyalty to the Catalan language during the strenuous early years of Francoism, when the Spanish state aimed to reduce Catalan to a provincial and domestic dialect, and Espriu's literature contributed to maintaining Catalan as a literary language. As she points out, thanks to Espriu's generation, she and other authors have been able to 'recuperar el fil de la literatura estroncada' [recover the thread of the severed literature] (1976: 25). Roig's arguments revolve around two key *resistentialist* notions: the importance of political unity among Catalans due to the external threat posed by the Spanish (post-)Francoist state, and the respect due for canonical authors whose texts have been pivotal to the very existence and continuity of Catalan literature under Francoism. In fact, Roig remarks that the influence of the Francoist period is essential to understanding this controversy. From her point of view, the lack of a sense of humour and the inability to respect others' opinions are Francoist remnants still pervading Catalan culture. In a clear reference to Monzó's cartoon, she declares that, '[q]uan no ens agrada una idea que no s'adiu amb el nostre món mental, no la discutim: la triturem, la reduïm a la paròdia' [when we don't like an idea which doesn't fit within our mental framework, we don't discuss it: we destroy it, we reduce it to parody] (1976: 25). Roig closes her article by observing that such debating style is an idiotic, foreign-born trend imposed on Catalonia, in what is a clear reference to Spain: 'En podem discutir, en podem discrepar, però no l'hem de vexar. Si ho fem, és que acceptem la subnormalitat que ens ha estat imposada des de fora' [We can discuss it, we can disagree about it, but we shouldn't vex it. If we do so, we're accepting the idiocy that has been imposed on us from outside] (1976: 25). Through these discourses, Roig is arguing that the bitter irony and outright critique deployed by Monzó in his cartoon should not be used in debates within Catalan culture. By doing so, Roig locates Monzó's (unexpected) criticism outside the framework of customary Catalan cultural debates.

The polemic continued two weeks later, on 29 November 1976, when *Arreu* published a two-page special on the topic. Under the heading 'Debat', this consisted of a brief preamble by the editors introducing the controversy, Monzó's public riposte in the form of a letter to the director and a longer article on the topic signed by the poet and socio-linguist Francesc Vallverdú, a member of the PSUC and public intellectual of reference for the party at the time. Monzó's cartoon was also reproduced, thus gaining yet more visibility and notoriety. In their text, the editors present Monzó as the winner of the *Premi Prudenci Bertrana de Novel·la* 1976, and state that they wanted to reproduce the cartoon to show that, from their point of view, the attack to Salvador Espriu had been completely unfair, given how 'tota l'obra de Salvador Espriu és un constant, fecund i rigorós homenatge a la llengua catalana' [Salvador Espriu's oeuvre is a constant, fertile and rigorous homage to the Catalan language] (1976: 34). Tellingly, this introductory text does not mention Vallverdú's article, published right next to Monzó's, which Agustí Pons, Espriu's biographer, interprets as illustrating how the editors of *Arreu* did not want Monzó to have the last word on the matter (2013: 658). As a matter of fact, we can infer that the special was published because the editors did not want to publish solely Monzó's right of reply to Roig's article which, in itself, reveals a guarded, *resistentialist* conception of cultural debates. Moreover, Vallverdú may have wanted to have his say and defend Espriu because he had arranged Batista's interview with Espriu, as Batista himself recounts in the introduction to the interview in the PSUC book (Batista and López Raimundo 1976: 167).

If Roig's piece made use of *resistentialist* discourses and vocabularies, Monzó's answer is radically different, mordant and unabashedly ironic, just as his political cartoon. After declaring his intention to answer to the obvious allusions to his cartoon, Monzó's second paragraph opens with a forthright statement in which he mentions Roig directly: 'És evident, Sra. Roig, que quan parleu de manca de sentit de l'humor només podeu estar referint-vos a la vostra, palesada ben clarament en la reacció que heu tingut davant l'acudit' [It is clear, Sra. Roig, that, when you talk about a lack of sense of humour, you can only be referring to yours, given your reaction to the joke] (1976b: 34). This is followed by a sarcastic couple of sentences between brackets where Monzó wonders if Roig was perhaps pretending that the 'llibre del PSUC' in which Espriu had declared his support for co-officiality was 'un annexe de la revista "Por Favor"' [a supplement of the magazine *Por Favor*], the mythical satirical magazine of political humour published in Barcelona between 1974 and 1978, with contributors such as Jaume Perich, Manuel Vázquez Montalbán and Forges. If this was the case, Monzó adds, '[a]leshores — i només aleshores — sí que reconeixeria el meu error per no haver-me-les pres en conya' [then — and only then — I would acknowledge my mistake of having taken the declarations seriously] (1976b: 34). This excerpt reveals Monzó's provocative and direct style in the context of the heated Transition debates, directed here not only at Roig but also at the PSUC by suggesting that the book edited by the party could be disguised as a section of the satirical *Por Favor*. In the next couple of paragraphs, Monzó argues that a clear remnant of Francoism is the tendency to create untouchable personalities, thus challenging the parochial idea that foremost cultural figures should not be the object of criticism and public debate. Monzó also engages with Roig's argument about Espriu's vital role for Catalan language and literature by arguing that it is precisely because of Espriu's historic role and relevance that his statement is so dangerous (1976b: 34). In the closing paragraph, Monzó directly addresses Montserrat Roig again, contending that irony should not be confused with insult. In his own words,

> Si confoneu ironia amb insult, si enteneu que fer un acudit sobre Espriu és vexar-lo, malament rai; ha tornat l'època dels mites intocables, de les sacrosantes presències sobre les quals no ens és dat opinar. Creia que anàvem cap a la llibertat, no cap al Decreto de Unificación (1976b: 34)

> [It is a problem that you mistake irony for insult, that you think that making a joke about Espriu is vexing him; the time of the untouchable myths, of the sacrosanct personalities about whom we can't give our opinion, has returned. I thought we were going towards freedom, not towards the Decree of Unification]

Monzó's grandiloquent terms 'mites intocables' and 'sacrosantes presències' clearly depart from the balanced and serene rhetoric and vocabularies of the oppositional model, exemplifying his refusal to abide by the (alleged) rules of the Catalan cultural field as discussed in Roig's piece and Espriu's interview. This is further illustrated by Monzó's hyperbolic closing sentence, in which he wonders if the end point of the Transition is the Decree of Unification, in reference to the law passed by Franco's provisional government on 19 April 1937, which merged the fascist Falange Española and the Carlist Comunión Tradicionalista into a new political party under the name the Falange Española Tradicionalista y de las Juntas de Ofensiva Nacional Sindicalista. While the use of the third person plural in Monzó's closing line is polysemic, in view of the rest of the letter, it can be suggested that the sentence alludes to the desire for unity within Catalan culture as proposed by Roig. Monzó's letter, therefore, seems to suggest that Roig's call for unity may ultimately contribute to suppress public debate within the Catalan cultural field.

Vallverdú's article seizes the opportunity offered by the controversy to comment on the argumentative lines that define public debates in Catalonia after Franco's death, and to denounce what he perceives as the growing tendency to use demagogy and gratuitous insults against those who defend democratic, fair and totally justifiable political positions, in what is a clear hint at the growing divisions amongst the democratic opposition. Entitled 'Una plaga que cal aïllar: el "terrorisme intel·lectual"', the article nevertheless engages with Monzó's cartoon, albeit without mentioning his name. Vallverdú briefly discusses Espriu's statement on co-officiality, observing that co-officiality should not prevent Catalan language's full normalization, an aspect that certain advocates of co-officiality sometimes forget. Vallverdú is therefore remarking on his party's support for the promotion and full normalization of the Catalan language. Vallverdú then moves on to defend Espriu from the attacks he received in response to his statement in favour of co-officiality (Monzó's cartoon was one among others), arguing that Espriu is a writer and citizen that has done 'molt més pel nostre país i per la nostra cultura que els qui ara l'escridassen' [much more for our nation and our culture than those who now heckle him] (1976: 35). Subsequently, Vallverdú asks rhetorically what is the aim of publishing 'un acudit malintencionat en què un ninot diu en "bilingüe" uns memorables versos seus?' [a malicious joke in which a figurine recites one of his memorable verses 'in bilingual'?] (1976: 35). For Vallverdú, this is an example of an irresponsible intellectual terrorism, which is as irrational as any other type of terrorism, therefore associating Monzó's argumentative style to one of the critical problems that defined the Transition to democracy. Partly echoing Roig's arguments, Vallverdú adds that intellectual terrorism is defined by a lack of respect for others' opinions and, more importantly in this case, by its aim to wipe out the colossal contribution of a writer and citizen 'que ha donat proves de fidelitat al seu poble i a la seva llengua (i que entre altres coses mai no ha escrit en "bilingüe"!)' [who has always demonstrated his loyalty to his people and his language (and who has never written in bilingual!)] (1976: 35). In the remainder of the article, Vallverdú elaborates on and defends the balanced and prudent stance that the PSUC is taking in these debates, contrasting it with the demagogic and irresponsible positions that delay the democratic rupture with the structures of Francoism.

Monzó's cartoon on Espriu and the ensuing controversy offers a prime example of the conflict between two opposing stances in the debate over the configuration of an autonomous Catalan cultural field in the post-Francoist period. A key point of divergence between Monzó and both Roig and Vallverdú concerns the role of irony and sarcasm in art as political critique. If Monzó deploys and argues for irony and wit as politico-cultural tools, Roig and Vallverdú regard them as signs of disrespect. Discussions about the role of humour and irony in public debates had been rife in Catalan culture since the late 1960s. In cultural debates of the time, as analysed by Mercè Picornell, the work and values of young and up-and-coming authors were associated with the new sociocultural spirit as represented by mass culture, consumerism, artificiality, scepticism, irrationality and irony, even nihilism (Picornell 2013: 124–33). In 1969, for instance, established figures within the Catalan cultural system such as the author Josep M. Carandell or the philosopher Eugeni Trias published articles in *Destino* and *Tele/eXprés* in which they criticized the negative impact that television and mass culture were having on young artists (Picornell 2013: 124–33). For Trias, their creations and values were defined by a rupture with the Marxist and humanist traditions, a break which distanced their views and work from rational stances (Picornell 2013: 133). The discourses and vocabularies put forward by Montserrat Roig and Francesc Vallverdú in this controversy reveal how these ideological manoeuvres were still operative in the mid-1970s. In her article, Roig emphasizes Espriu's liberalism and openness to debate. In her own words, 'Salvador Espriu ha estat sempre un home liberal, que s'ha obert a la discussió, a la polèmica, a les discrepàncies' [Salvador Espriu has always been a liberal man, open to discussion, difference and discrepancy] (1976: 25). Vallverdú, for his part, notes that, in recent discussions, 'les deformacions demagògiques s'han imposat sobre els plantejaments reals, els insults sobre els arguments' [demagogical distortions have prevailed over real proposals, insults over arguments] (1976: 34). Through the contrasting narratives of rationality/irrationality, arguments/insults, ponderation/irony and liberalism/extremism, Roing and Vallverdú seem to suggest that Monzó and those with similar stances do not take into consideration the critical challenges that Catalan culture is undergoing in the context of the Transition. This can help understand why the eruption of humour, irony and (self-)parody in the Catalan cultural field of the 1970s was so unwelcome and controversial. At stake in this debate were the different ways of conceiving a (proto-)institutional cultural field, with *resistentialist* practices inspired by a respect for tradition on one side, (a hierarchical model in which due consideration for major cultural figures is of the utmost importance), and postmodernist, self-referential and satirical modes on the other (a model that favours provocation, (self-)criticism and disrespect for authority). As such, Monzó's cartoon of Espriu and the prolonged public controversy it aroused is not only a prime example of Quim Monzó's countercultural challenge to the Catalan oppositional model in the mid-1970s, but also of the tensions and anxieties that defined the (re-)configuration of the Catalan cultural field after *resistencialisme* entered into crisis.

The controversy, however, did not end with the spate of public opinion articles in the wake of Monzó's cartoon. In a piece published in *La Vanguardia* in 2013, Julià Guillamon explains how, digging in the Arxiu Nacional de Catalunya for a completely different project, he came cross two cards sent by Espriu to Roig, where the poet talked about the dispute. As Guillamon tells us, in the first one, Espriu 'es declara vexat, fastiguejat i ple de menyspreu per la mala bava estúpida' [says that he feels vexed, disgusted and full of contempt for the stupid malicious talk], and defends the co-officiality of Catalan and Spanish, attacking those who 'volen entrar per la finestra quan encara no som al llindar de la porta' [want to enter through the window when we're not even at the doorstep] (2013: 38). In these cards, Espriu also resorts to the above-mentioned dichotomies, confiding in Roig that he feels 'assejat pels primaris, que amb els seus exabruptes demanen a crits una nova dictadura' [harassed by the primitives, who, through their harsh remarks, are demanding a new dictatorship] (2013: 38). In the second one, Espriu thanks Roig for her article and reveals that he does not know who Quim Monzó is. Espriu's words illustrate the division between the Catalan model of the public intellectual who participates in the values of *resistencialisme* and the new attitudes and ideologies promulgated by emerging countercultural writers and artists, whom are defined as 'primitives' by the poet. Espriu's support for co-officiality in post-Francoist Catalonia and his horror at the divisive cultural practices promoted by Monzó's cartoon belies the bigger question of Catalan intellectuals' stances in the construction of Spanish and Catalan consensus during the Transition. According to Paloma Aguilar, the traumatic memory of the Civil War played a major role 'in the institutional design of the Transition by favouring negotiation and inspiring a tolerant attitude on the part of the main actors' (2002: 25). The memory of the Civil War's atrocities and the early years of Franco's regime induced political and intellectual leaders in Catalonia and Spain as a whole to prioritize stability and consensus. Hence, Espriu's position in this debate ought to be partly linked to the fact that he had lived through the Civil War and the subsequent brutal political and cultural repression of the post-war years, during which time the publication of books in Catalan practically disappeared. This is exemplified in his interview in *Arreu*, where Espriu remarks his desire that 'tothom procuri d'entendre's, de vèncer les seves divisions i que busquin un comú denominador per viure. Tot el que sigui portar a la guerra civil, jo n'estic contra' [everyone tries to understand each other, overcome the divisions and work towards finding a shared framework to coexist. I'm against anything that may provoke a civil war] (Batista and López Raimundo 1976: 171). Espriu had already expressed a similar idea in an interview published in *Destino* in the summer of 1975, a few months before Franco's death: 'Lo que no quiero ni deseo, de ninguna manera, es la horrible y estúpida tragedia de otra guerra civil' [What I don't want, nor desire in any manner, is the horrible and stupid tragedy of another civil war] (qtd. in Pons 2013: 652). Monzó's generation, by contrast, had not been directly affected by the traumatic events of the war and its immediate aftermath, nor were their cultural influences and political alliances the same as those of the Catalan post-war literary writers. Rather, as Teresa Vilarós notes, Barcelona's countercultural artists were a part of the 'minorías subterráneas, marginales, compuestas de gente joven que no estaba abrumada por ningún compromiso intelectual contraído previamente a la muerte de Franco' [underground, marginal minorities, formed by young people who were not burdened by intellectual commitments taken on before Franco's death] (1998: 25). If Monzó's attitude towards the Catalan–Spanish pacts of the Transition was more disaffected than that of Espriu, this is partly because Monzó and other countercultural artists did not see themselves as enfranchised by or committed to these pacts. This difference emerges as key to understanding Monzó's critique of the national politics of the Transition in Catalonia.

CHAPTER 2

❖

Political Cartooning during the Spanish Transition

'—Albert Abril: Països Catalans?
—Quim Monzó: Uns, grans i lliures.'

[—Albert Abril: Catalan Countries?
—Quim Monzó: One, great and free]

Interview in *Canigó*, 17 July 1976 (Abril 1976: 26).

Consensus was the fundamental concept underlying the Spanish Transition to democracy. The Transition's consensus was a carefully crafted discursive, cultural project that made it possible for a group of extraordinarily divergent political parties to work together in establishing the institutional basis of the post-1978 Spanish state. The term *ruptura pactada* epitomizes how the consensus of the major political parties overcame the legacy of the Francoist period and started a political process that, at the same time, did not entail a profound break with the dictatorial regime. In Paloma Aguilar's words, 'the institutionalization of consensus was, perhaps, the most outstanding process witnessed during the Transition. It was a question of establishing a new pattern of resolving problems and inaugurating a new era governed by new principles (2002: 210). For decades, the Spanish Transition was seen internationally and analysed academically as a successful and exemplary process of transition from a dictatorial regime to a fully-fledged democracy (Guibernau 2004; Montero 1995; Preston 1987; Romero-Salvadó 1999; Tusell 2007). In the early 2010s, however, the mainstream narrative of the Transition entered into a crisis triggered primarily by the 15-M protests in 2011 and the birth of the modern Catalan independence movement. This fading hegemony was epitomized by the rapid popularization of the term 'Régimen del 78'. After the *Indignados* occupied squares all over the country on 15 May 2011, a number of authors and intellectuals analysed the Transition's consensus as a political culture that was institutionalized as the only way to solve (and eclipse) political conflict in Spain. Guillem Martínez's edited collection *CT o la Cultura de la Transición* (2012) and Luisa Elena Delgado's *La nación singular: Fantasías de la normalidad democrática española (1996–2011)* (2014) are the most thorough critiques of the political culture instituted during the Transition.

Guillem Martínez influentially coined the catchy acronym 'CT' to describe the politico-cultural paradigm operating in Spain since the Transition, characterized by a silencing of political and cultural dissidence and the concomitant favouring of a sense of political stability and social cohesion (2012: 15). Martínez identifies the *Indignados* protests as the moment when the CT paradigm began to be widely challenged. From his point of view, the cultural paradigm arising from the 15-M protests had the potential to challenge the state's cultural monopoly (2012: 23). Other contributors, such as Amador Fernández-Savater, Raúl Minchinela and Guillermo Zapata, highlight the economic and sociocultural dimensions of this shift, which undeniably comprises the 2007–2008 global financial crisis, the housing and job crisis and, finally, the new habits in cultural consumption emerging among young Spaniards, dramatically transformed by globalization, digital and social media and the consequently declining influence of printed media and television (Fernández-Savater 2012: 39; Minchinela 2012: 158; Zapata: 142–43). Tellingly, the impact of the pro-independence cycle of mobilizations of 2005 to 2010 and the deep socio-political discontent arising in Catalonia after the 2010 Constitutional Court ruling on the Statute are hardly mentioned in Martínez's edited collection. Delgado's book also pinpoints 2011 as the decisive moment in which the politics of consensus sealed during the Spanish Transition entered a phase of crisis (2014: 19). The book continues by arguing in favour of a new political culture for Spain that leaves behind consensus as the driving democratic principle, favouring instead the continual enfranchising of all parties involved through a democratic and interrelational process which accepts conflict as a necessary element (2014: 292–301). For her, the post-Francoist institutional system can be seen as a limited democracy in which the 'sentido común nacional' unremittingly othered its detractors, in particular Catalan and Basque nationalisms, which have been consistently depicted as irrational, inflexible and ever-demanding (2014: 20). In view of this, Delgado proposes a new political culture which extends the narrow limits of the Spanish democracy in order to accommodate diverse and even contrasting political and territorial projects; in this regard, Delgado's book pays due attention to the national disputes that have characterized Spain in recent decades. As a matter of fact, the modern Catalan independence movement has led the most consistent threat to the Spanish post-Francoist institutional framework, sparking the deepest political crisis seen in the country since 1978. The events of October 2017 in the Catalan region were the peak of this critical situation, a moment in which Catalonia's secession from Spain seemed a plausible possibility. Given how debates about the nature of the 'Régimen del 78' and the interpretation of the Transition vis-à-vis the Catalan pro-independence push have been at the core of political clashes in the 2010s, revisiting how one of the main public intellectuals in post-Francoist Catalonia represented the Transition as it unfolded helps achieve a better understanding of this political process in Catalonia as well as the recent political crisis regarding Catalonia's relation with Spain.

In the midst of the Transition, between September 1976 and April 1978, Quim Monzó published sixty-one political cartoons and satirical collages in the magazine *Canigó*. Founded in Figueres in 1954 as a monthly cultural magazine for the Catalan region of Empordà, *Canigó* moved its editorial office to Barcelona in 1975 after the journalist Isabel-Clara Simó had become its director a year earlier. In this new stage, *Canigó* transitioned into a weekly magazine and transformed to become more influential politically, associating itself with the Catalan radical-left independence movement in favour of the political unity of the Països Catalans. In fact, the weekly's subtitle became 'Setmanari independent dels Països Catalans'. Strongly associated with the politico-cultural climate of the Transition, *Canigó* was unable to sustain the project in the democratic period, defined by the normalization of the relations between Catalonia and Spain, and thus closed down in 1983. Nevertheless, *Canigó* has retained a cult status among Catalan independence activists who opposed the Transition's consensus (Meroño i Cadena 2011). Although Monzó's satirical production is not negligible, this body of work has only been mentioned briefly in passing by Antoni Maestre (2010: 238–39; 2012b: 99; 2012c: 156–57). The fact that Monzó's pre-1978 work has attracted little critical attention to this day should be, to a certain extent, connected to the abovementioned mainstream narrative of the Transition as well as the discourses of cultural normalization. Antoni Maestre has observed that the notion of Catalan cultural and linguistic normalization can be associated with the narratives of democratic normality developing in Spain after Franco's death. For Maestre, both politico-cultural frameworks displaced the radical and maximalist proposals of the independence movement, counterculture and the radical left; in short, any political project that dared to oppose or question the consensus of the Transition (2015: 39–43). Hence, it can be suggested that there has been a tendency to focus on Quim Monzó's post-1978 work precisely because earlier creations disrupt the representation of the Transition to democracy as a smooth and fully consensual process resulting in the normalization of political relations between Catalonia and Spain.

Monzó's work usually appeared in two different sections of *Canigó*. His political cartoons normally featured in 'Llobarreria' (from 11 September 1976 until 8 January 1977) and his pieces that combined cartooning, collage and written components appeared in 'Politicafliccio' (from 15 January 1977 until 1 April 1978). All in all, Monzó published fifteen cartoons in 'Llobarreria' and forty-six pieces in 'Politicaflicció' (of which forty-four were single-authored, while the remaining two were composed in collaboration, one each with artists Lluís Mayol and Lluís F. Calpena).[1] Monzó also produced some front-covers for *Canigó*, although the exact number has remained difficult to determine due to the fact that he left them unsigned (Simó qtd. in Guillamon 2009: 143). Quim Monzó's cultural production in *Canigó* can be read as a chronicle of the Spanish Transition to democracy in Catalonia and it illustrates the author's ardent support for Catalonia's independence. Monzó's combative work puts forward a staunch critique of the principles informing the Transition, which are depicted as in line of continuity with Francoism, in particular concerning the debate over the political status of Spain's historical regions. Tellingly, Monzó's creations attack both Spanish and Catalan political parties and personalities who endorsed or abided by the Transition's politics of consensus, including Catalan mainstream nationalism. Monzó's artistic production in *Canigó* is another example of his critique of the consensual politics at the core of the emerging Catalan cultural and political fields. Further, this satirical work not only displays Monzó's most political facet, but also offers an insight into how major political activists and rising Catalan young artists experienced the development and outcome of the Transition, with a focus on Catalonia's relation with Spain. Some of the prominent intellectual and political figures of the current Catalan independence movement were possibly readers of *Canigó* during the Transition. Political leaders like Josep-Lluís Carod-Rovira, Josep Bargalló and Josep Huguet (Esquerra Republicana de Catalunya, ERC), as well as Eva Serra and Carles Castellanos (Candidatura d'Unitat Popular, CUP) were members of the Partit Socialista d'Alliberament Nacional (PSAN), which was part of the political space of *Canigó* and occupies a special place in the imaginaries of the independence movement (Buch 2012).

It is not surprising that an up-and-coming Quim Monzó, working as a graphic designer at the time, experimented with political cartooning as a suitable genre for critically engaging with the historical moment of the Spanish Transition to democracy. From the late 1960s, with Manuel Fraga's Ley de Prensa e Imprenta [Printing and Press Law] (1966) and the relaxation of censorship, political cartooning experienced a revival, becoming a key form of politico-cultural protest across Spain but especially in Barcelona, that period's 'capital of the humour publication industry in Spain' (McGlade 2016: 207). Published in Barcelona, humour publications such as *Barrabás*, *El Papus* and *Por Favor* played a central role in providing social discontent with a platform during the late Francoist period and the Transition. These magazines, however, were not released solely for a Catalan readership; they were published in Spanish and aimed at audiences across the country. By contrast, publications like *Canigó* or *Oriflama* used the Catalan language exclusively and were thus closer to the demands and interests of Catalan nationalism (as well as better displaying its internal conflicts). It was in *Oriflama* throughout 1967 and 1968 that Enric Sió and Emili Teixidor published the controversial serialized comic *Lavínia 2016 o la guerra dels poetes*, which allegorically represented Catalan people's will to maintain the Catalan language under the Francoist regime. The comic was discontinued after it included a satirical drawing depicting the Montserrat abbot and symbol of the opposition to Francoism, Aureli Maria Escarré, and the iconic early-twentieth-century nationalist politician and intellectual Enric Prat de la Riba (founding member of the Lliga Regionalista de Catalunya in 1901, first president of the Mancomunitat de Catalunya beginning in 1914 and author of the seminal book and political manifesto *La nacionalitat catalana* [1906]). In *Lavínia 2016*, both personalities were described as 'patricis que dirigien l'ànima col·lectiva d'aquell poble treballador' [patricians who led the collective spirit of the Catalan working class] and depicted with a totem pole alongside a number of little angels wearing the Catalan *barretina* (Sió and Teixidor qtd. in Huertas 1987: 56). Circulated at a heated time for Catalan nationalism after the publication of Jordi Solé i Tura's *Catalanisme i revolució burgesa* in 1967, the comic can be seen as one of the first self-critical cultural products within Catalan nationalism. Its discontinuation reveals the clash between conservative and progressive nationalism, as well as the rising influence of an emerging generation no longer in sync with the values of *resistencialisme*. *Lavínia*

2016 can be seen as part of the long history of Catalan satire, excellently analysed by Rhiannon McGlade in *Catalan Cartoons. A Cultural and Political History* (2016). One of McGlade's most innovative arguments is that cartoon humour has played a central role in reinforcing a sense of identity difference between Catalonia and Spain throughout the twentieth century (2016: 245–49). Strongly embedded in the Catalan satirical tradition, Monzó's pictorial work in *Canigó* provides an excellent platform from which to explore the sense of Catalan national difference from Spain and the clashes within Catalan nationalism during the acrimonious period of the Transition to democracy.

2.1. Debunking the Transition's Consensus

The ideologue and main leader of the Transition process in Spain was the former Francoist minister and civil servant Adolfo Suárez, appointed as Prime Minister of Spain by King Juan Carlos I on 3 July 1976 after Carlos Arias Navarro's resignation on 1 July. Suárez's policies were no doubt facilitated by the politics of reconciliation embraced by the Partido Comunista de España (PCE) and the PSOE, as well as by Catalan and Basque conservative nationalism. The economist Ramon Tamames, a member of the Central Committee of the PCE during the Transition, wrote in his memoirs that, by mid-1976, 'ya quedó claro que, en vez de ruptura con el régimen anterior, habría negociación y pacto con sus elementos más aperturistas, ya formalmente encabezados por Adolfo Suárez' [it was already clear that, instead of a rupture with the previous regime, there would be negotiation and pacts with the reformists, formally led by Adolfo Suárez] (2013: 571). The roles played by the leaders of the PCE as well as by Catalan and Basque nationalists have been generally lauded for their responsibility, goodwill and willingness to avoid the politics of confrontation in order to accomplish a negotiated and relatively peaceful Transition (Preston 1987: 120–21; Romero-Salvadó 1999: 161–67). However, certain voices and political organizations also harshly criticized these actors' roles because the Transition materialized in such a manner that it enabled the process to be directed by recycled Francoist politicians and institutions and, for this reason, did not meet all the necessary democratic guarantees (Falcón 1999; López Crespí 2001; Muniesa 2006). As we will see in this chapter, Monzó's pictorial work in *Canigó* severely criticized them all.

On 25 September 1976, less than three months after Adolfo Suárez took office, the Spanish Prime Minister featured on *Canigó*'s front page. The magazine opened with the headline 'A Madrid fan dissabte' and an illustrated caricature of a smiling Adolfo Suárez wearing an apron and hand-washing a stamp with Franco's face on it (Figure 2.1). A touch of humour is added by the name of the detergent, 'Reformil', an obvious pun on the term 'Reforma', which featured prominently in the ongoing political and legislative process led by Suárez (Monzó 1976a). The cartoon's humour also relies on the fact that Suárez, a political leader who was always perfectly suited and booted in his public appearances, is depicted with rolled-up shirt-sleeves, a rare image of a statesman who strongly capitalized on his youthful and unblemished

FIG. 2.1. *Canigó* 468. 25 September 1976.

image, representative of the new Spain that was allegedly leaving behind its Francoist past. Although unsigned, the author of the front-page's illustration was Quim Monzó. Addressing the early days of Suárez's term in office, the cartoon engages with the new political vocabularies that were to become his signature discourse, with terms such as 'democracy', 'pluralism', 'moderation' and 'consensus' being used to push through a reform that did not break neatly away from the Francoist structures (Aguilar 2002: 49; Molinero and Ysàs 2014: 94). Conveying this critique of the Transition as it unfolded, Monzó's cartoon draws a line of continuity between the new regime and the previous one, embracing the view held by sectors of the population, including *Canigó*'s readership, that the process towards democracy in Spain did not imply a clear-cut break with the previous regime. Suárez perfectly symbolized the deficits of the Transition as experienced (and denounced) by the radical left-wing sections of the Spanish and Catalan population (as well as the pro-independence segments in the latter). First, although now seen as a champion of democracy, Suárez was a man of the regime: not only had he been a Francoist minister, but also General Secretary of the 'Movimiento Nacional'. And second, his political proposals and vocabularies were archetypal of the new culture of consensus underpinning the Spanish Transition to democracy. This new political culture defined Suárez's political party, the Union de Centro Democrático (UCD), founded under his leadership on 3 May 1977. As Paloma Aguilar puts it: 'La UCD se presentó a la sociedad española como la encarnación misma de la moderación' [UCD was introduced to Spanish society as the embodiment of moderation] (2008: 351). Similarly, Antonieta Jarné highlights how Suárez's political past, ambiguity and calculation as well as ideological strategies, 'el feien l'home més adequat per a la tasca tan complexa de transformar la dictadura en democràcia i suavitzar la ruptura' [made him the perfect candidate for the complex endeavour of transforming the dictatorship into a democracy and alleviating the rupture] (2006: 14). *Ruptura*, however, was what Monzó desired at the time, as demonstrated by his cartoons. It is not by chance, therefore, that Adolfo Suárez was among his preferred targets, as shown by the fact that he authored at least four cartoons portraying the Spanish president. In this criticism he was not alone, as other Catalan satirical magazines such as *Por Favor* focused on debunking the emerging political reform 'and dedicated countless pages to the satirising of Adolfo Suárez' (McGlade 2016: 208).

   This caricature of Adolfo Suárez brought about legal trouble for Monzó and *Canigó*. A snippet published in *Canigó* on 27 November 1976 entitled 'Exhort a Canigó' recounts that the magazine's director, Isabel-Clara Simó, received an exhortation from the Barcelona Court of Instruction Number 5 to communicate the name of artist of the front cover's drawing. The text's last sentence disclosed the artist's name: 'L'autor de l'esmentada portada és Quim Monzó, el jove novel·lista guanyador del darrer premi "Prudenci Bertrana"' [The front cover was drawn by Quim Monzó, the young novelist who won the last 'Prudenci Bertrana Prize'] ('Exhort a Canigó' 1976: 11). In spite of this, neither Monzó nor the magazine suffered any legal consequences in the end. As Simó recalls in the book *Monzó, com triomfar a la vida* (2009), she and Monzó went to the courthouse together, 'i la sorpresa d'ell va ser, en arribant als jutjats, que haguéssim d'anar al Departamento de lo Criminal. Van demanar qui era l'autor de la portada, en van prendre nota i *nunca más se supo'* [and he was surprised that we had to go to the Criminal Investigation Department. They asked who had drawn the front cover and then we never heard anything else about it] (Simó qtd. in Guillamon 2009: 143. Italics in original). Despite the fact that Monzó was not eventually tried, it could be suggested that this instance of repression demonstrates that Monzó's critique of the continuity between Francoism and the newly formed Spanish democracy was not entirely unfounded. However, a more historical reading of this controversy would contend that Monzó was ultimately spared a court trial because the Spanish institutions were gradually developing a more democratic approach to the solving of conflicts. As a matter of fact, political cartoons can only thrive in an atmosphere of political freedom and democracy (Hess and Northrop 2011: 186). For this reason, Katherine Roeder argues that the state of comic art in any particular moment offers a good insight into the quality of the democratic institutions surrounding it (2008: 7). The liberalizing of Spain's democratic standards is illustrated by the fact that Monzó continued to publish drawings against the Transition's consensus in general and Adolfo Suárez in particular without any legal problems. Accordingly, this front cover drawn by Monzó and its reception can be seen as a litmus test for the solidity of the advances towards democracy and the concomitant freedom of expression in Spain.

It was in the same November of 1976 when the Spanish Francoist Cortes approved the Political Reform Act, then voted on in the Spanish Political Reform Referendum of 15 December 1976. The main aim of this law was to transition, without any institutional break, from the Francoist regime to a constitutional monarchy with a parliamentary system based on representative democracy (Balcells 1996: 170). Four days before the referendum, Monzó published a cartoon in *Canigó* showing the image of a well-dressed middle-aged man with a moustache and sunglasses, who seems to stereotypically represent a Francoist politician now in charge of overseeing the Transition (Figure 2.2). This was a customary depiction of members of the state apparatus in political cartooning during the Transition, as analysed by McGlade, who notes how the foremost Catalan comic artist Cesc generally portrayed 'his typical apparatchik figures with medals, moustache and dark sunglasses' in order to symbolize the repressive side of the Transition (2016: 212). In Monzó's cartoon, a speech balloon indicates the political leader's viewpoints on the Transition in Catalonia, focusing on the concessions granted by the central government, namely the deposing of Rodolfo Martín Villa as Civil Governor of Barcelona in December 1975, the recognition of pre-War Catalan cultural institutions such as the Institut d'Estudis Catalans (legalized in November 1976 by the Spanish Cabinet of Ministers) and the implementation of co-officiality for Catalan and Spanish in the field of language policy, which was not officially legalized until the Statute was approved in 1979 though the principle was accepted by the Spanish government in December 1976 (Molinero and Ysàs 2014: 133) . These three political measures (all historically verifiable) stand in contrast to the facetious 'us passarem Lluís Llach per la TV' [we'll allow Lluís Llach to appear on

FIG. 2.2. *Canigó* 479. 11 December 1976, p. 7

TV] featuring in Monzó's vignette, seemingly used to downplay the significance of the preceding agreements while also bringing to mind the Francoist veto to Joan Manuel Serrat's singing in Catalan at the Eurovision contest in 1968; Serrat would not feature in Televisión Española (TVE) until 1974 (Monzó 1976g: 7). Alongside these thoughts, the politician visualizes a group of sheep placing a vote in a ballot box, a clear reference to how Monzó saw the mindset of the Catalan people in the imminent referendum.

The cartoon's critical message is twofold. On the one hand, the changes imple-mented in Catalonia by the political elites are represented as insufficient and cosmetic. On the other hand, the Catalan population is itself depicted as gleefully legitimizing the process with their vote, therefore doing what the political elites both desired and expected — it is not by chance that the sheep is inside the thought-bubble, showing that the big-shot politician sees the Catalan population as such. The contrast between the statesman and the Catalan population can be seen as resting on an 'us' (the people) versus 'them' (the political leaders) binary structure, characteristic of political cartooning, a genre that often criticizes by exposing dichotomies and polarities (Medhurst and DeSousa 1981: 205). However, the 'us' versus 'them' opposition underpinning the political message in this cartoon is exposed for its contradictions. Firstly, it shows how the political leaders, represented in Monzó's caricature through a member of the state institutions, are happy to grant those concessions (mainly in the cultural realm) through the medium of Catalan, showing a sense of proximity to, and benevolence with, the Catalan population. Secondly, it depicts the Catalan population itself, lured in by the apparent significance of those concessions and happy to endorse the political pacts of the Transition. The referendum's result proved Monzó's cartoon right, as 97.7% of the Catalan population voted in favour of the Political Reform Act.

Both cartoons discussed here (Figures 2.1 and 2.2) exploit a series of images and metaphors which reflect ideological assumptions shared by the cartoonist and his readers. According to Will Eisner, author of the seminal work *Comics and Sequential Art* (1985), 'comprehension of an image requires a commonality of experience [...] An interaction has to develop because the artist is evoking images stored in the minds of both parties' (13). Monzó was creating his vignettes for a particular readership, that is, the readers of *Canigó*, a community of highly politicized people leaning towards the Catalan pro-independence left. The magazine's political stance was clearly manifested in an editorial published on 4 March 1978, which explicitly situates itself on the side of the fringe political parties that mushroomed in Catalonia during the Transition: 'com que la nostra és una revista "extraparlamentària", entre les catacumbes i la marginació, és clar, ens interessen els temes, les persones i les organitzacions extraparlamentàries; qüestió de simpatia entre semblants' [since ours is an 'extraparliamentary' magazine, fringe and underground, we are interested in themes, personalities and organizations that are extraparliamentary; affinities and connections between similar people] (qtd. in Meroño i Cadena 2011: 157). While the pro-independence left performed particularly badly in the elections during the Transition and thereafter, its politico-cultural influence was significant during the early stages of the Transition and its impact should not be ignored. Quim Monzó, described by Salvador Espriu's biographer, Agustí Pons, as the 'ninotaire diguem-ne oficial de la revista' [official caricaturist of the magazine] (2013: 656), was undoubtedly part of the *Canigó* community and, therefore, close to this political movement during the early stages of the Transition. Moreover, his particular role or influence in the magazine is likely to have been significant, since cartoonists tend to play a key function in the media to which they contribute because of the conspicuousness of their creations (Edwards 1997: xii). Monzó's pictorial work, therefore, contributed to creating a sense of Catalan difference with, and opposition to, Spain at a time when the status of Catalonia was at the centre of political discussions across the country. Overall, Monzó's critique of the Transition's consensus in these two cartoons reveals that, while a significant majority of the Catalan population voted in favour of the process of political reform led by Suárez from 1976 onwards, this process was also met with solid opposition, in particular from pro-independence political activists.

2.2. A Peaceful Transition?

Monzó's satirical work was not only critical of the political and institutional transformations developing in Spain at the time, but also of the physical violence carried out by the security forces of the state and far-right groups during the Transition. This violence has tended to be concealed by the mainstream narrative of a peaceful Transition (Aguilar 2008: 398, 475), which the former PCE member Lidia Falcón defined in 1999 as 'la falsa y endulzada versión que las castas dirigentes de nuestro país han impuesto' [the fake and sugar-coated narrative imposed by the ruling classes of our country] (1999: 95), using vocabularies that were to become mainstream in the post-15-M paradigm. Monzó's cartoons especially denounced the violent attacks suffered by Catalan cultural associations and pro-independence activists in the Valencian region, a hotbed of extreme-right violence in Spain at the time. The Transition in the Valencian Community was determined by the conflict about Valencian identity and its symbols that took place in the region from the late 1960s until the early 1980s, which is known as the Battle of Valencia. Particularly heated and violent in many instances, the conflict deeply divided Valencian society into two opposing blocs that have defined politics in region in the post-Francoist period. I will analyse two of Monzó's pertinent cartoons, both published in late 1976.

The first illustration came out on 16 October and deals with the Spanish government's prohibition of the Valencian national day on 9 October. Opening with the text 'Prohibit el Dia Nacional del País Valencià', Monzó's drawing resorts again to the stereotype of the apparatchik figure, who appears here together with a far-right militant reflecting on the government's ban (Figure 2.3). In a condescending way, the politician claims that, 'más que nada os lo hemos prohibido para evitaros accidentes mortales provocados por comandos incontrolados e inidentificados, verdad Manolo?' [more than anything else, we've banned it to prevent deadly accidents provoked by uncontrolled and unidentified gangs, isn't that true, Manolo?] (Monzó 1976e: 9). Manolo, the far-right militant, curtly answers 'sí'. The political leader carries copies of two Valencian regional newspapers, *Las Provincias* and *Levante*, each known for its anti-Catalanist editorial line; *Las Provincias*, for instance, used to spread accusations of Catalan imperialism (Buffery and Marcer 2011: 83). The apparatchik figure is also wearing two medals on his chest, one of the fascist party Falange Española, the other a swastika, thus bringing to mind the military nature of the Francoist regime and suggesting a link with the political leaders who were now leading the Transition towards democracy. Exaggerated as the swastika may seem, during the Transition political leaders such as Rodolfo Martín Villa, mentioned in the previous cartoon (Figure 2.2), were frequently portrayed as Nazis in satirical magazines (McGlade 2016: 208–09). Manolo, for his part, carries a gun and tries to conceal his identity by wearing sunglasses and having his collar upturned, which clearly hints at his involvement in violent attacks. The political leader offers further reasons why the government prohibited the celebrations, such as the fact the demonstrators would neither be displaying flags of the Falange nor singing the 'Cara al sol'. If this were not enough, he further highlights the fact that

Llobarreria

FIG. 2.3. *Canigó* 471. 16 October 1976, p. 9

protesters will want to chant in Catalan, to which a further speech bubble adds, 'què [*sic*] digo en catalán, en valenciano! que es peor!' [worse, not in Catalan but in Valencian!] (1976e: 9). The cartoon's narrative and symbology clearly represent *blaverisme*, the anti-Catalanist socio-political movement that rose during the 1960s in the Valencian region in reaction to the growing nationalist and progressive demands developing within the Valencian anti-Francoist opposition. Inspired by Joan Fuster's *Nosaltres els valencians*, published in 1962, significant sections of the Valencian left embraced the cultural and political project of the Països Catalans (Archilés 1997: 28–30; Dowling 2018: 42). It was this association between the left and Catalanism that *blaverisme* combated, generally through violent means. A movement with deep roots in Valencian society, in particular among the conservative middle classes, *blaverisme* had strong links with the Spanish extreme-right in the region, which engaged in violent activities against anything related to Catalan culture and pro-independence positions, as well as against left-wing activists (Buffery and Marcer 2011: 83; Cucó 2002: 12–14, 76; Viadel 2009). According to Alfons Cucó, such violent actions were carried out with rampant impunity thanks to the connivance and even protection of the security forces and the state institutions (2002: 76). This is precisely what Monzó's cartoon denounces through its depiction of the political leader entirely in cahoots with Manolo, seemingly a member of the *uncontrolled* far-right squads involved in violent activities during the period.

The cartoon clearly engages with the basis of the Battle of Valencia, that is, whether Valencia's vernacular language, culture and identity are connected with Catalonia's or not. One of the main sites of conflict was the name of the regional language: Valencian or Catalan? For *blaverisme*, the vernacular language of Valencia is Valencian, a language completely unrelated to Catalan. For this reason, they heavily opposed the use of the term Catalan to refer to Valencia's regional language. However, Valencian nationalists argued that *blaveros* did not aim to defend the vernacular language of Valencia, regardless of its name, but to stop the language's recuperation developing from the 1960s. For this reason, they regarded *blaverisme* as a divide and conquer strategy pushed by Spanish nationalism to block the advances of Valencian nationalism. This is the reason why, in Monzó's cartoon, the political leader states that chanting in Valencian is even worse than chanting in Catalan, therefore representing the view held by Catalanism that the ultimate aim of *blaverisme* was far from promoting Valencia's language but, instead, to subordinate the region's vernacular language and culture to the Spanish state.

One month later, Quim Monzó published another cartoon representing this conflict after the Valencian bookshop Tres i Quatre was partially destroyed by a bomb, which *Canigó*'s editorial in the same issue linked to far-right extremists (Figure 2.4). The editorial contextualizes this assault as part of a broader climate of political violence and repression in the Valencian region, as does Monzó's drawing, which includes a newspaper clip reading 'seté atemptat a "Tres i Quatre". El gerent de la llibreria acaba de ser multat a causa dels "Premis Octubre"' [seventh attack to 'Tres i Quatre'. The library's manager has just been fined due to the 'Premis Octubre'] (Monzó 1976f: 6). The newspaper subheading refers to the penalty of half-a-million pesetas imposed days earlier by the Civil Governor of Valencia, Mariano Nicolás, to the bookshop for organizing the *Premis Octubre*. According to the notification, a number of speakers spoke in favour of the 'día del país valenciano', condemned the Francoist dictatorship, supported Catalan separatism and advocated 'la ruptura como fórmula de oposición a la reforma que propone el Gobierno' [rupture as a way to oppose the reforms proposed by the Government] (Millas 1976). The cartoon includes a caricature of Eliseu Climent, founder of the bookshop, whose depiction with a plaid corduroy blazer evokes the *progre* style of the Transition and stands in stark contrast to the previously analysed portrayals of the Transition's leaders. Holding the notification in his hands, Climent wonders: 'No sé si pagar la multa al Govern Civil i demandar els "Comandos Incontrolados" o demandar el Govern Civil i pagar als "Comandos Incontrolados" o...' [I don't know whether to pay the fine to the Civil Government and sue the 'Uncontrolled Gangs' or sue the Civil Government and pay the 'Uncontrolled Gangs' or...] (Monzó 1976f: 6). While the newspaper clip and *Canigó*'s editorial hints at conceivable links between far-right violent commandos and the governmental penalty, Monzó's cartoons goes further and indicates that the proto-democratic state's institutions are working in complete collusion with violent extremists. It is important to note that the text in the speech bubble ends with an ellipsis, implying an endless loop and an infinite reproduction of the adverse situation for Catalan cultural nationalism in the Valencian region.

Llobarreria

FIG. 2.4. *Canigó* 475. 13 November 1976, p. 6

Aguilar's analysis of the Transition discloses the key impact of fascist violence and points to the links between extremists, the judiciary and state security forces:

> la ausencia de reformas profundas en varias instituciones españolas clave, particularmente en la policía y la judicatura, explica las elevadas cifras de represión estatal a lo largo de la transición, así como la impunidad con la que la extrema derecha actuó en dicho período. Los ejemplos de connivencia entre la ultraderecha, los jueces y las fuerzas de seguridad del Estado son abundantes. (2008: 470–71)

> [the lack of deep reforms in various key Spanish institutions, in particular the police and the judiciary system, explains the prevalence of state repression throughout the transition, as well as for the impunity of the far right during the period. The instances of collusion between the far right, judges and State security forces abound]

These two cartoons show, on the one hand, how one year after Franco's death, the political climate in the Valencian region was defined by conflict and low-intensity violence; on the other, Monzó's real-time criticism of this political violence and its effects on Valencian nationalism. Furthermore, the cartoons illustrate how Monzó's work in *Canigó* directly engaged with the conflictive socio-political reality of the

Països Catalans, which can certainly be seen as one of the main sites of national conflict during the Transition in Spain. It is worth pointing out that Monzó's satirical work also embraced the terminology of the pro-Països Catalans political movements, referring to the Autonomous Community of Catalonia as 'Catalunya Sud' or 'Principat', to the Valencian region as 'País Valencià' and to the anti-Catalanist movement in Valencia as 'franja blava', in reference to the conflict about whether the flag of the Valencian region should have a blue stripe on its top. The movement in favour of the cultural and political unity of the Catalan-speaking territories was influential during the late 1960s and 1970s when a number of political parties and organizations, cultural institutions and public intellectuals adopted and defended the Catalan Countries as their politico-cultural frame of reference (Lladonosa 2006: 40). However, this political position suffered a major defeat during the Transition, owing to the fact that the majority of citizens of the Valencian Community and the Balearic Islands voted for political parties that rejected such proposal. This may explain why, from the early 1980s onward, Monzó's opinion work has dedicated significantly less attention to this issue. Hence, Monzó's representation of the socio-political and cultural clashes around the Catalan Countries' project in *Canigó* should be analysed within the specific context of the Spanish Transition and, perhaps more importantly, read vis-à-vis the affinities and connections developed between his political cartoons and *Canigó*'s readership.

2.3. One Sole Aim: Catalonia's Right to Independence

Monzó's contribution to 'Llobarreria' came to an end on 8 January 1977. A week later, Monzó launched the section 'Políticaflicció', which lasted until 1 April 1978. Whereas 'Llobarreria' was a political cartoon occupying a little less than half a page, the new output was almost a full-page and was formed by a cartoon or collage paired together with a satirical written piece also authored by Monzó. These texts were generally fictional, grotesque pieces typical of the countercultural satirical magazines of the time. The fact that Monzó started a new and larger section illustrates the success of his satirical work in *Canigó*. If 'Llobarreria' focused on the early stages of Suárez's presidency, 'Políticaflicció' covered the period in which the PCE was legalized, the first democratic elections of June 1977 were held, the Constitution was drafted and associated debates about the status of Spain's historical autonomies were conducted. The Constitution would be approved on 6 December 1978, months after Monzó's contribution to *Canigó* had come to an end. While in this new section Monzó continued to condemn the ideology of consensus, his work put more emphasis on Catalonia's right to independence from Spain and, for this reason, criticized the Spanish and Catalan political parties that abided by the politics of *ruptura pactada*.

Monzó's second contribution to 'Políticaflicció' came out on 22 January 1977 and it put forward a criticism of the national politics of the PCE and the PSOE as well as denouncing the essential collaboration of Jordi Pujol's Convergència Democràtica de Catalunya (CDC) in building the new Spanish institutions. Entitled 'Madrid

Madrid la nuit

FIG. 2.5. *Canigó* 485. 22 January 1977, p. 14

la nuit', it is formed by a collage showing the image of Santiago Carrillo and a surrealist short story rife with irony starring Carrillo himself and Pujol (1977c: 14). The collage exhibits a photograph of the PCE's leader with a Spanish flag painted on his shirt, thus displaying the cartoonist's intervention in a real image (Figure 2.5). A speech balloon emerging from Carrillo's mouth illustrates his opinion on the Països Catalans: 'Els Països Catalans són un invent expansionista de la burgesia catalana maçona atea jueva trotsquista i sexualment perversa' [The Catalan Countries are an invention of the expansionist Catalan Freemason atheist Jewish Trotskyist and sexually perverse bourgeoisie] (1977c: 14). During the Transition, the PCE official line considered that regional nationalisms in Spain brought about a divisive politics among the working class, a political stance which was strongly criticized and rejected by Catalan independence activists (Archilés 2009: 112–18; Quiroga 2009: 25–27). Relatedly, they also denounced that the PCE generally regarded the Països Catalans as maximalist proposals coming from 'avatguardes intel·lectuals desconnectades de la realitat popular' [intellectual vanguards detached from the reality of the ordinary people] (López Crespi 2001: 234). Monzó's phrasing clearly interacts with the Partit Socialista Unificat de Catalunya's harsh criticism of the Països Catalans expressed as early as 1961 in *Nous Horitzons*, the intellectual journal of the party. At that time, it had conspicuously stated that 'la idea de Països Catalans és una reminiscència de la ideologia imperialista de la gran burgesia catalana, és una idea reaccionària' [the idea of the Catalan Countries is a reminiscence of the imperialist ideology of the big Catalan bourgeoisie; it is a reactionary idea] (qtd. in Dowling 2015: 234). The success of the PSUC's critique is demonstrated by the fact that Monzó's work critically interacted with it more than fifteen years after it was released, revealing that it was already part of the collective political imaginary in Catalonia. Although Monzó's text initially engages with this scathing attack on the concept of the Països Catalans, his cartoon subsequently goes on to mention other adjectives that bring to mind and parody Francoism's rabid discourse against the so-called 'anti-Spain.' Through these discursive echoes, Monzó's cartoon criticizes the PCE's position as not too different from the Francoist discourses on the subject of Spain's national conflicts, in particular when maximalist proposals such as the Catalan Countries are put on the table.

The Spanish flag sewn on Carrillo's sweater is a key visual prop for the cartoon's political message. In mid-January 1977, the PCE still considered the Republican flag as Spain's legitimate emblem and the *rojigualda* as a Francoist symbol (Juliana 2014). For this reason, attaching the *rojigualda* to Carrillo at the time could be read as an excessive and unfair criticism. In this regard, Monzó's depiction exemplifies how cartoons tend to exaggerate popular opinions through a hyperbolic and highly manipulative style (Hess and Northrop 2011: 12). Nevertheless, this portrayal of Carrillo reinforces the excessive political message of the cartoon, that is, that the PCE and Francoism largely agree on the question of Spanish national unity — and that they resort to similar discourses to protect it. There is little denying that this is an entirely unnuanced and unfair depiction of the national politics of PCE. However, it is also essential to note how Monzó's cartoon, by associating the Spanish flag with the PCE, was also representing (and interacting with) the political transformations embraced by the PCE in the months to follow in order that it be legalized by Adolfo Suárez's government. The PCE was eventually legalized on 9 April 1977 and, on 16 April, less than three months after this cartoon was published, the PCE Central Committee announced that the party recognized the Monarchy and the Spanish *bicolor* flag. Fernando Soto, a member of the party's Central Committee at the time, recalls in his memoirs how difficult it was to accept such a flag because of its strong identification with Francoism: 'la bandera bicolor la utilizó el franquismo para acusar a los demócratas de antipatriotas, la manipuló sin recato alguno' [the bicolour flag was used by Francoism to accuse the democratic opposition of being anti-patriotic; they manipulated the flag without shame or remorse] (1996: 115). Similarly, Carrillo's justification of this political decision reveals the Francoist undercurrent of such a flag during the Transition: the bicolour flag 'no puede ser monopolio de ninguna fracción política, y no podíamos abandonarla a los que quieren impedir el paso pacífico a la democracia' [cannot be the monopoly of any political fraction, and we couldn't leave it to those who aim to block the peaceful road to democracy] (qtd. in Prieto 1977). The decision was fairly controversial at the time and, for many like Monzó, illustrative of the communist party's acceptance of the *ruptura pactada*. Excessive as Monzó's drawing may be in its likening of the PCE to Francoism on the question of national unity, its metaphors can be seen as partly foreshadowing the PCE's political shifts by focusing on Santiago Carrillo, the party's leader, who has been described by ex-members of the party such as Lidia Falcón as 'el padre inventor de aquellas componendas que se establecieron entre los partidos parlamentarios y los gerifaltes de la dictadura' [the mastermind behind the deals between the parliamentary parties and the leaders of the dictatorial regime] (1999: 115). Accordingly, Monzó's cartoon activates a narrative that reveals and strongly condemns both the role played by the PCE during the Transition and the crucial function of Santiago Carrillo.

The text accompanying this illustration extends this critique to a number of Catalan and Spanish politicians. Monzó's piece is an obviously fictional (and surreal) account of Jordi Pujol's trip to Madrid to meet with a series of Spanish politicians, including Carrillo himself, Felipe González, the leader of the PSOE at the time, and Enrique Tierno Galván, who was the main figure of the Partido Socialista Popular (PSP), which merged with the PSOE in 1978. Despite the fact that this was a politico-professional trip to Madrid, Jordi Pujol, away from his country and family, goes to a bar at night and is seduced by Ingrid, an attractive Swedish model. Less than an hour later, Ingrid and Pujol are in a suite at the latter's hotel, the five-star Melià Castilla, in the centre of Madrid, where they address each other as 'Amor' and 'Carinyu' (Monzó 1977c: 14). Pujol then caresses Ingrid's hair, a move described by the narrative voice as 'un gest sobtat –– d'impetuós erotisme bancari' [a sudden gesture –– of impulsive erotic banking] (1977c: 14). However, Pujol soon realizes that Ingrid is, in fact, Santiago Carrillo, dressed up a woman. Suddenly, 'de darrera de les cortines surten tres goril·les (dos boxadors i un karateca). Carrillo fa les presentacions. Pujol comença a cordar-se els pantalons' [three gorillas (two boxers and a karate fighter) appear from behind the curtains. Carrillo introduces them to Pujol, who begins to button his trousers] (1977c: 14). Afterwards, Carrillo and Pujol leave the hotel for a political reunion in the country's capital.

Monzó's text intertwines Pujol's personal and political life in a clearly sarcastic but critical manner. By connecting the leader's political trips to Madrid with hints to extramarital sexual affairs and his occupation as a banker, Monzó's text pokes fun at the representation of Pujol as a devoted Catholic family man and a middle-class banker, a representation on which the Catalan political leader capitalized. This depiction of Jordi Pujol triggered an angry response from a reader of Canigó: published two issues later, a letter signed by Lloreç Volonte rejected Monzó's contribution for its lack of taste and ethics, to the point that it 'fa enrogir d'indignació' [makes you flush with anger] (1977: 2). After continuing to denounce the portrayal of the Catalan nationalist leader on similar grounds, Volonte concluded that Monzó's piece was 'estúpida i baixa' [stupid and tawdry], a response which is highly reminiscent of Salvador Espriu's reaction to Monzó's cartoon in his postcard to Monserrat Roig, as analysed in the previous chapter. What is more, if Espriu denied having ever heard of Quim Monzó, Volonte similarly begins his letter by stating that he would like to comment on 'l'articulet "Madrid la nuit" que signa un tal Quim Monzó' [that shabby article 'Madrid la nuit' signed by some Quim Monzó], thus presenting Monzó as a newcomer who is not cognizant of the conventions of Catalan political debates as well as downplaying his relevance in the Catalan cultural field (1977: 2). Although Volonte's letter claims that all opinions should be respected, he points out that the private life of a political leader should not be mentioned, nor should someone ridicule the religious convictions of public figures. By saying this, Volonte's letter illustrates the generational and cultural clash taking place within Catalan culture in the mid-1970s. More importantly, however, Volonte's letter is yet another example of the crisis experienced by the monolithic and hierarchical Catalan oppositional cultural model from the late 1960s. Monzó's criticism of the consensual and bourgeois politics of Jordi Pujol from a radical pro-independence left perspective reveals the internal clashes within Catalan nationalism during the Transition to democracy, as exemplified by the dichotomy of 'rupture and independence' versus 'consensus and autonomy'.

This line of criticism is further developed and expanded in the remainder of the text, where Carrillo and Pujol head to a meeting with González and Tierno Galván. This seems to refer to the Comisión de los Nueve, the committee created on 1 December 1976 to negotiate the steps towards democratization with Suárez's government and, perhaps more importantly, to suggest solutions to 'la cuestión de las nacionalidades' [the issue of nationalities] (Molinero and Ysàs 2014: 15). The committee comprised six representatives of the main opposition parties and one from each of the historical regions (the Basque Country, Catalonia and Galicia). Carrillo, González, Tierno Galván and Pujol sat on the committee, wherein the latter played a significant role (Molinero and Ysàs 2014: 135–47). In his characteristically biting style, Monzó's article ridicules both the political leaders and the committee's debates on the national question. In Monzó's piece, Tierno Galván tells Pujol that 'lo mismo que vosotros, también un extremeño o un conquense querrían formar parte de la comisión' [anyone from Extremadura or the city of Cuenca would want to be part of the committee too, just like you do], a comment which Carrillo and Tierno Galván find quite amusing, as the narrative voice sarcastically remarks that 'Santiaguito i Enriquito riuen a cor què vols' [little Santiago and little Enrique burst out laughing] (Monzó 1977c: 14). The article therefore depicts the Spanish left-wing political leaders watering down Catalonia's claims for self-governance and historical difference. Felipe González remarks that, 'si seguimo asín, noh quedaremo namà que con Cuenca' [if we go on like this, we'll only keep Cuenca], which can be seen to illustrate Monzó's view that the mainstream political parties' main concern was, ultimately, the unity of the country and thus, that granting the historical regions a seat at the committee was nothing more than a superficial move (Monzó 1977c: 14). The specific characteristics of González's language, which mimics the socialist leader's Andalusian accent through deliberately altered orthography, is another example, alongside exaggeration and sarcasm, of Monzó's use of satirical conventions to build a sense of Catalan difference. By representing Pujol as a member of such an allegedly ineffectual committee, the piece reveals further Monzó's critique of Pujol's consensual strategy, given that in the early stages of the Transition 'CiU abandoned independence to advocate full development of regional devolution to Catalonia' (Núñez Seixas 2000: 318).

In the text, Monzó returns to the debate about the Països Catalans. The narrative voice emphasizes that, 'un eldenc i un manacorí tracten, endebades, d'aconseguir formar part de la comissió negociadora' [a man from Elda and a man from Manacor try in vain to be part of the negotiating committee] (1977c: 14), referring to the

Valencian region and the Balearic Islands through figurative references to the cities of Elda and Manacor. By representing the exclusion of the Valencian and Majorcan representatives from the committee, the piece symbolically represents the lack of recognition, and subsequent marginalization, of the political project in favour of the Catalan Countries in the Transition's negotiations. Whereas this could be seen as part of the central government's policy at the time, Monzó's text represents Carrillo as in agreement with such posture, since the PCE leader remarks that 'esta gente, mallorquines i levantinos, son como críos' [these guys, Majorcans and Levantines, are like babies] (Monzó 1977c: 14). Not only does Carrillo define the claims in favour of the Països Catalans as political infantilism, reflecting Leninist vocabularies, but also employs the term 'levantinos', vocally rejected by Valencian nationalists. Monzó is also critical of Pujol's stance in this matter: when Carrillo asks Pujol for his opinion, the Catalan politician only manages to mumble the response 'Jo..., doncs...' [I... well...] (Monzó 1977c: 14). By appearing reluctant to answer, Pujol is represented as avoiding this controversial topic and, in so doing, as abiding by the Transition's consensual politics. Luisa Elena Delgado and Amador Fernández-Savater have recently observed that the paradigm of the *Cultura de la Transición*, hegemonic in Spain since the political and socio-economic pacts that Monzó's cartoons so pointedly criticized, classifies and subsequently discriminates between the topics that are open to public debate and those that are not (Delgado 2014: 19; Fernández-Savater 2012). In Delgado's words, the CT paradigm encompasses the 'ámbito de lo decible, visible y pensable' [that which can be said, visibilized and thought] (2014: 19). Accordingly, through the portrayal of both Carrillo's and Pujol's stances on the Catalan-Spanish territorial question and the Països Catalans as either ambiguous or uncomfortable, Monzó's work denounces the maximalist proposals as falling outside of the framework for consensus reached by both Spanish and Catalan mainstream parties during the Transition.

In Monzó's work in 'Políticaflicció', the strong argument for Catalan independence generally appears hand in hand with a firm criticism of Spanish nationalism. In fact, Monzó's satirical work in 1977 and 1978 puts forward an ideological construct that depicts diverse Spanish and Catalan political parties across the spectrum as forming a Spanish unionist continuum. In the remainder of this section, I will examine this construct through the analysis of three examples from 'Políticaflicció'. The first one was released on 30 April 1977, three weeks after the legalization of the PCE, and it ridicules a range of Spanish and Catalan politicians who had expressed their opposition to Catalan independence, including Carrillo, Gregori López Raimundo, leader of the Partit Socialista Unificat de Catalunya (PSUC), and Laureano López Rodó, a former Minister under Franco and candidate of the post-Francoist coalition Alianza Popular (AP) in the general elections of June 1977. In Monzó's piece, entitled 'Drama en un acte', Carrillo and López Raimundo celebrate Spain's unity and the *bicolor* flag, while López Rodó insults the President in Exile of the Generalitat de Catalunya, Josep Tarradellas, who at the time was immersed in negotiations with Adolfo Suárez to re-establish the Generalitat and return to Catalonia. The text concludes with Carrillo and López Rodó dancing a *sardana* in harmony together. This piece offers a prime example of Monzó's viewpoint regarding the connections between the national politics of the PCE and AP. He presents them here as strongly related. There is little doubt that Monzó's satirical work tends towards oversimplification in its political message. In this instance, it is demonstrated not only because, by placing the emphasis on the critique of an alleged Spanish unionist continuum joining some Catalan and Spanish political leaders, the significant differences between Carrillo and López Rodó are lost, but also because the PCE and the PSUC were far from interchangeable parties. The PSUC, in fact, was a Catalanist party that, from the 1960s onwards, played a key role in galvanizing migrants from other parts of Spain to support Catalan language and culture as well as demands for greater devolution (Balcells 1996: 180–81; Dowling: 2013: 108–11; Molinero and Ysàs 2014: 9). As far as satirical conventions are concerned, it is interesting to notice how Monzó re-utilizes tropes already used in previous works, in particular regarding the PCE criticism of the Països Catalans and their acceptance of the *bicolor* flag. These reverberations reveal Monzó's expertise as a satirical cartoonist: 'The great cartoonists have achieved lasting recognition because they have a political or social point of view and have kept that perspective continually before the audience, constantly inventing new ways to present the same message' (Hess and Northrop 2011: 12).

The cartoon that accompanies the text exemplifies further how Monzó's satirical work reiterates his political messages in new and different manners. The drawing depicts a nurse telling a new-born baby 'catalanet que vens al món, qualsevol de les dues Espanyes et tocarà els pebrots' [little Catalan just now coming into the world, both Spains will give you a hard time] (Figure 2.6). The cartoon deploys a deep cultural symbolism by engaging with the well-known lines of Antonio Machado's LIII poem in 'Proverbios y cantares', included in *Campos de Castilla* (1912): 'Españolito que vienes | al mundo, te guarde Dios. | Una de las dos Españas | ha de helarte el corazón' [Little Spaniard just now coming | into the world, may God keep you. | One of the two Spains | will freeze your heart] (1997: 246). During the 1960s and 1970s, Machado's poetry had become a symbol of resistance against the Francoist dictatorship and, in 1969, a year after the ban at the Eurovision contest, Joan Manuel Serrat published the album *Dedicado a Antonio Machado, poeta*, paying tribute to the most relevant poet of the Generation of 1898 and one of the creators of the myth of Castile as the soul and heart of Spain (Driever 1997; Labanyi 1994; Resina 2011; Ribbans 2009). As exemplified by Serrat's album, in the late stages of Francoism Machado's work came to symbolize the healthy and fruitful dialogue between the diverse Hispanic cultures, as well as the belief that another Castile and thus, another Spain, completely different from the Francoist model, was possible. Monzó's cartoon, by suggesting that both Spains will be detrimental to Catalonia, precisely aims to debunk this idea, therefore making an argument for Catalonia's independence. Overall, Monzó's piece implies that, healthy and fruitful as the dialogue between Spain and Catalonia may be, it will always be unbalanced in terms of power relations.

If in 'Drama en un acte' Monzó equates the PCE to ex-Francoist ministers, the

FIG. 2.6. *Canigó* 499. 30 April 1977, p. 17

issue of 'Políticaflicció' published on 16 July 1977 associates the anarcho-syndicalist trade union Confederación Nacional del Trabajo (CNT) to the Francoist territorial model for Spain. Entitled 'Don José Peirats, anarcolerrouxista i de les JONS', the text and political cartoon engage with the anarchist historian and leader of the CNT in exile Josep Peirats, who returned to Spain in 1976. On 2 July 1977, the CNT organized its first mass rally in Spain since 1939. Held in Barcelona, the public meeting was an enormous success, attended by 300,000 people who listened to the speeches of formerly exiled militants such as Peirats and Federica Montseny. Peirats was particularly critical of regional nationalisms in Spain, to the point that his speech had been revised and tweaked by the Catalan Regional Committee of the anarcho-syndicalist trade union after a controversial and heated debate in one of the committee's meetings (Ucelay-Da Cal 2009: 108–09). This event not only shows the distance between the CNT's exiled generation and the younger members who had been politically socialized in late Francoist Catalonia, but also the legitimacy

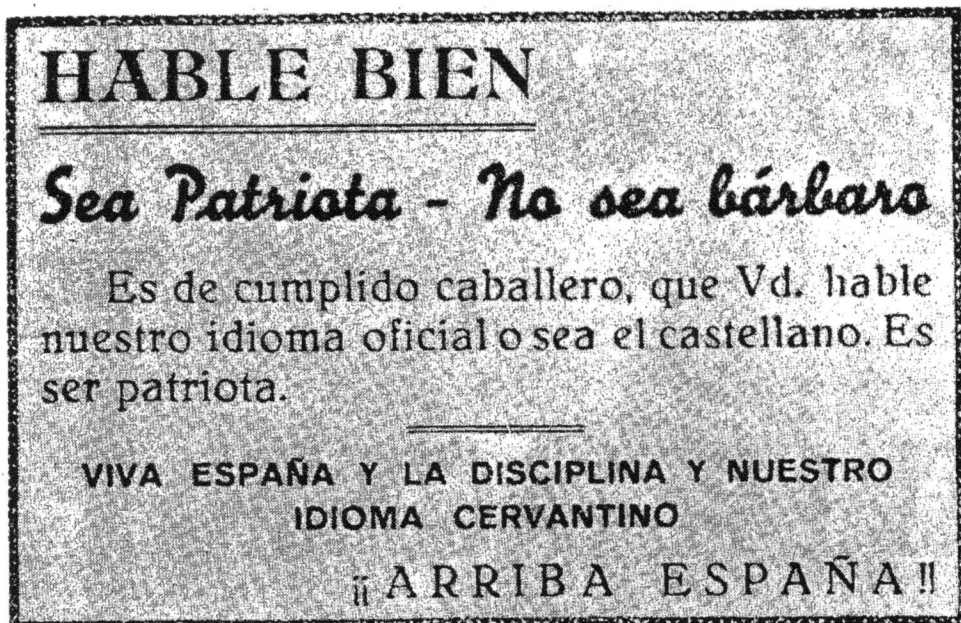

HABLE BIEN

Sea Patriota – No sea bárbaro

Es de cumplido caballero, que Vd. hable nuestro idioma oficial o sea el castellano. Es ser patriota.

VIVA ESPAÑA Y LA DISCIPLINA Y NUESTRO IDIOMA CERVANTINO

¡¡ARRIBA ESPAÑA!!

Model de pancarta que el senyor Peirats vol col·locar a la façana de la Soli, bon punt li retornin l'edifici.

FIG. 2.7. *Canigó* 509. 16 July 1977, p. 17

enjoyed by Catalan nationalism as a force of opposition against the Francoist regime. In spite of the changes introduced, Peirats's speech was received as 'un duro ataque a las nacionalidades' [a strong attack on regional nationalities] and days later the CNT's Catalan regional branch issued a press statement remarking that Peirats's comments on the national question were expressed in a personal capacity and did not reflect the position of the regional committee (Canals 1977). Two weeks after the rally, Monzó's cartoon in *Canigó* satirically connected Peirats's stance to Francoist ideals by reproducing, alongside another surrealist text, an unmistakable regime poster against the public use of regional languages in Spain: 'Hable bien. Sea patriota –– No sea bárbaro. Es de cumplido caballero, que Vd. hable nuestro idioma oficial o sea el castellano' [Speak well. Be a patriot –– Don't be a barbarian. A true gentleman speaks Spanish, our official language] (Figure 2.7). At the bottom of the Francoist poster, Quim Monzò adds an explanation text stating that Peirats wants to display it in the CNT headquarters in Barcelona: 'Model de pancarta que el senyor Peirats vol col·locar a la façana de la Soli, bon punt li retornin l'edifici' [Example of the banner that Mr Peirats wants to put at the front of the Soli as soon as the building is returned] (1977b: 17). The text on the side depicts Peirats declaring that 'no hay ninguna nacionalidad limpia' and 'mi patria es la Tierra' [there isn't any immaculate nation [...] Planet Earth is my motherland] (Monzó 1977b: 17). Peirats is observed from heaven by the seminal anarchist philosophers Peter Kropotkin and Pierre-Joseph Proudhon, who, utterly surprised, remark that 'caldria jubilar-lo' [he should be retired], thus seemingly implying that Peirats is out of touch with the political situation in mid-1970s Catalonia (Monzó 1977b: 17). Also in heaven, General Franco shows his admiration and respect for the anarchist figure: ¿I aquest home era exiliat mentre jo manava? Si arribo a conèixer els seus pensaments, el faig director, no de **Soli** sinó del **Pueblo**' [And this man was in exile when I was in power? If I had known his ideas, I would have made him editor in chief of the newspaper Pueblo instead of the Soli], in reference to the Falangist newspaper *Pueblo* and the anarchist *Solidaridad Obrera* (Monzó 1977b: 17. Bold in original). As with the PCE/PSUC, Monzó's depiction of the national politics of the CNT is both hyperbolic and partisan. More importantly, however, these depictions reveal the ways in which Monzó's work constructs a clear ideological boundary between those who support Catalonia's right to self-determination and those who oppose it, offering a framework to interpret the Transition's political clashes and discussions in the Catalan region.

The first democratic elections held on 15 June 1977 were a definite step in the consolidation of the process towards democracy. The Spanish electorate favoured the political parties that were leaning towards the centre of the political spectrum, such as the UCD and the PSOE, and penalized those that were seen as too extremist and radical, such as the PCE and the AP (Balcells 1996: 170–71; Preston 1987: 118–23; Romero-Salvadó 1999: 167–68). Through these results, the Spanish population was once again endorsing the politics of consensus and *ruptura pactada*. Catalonia, however, presented a different political landscape: while the Transition's consensual paradigm was also widely ratified, the UCD did not win and the Catalan electorate backed either leftist parties which advocated higher degrees of devolution or Catalan conservative nationalism (Balcells 1996: 170–71; Romero-Salvadó 1999: 167–68; Ysàs i Solanes 1997: 12). Negotiations to draft a Constitution for Spain started in mid-1977. Approved by a popular referendum on 6 December 1978, the Constitution was the legal framework that would prevent Catalonia's secession from Spain in the post-Franco period, as illustrated nearly thirty years later on 27 October 2017 when the Spanish government took control of Catalonia's autonomy thanks to Article 155 of this legal charter. On 18 February 1978, eight months before its approval, Quim Monzó's work in 'Políticaficció' criticized the national politics of the Constitution; its content had been made public in November 1977 after being leaked to a newspaper (Tussell 2007: 296). The cartoon shows a jester holding a large placard with a clear and simple slogan on the subject that reads as follows: 'El que es fia de constitucions acaba pobre i no sap com' [He who trusts in constitutions will be conned] (Figure 2.8). By deploying a jester, Monzó's drawing interacts with a typological character who, in the artistic world, commonly questions the prevailing order and is generally associated with mockery, laughter, paradoxes and absurdity (Janick 1998: 1–17). In view of this, it can be suggested that the message conveyed by Monzó's jester intends, on the one hand, to question the prevailing order by opposing the Spanish Constitution that mainstream Spanish and Catalan political parties were drafting at the time; and, on the other hand, to engage with the notion

FIG. 2.8. *Canigó* 541. 18 February 1978, p. 35

of absurdity and foolishness by warning the Catalan population that, if it accepted the political status of Catalonia within Spain as expressed in the Constitution talks, it would be, in the cartoonist's view, conned.

This argument is emphasized in the accompanying text, entitled 'Escenes de plaça'. The piece is an allegorical representation of Monzó's take on the negotiations about Catalonia's political status. The negotiations are portrayed as a dialogue in a market between a fishmonger and her client, Donya Principat. When the latter orders two pounds of independence, the fishmonger quickly points out that this is strictly prohibited by the Constitution and offers her 'una autonomia ben arregladeta' [a cute little autonomy] (Monzó 1978: 35). Donya Principat then requests an autonomy like the one enjoyed by the US states or, at least, 'una autonomieta com la que teníem el 32' [a little autonomy like the one we had in 1932], in reference to the Catalan Statute of Autonomy approved during the Second Republic, an option rejected by the fishmonger on the grounds that that was a Republican Constitution and this one should be Monarchic (Monzó 1978: 35). The bargaining continues and, in the end, after the fishmonger has made her last offer, 'mig quilo de preautonomia estàndard', Donya Principat replies '¿perquè [sic] no es queden vostès amb aquesta [Constitution] que tant els plau i ens deixen a nosaltres fer la nostra' [half a kilo of standard pre-autonomy [...] if you like it so much, why don't you have this one for you and let us do ours?] (1978: 35). The overall message is clear: the competences of a potential Statute of Autonomy emerging from this Constitution will be fairly limited and thus, superficial. Monzó's work seems to suggest that the Constitution will not respect Catalonia's national rights and, consequently, independence is the best option. Perhaps this is the reason why, in the end, the fishmonger calls the police, who violently arrest Donya Principat, alluding again to the critique put forward by Catalan independence activists that their political stances were either rejected as illegal or aggressively repressed (Buch 2012: 29–32; Usall 2006: 172–85; Vilaregut 2004: 65–68). Hence, Monzó's cartoon and text illustrate the threat of institutional violence and repression during the Transition and the limits that the new Spanish Constitution, on not including the right to self-determination, placed on the process of regional devolution.

Quim Monzó's work in *Canigó* reveals how the author's concern during the Transition focused almost exclusively on the national question and associated debates on democratization, two matters that are clearly prioritized over other key conflicts of the time, such as working-class and feminist demands. This is Monzó's most overtly and consistently political work and which most clearly reveals his aim to build a Catalan politico-cultural sphere different from and opposed to that of Spain. Monzó's separatist stance is at the core of his critique of the consensual elements that define cultural normalization, which his work criticized during the 1980s and 1990s. This illustrates how analysing and understanding Monzó's pre-1978 work is essential to achieving a deep understanding of his cultural project. Although not so conspicuously and regularly as in his two-year stint at *Canigó*, in the autonomous period Monzó's opinion pieces, public statements and mass-media participation have continued to criticize the status of Catalonia within Spain and the unbalanced power relations between Catalan culture and the Spanish state, as well as showing his ardent support for Catalonia's separation from Spain. From the present perspective, it is not as relevant whether Monzó's denunciations were partly unfounded or lacked nuance as it is important how his satirical work offers a glimpse into the ways in which Catalan separatists experienced the development and outcome of the national conflict during the Spanish Transition to democracy. Regardless of the indisputable advances and improvements for Catalonia's language, culture and political status, the Transition was, for independence activists, a political defeat. While the political stance and critique depicted in Quim Monzó's artistic production in *Canigó* was a minority view at the time, with historical hindsight there is little denying that the points it raised about Catalonia's status within Spain were germane, given how the conflict has unfolded since 2010. This is not only illustrated by the outcome of the October 2017 referendum and subsequent Unilateral Declaration of Independence, but also by how, in their critique of the

Spanish state, public discourses of independence parties in post-2017 Catalonia follow some of the lines suggested by Monzó's satirical work, in particular the depiction of Spain as an undemocratic state which does not respect the right of self-determination.

Note

1. After Monzó's last contribution to 'Llobarreria' on 8 January 1977, and until the section came to an end on 18 June 1977, the cartoons were co-authored by two artists who also participated in Barcelona's countercultural scene: the actor and musician Quim Sota (signing as 'El Quim') and the film-maker Antoni Martí (signing as 'Toni') (Quim Monzó, personal communication, 9 December 2015). In 1976, Monzó, Martí and Sota had worked together in the experimental film *Hic Digitur Rei*. Monzó and Roser Fradera wrote the script, Martí directed the film and Sota was a member of the acting crew as well as being charge of the music and lighting. Martí and Monzó worked together again in 1983, when the former made a short film of Monzó's short story 'Underworld' (*Uf, va dir ell*), which Monzó adapted for the screen (Dorca 2013: 49–50).

CHAPTER 3

❖

An Authoritative Cultural Mediator

'Vaig anar a Nova York l'any 1982 amb una beca per estudiar la literatura
nord-americana contemporània. Vaig triar d'estudiar aquella literatura perquè,
en aquella època, resulta que els americans eren tan dolents i tan perversos [...]
que s'afirmava amb total impunitat que no podien tenir una bona literatura.
[...] Però només calia llegir-la sense prejudicis per veure que, evidentment, n'hi
havia de ben bona.'

[I went to New York in 1982 with a scholarship to study contemporary
American literature. I chose to study that literature because, at the time, the
Americans were so bad, so depraved [...] that people were claiming with total
impunity that they couldn't produce good literature. But you just had to
read it without prejudice to see that, naturally, there was some really good
stuff there]

Interview in *L'Avenç*, June 2007 (Ollé 2007: 19).

The 11 December 2002 issue of *La Vanguardia Cultura/s* revolved around the literary
and cultural relations between Barcelona and New York, and included a full-
page article by Quim Monzó talking about three significant visits he took to the
American city (2002: 10). He first travelled to New York in the summer of 1975;
General Franco was still alive and Monzó was an up-and-coming author who
still had not published his first novel, *L'udol del griso al caire de les clavegueres* (1976).
His longest stay took place in 1982 when he was awarded a grant by the Fundació
Congrés de Cultura Catalana to spend a year abroad and chose New York in order
to further familiarize himself with contemporary American literature. During his
American sojourn, Monzó wrote the novel *Benzina* (1983), numerous scenes and
the overall plot of which are inspired by his own experiences in the US. Finally, a
few days after 11 September 2001, Monzó travelled to New York to write a series
of chronicles for *La Vanguardia*, some of which were later collected in *Catorze ciutats
comptant-hi Brooklyn* (2004). The relevance of Monzó's work and career for the
relations between both cities is also exemplified by the fact that he is mentioned
in two other articles of the same issue of *La Vanguardia Cultura/s*. Talking about his
experiences in New York during the 1980s, Xavier Rubert de Ventós highlights
the pleasant evening gatherings at his flat, attended by Monzó and other Catalan
artists and authors as well as American Catalanophiles such as the New York
University Professor Mary Ann Newman (2002: 12). Julià Guillamon authors a brief
text on the representation of the US in Catalan culture since the late nineteenth

century and Monzó's work during the early 1980s features prominently (2002: 16). Guillamon first observes that 'los artículos de Quim Monzó, en 1982, introdujeron en Catalunya el debate sobre el postmodernismo o la recuperación del prestigio de la vida urbana' [in 1982, Monzó's articles introduced the debate about postmodernism and the rising prestige of urban life in Catalonia], and subsequently elaborates on how *Benzina* depicted life in the New York of its time (2002: 16).

Monzó's prominent position in this issue of *La Vanguardia Cultura/s* attests to the key function played by the author in the cultural connections between Barcelona and New York and, more generally, to the influence of American culture in 1980s Catalonia. In his piece, Guillamon credits Monzó with having introduced the debate about postmodernism into Catalan culture through his regular press articles during his stint in New York. Pivotal to the impact of American postmodernist fiction in Catalonia are Monzó's translations of John Barth's essays 'The Literature of Exhaustion' (1967), widely regarded as the manifesto of postmodernism, and 'The Literature of Replenishment — Postmodernist Fiction' (1980), published in *Els Marges* in 1983. In an article published in 1999 in *Revista de Catalunya*, Guillamon noted the deep impact that both essays had on early 1980s Catalan culture; in his own words, 'quan el 1983 van aparèixer a *Els Marges*, les reflexions de Barth es van incorporar al discurs habitual de la crítica i van generar molts llocs comuns' [in 1983, when they were published in *Els Marges*, Barth's ideas were incorporated into the critics' regular discourses, generating shared imaginaries] (Guillamon 1999: 124). In the collectively-authored book *70–80–90 Literatura (Dues dècades des de la tercera i última)*, published in 1992, the author and literary critic Francesc Calafat also pointed out that both essays were highly influential in 1980s Catalan literary circles (1992: 124). Monzó's 1982 stay in New York emerges as a pivotal moment not only for the author's career but also for Catalan literature and culture. During his stay in the US, he became fascinated with American postmodern authors such as John Barth, Donald Barthelme and Robert Coover (Blake 1997; Miralles 2004; Ollé 2007: 19–21). The influence of these authors has been considered key for the development of Monzó's innovative postmodern literary aesthetics — aesthetics which would be decisive in the transformations that Catalan literature would experience during the 1980s (Bou 1988: 409; Cònsul 1995: 174; Lunati 2008: 218; Marrugat 2014a: 33–35; Nogués 1998: 37–38; Ollé 1998: 50).

John Barth's articles are not the only American texts that Monzó has translated into Catalan. In fact, Monzó was quite prolific in his translational activities throughout the 1980s as well as beyond, albeit with significantly less intensity after 1990. Between 1981 and 2002, Monzó translated nineteen texts from English into Catalan, most of them short stories but also novels and theatre plays, a preponderance of which were by American writers. In 1981, Monzó published the translation of two of Dorothy Parker's short stories, 'Vides corrents' ('The Standard of Living') and 'El vals' ('The Waltz'). Barthelme's short stories 'Alguns de nosaltres havíem estat amenaçant el nostre amic Colby' ('Some of Us Had Been Threatening Our Friend Colby') and 'El nou membre' ('The New Member') came out in 1982. During his spell in the US, Monzó had probably been working on the six translations that he published in 1983, namely: the novels *Jude, l'obscur* (*Jude the Obscure*) by Thomas Hardy and *Frankenstein o el Prometeu modern* (*Frankenstein, or the Modern Prometheus*) by Mary Shelley, the short-story fixup *Les cròniques marcianes* (*The Martian Chronicles*) by Ray Bradbury, the play *Tres boleros* (*The Torch Song Trilogy*) by Harvey Fierstein and John Barth's essays. Hemingway's novel *El sol també s'aixeca* (*The Sun Also Rises*) was published in 1984, and Salinger's short-story collection *Nou històries* (*Nine Stories*) in 1986. In 1988, Monzó rendered three stories by Roald Dahl into Catalan, which he published together in a book entitled *L'autostopista*: 'El nen que parlava amb els animals' ('The Boy Who Talked With Animals'), 'L'autostopista' ('The Hitch-Hiker') and 'El tresor de Mildenhall' ('The Mildenhall Treasure'). He also translated Truman Capote's short-fiction collection *Música per a camaleons* (*Music for Chameleons*) the same year and, in 1989, he compiled a number of Capote's short stories in a book entitled *El convidat del Dia d'Acció de Gràcies*: 'Un record de Nadal' ('A Christmas Memory'), 'El convidat del Dia d'Acció de Gràcies' ('The Thanksgiving Visitor') and 'Un Nadal' ('One Christmas'). His translation of Robert Coover's short story 'La primeria de la vida de l'artista' ('The Early Life of the Artist') came out in 1990. After this, Monzó's translational output decreased significantly, probably because of his gradual consolidation as a literary author. 1995 saw the publication in Catalan of James Finn Garner's short-story collection *Politically Correct Bedtime Stories* in Catalan, translated jointly by Monzó himself and Maria Roura as *Contes per a nens i nenes políticament correctes*. At the turn of the twenty-first century, Monzó published his last two translations from English into Catalan, the theatre plays *Tots eren fills meus* (*All My Sons*) by Arthur Miller in 1999 and Howard Barker's *Escenes d'una execució* (*Scenes from an Execution*) in 2002.

Quim Monzó's sustained translation of American authors is too important to be ignored. In this chapter I argue that Monzó has been a cultural mediator through his translational activity, advancing the transmission of American literary, cultural and political trends into Catalonia. In the first part of this chapter, I explore the impact of John Barth's essays on Monzó's postmodernist literary fiction through the analysis of *Benzina* vis-à-vis Barth's texts. Existing scholarship has generally limited the links between Monzó's work and American cultural trends to the postmodern elements of his fiction which modernized Catalan literature from the early 1980s onwards. This chapter, however, shows that Monzó's channelling of American sociocultural trends goes beyond this specific link. As I show in the second section, Monzó continued to be a mediator of American ideas through the 1990s with his translation of James Finn Garner's *Politically Correct Bedtime Stories* (1994), importing the American parody of political correctness into the Catalan context of the mid-1990s. By exploring the transnational connections between Quim Monzó's work and American trends, this chapter continues to problematize and move beyond the interpretation of Monzó's oeuvre within a narrow, nationally defined Catalan literary canon. Monzó himself has asserted that translated works were key literary and cultural influences during his formative years and, for this reason, he has been critical of the tendency to see the network of literary influences on Catalan authors as to be located mainly within the national tradition. In the late 1980s Monzó declared, in his well-known sarcastic style, that some critics still think that 'vivim en una mena de edat mitjana imaginada, i que no hi ha altre cap altre mitjà de comunicació que no siguin els sermons dominicals i els llibres catalans, i on les traduccions, evidenment, no existeixen' [we live in a kind of imagined Middle Ages in which there aren't media outlets apart from Sunday sermons and Catalan books, and in which translations, of course, don't exist] (Castillo 1989: 71). This statement not only reveals Monzó's interest in translated literature, but also, and perhaps more importantly for this chapter, his awareness of the impact that translated works can have on the target literary and cultural system.

3.1. *Benzina*, or the Catalan Literature of Replenishment

Kathryn Crameri has analysed how the translation of major authors into Catalan has been pivotal to the main Catalan literary movements since the late nineteenth century, when foremost authors associated with *Modernisme* and *Noucentisme* such as Joan Maragall, Josep Carner, Jacint Verdaguer, Santiago Rusiñol and Carles Riba translated a number of foreign works into Catalan, thus operating as authors/translators. Their aim was to promote Catalan as a literary language and to 'strengthen Catalan culture through the influence of European thought and literature' (Crameri 2000b: 172–73). While the publication of translations into Catalan came to a halt in the 1940s due to the Francoist policies, by the 1960s, the 'number of translations being published increased dramatically, and in certain years accounted for nearly half of all the production in Catalan' (Crameri 2000b: 173). For this reason, as Crameri argues, the new generation of authors who emerged in the 1970s, such as Terenci Moix, Biel Mesquida, Quim Monzó and Oriol Pi de Cabanyes, 'turned to a large number of European and American literary models when nothing suitable was found in the tradition of either Catalonia or Spain' (2000b: 175). Monzó's public statements support Crameri's observation. In a 1977 interview he claimed that,

> hi ha tota una sèrie de gent que ha començat a escriure sense tenir en compte la tradició literària d'aquí, cosa que considero positiva perquè permet partir d'uns altres punts que no necessàriament han de ser els de la tradició cultural nostra (X.M. 1977: 12)

> [there's a group of people who have started writing without taking the local literary tradition into account, something which I consider positive because it allows one to set off from points which are not necessarily those of our cultural tradition]

Crameri notes how, while translations plummeted in the 1970s, they rose sharply again in the 1980s (2000b: 173). To throw light on this surge Crameri draws upon Itamar Even-Zohar's influential essay 'The Position of Translated Literature within the Literary Polysystem', wherein Even-Zohar theorizes the crucial function that translation plays in literary polysystems as channel for innovation, expansion and renewal, particularly in minority or non-state cultures (2000). As Even-Zohar observes, 'when new literary models are emerging, translation is likely to become one of the means of elaborating the new repertoire. Through the foreign works, features (both principles and elements) are introduced into the home literature' (200: 193). He lists three major circumstances in which translated literature can act as a catalyst for change in the receiving literary system: first, when the literary polysystem 'has not yet been crystallized' or is 'in the process of being established'; second, when it is peripheral, as opposed to a majority, central or hegemonic culture; and third, when 'there are turning points, crisis or literary vacuums' in the polysystem (2000: 193–94). In the early 1980s, Catalan literature fulfilled the three cases. While the Catalan literary system had existed for centuries, it was now re-emerging from an epoch of significant disruption, one in which its very existence was threatened. As such, it was at a turning point, in the process of being (re-)established and (re-)defined following the gradual consolidation of democracy in Spain and the restitution of the Catalan autonomous institutions. However, in spite of the recovery of Catalonia's autonomy, Catalan literature and culture were still peripheral and minoritized due to its subordinate position vis-à-vis the Spanish state. It was in this context that Quim Monzó operated as an author/translator, following the tradition initiated by *Modernistes* and *Noucentistes*.

Monzó's most influential translations during the decade are those of Barth's essays, which came out together in a special issue of *Els Marges* in 1983. This issue is particularly relevant when considering the role of translated works in early 1980s Catalonia. As specified in the editorial, the economic support granted by the Generalitat de Catalunya was essential to publish this longer, first special issue of *Els Marges*, fully dedicated to essays translated into Catalan on the topic of 'modernity'. In the words of the editors: 'Posats a fer —— amb el suport econòmic de la Generalitat de Catalunya —— un primer número extraordinari, de gruix i de contingut, de la revista "Els Marges", hem volgut que aquest fos íntegrament constituït per traduccions' [We have wanted to dedicate this first special issue, both in length and theme, of *Els Marges* —— published thanks to economic support of the Catalan Generalitat —— to translated works] (*Els Marges* 1983: 3). The list of translated authors includes, among others, Karl Marx, Friedrich Nietzsche, Sigmund Freud, György Lukács, Ludwig Wittgenstein, Paul Valéry, Roman Jacobson, Jean-Paul Sartre, Martin Heidegger, Theodor W. Adorno, Claude Lévi-Strauss, Jacques Lacan, Jacques Derrida, Michel Foucault, Roland Barthes and John Barth's essays. Finally, the editors assert that their two main aims with this issue are to foster up-to-date intellectual debate within Catalan literature and stimulate further translations into Catalan (1983: 4). This illustrates how, in the early 1980s, Catalan literature was ripe to welcome new literary and cultural models and, to use Even-Zohar's terminology, translation was seen as essential to the development of new principles and elements.

John Barth is widely regarded as one of the key representatives of American postmodern literature (Clavier 2007: 14; Hoberek 2007: 235; Ziegler 1987: 89). During the 1960s, American fiction went through deep transformations owing to the sociocultural shifts developing at the same time. A generation of writers, Barth, Donald Barthelme and Robert Coover among them, turned to experimentalist modes and produced 'fiction which was primarily about fiction itself' and which was 'profoundly intertextual, constantly referring directly or indirectly to other texts and genres, obsessively indulging in parody and pastiche' (Nicol 2009: 72–73). As Larry McCaffery has noted, authors like Barth, Barthelme and Thomas Pinchon engaged in a type of metafictional literature which shares a wilful artificiality and 'a sense of playfulness and self-consciousness' in ways that betray fully their postmodernist essence (1982: 4). In this context, John Barth's essays on postmodernist literary aesthetics, in particular 1967's 'The Literature of Exhaustion', have been received as veritably crucial and representative works of a literary era (Clavier 2007: 167; Lodge 1992: 298; Nicol 2007; 50; Ziegler 1987: 17).

In his translations into Catalan, Monzó is aware of his role as a cultural mediator, drawing upon his extensive knowledge of contemporary American literature and its theoretical debates. Both essays offer a brief critical comment on the first page and include a few translator's notes. In his comments on 'La literatura de l'exhauriment', Monzó highlights that, due to its cultural impact, Barth's essay had been considered the literary manifesto of the 'corrent narratiu dit "de l'exhauriment"' [narrative trend known as 'exhaustion'], of which Barth and Thomas Pynchon were the main representatives (1983b: 269). Subsequently, Monzó discusses the reception of the essay in the US: while some critics believed that it had a depressing and confusing effect on American literature, others saw it as a key piece to reflect upon in regards to narration and literary creation at a time pervaded by debates about the death of the novel (1983b: 269). In his introduction to the second essay, Monzó asserts that, when Barth's text was published in 1980, 'el terme *postmodernism* havia deixat de ser patrimoni exclusiu dels arquitectes i havia esdevingut d'ús ben comú en el món literari dels Estats Units' [the term postmodernism was no longer exclusive to architecture and had become of common use in the American literary world] (1983c: 279. Italics in original). Monzó also explains his translation of the terms modernist/postmodernist and modernism/postmodernism into Catalan: while he translates the former as 'modern/postmodern', he leaves *modernism* and *postmodernism* in English and italics because the Catalan term 'modernisme' may have led to confusion because of its connotations (1983c: 279). As far as translation strategies are concerned, Monzó does not significantly intervene in the text; he makes the text readable to a Catalan audience and translates the titles of books into Catalan when they would not be readily known or understood by Catalan readers. In the first essay, for instance, Barth discusses a catalogue of playful and surrealist books, listing a few authors and titles such as 'Robert Filliou's *Ample Food for Stupid Thought*', 'Ray Johnson's *Paper Snake*' and 'Daniel Spoerri's *Anecdoted Typography of Chane*' (1984: 65). In these cases, Monzó translates the titles into Catalan as 'Queviure Ample per a Pensament Estúpid, de Robert Filliou', 'Serp de Paper, de Ray Johnson' and 'Tipografia Anecdòtica de l'Atzar, de Daniel Spoerri' (1983b: 270). On the very same page, however, Barth mentions James Joyce's *Finnegans Wake* and Monzó leaves the title in English, as the book would be recognizable to Catalan readers.

The key idea underpinning 'The Literature of Exhaustion' is that techniques of literary representation have become exhausted and, for this reason, authors must come up with new fictional forms better adapted to the present day. From the very first page of the essay, Barth's celebratory tone welcomes the changes occurring in Western literature and rejects a nostalgic view of past literary production: 'by "exhaustion" I don't mean anything so tired as the subject of physical, moral, or intellectual decadence, only the used-upness of certain forms or the felt exhaustion of certain possibilities –– by no means necessarily a cause for despair' (1984: 64). Barth connects this feeling of 'exhaustion' to the changes triggered by a variety of rising multidisciplinary artistic forms combining textual and visual culture, such as pop art, drama, musical happenings and performance art. Key to his argument is how these new artistic forms have contributed to transforming the notion of the artist in the West, disrupting the traditional Aristotelian conception of the creator as an individual endowed with uncommon, otherworldly talent and virtuosity. This disruption had a profound impact on literary creation, as it problematized the omniscient narrative voice of realist fiction and the idea of the controlling narrator in general (1984: 65). Barth then moves on to consider what makes a 'technically-up-to-date' artist and offers examples such as James Joyce and Franz Kafka in the recent past and Samuel Beckett and Jorge Luis Borges in the present times (1984: 66). For the remainder of his essay, Barth discusses the main traits of Borges's fiction, while also offering a couple of examples from Beckett's that exemplify his literary theories as well. Barth contrasts both authors against the 'technically-old-fashioned' artists, those who, in the 1960s, continue to write as if the literary movements and transformations of the twentieth century had not taken place, falling back into the realist techniques of literary representation. In Barth's own words: 'it is dismaying to see so many of our writers following Dostoevsky or Tolstoy or Balzac, when the question seems to me how to succeed not even Joyce and Kafka, but those who *succeeded* Joyce and Kafka' (1984: 67. Italics in original).

For Barth, Borges is an essential author not merely for his aesthetics but, more importantly, for his innovative metaphysical conception of literary creation (1984: 64). As Barth sees it, the main features of Borges's original literary programme are encapsulated in his 1939 short story 'Pierre Menard, autor del Quijote' (1984: 68–69). Borges's text revolves around a French symbolist author who, 'by an astounding effort of imagination, produces –– not *copies* or *imitates*, but *composes* –– several chapters of Cervantes' novel' (1984: 68. Italics in original). For Barth, this is a serious intellectual project which interrogates the history of Western literature by challenging one of its main tenets, that of originality –– a challenge which Barth equates to that of Andy Warhol's *Campbell's Soup Cans* in the artistic field. Borges's highly ironic yet serious text questions 'the difficulty, perhaps the necessity, of writing original works of literature' (1984: 69). Borges encountered the dead-end faced by creative originality and confronted it, finding an innovative solution by using originality against itself, thus opening a new artistic avenue. Subsequently, Barth discusses the specific characteristics that make Borges an up-to-date artist, namely, the ironic and self-aware perspective, the 'contamination of reality by dream', the 'story-within-the-story' and the 'literary illustration of the *regressus in infinitum*' which precludes fixed closures in literary texts (1984: 71–73).

The literary features that Barth associates with Borges form the basis of what came to be known as postmodern fiction. The identification of Borges — and also Beckett — with postmodern literature has been a matter of debate among scholars for many reasons, not least because postmodern literature is considered to have emerged in the late 1960s, when both authors had already been active for decades. In *The Cambridge Introduction to Postmodern Fiction* (2007), Bran Nicol observes how Borges and Beckett were particularly influential for postmodern authors in the late 1960s because their work seemed to suggest solutions to the two questions underpinning Barth's essay: 'how to remain in tune with significant developments in the modern world and how to continue writing despite the apparent exhaustion of a literary form' (2007: 51). Michael Wood, for his part, highlights how Borges's concerns about fictionality and distrust of literary realism were particularly relevant for poststructuralist thinkers. Trying to answer whether Borges should be defined as modern or postmodern, he states that 'the only credible answer to this question is the unhelpful "both"' (2013: 33). Similarly, and in terms of literary historiography and periodization, Nicol conceives of Borges and Beckett as 'key transitional figures in the passage from modernism to postmodernism' (2009: 51). The reception of Borges's and Beckett's as transitional authors moving towards postmodern literature is also relevant for the critical manoeuvres associating Quim Monzó's fiction to Pere Calders and the Grup de Sabadell, as their work could also be seen as prefiguring certain features of postmodern fiction in Catalan.

The novel *Benzina*, published in 1983 like the translation of Barth's essays, offers an excellent case study to analyse the connections between Monzó's translational activity and the literary and aesthetic debates with which he engaged as a result of this activity. More specifically, my analysis of *Benzina* illustrates, on the one hand, the interrelations between Barth's essays and Monzó's literary programme and, on the other, the relevance of the American transnational framework to a deeper understanding of Monzó's modernizing project. Revolving around the vicissitudes of two Catalan painters of global renown, resident in New York in the early 1980s, Heribert and Humbert, *Benzina* displays the artistic world and postmodern debates about culture and art taking place in the city at the time. Through a focus on individualism, consumerism, eccentric behaviours and the immediate fulfilment of personal desires, the characters are depicted socializing in expensive New York restaurants and engaging in obsessive consumption of all type of objects and experiences — from works of art and fashionable items such as Cadillacs, Chevrolets and Cartier watches to stamps and historical coins, as well as trips to cosmopolitan destinations such as Paris, Hong Kong, Munich, Tokyo, Milan, Karachi, the Caribbean and the island of Samoa. The novel's tone, in typical Monzó style, is aloof and detached, clearly ironic at times, and depicts the commodification of art associated with the postmodern era. As Josep-Anton Fernàndez has observed, *Benzina* portrays art 'as a part of a larger economic system in which culture is commodified: it is more a matter of supply and demand than of sincerity, originality and authenticity' (1998: 265). The publication of *Benzina* had a deep impact on Catalan literature and, in particular, among a young generation eager for new urban and international references for Catalan culture, as Jordi

Puntí has observed, defining it as 'la primera novel·la postmoderna en català' [the first postmodern novel in Catalan] (2010: 72). *Benzina* not only broadened the traditional borders of Catalan culture by (re-)locating its plot to New York, but also contributed to the modernization of Catalan fiction by engaging with the key literary and cultural debates taking place in the Western world at the time. The novel situates Catalan culture within the American cultural sphere both literally and symbolically. Hence, there is a clear thread that connects *L'udol del griso al caire de les clavegueres* and *Benzina*: their (re-)location of the story to culturally leading cities and their engagement with the sociocultural spirit of their times in the West and, in particular, with American culture and lifestyles. If *L'udol* depicts the world of counterculture and May 1968 at the end of the 1960s, *Benzina* portrays the zeitgeist of postmodernism in the 1980s.

Being set in New York, the novel is packed with American imagery that undoubtedly excited a Catalan readership eager for cosmopolitan cultural references. The art world is represented through painters such as Edward Hopper, Stuart Davis and Tamara de Lempicka, the sculptors Alexander Calder (and his 'The Brass Family') and Gaston Lachaise (and his 'Standing Woman'), the jazz band Dave Brubeck Quartet and institutions such as the Whitney Museum of American Art, the Art Institute of Chicago and the Metropolitan Opera. Well-known NYC neighbourhoods and landmark sites which Catalan readers would identify from films and other cultural products are portrayed: Greenwich Village, SoHo, TriBeCa, the World Trade Center, Staten Island. The novel's characters socialize in some of the city's legendary bars and restaurants in which famous artists, Andy Warhol amongst them, mingled: Les Pleiades, Sardi's, The Odeon, Ballato, Da Silvano. References to artistic and cultural movements are also a constant: conceptualism, hyperrealism, New Journalism, minimalism, new Dadaism, new cubism and, of course, postmodernism. All this cultural excitement is interspersed with numerous Catalan references, especially in the second part of the novel when Humbert's path to global stardom is narrated. Through an interview in an American art magazine, we learn that, at the age of fourteen, Humbert went to the Escola Massana Art School in Barcelona and, three years later, to the Escola Llotja. The journalist conducting the interview, however, does not recognize these references and Humbert quickly points out that Picasso, in his youth, had attended the Escola Llotja, which excites the reporter. Humbert then continues talking about his beginnings in the art world but must constantly provide clarifications about the references he makes, from *Serra d'Or*, *El Capitán Trueno*, *La Vanguardia Española* and the drawing competitions Ynglada-Guillot and Joan Miró to Barcelona's La Sagrera neighbourhood and the city of Granollers, among many others. In this interview, Humbert acts as a cultural mediator to introduce and describe Catalonia and its cultural world to the journalist and, by extension, to the implied American readership, in what is an inversion of what Monzó does with *Benzina*, where he portrays New York and American culture for the Catalan readership. Humbert later talks about how he moved to New York at the age of twenty-three thanks to a grant he was awarded for a year-long project to study art in the American city. Humbert is partly Monzó's alter ego, as the author himself attended graphic design classes at the Escola Massana in his youth and won a grant to study literature in New York. Precisely because of this, Humbert's reasons for moving to New York shed light on Monzó's connection with the US and its implications for Catalan culture. As Humbert recounts, he hesitated between New York and Paris: while the former had been the leading centre for artistic creation for decades, the latter had a sentimental appeal for him, since, as his mother said, Paris 'és una segona casa pels catalans' [is a second home to Catalans] (1983a: 144).[1] Eventually choosing New York, Humbert had a big argument with his mother, who was scandalized by the image she had made herself of the city through the films of the 1940s and 1950s and, more recently, by television. Nevertheless, Humbert stood firm in his choice because, as he repeatedly told his mother, a sojourn in the capital city of contemporary art would be highly beneficial for his career. Through the dichotomy of Paris/mother/sentiments versus New York/Humbert/career, the novel can be seen as engaging with the debates we saw in Chapter 1 about the substitution of Paris by New York as the global leading cultural centre in the West. This excerpt can be seen as depicting New York as the thriving future and Paris as the nostalgic past, a dichotomy that, in the context of early 1980s Catalonia, can be extended to New York as representing the project of Catalan cultural normality in the democratic period, wherein Paris stands for the oppositional paradigm of cultural *resistencialisme* under Francoism. Like Humbert, Monzó went to New York and, while it is not known whether the author also considered Paris, this would have certainly been a possibility, given the inspirational role played by the French capital for Catalan culture under Francoism.

Alongside its interrelations with American culture, *Benzina* contains some literary traits reminiscent of Borges, as discussed by John Barth. To start with, the novel is divided into two clear sections of similar length, entitled January and December. The first one describes the fall of Heribert, who seems to have lost his inspiration after having achieved world renown, and the second depicts the rise of Humbert, whose profile quickly rises and who replaces Heribert as a world-leading figure in modern art. Covering one year, the plot begins with Heribert waking up on New Year's morning with his lover Hildegarda instead of his partner and agent Helena. The second part opens with Humbert sleeping by Helena, now his partner and agent, who has played a key role in catapulting him to fame. Hence, Humbert comes to replace, even to supplant, Heribert's career and life. What is more, as the story progresses, Heribert begins an affair with Hildegarda. The book ends with Heribert and Hildegarda going to bed after having attended a New Year's Eve party together. This circular plot structure can be linked to Borges's *regressus in infinitum* as analysed by Barth, which does not allow for a fixed closure to the story. Alfonso de Toro reads Borges's *regressus in infinitum* in relation to the notion of infinite, linking it to repetition, proliferation, postponement, as in a series without beginning or end (2018: 9). Owing to its circular (and thus postponed) plot, *Benzina* can be read as an ironic critique of the commodification and shallowness of the postmodern art world, a superficiality that constantly repeats itself through the incorporation of new artists and vocabularies. The circular plot structure without a definite closure is a recurrent and pivotal trend in Monzó's fiction, as my next two chapters analyse.

Barth also highlights how Borges's literature tends to combine reality and dream, which he refers to as the 'contamination of reality by dream' (1984: 7). The amalgamation of reality and dream is at the very core of *Benzina*; the novel is rife with constant references to dreams and long oneiric sections which enter the realm of the surreal. Both parts of the novel start with a lengthy description of a dream, Heribert's in the first one and Humbert's in the second. In fact, the novel opens with a sentence in which reality and dream are fused: 'Torna a tenir la sensació d'estar adormit i despert alhora, i si hi para atenció li sembla estar adormit del tot' [Once again, he feels as if he were asleep and awake at the same time, yet if he concentrates he feels as if he were fast asleep] (1983a: 11). A few lines later, the narrator tells us that Heribert wastes time wondering if he is awake or asleep, and the next pages describe Heribert's dream and reflections about it: if, after some struggle, he feels he is dreaming freely and decides to let his imagination flow, later on he is bored by that dream and tries to stop it or, as the narrator tells us, to 'somiar, ara, un altre somni' [start dreaming another dream] (1983a: 14–15). This beginning sets the novel's frame of reference, in which the reader struggles to know whether the subject of the narration is real or merely another dream. In his essay Barth also points out how Borges's fiction is interested in the story-within-the-story (1984a: 73), which can be linked to the metafictional quality of postmodern literature. Whereas several of Monzó's short stories follow the story-within-the-story structure, it is worth noting how *Benzina* turns it into a dream-within-the-dream structure. At some point in the novel, Humbert and his lover Hildegarda fall asleep and 'Humbert, en el somni que somia en el somni, somia que va en cotxe, amb la Hildegarda al costat' [Humbert, in the dream he is dreaming in the dream, dreams that he is in a car at Hildegarda's side] (1983a: 191). *Benzina*'s literary traits therefore proffer a sense of expansion and endless repetition similar to the one which Barth detected in Borges's work.

Barth closes his essay discussing how Borges's short story 'The Library of Babel', which revolves around a vast library containing every possible book thanks to its adjacent hexagonal rooms, signals the sense of infinite and, due to its physical shape, suggests the idea of a labyrinth (1984: 75). Barth remarks that a labyrinth, 'after all, is a place in which, ideally, all the possibilities of choice (of direction, in this case) are embodied' (1984: 75). In the face of exhaustion, the labyrinth opens up boundless possibilities for literary authors, though they must be aware of the existing literary tradition and acknowledge it; only then can they start working on their texts (1984: 76). *Benzina* literally enacts the debate about exhaustion and originality at the core of Barth's essay. In the midst of his creative stagnation, Heribert struggles to produce a canvas for his forthcoming exhibition and the narrative voice describes his (self-)reflections on originality, creativity and innovation vis-à-vis art history:

> Alineà totes les teles en blanc que tenia a l'estudi i se les mirà. ¿I si exposés allò: teles en blanc, sense ni el més mínim traç humà? Ja s'havia fet. Minimal. A més, si les firmava ja hi hauria col·locat uns traços propis. Podia no firmar-les. També ho devia haver fet algú. ¿Hi havia res d'original a fer? Ni tan sols omplir tots els quadres d'una exposició sense ganes no era un acte original. ¿Calia fer coses

originals? ¿Per què? ¿Calia ser honest i fer coses originals? Per honestedat, molta
gent no havia fet res d'original. (1983a: 75)

[He lines up all the blank canvases he has in the studio and examines them.
What if he showed just that: white canvases without the slightest trace of a
human hand? It's been done. Minimalism. And anyway, if he signs them he will
have placed a few strokes of his own. He could not sign them. Someone must
have done that, too. Is there anything original left to do? Even half-heartedly
filling up all the walls of an exhibition isn't new. Do you really have to do
something new? Why? What is more important, to be honest or to be original?
Out of honesty, people often refused to be original]

Heribert's thoughts not only depict the dead-end and used-upness analysed by
Barth but also hint at how an artist can acknowledge it and produce an up-to-
date self-aware text by turning the notion of originality against itself. This
excerpt also reveals a key characteristic of artistic creation under the postmodern
aegis as analysed by Mike Featherstone in his seminal work *Consumer Culture and
Postmodernism* (1991), namely that, given postmodernism's attack on the historically-
established transformative role of art within society, artists should stay away from
lofty pretensions about their work. In his own words, 'everything is already
seen and written, the artist cannot achieve uniqueness but is doomed to make
repetitions, which he/she should do without pretension' (1991: 123). Taken together,
this fragment illustrates Monzó's theoretical awareness of what makes an up-to-
date, and thus postmodern, artist in the final decades of the twentieth century in
the West.

In 1980, thirteen years after the publication of his landmark essay, Barth
added more arguments to the debate in 'The Literature of Replenishment —
Postmodernist Fiction'. In this second essay, which has not been as influential as the
first one, Barth aims to set out his programme for postmodernist fiction vis-à-vis
modernist literature. As Barth sees it, postmodernism is a complex, multifaceted
and sometimes contradictory term within literary studies. He asserts that, in order
to offer a sound genealogy and definition, it is crucial to analyse postmodernism's
interrelations with modernist fiction. For Barth, postmodernism 'is in some respects
an extension of the program of modernism, in other respects a reaction against it'
(1984: 197). Subsequently, he discusses modernism as a literary movement whose
main aim was to subvert the bourgeois order portrayed by nineteenth century
realist fiction. As such, the modernist literary programme disrupted the linear flow
of the narrative, problematized the unity and coherence of plot and characters,
deployed a self-aware ironic perspective to call into question the bourgeois narrative
of progress and development, and favoured subjectivism and inward consciousness
to problematize the alleged objectivity and rational aspiration of bourgeois realist
literature. At the heart of most modernist fiction is the insistence, 'borrowed
from their romantic forebears, on the special, usually alienated role of the artist in
his society' (Barth 1984: 199). For this reason, Barth observes, certain modernist
authors tended to produce difficult and complex works which were well-received
in intellectual and academic circles but remained fairly unpopular outside them
(201–02). After discussing the traits of modernist fiction, Barth proclaims that the

modernist aesthetic belongs to the first half of the twentieth century, while the second half is the age of postmodernist literary aesthetics. For him, postmodernist fiction should neither repudiate modernism or realism nor imitate them or fall into the temptation to behave as if both literary movements never took place. Instead, postmodernist fiction should combine features from both modernism and realism, becoming 'the synthesis or transcension of these antitheses, which may be summed up as premodernist and modernist modes of writing' (Barth 1984: 203). In light of this, the ideal postmodernist novel 'will somehow rise above the quarrel between realism and irrealism, formalism and "contentism", pure and committed literature, coterie fiction and junk fiction' (1984: 203).

Barth's definition of postmodern literature is pivotal to an understanding of the continuities and discontinuities in Quim Monzó's fictional oeuvre. As we saw in Chapter 1, Catalan literature in the 1950s and 1960s was permeated by the themes and aesthetics of social realism or *realisme compromés* (Picornell 2007: 90–95; Simbor 2005: 9–14). In the 1970s, however, Monzó's generation sought to escape from social realism through the highly experimentalist aesthetics en vogue at the time, which came to be known as *textualisme* in Catalonia. *L'udol del griso al caire de les clavegueres* is an excellent example of how Catalan experimentalist fiction challenged realist techniques of representation through a highly fragmented narrative, the disruption of language and syntax and the destabilization of characters' fictionality (among other experimentalist features). Although, as previously discussed, *L'udol* did not fully break away from realist representation, the novel lacks the balance between experimentalism and realism indicated by Barth. Monzó, however, would progressively detach himself from the highly experimentalist aesthetics of *textualisme*, which he considered an exhausted literary form, as illustrated by the following quotation taken from a lengthy interview in the magazine *Jot Down*:

> Quan vaig començar a escriure, parlo dels vint anys, a escriure sense publicar, aquí la pauta era el textualisme. S'havia d'escriure i que ningú no t'entengués. Perquè si algú entenia que a la història apareix un senyor amb una llibreta de paper groc assegut davant d'un altre senyor i amb unes ulleres al damunt del full de paper groc, i tots dos estaven conversant...si s'entenia tot això, eres gairebé un feixista decrèpit. No s'havia d'entendre una puta merda! Allò sí que era literatura. Tu, això ho vas viure? Allò sí que era revolucionari. Que no s'entengués què collons hi passava, al relat, i que anessis avançant i res. (González 2012)

> [When I was twenty years old and started to write but did not publish yet, *textualisme* was the trend here. You had to write in a way that no one understood what was going on. Because if someone understood that the story talked about a man with a yellow-paper notepad who was sitting in front of another man, with a pair of glasses on top of the yellow paper, and both were having a chat... if the reader could understand this, you were a decrepit fascist. Nothing should be understood! That was real literature. Did you experience it? That was really revolutionary. You were reading the text and you didn't understand shit about the plot]

In this comment, Monzó is highly critical of the literary project of *textualisme*, sarcastic almost to the point that it seems that he never published experimentalist fiction. This scathing disapproval may partly explain why he has never allowed for the re-publication of his early works associated with *textualisme*, namely, *L'udol del griso al caire de les clavegueres* and *Self-service* (1977). While Barth criticizes the elitism of certain modernist authors, here Monzó disapproves of highly experimentalist techniques of representation and advocates a more accessible fiction which does not aim to disrupt language representation. In spite of this unsympathetic analysis of *textualisme*, Monzó's fiction from 1978 onwards has kept certain experimentalist trends as discussed by Barth, thus transcending the dichotomy of realism versus experimentalism. *Benzina*, having one foot in realism and another in dream and fantasy, is a brilliant example of how Monzó's postmodern fiction combines elements from both modernist and pre-modernist fiction. The novel brings together straightforwardness and artifice, combining a realist mode of writing with lengthy surreal enumerations and playfulness through its circular structure. It also intermingles references to high art such as painting, sculpture, opera and literature with female beauty magazines, pornographic imagery and comic art. Furthermore, while *Benzina* clearly stays away from political commitment, it nevertheless engages with the subaltern position of Catalan culture by locating it within the American sphere on an equal basis, though this is represented in a matter-of-fact way, detached from any kind of political activism. In this light, Jordi Puntí's description of *Benzina* as the first postmodern novel in Catalan becomes relevant not so much as to whether *Benzina* was actually the first one or not, but as to how it was perceived when it came out and how it continues to be perceived today: a thematically, stylistically and metaphysically ground-breaking novel for the early democratic period in Catalonia. As such, *Benzina* can be seen as an example of the Catalan literature of replenishment.

3.2 Importing the American Parody of Political Correctness to Catalonia

After 1990, Monzó's translational activity nearly screeched to a halt but, in 1995, he and Maria Roura published the translation of a ground-breaking American short story collection, *Politically Correct Bedtime Stories: Modern Tales for Our Life and Times* by James Finn Garner, first released in the US in 1994. Monzó and Roura's translation into Catalan was published by Quaderns Crema with the suggestive title *Contes per a nens i nenes políticament correctes*. If the publication of Barth's essays in Catalan had a profound influence on the configuration of post-Francoist Catalan literature, *Contes* is, without a doubt, Monzó's most socially and politically influential work of translation, continuing to feature prominently in Catalan socio-political debates well into the twenty-first century. In *Politically Correct Bedtime Stories*, Garner satirized the rising trend of political correctness through the rewriting of thirteen children's stories and fairy tales in way that supposedly represented a politically correct version. From 'Little Red Riding Hood' and the 'Three Little Pigs' to 'Snow White', 'Cinderella' and 'Rapunzel', Garner's short-stories have been received as an excellent exercise of political satire, with a reviewer praising the book as 'a delightful and lucrative exercise in absurdist literature' (Gring-Pemble and Watson 2003: 132–33). *Politically Correct Bedtime Stories* quickly became a runaway bestseller and a sociocultural hit in the US. First published in April 1994, it had sold more than 100,000 copies by July and would remain on *The New York Times* bestseller list for sixty-four weeks (Gring-Pemble and Watson 2003: 132; Pleguezuelos 2009: 130). One year later 'there were almost 1.5 million copies of *Politically Correct Bedtime Stories* in print as it continued to excite public commentary' (Gring-Pemble and Watson 2003: 132). Almost immediately, Garner published two similar and also highly successful sequels under the titles *Once Upon a More Enlightened Time: More Politically Correct Bedtime Stories* and *Politically Correct Holiday Stories: For an Enlightened Yuletide Season*, both released in 1995. Garner's first book, *Politically Correct Bedtime Stories*, continues to be popular today, having sold more than 2.5 million copies and having been translated into twenty languages (Pleguezuelos 2009: 130; Sauder 2009: 273–74).

Debates around the notion of political correctness emerged in the US in the early 1990s, and quickly spread to other Western countries (Friedman 1995: 1; Weigel 2016; Wilson 1995: 1). Since then, the clashes and controversies surrounding political correctness have been recurrent and persistent. A fluid and difficult-to-define concept, political correctness is largely a negative term used as an accusation. As Moira Weigel aptly puts it, 'if you go looking for the origins of the phrase, it becomes clear that there is no neat history of political correctness. There have only been campaigns *against* something called "political correctness"' (2016). In most cases, political correctness is an accusatory term used by conservative commentators to criticize and ridicule progressive discourses of equality, diversity and inclusivity, generally through bombastic exaggerations and distortions (Beckwith 1994: 331; Berman 1992: 6; Browne 2006: 3; Weigel 2016; Wilson 1995: 1, 10–13). For Marilyn Friedman, the term encapsulates the different ways in which 'the left has challenged European, American, heterosexual, and masculine biases' in research, education and politics (1995: 2). Lawrence Keller, for his part, argues that debates around political correctness are 'in large part developed from contemporary efforts to ease racism and sexism in modern society' (1993: 37). At its core, the controversies surrounding political correctness are clashes about 'power, who has it and what they do with it' (Dunant 1994: ix). Debates around political correctness reveal tensions and anxieties about sociocultural change unfolding since the 1970s, and which can be seen as the tip of the iceberg of the culture wars linked to the growing influence of the New Right in the 1980s and 1990s, as the cultural theorist Stuart Hall has observed (1994: 168). Writing in 1995, Harold Bush Jr. asserts that the year 1994 was key to the debates about political correctness as 'it was clear that political correctness had hit the big time as at least a semi-permanent signifier in the mainstream American idiom' (1995: 42). One of the examples he provides to support this statement is the widespread and rapid success of Garner's *Politically Correct Bedtime Stories*, which, immediately following its publication in April 1994, became a key contribution to the burgeoning debate.

Contes per a nens i nenes políticament correctes came out in October of the following year. The translation illustrates Monzó's aim to import the American critique of political correctness to the Catalan cultural and political fields at a time in which this was an uncharted discussion in Catalonia and the rest of Spain. In so doing, Monzó continued to channel American political ideologies and cultural trends into Catalonia. Written by a consolidated and popular author, the publication of *Contes* was widely reported in the Catalan press and one of the rewritten tales, 'La Blancaneu', was published in *Avui* alongside a favourable review by Eva Piquer, who praised the excellent Catalan translation and quoted Monzó's critical views of political correctness (Gironell 1995: 36; Monzó and Roura 1995b: viii–ix; Piquer 1995: ix). On 3 November 1995, *La Vanguardia*'s cultural section opened with an article by Rosa María Piñol on *Contes* entitled 'Caperucita, los tres cerditos y el "pc"', in which the journalist discusses the book and introduces political correctness to the Catalan readership, highlighting its American origins. As Piñol tells us, Monzó learnt about the original book and contacted Jaume Vallcorba to discuss its publication in Catalan with Quaderns Crema. In the article, Monzó is quoted as an authority on the origins and development of political correctness in the US. He links the trend to 'ciertos movimientos pretendidamente progresistas y de izquierdas, que han dado totalmente la vuelta al tema' and, more specifically, to 'un cierto feminismo, hoy convertido en un feminismo de derechas, puritano' [some allegedly leftist and progressive movements, which have completely turned the topic around [...] a certain strain of feminism, now turned into conservative, puritanical feminism] (Piñol 1995: 48). One of the headlines quotes Monzó associating political correctness with totalitarianism and dictatorships: 'el "pc" llega a una presión dictatorial' [political correctness has become a dictatorial pressure] (Piñol 1995: 48). Taking a similar perspective, Vallcorba notes that, from his point of view, 'esto de lo "políticamente correcto", llevado al límite, puede ser un maccarthysmo de pretendida izquierda' [this political correctness thing, taken to the extreme, can become a McCarthyism of the alleged left] (Piñol 1995: 48). Three months later, a three-page article on political correctness authored by David Duster came out in *La Vanguardia Revista*. Entitled 'La dictatura del PC', the piece observes that the expression first appeared in the US around 1990 and added that, 'en España empiezan a hacerse familiares las iniciales PC entre la incomprensión, la perplejidad y la burla' [the initials PC are becoming common in Spain in a combination of incomprehension, bewilderment and mockery] (Duster 1996: 2). The text's perspective is generally critical and Duster describes political correctness as a 'tópico maniqueo' and 'moda excéntrica' [Manichean topic [...] eccentric trend] (1996: 1).

The way political correctness is discussed in these articles by Monzó, Vallcorba and the journalists echoes American discourses against the trend, which largely connected it to totalitarianism and ideological persecutions, to a new form of McCarthyism or Stalinism and to moral crusades (Browne 2006: 2; Dunant 1994: vii; Keller 1993: 44). In so doing, American anti-PC commentators represented themselves as the victims of ideological purges promoted by identity politics, amongst which feminism used to play the leading part in the 1990s (Feldstein 1997: 55, 75; Weigel 2016; Wilson 1995: 16). British journalist Anthony Browne, for instance, declared that, although PC started 'as a reaction to the dominant ideology, it has become the dominant ideology. It defines the terms and parameters of any national debate. Anything that is not PC is automatically controversial' (2006: xxi). His statement illustrates how conservative commentators present political correctness as an oppressive mainstream ideology which silences disagreement and prevents more open political discussions, a viewpoint that has become widespread in the public arena, thus illustrating the success of the conservative agenda (Bush Jr. 1995: 45; Cameron 1994: 16; Feldstein 1997: 63; Wilson 1995: 2). However, as Weigel states in her analysis of Donald Trump's uses of political correctness, 'there is an obvious contradiction involved in complaining at length, to an audience of hundreds of millions of people, that you are being silenced' (2016). Similarly, anti-PC positions enjoy visibility in the Catalan public sphere through generous media coverage on mainstream newspapers and media platforms, as the immediate visibility enjoyed by *Contes* illustrates, to offer just one example.

Albeit a polyvalent parody with a satiric bent, Garner's *Politically Correct Bedtime Stories* can be seen as part of the conservative continuum against political correctness. Through its rewriting of thirteen children's stories and fairy tales, the book satirizes feminism and inclusive language, multiculturalism, environmentalism, vegetarianism, reproductive rights, the promotion of healthy lifestyles, animal rights, discourses of equality and anti-colonial struggles. Garner's hilarious versions generally rely on the *reductio ad absurdum* technique, bizarre plots twists, parodies of PC buzzwords and a purposely stiff moralizing perspective with a view to representing PC as nonsensical and out of touch with reality. In Garner's 'Little Red Riding Hood', for instance, the woodsman is represented as a sexist and speciesist man who assumes that 'womyn and wolves can't solve their own problems without a man's help!' (Garner 2011: 4). The story closes with Grandma killing the woodsman and setting up, together with Red Riding Hood and the wolf, 'an alternative household based on mutual respect and cooperation' (2011: 4). In 'Rumpelstiltskin', the straw is not turned into gold by magic but, instead, is taken to a local farmer's cooperative, where it is used to thatch the roof of poor farmers' houses. Thanks to this, the farmers become 'healthier and more productive' (2011: 15) and the overall life-quality of the kingdom improves. The prince, by contrast, is captured 'by an angry mob and stabbed to death with pitchforks outside the palace' (2011: 15). In 'Snow White', to offer an example of Garner's burlesque of politically correct vocabularies, the Seven Dwarfs are referred to as 'vertically challenged men' (2011: 46). In light of this, James Finn Garner's book works 'against the (re-)building of community in the face of social change' by suggesting that politically correct attitudes merely 'reinscribe existing institutions, albeit with new leaders in positions of power' who 'perpetuate violence, hierarchy, and intolerance for opponents' (Gring-Pemble and Watson 2003: 145).

Given political correctness's focus on ideology and language representation, translation issues are intricate and culturally relevant. As Sergei Pshenitsyn puts it, 'the problems of PC translation demonstrate the complexity of relationships between language and culture' (2011: 242). This is illustrated by the Catalan translation of *Politically Correct Bedtime Stories*, in which Monzó and Roura splendidly bring the

American parody of PC to the Catalan sphere through the deployment of a number of translation strategies to increase the satirical perspective of Garner's text. The translation is particularly successful because it conveys the humorous effect of Garner's book to the Catalan reader by adroitly exaggerating inclusive-language strategies and by domesticating the source text in its translation of culture-bound terms through a number of adaptive translation strategies. Moreover, as I will show, *Contes* manipulates the original text by inserting a series of references to national politics in the Catalan version, thus making the question of nationalism more visible for the Catalan readership.

Monzó's and Roura's skilful translation strongly relies on the most polemical issue concerning inclusive language in Catalan, that of grammatical gender, a central component of the feminist critique of Romance languages. Feminist language strategies have been met with remarkable resistance in Catalonia and Spain, both from university language lecturers and institutions such as the Real Academia Española de la Lengua (RAE), which have generally depicted inclusive language as absurd social engineering, even as a crusade. In 2009, the linguist Gabriel Bibiloni, from the University of the Balearic Islands, argued that the 'croada contra la denominada — sovint precipitadament — discriminació sexista del llenguatge [...] pretén una operació d'alta enginyeria orientada a la utopia de canviar aspectes essencials de l'estructura de la llengua' [crusade against the so-called — usually hastily — sexism in language [...] is a project of social engineering with the utopian aim of changing essential structures of the language] (2009). Similarly, the Catalan linguist Carme Junyent defined the 'desdoblaments' (the use of both the masculine and feminine word in cases such as 'els ciutadans i les ciutadanes', known in English as splitting) as a 'comèdia' (Zaballa 2013). The RAE, for its part, has published several notes and reports against inclusive language; in 2012, for instance, they stated that, if gender-inclusive proposals were incorporated in the dictionary, speakers would be unable to communicate (*Público* 2012). If the critique of non-sexist language as artificial is recurrent in Catalonia and Spain, *Contes* goes above and beyond in exceptionally creative ways to portray it as gratuitously convoluted and impenetrable.

In *Politically Correct*, Garner uses the alternative spellings of 'woman' and 'women', 'wommon' (2011: 31, 33, 40) and 'womyn' (2011: 4, 33, 56), which in the Catalan version appear as 'persona femenina' (1995a: 49, 52, 58) and 'persones femenines' (1995a: 16, 52, 78), thus using a term that aims to convey the sarcastic slant of the original. However, *Contes* also deploys (sarcastic) inclusive language strategies which are not present in the original text. For instance, the following string of examples can be seen as a way to emphasize the intricacy of feminist and queer language strategies. In *Contes*, 'young woman' (2011: 13) is translated as 'persona femenina jove' (1995a: 27) and 'girl' (2011: 55) as 'persona femenina' (1995a: 77), instead of the more straightforward 'dona jove' and 'noia'. Similarly, 'man' (2011: 32, 78) is rendered as 'persona masculina' (1995a: 50, 102) and 'men' (2011: 36, 47) as 'individus masculins' (1995a: 55) and 'persones masculines' (1995a: 67), instead of 'home' and 'homes'. Furthermore, the masculine and feminine forms of articles, nouns and adjectives are persistently inserted in *Contes* through the combination of different strategies taken to the extreme without reason or clear convention, even in instances where the original English uses epicenes. For instance, the sentence 'the children of the kingdom grew strong and tall' (2011: 15) is translated as 'els i les nens i nenes del reialme van créixer alts i altes i valents i valentes' (1995a: 29), and the expression 'an indelible mark on our children' (2011: viii) is rendered into Catalan as 'una empremta inesborrable en els/les nostres/nostres nens/nenes' (1995a: 12), thus including the word *nostres* twice. Similarly, in the Catalan version 'everyone' and 'all except one small boy' (2011: 8) become 'tothom i totdon' in both instances (1995a: 22). The phrase 'free markets are the only way to give people the personal incentive to build a better society' (2011: 78) appears in the Catalan version as 'el mercat lliure és l'únic sistema segur de proporcionar al/la ciutadà/ ciutadana els incentius personals' (1995a: 102), thus choosing a *desdoblat* term instead of the suitable epicene 'gent'. A particularly relevant example to illustrate Monzó and Roura's dexterous enhancement of the original text's sarcasm towards inclusive language through convoluted combinations is the translation of the phrase 'the town leaders could hear the children talking earnestly to each other' (2011: 78) as 'els/les regidors/res sentien que parlaven amb molta seriositat els/les uns/nes als/les altres' (1995a: 102). At some point, Monzó and Roura even coin the term *habitantes* to split the masculine and feminine forms further: the phrase 'the empire and its inhabitants' (2011: 6) is translated as 'l'imperi i els/les seus/seves habitants/ habitantes' (1995a: 20. My italics). Monzó and Roura's playful, seemingly endless and (il)logical combinations of words intend to expose the presumed haphazardness of inclusive language strategies. These diverse translation strategies reveal Monzó and Roura as empowered translators aware of their role as cultural agents, in line with the cultural turn developing in Translation Studies since the mid-1980s, which has emphasized the need to empower translators to make their own choices (Bassnett 2002; Hermans 1985: 9; Pym 1998; Tymoczko 2002). As André Lefevere and Susan Bassnett argue, translation is both a creative and necessarily 'manipulative' process (1998: 1–11). In view of this, Quim Monzó and Maria Roura are not only mediating as intercultural agents to convey Garner's sarcastic depiction of non-sexist language to a Catalan readership, but they are, in fact, intensifying, even improving, Garner's burlesque by making inclusive language strategies absurdly ubiquitous and apparently limitless.

Culture-bound terms are another area in which Monzó and Roura develop imaginative and manipulative formulas in order to adroitly convey Garner's satire to the Catalan readership. A culture-bound term is a word or expression that 'has a meaning that is particularly associated with a given culture' (Palumbo 2009: 31). As Bassnett states, culture-bound terms encapsulate 'the difficulty of achieving total equivalence between languages' and thus, illustrate why empowering translators is essential to ensure 'that what has meaning in one context will have the same meaning in another' (2011: 95). The ingenious solutions to translation challenges put forward in *Contes* do not only illustrate Monzó's and Roura's full awareness and understanding of the key cultural differences between the target and source cultures, but also their ability to produce a fully functioning parody of political correctness in the Catalan language. Garner's version of 'The Three Little Pigs' is reimagined as a story of resistance to imperial expansionism. The pigs accuse the Big Bad Wolf's of being a 'carnivorous, imperialistic oppressor' who wants to take their home and conquer their land, while the wolf argues that 'progress cannot be stopped' (2011: 10). At some point during their resistance, 'the little pigs sang songs of solidarity and wrote letters of protest to the United Nations' (2011: 11), which in *Contes* is rendered as 'els porcs van cantar cançons de solidaritat i van enviar cartes de protesta a les Nacions Unides *i a diverses ONGS*' (1995a: 25. My italics). Garner's reference can be read as a mockery of the geopolitical role of the United Nations, whose mission to promote international peace and human rights has been strongly criticized by American neoconservative thinkers for allegedly being anti-American and anti-Western (Kagan 2008: 22–33; Kirkpatrick 2004: 237; Rand 1964: 91–92; Vaïsse 2010: 5). Given that such critical perspective of the UN is largely unknown in Catalonia, Monzó and Roura insert the reference to the NGOs with a view to conveying Garner's satirical reference to the policies of international security and humanitarian aid to Catalan readers.

'Cinderella' provides three further examples of Monzó's and Roura's mediation. First, in Garner's text, when Cinderella is arriving at the palace, the narrator recounts that 'many, many carriages were lined up outside the palace that night; apparently no one had ever thought of car-sharing' (2011: 33). 'Car-sharing' was possibly an unknown term in Catalonia in 1995 and Monzó and Roura bring the term into Catalan and include three extra clauses to convey Garner's mockery of environmentalist discourses: 'Era evident que ningú no havia pensat en la possibilitat de compartir cotxe per contribuir així a la fluïdesa del trànsit, l'estalvi de recursos energètics i la minva de la contaminació ambiental' (1995a: 51). Second, idiomatic expressions are particularly challenging for translators (Bassnett 1991: 23) and Garner's 'Cinderella' includes the following: 'Cinderella was working harder than a dog (an appropriate if unfortunate speciesist metaphor)' (2011: 32). In *Contes* this reads as 'la Ventafocs treballava com una persona femenina d'ètnia africana (una metàfora apropiada i tanmateix desafortunadament racista)' (1995a: 50). This phrase condenses a number of translation strategies deployed by Monzó and Roura in *Contes*. To start with, they turn the English-language idiom 'to work like a dog' into the genuinely Catalan expression 'treballar com un negre', thus domesticating the original idiom for the Catalan context. Second, in opting for 'persona d'ètnia africana' as a substitute for 'negre', they reword the Catalan idiom to satirize non-sexist language strategies. Finally, it is remarkable that Garner's parody of political correctness through a sarcastic reference to animal rights can be genuinely conveyed in Catalan through an idiom that betrays the inherent racism of the vernacular expression. Giuseppe Palumbo asserts that translators should interact 'with social and political trends of the moment' (2009: 59) and, in this regard, Monzó's and Roura's translation is particularly adept, as it can be argued that in mid-1990s Catalonia a reference to animal rights would not convey the same force and meaning vis-à-vis political correctness as the inherently racist idiom they opted for. Further evidence of this and of Monzó's and Roura's mediation is their translation of the term 'speciesist' (2011: 4) from Garner's 'Little Red Riding Hood' as 'discriminador d'espècies animals' (1995a: 16) instead of 'especista', a term which would probably not have managed to transmit the desired meaning in mid-1990s Catalonia. The final example of a culture-bound term in 'Cinderella' concerns the American singer-songwriter and feminist activist Holly Near. In Garner's rewriting, feeling sad about the way in which her stepmother and stepsisters treat her, Cinderella 'contented herself with her Holly Near records' (2011: 32). Given that Holly Near is largely unknown in Catalonia, in *Contes* Cinderella is depicted as listening to 'els seus discos de Sopa de Cabra' (1995a: 50), one of the leading bands of the Rock Català movement which flourished in Catalonia during the 1990s linked to grassroots organizations promoting Catalan language and culture.

Monzó and Roura's integration of a reference to a music band associated with Catalan nationalism is not casual but part of a wider translation strategy to bring to the fore nationalist politics by integrating a number of cultural references in the Catalan version. Garner's reimagining of the 'The Three Little Pigs' as an anti-colonial fable in which the three pigs are turned into freedom fighters offered Monzó and Roura an excellent opportunity to hint at (Catalan) nationalist discourses. When the Big Bad Wolf tries to break into the pigs' house, the latter shout back, 'your gunboat tactics hold no fear for pigs defending their homes and culture' (2011: 10). Monzó and Roura, instead of translating the word 'homes' as 'cases', opt for 'terra', a term strongly associated with Catalan nationalist rhetoric, as illustrated by the popular motto 'Defensem la terra': 'les teves tàctiques bèl·liques no ens fan por. Som porcs que defensem la nostra terra i la nostra cultura!' (1995a: 24). Monzó and Roura's translation goes even further in manipulating the source text by inserting a series of references to national oppression and linguistic discrimination which are not present in Garner's text. *Politically Correct* opens with a hilarious introduction in which Garner communicates his intention to rewrite a number of fairy tales in order to amend the oppressions and discriminations that they display. Subsequently, he states that, 'however much we might like to, we cannot blame the Brothers Grimm for their insensitivity to womyn's issues, minority cultures, and the environment' (2011: vii). In *Contes*, this sentence is rendered as 'tot i que ens agradaria molt, no podem culpar els germans Grimm de la seva falta de sensibilitat cap als problemes de la persona femenina, les cultures minoritàries, *les nacions oprimides* i el medi ambient' (1995a: ii. My italics). In like manner, the narrator of 'Rumpelstiltskin' tells us that, thanks to the generosity of the miller's daughter and the effective organization and solidarity of the community –– which included killing the prince –– the kingdom was gradually turned 'into a model democracy with no economic or sexual injustice and low infant mortality rates' (2011: 15). In Catalan this sentence reads as 'van fer del reialme una democràcia modèlica, sense injustícia sexual, econòmica o *lingüística*, i amb un índex de mortalitat infantil francament baix (1995a: 29. My italics). These examples reveal how Monzó and Roura's translation inserts references that echo the particular terminology of anti-colonial nationalism and which, in the Catalan context, brings to mind the specific discourses of Catalan resistant nationalism.

This strategy can be read from two different interrelated perspectives. On the one hand, by inserting references to national liberation and linguistic discrimination which are not present in the original text, *Contes* interpolates non-state nations and minority languages as a subaltern subject associated with identity politics. On the other, however, references to the specific terminology of Catalan nationalism are inserted through a satire of its rhetoric, in what is an example of postmodern polyvalent (self-)parody. By integrating (Catalan) nationalism as identity politics, Monzó and Roura not only dexterously bring Garner's satirical perspective to the Catalan sphere and readership, which would readily recognize the references, but also increase the visibility and centrality of (Catalan) nationalism from a (self-)ironic perspective in line with Quim Monzó's postmodernist cultural programme. As such, *Contes per a nens i nenes políticament correctes* emerges as yet another example of Monzó's aim to build a Catalan national identity distinct from that of Spain.

Like its source material in the US, *Contes per a nens i nenes políticament correctes* was immediately successful and highly influential. Published in late October 1995, it was still at the top of the most sold books in Catalan in early February 1996, and by Sant Jordi's Day of the same year, it had already gone through five re-editions with 17,000 copies sold (*Avui* 1996a: xiv; *Avui* 1996b: xix–xi). In the 2000s, the book continued to be authoritative, shaping debates on the topics encapsulated by the term 'political correctness' (Aymerich 2009: 2; Cardús 2007: 29; Masanés 2001: 27; Moliner 2008). Two articles stand out, one by the prominent intellectual Salvador Cardús in 2007 and the other by author Empar Moliner in 2008. Entitled 'De lo correcto a lo biempensante', Cardús's article criticizes the apparently populist positions regarding the early twenty-first century culture wars on immigration and meritocracy, which he describes as mere rhetoric wars between pseudoprogressives and pseudoconservatives (2007: 29). Cardús's piece, published in *La Vanguardia* during the campaign for the Spanish 2007 Local Elections, included a criticism of the former Mayor of Barcelona, Joan Clos (Partit dels Socialistes de Catalunya–PSOE). Perhaps overstating the book's impact, Cardús states that, in the mid-1990s, the publication of Garner's *Politically Correct Bedtime Stories*, 'traducidos magistralmente al catalán por Quim Monzó' [masterfully translated into Catalan by Quim Monzó] (2007: 29), had put an end to the intellectual project of political correctness (tellingly, in relation to debates around language representation and sexism, the female translator Maria Roura is not mentioned by Cardús). In his own words, Monzó's translation 'por lo menos desde el punto de vista intelectual acabó con ella [political correctness]. Luego siempre quedan algunos iletrados que no se han enterado, pero el combate ideológico en contra de la corrección política ya estaba ganado' [totally debunked it, at least from an intellectual perspective. Some ignorant individuals pretend this did not happen, but the ideological battle against political correctness had already been won] (2007: 29). Following the traditional lines of critique, Cardús connects political correctness to totalitarianism and detaches it from progressive politics. He sees political correctness as a 'pseudoprogresismo autoritario' [authoritarian pseudo-progressiveness] which acts as a 'una verdadera policia del pensamiento' [a real thought police] (2007: 27). One year later, in 2008, Empar Moliner published the article 'Las y los ratas y ratos' in *El País*, in which she discusses Pilarín Bayés adaptation of 'The Vain Little Mouse' into an animated film under the title *El ratolí que escombrava l'escaleta*. As the title suggests, in Bayés version the protagonist is a male mouse instead of a female one, as it is in traditional renderings of the story. Bayarés re-writing, however, introduces further modifications to turn the moral of the story into a claim against racial prejudices. The seducers that the he-mouse turns down, therefore, are a South-American immigrant she-mouse, a female camel, a female duck and a Romani hen. Pointing out that she does not disagree about educating kids on racial discrimination, Moliner criticizes Bayés's version because, as she argues, its theme is completely different from that of the Brothers Grimm's tale. From her point of view, Bayés should have written a new story instead of modifying the theme of the Brothers Grimm's tale: '¿Por qué no inventar un cuento nuevo, si queremos hablar de racismo? Pues porque si adaptas un cuento clásico quedas mucho más guay y enrollado' [Why not write a new tale, if you want to talk about racism? Well, simply because adapting a classical fairy tale is cooler and trendier] (2008). In light of the growing tendency to make new versions of classical narratives, in the final paragraph of her article Moliner urges people to read *Contes*, 'traducido por Quim Monzó y Maria Roura. Aunque les advierto que deben darse prisa. Pronto dejarán de ser humor para convertirse en realidad [translated by Quim Monzó and Maria Roura. Although I urge you to hurry up. Soon they will not be parody but reality] (2008).

Monzó's and Roura's translation was met with two enthusiastic articles by high profile commentators in the Catalan cultural and political system. Published in 2007 and 2008, both pieces came out at a time in which discussions around political correctness had again come to the fore, after the Catalan Tripartit government (2003–2010) and the Spanish government led by José Luís Rodríguez Zapatero (2004–2011) adopted many of the discourses and vocabularies associated with political correctness. It was in this context that Cardús and Moliner wholeheartedly welcomed the publication of Garner's book into Catalan, while recognizing and celebrating Monzó's role as an authoritative mediator in this debate. Viewed together, the American transnational and translational scope of Quim Monzó's work emerges as key to understanding the main features, continuities and discontinuities of his literary programme, as well as the political impact and uses of his cultural production.

Note to Chapter 3

1. In this book, all translations of *Benzina* are taken from Mary Ann Newman's translation in *Gasoline* (Monzó 2010a).

CHAPTER 4

❖

The Influence of
American Libertarianism

'Hoy ya no creo en muchas de las cosas en las que creía a principios de
los ochenta'

[Today I no longer believe in many things I believed at the beginning
of the 1980s]

Interview in *Quimera*, March 2008 (Sarret 2008: 39).

In his ground-breaking monograph *La ciutat interrompuda* (2001), Julià Guillamon
charts the cultural shifts taking place in Barcelona from the early 1970s to the mid-
1990s, that is, from the countercultural movement to the post-Olympic period.
Guillamon argues that the post-Transition period is defined by a progressive
detachment from collective ideals in favour of individualism and hedonism
(2001). The 1980s and 1990s were decades of quick socio-political and cultural
transformations in the Catalan, Spanish and Western contexts. In the West, the
1980s saw the beginning of the neoliberal agenda of free markets, privatization
of state-owned companies and withdrawal of the welfare state, championed by
Ronald Reagan in the US and Margaret Thatcher in the UK (Robertson 2004: 348;
Vincent 2009: 339). In Spain, despite the fact that the government was led by the
PSOE, left narratives also underwent a deep crisis and were no longer able to offer
meaningful alternatives to the status quo (Balibrea 1999: 110–20). As Elías Díaz puts
it, post-Transition Spain is defined by 'market ideology, economic individualism,
and extreme competition fostered by the "new" right' (1995: 289). In Catalonia,
while the left dominated the Catalan political and intellectual climate during the
Transition, conservative nationalism became hegemonic in the post-Transition
period thanks to CiU's electoral victories (Dowling 2013: 112–13). Owing to
globalization, the fall of the Berlin Wall and the disintegration of the Soviet Union,
neoliberal discourses and policies rose exponentially in the 1990s (Gabilondo 2002:
238–52; Harvey 2005: 13; Klein 2007: 14–15). In Spain, neoliberal discourses grew
particularly in the second half of the decade, after the conservative Partido Popular
was able to form a coalition government in 1996, thus removing the PSOE from
power (Balibrea 1998: 195–96). Analysing a number of Quim Monzó's texts — the
short story 'Fam i set de justícia' (*Guadalajara*, 1996) and the compilation of opinion
pieces *Esplendor i glòria de la Internacional Papanates* (2010) — through the lenses of
socio-political theory, this chapter argues that, from the mid-1990s, Monzó's work

has responded to this changing politico-cultural situation by displaying a series of ideological interplays with the American political philosophy of libertarianism.

Libertarianism can be seen as the American political doctrine par excellence, placing as it does the defence of individual freedom and market economy at its very core (Doherty: 2007: 22–31; Rothbard 2006: 23). While the principle of individual freedom is shared by anarchism, libertarianism radically departs from anarchist thought in claiming that market economy is a necessary condition for the development of individual freedom, accepting the need for a state and considering 'any collective action as purely contractual and based on coincidence of sheer self-interest' (Robertson 2004: 285). According to Milton Friedman's *Capitalism and Freedom* (1962), a foundation stone of libertarian thought, society is not formed by collectives but by individuals (1962: 1). Conceiving social life as a constant struggle between the individual and the state, Friedman advocates for a minimal state role, with the limited function of protecting individuals' freedom 'from the enemies outside our gates and from our fellow citizens: to preserve law and order, to enforce private contracts, to foster competitive markets' (1962: 2). Given that libertarians consider transnational economic markets to be the main elements of political freedom, they claim that the liberty of the individual is best protected in a capitalist society or, as Friedman puts it, 'history suggests that capitalism is a necessary condition for political freedom' (1962: 10). Robert Nozick, in his classic *Anarchy, State, and Utopia* (1974) expresses a rejection of concepts like equality, solidarity and even human rights because the state 'may not use its coercive apparatus for the purpose of getting some citizens to aid others, or in order to prohibit activities to people for their *own* good or protection' (1974: ix. Italics in original). For libertarians, humans are entitled to what they see as natural rights, that is, the right to life, the right to property and the right to liberty (Boaz 1997: 2).

Crucially for my analysis of Monzó's work, libertarians maintain that individuals must be free to live according to their own ideas as long as they do not interfere with the rights of other human beings. Hence, libertarian philosophy rejects the interference of moral and religious beliefs in governmental policies and legislation as well as in political debates. In Susumu's Morimura's words, 'each individual should be free to decide on the nature of happiness or human good as well as on such personal matters as religion and hobbies' (Morimura 2007: 4). By virtue of this, libertarian thinkers argue that the political categories of left and right are outdated and claim to occupy a third space between conservative and progressive ideals (Doherty 2007: 30 336–42; Machan 2001: 95; Rothbard 2006: 27–28). The philosopher Alan Haworth, however, contends that, while the original meaning of the term libertarianism referred to any ideology in which 'central importance is attached to freedom', nowadays it mainly indicates a 'certain assertively right-wing, pro-free market ideology' (1994: 3). This ideological stance is acknowledged by certain libertarian philosophers, such as Llewellyn H. Rockwell, who notes that libertarianism 'is certainly antileftist [...] and antisocialist' (2006: x).

Libertarianism has remained a little known, and sometimes inaccurately described, political concept in Spain, where scholarly studies or media references to it are still scarce. The scant influence of libertarian thought in Spain is exemplified by the problems that the translation of the term 'libertarian' into Spanish poses: José María Marco, for instance, observes that 'sería conveniente distinguir entre "libertarios" (en el sentido norteamericano) y "liberales" o "liberales clásicos"' [it is important to distinguish between 'libertarios' in the American sense and 'liberals' or 'classic liberals'] (2005: 129–30), while Pineda, Labio and Romero remark that 'utilizamos el término "libertario" como traducción del inglés *libertarian*, que no debe confundirse con el libertarianismo de extrema izquierda anarquista' [we use the term 'libertario' to translate the English word 'libertarian', which should not be confused with the anarchist, extreme-left libertarianism] (2009: 2971. Italics in original). In fact, the term 'libertario' is conventionally used in Spanish cultural studies and history to refer to anarchist ideas. In their seminal work *Spanish Cultural Studies: An Introduction*, for instance, Helen Graham and Jo Labanyi point out that they use the term libertarian to refer to 'anarchist beliefs/movement' (1995: 423). In like manner, Stanley Black, commenting on Juan Goytisolo's *Disidencias* (1977), observes that the author's 'allegiance to a libertarian philosophy [...] sees the re-affirmation of the corporal as the only means of combating reification in modern society both of the capitalist and socialist type', thus using the term to refer to countercultural philosophies (2001: 23). In Spain, libertarian viewpoints are only disseminated through the online newspaper *Libertad Digital* and the think tank Instituto Juan de Mariana (Carmona, García and Sánchez 2012: 64–65, 131–32; Pineda, Labio and Romero 2009: 2977). In fact, many contributors to *Libertad Digital* advocate libertarian ideas in the economic arena but not in the area of religion and morals (Carmona, García and Sánchez 2012: 26–29); for this reason, the term neoconservative seems more suited to refer to their ideology.

Emerging in the US during the 1980s as a reaction to the apparent rising influence of progressive and countercultural discourses, neoconservatism steadily gained relevance and impact from the 1990s and, in particular, in the early 2000s during the George W. Bush administration (Harvey 2005: 83; Klein 2007: 322; Record 2010: 47–50; Vaïsse 2010: 1–21). Libertarian and neoconservatives share elements such as the defence of economic neoliberalism and free markets, a hostility towards the welfare state, an opposition to significant government regulation and spending and the promotion of political individualism instead of collective action. They particularly differ, however, on the role of morality and religion in public life, in particular in topics such as abortion and drug legalization (Wolfson 2004: 215–31). Neoconservatism, after all, has 'a strongly traditional approach to matters of religion and morality and rejects the trends associated with the 1960s youth movement' (Robertson 1993: 341–42). Furthermore, most libertarians generally dislike neoconservatism's excessive focus on nationalism and patriotism (Harvey 2005: 82, 195; McGirr 2001: 10; Vincent 2009: 67). In the early 2000s, during José María Aznar's second term of office, the Spanish government developed closer ties with the Bush administration. Owing to this, Spanish conservative discourses and political practices were significantly influenced by the American neoconservative agenda. As I show in this chapter, while Monzó's own views are generally distanced from neoconservative stances, in particular regarding religion, morals and Spanish nationalism, his distaste of certain aspects of the legacy of the countercultural

movement concurs with specific features of the neoconservative programme gaining force in Spain in the early twenty-first century.

4.1 Debunking the Myth of Robin Hood

In three of the short stories included in *Guadalajara* (1996), Monzó rewrites canonical
texts and traditional myths of the Western world: 'A les portes de Troia' is a version
of the Trojan Horse tale; 'Les llibertats helvètiques' relates the legend of William
Tell from the perspective of Walter, William's son; 'Fam i set de justícia' rewrites the
story of Robin Hood; and 'Gregor' is Monzó's adaptation of the Franz Kafka's *The
Metamorphosis*. For Montserrat Lunati, these short stories are politically transgressive
insofar as they offer critical revisions of the past and challenge the traditional
concept of authorship (1999). Lunati's reading draws upon Linda Hutcheon's
analyses of postmodern parodies as ironic, self-conscious and contradictory texts,
'both deconstructively critical and constructively creative' (2002: 94). As Hutcheon
puts it, 'as a form of ironic representation, parody is doubly coded in political terms;
it both legitimizes and subverts that which it parodies' (2002: 97). Inferring from
Hutcheon, Lunati points out how Monzó's short stories problematize specific grand
narratives of the Western world, questioning its values and legitimizing discourses
(1999). 'Fam i set de justícia', for instance, disrupts the notion of moral progress and
human emancipation that emerged during the Enlightenment era and which was
subsequently furthered by Marxism (Lunati 1999).

Lunati's analysis highlights a key aspect of Monzó's fiction in particular and
postmodern parodies in general: the political function of irony. This debate
is epitomized in 'Fam i set de justícia', Monzó's postmodern version of Robin
Hood. An intertextual piece in which irony is an essential element, Monzó's text
alternatively evokes two historically discontinuous time frames, the Middle Ages
and the contemporary period, thus problematizing linear time in a characteristically
postmodern fashion (Smethurst 2000: 175). Further, its circular plot remains open-
ended, thus conveying the idea that the problem at hand, poverty and social
justice, remains unresolved. Monzó's literary adaptation of the myth of Robin
Hood debunks the legend's message on redistribution of wealth from a perspective
that partly incorporates libertarians' critique of altruism. In fact, Robin Hood is
a symbolic text for libertarians, who tend to bring it up in debates to challenge
progressive discourses about wealth inequality, in particular after it was harshly
criticized by the Russian-American novelist and philosopher Ayn Rand, one of the
'founding mothers of modern libertarianism' (Doherty 2007: 18). In her influential
novel *Atlas Shrugged* (1957), which presents a dystopian US where entrepreneurs and
successful businesspeople are coerced by the state, Robin Hood is defined as the
'most immoral and the most contemptible' of all human symbols (Rand 2007: 577).
Although a much more nuanced text, Monzó's short story echoes the libertarian
critique of the myth of Robin Hood and, as such, is a salient example of the
interlinks between his work and cultural libertarianism.

Since it first appeared in the late Middle Ages, the representation of Robin Hood
has been far from static. Current depictions tend to present him as a nobleman

who robs the rich to give to the poor (Clouet 2002: 39–42; Knight 2003: 1–2, 44). However, the early ballads, dating from the mid-fifteenth century, tell a different story, one in which Robin Hood is not a nobleman but an outlaw yeoman and whose robberies are not as central to the plot (Clouet 2002: 38–39; Dixon-Kennedy 2006: 227; Knight 2003: 1–2). While the term yeoman refers to 'a free man who is not a bound serf' and who may have good earnings, yeomen were not members of the gentry, instead being part of the lowest ranks of society (Knight 2003: 2). Regarding the modern-day focus on Robin Hood's thievery, Joseph Falaky asserts that, in the early ballads, seldom do Robin Hood or his men 'commit an outright act of theft' and, perhaps more importantly, that he 'gives nothing without expecting something in return' (1980: 205–06). Knight agrees that Robin Hood was not charitable to the poor, though he notes that every now and then he stole from the rich, but for his own benefit (2003: 2). In line with most contemporary adaptations, Monzó's short story presents Robin Hood as a nobleman who resides in the forest and dedicates himself to stealing from the rich in order to spread the booty among the poor. This characterization seems to have first appeared in Elizabethan and Jacobean plays of the late sixteenth century, in which the figure of Robin Hood was gentrified and associated with charity to those in need (Dobson and Taylor 1976: 37–44; Knight 1994: 8). Nevertheless, in subsequent representations throughout the seventeenth century, Robin Hood 'remained an essentially plebeian legend' (Dobson and Taylor 1976: 45). It was in the Romantic period that the representation of Robin Hood as an aristocratic hero of the common people became more consolidated, initially by the highly influential compilation produced by Joseph Ritson in 1795 and then by Walter Scott's *Ivanhoe*, published in 1820 (Clouet 2002: 38–43; Dobson and Taylor 1976: 55–58; Knight 2003: 110). Twentieth-century films have mostly drawn on the Romantic plot, presenting Robin Hood as a nobleman and a Romantic hero who fights against social inequality, therefore depicting a 'Romantic illustration of Christian charity [that] is not so obvious in the early ballads' (Clouet 2002: 39). Whereas Monzó's 'Fam i set de justícia' draws on the Romantic depictions, the parodic perspective of his version is key to his project of demythicizing the legend by exploring its loopholes, thus calling into question 'notions of closure, totalization, and universality that are part of those challenged grand narratives' (Hutcheon 2002: 67). In Monzó's text, Robin Hood is a self-doubting nobleman, ironically introduced from the first paragraph as someone who deeply resents his aristocratic origins:

> El fet d'haver nascut en una família aristocràtica no impedeix que Robin Hood odiï profundament la desigualtat social. Des de petit l'ha indignat contemplar com, mentre els rics neden en l'excés, els pobres malviuen en la misèria. Aquest contrast, que deixa indiferents la resta dels seus familiars, a Robin Hood el revolta. (Monzó 1999: 527)

> [The fact he had been born into aristocratic family didn't mean Robin Hood couldn't hate social inequality. From his childhood, he'd always felt indignant when he saw the poor lived in abject poverty while the rich wallowed in luxury. Robin Hood was repelled by a contrast that left the rest of his family unfazed][1]

At first glance, this opening paragraph appears as though it could have been extracted from a Romantic depiction of the legend. However, Monzó's version soon problematizes this dichotomous portrayal through a clearly satirical re–writing. Robin Hood's outrage at wealth inequality prompts his philanthropic activities, and subsequently he loots a castle inhabited by the richest family in the country, who are holding a party. Monzó's irony relies on two elements here. On the one hand, the narrator lists the extraordinary booty stolen by the nobleman with disproportionate detail, which sarcastically points to the excessive and unnecessary abundance the aristocracy enjoys. On the other, the aristocratic hosts and guests are not worried at all but excited by the theft, as it has offered a distraction from their monotonous lives. Hence, they announce their intention to throw another party in order to entertain their guests with this unusual story: 'Per poder fer–los les explicacions amb tot detall els convidaran a casa i hi organitzaran una bacanal' [They invited them to an orgy in their castle, so they could tell them the whole story in detail] (Monzó 1999: 529). Their reaction to the theft, the cynical and polysemic term 'bacanal' and the overtly elaborate depiction of the wealth differences between the two sections of the population have an obvious ironic slant that attempts intertextually to question the altruistic message of the Robin Hood myth. In other words, through hyperrealistic descriptions of the stolen goods and the ludicrous attitude of the prosperous family, Monzó's short story debunks the monolithic representation of social class and wealth differences at the core of the traditional tale of Robin Hood.

Robin Hood brings the stolen goods to the poorest family in Sherwood, whom he has selected after weeks of research, as the narrator tells us. On his arrival, the family is terribly scared and refuses to open the door, which forces Robin Hood to bring it down, only to find them at the end of the single-room house, shuddering and begging for mercy. Since they do not trust the hero's plan of distributing stolen property to impoverished families, he has to reassure them that his intentions are noble and genuine. They eventually accept his presents, though the narrative tells us that they also find ways of making a quick profit out of them:

> Però els fruits del robatori desapareixen aviat. Una família pobra i nombrosa com l'escollida, amb gana endarrerida de segles, dilapida amb facilitat el menjar, els diners, les monedes, els canelobres, les arracades, els coberts de plata venuts a un preu indigne al mercat negre. (Monzó 1999: 530)

> [But the fruits of his robbery soon vanished. A poor, numerous family, like the one he'd chosen, with centuries–old hunger in their bellies, rapidly squandered the food, and the money, and sold the candelabra, earrings and silver cutlery on the black market for a pittance]

The way in which they quickly spend the money can be seen as satirizing the naive altruism at the core of the myth of Robin Hood, a line of thought that coincides with libertarian philosophy. In *The Virtue of Selfishness. A New Conception of Egoism* (1964), Ayn Rand lambastes the ethics of altruism, which she defines as 'evil' (1964: x). For her, altruism fails to bring about any positive change regarding social justice because of 'the enormity of the moral corruption it perpetrates' (1964: viii). Other libertarian thinkers agree with Rand and connect the topic to the failure of welfare policies adopted by Western countries after 1945. Brian Doherty observes that 'the incentives of the welfare state are apt to hinder, not help, people in becoming self-sufficient' (2007: 590), while Murray Rothbard emphasizes that the social welfare system 'actively discourages self-help by crippling the financial incentive for rehabilitation' (2006: 94). These three authors share the view that altruism neither solves the problem of poverty nor helps the impoverished become active agents of social transformation. Tellingly, Monzó's short story hints at these two points. Although the destitute family welcomes Robin Hood with joy on his second visit, the father impatiently remarks that 'ja era hora [...] estàvem a punt de defallir' [it was about time [...] we were on our last legs] (Monzó 1999: 532), thus signalling the extent to which they are beginning to take Robin Hood's deliveries for granted. They appear represented as passive and lacking initiative, even ungrateful: when Robin Hood third delivery materializes, the narrator informs us that 'n'hi ha un que mig es queixa perquè el botí és més discret que els altres dos cops' [one half complained because the booty was less bountiful than on the previous occasions] (199: 532). In light of this, Monzó's version of Robin Hood can be seen as exemplifying Rand's claim that altruism boosts moral corruption. In so doing, 'Fam i set de justícia' questions the apparently shallow message of mainstream versions of Robin Hood, which present altruism as a panacea to solve poverty and social inequality.

Monzó's text also focuses on the contradictions and loopholes of Robin Hood the character. The protagonist is portrayed as a selfless and sometimes naive character who, driven by a sense of guilt due to his own social position, takes action to redistribute wealth. However, such depiction is so hyperbolic that it acquires a clearly satirical slant. To help the poor, for instance, the legendary character 's'enfronta al xèrif, a les autoritats, als propietaris de terres, eclesiàstics o no. També per això procura tractar les dones, els pobres i la gent humil amb una cortesia especial' [confronted the sheriff, the powers-that-be, and the landowners, whether ecclesiastical or not. Similarly, he always tried to treat women, the poor, and the humble extremely courteously] (Monzó 1999: 530). Similarly, when the destitute family is confused by his actions and finds it difficult to come to terms with his benevolence, the short story resorts again to a farcical matter-of-fact description to bring to the fore the shallowness of contemporary versions of the plot:

> Robin Hood els explica que d'ell no han de tenir por i els repeteix que ve a donar-los el que ha robat als rics. Exactament aquesta és la idea, insisteix: robar els rics per donar-ho als pobres. Els ho repeteix diverses vegades, perquè a la primera no ho entenen. (Monzó 1999: 529)

> [Robin Hood told them they shouldn't be afraid and told them again that he was going to give them what he'd robbed from the rich. 'My idea is this,' he repeated, 'steal from the rich and give to the poor.' He repeated the idea several times because they didn't understand him at first]

In view of this, Monzó's text can also be read as a parody of bourgeois philanthropy, which is presented as a series of activities that well-off individuals pursue in order to feel better about themselves, rather than to bring about social change. This is the reason why the narrative voice stresses that Robin Hood 'no ho fa en benefici propi sinó pel bé dels altres' [didn't do so to benefit himself but to help others] (1999: 530).

This sentence satirically reframes the traditional representation of Robin Hood as a completely disinterested individual because it hints at the fact that he himself does not need to keep the stolen goods as he is already rich. Monzó's text is therefore alluding to the enormous gap between Robin Hood and the poor family, thus emphasizing the fact that inequalities continue to exist. Given that the short story's title is taken from Saint Matthew's Gospel, it can also be argued that 'Fam i set de justícia' aims to parody Catholic philanthropism. In the Sermon of the Mount, Saint Matthew says: 'Blessed are those who hunger and thirst for righteousness, for they will be filled', which in Catalan reads 'Feliços els que tenen fam i set de ser justos: Déu els saciarà'. Accordingly, 'Fam i set de justícia' signals a connection between Robin Hood's altruism and the charitable activities of the Catholic Church, none of which, according to Monzó's short story, helps find a long-lasting solution to the problem of social injustice at the core of contemporary versions of Robin Hood's legend. Through this link, Monzó's text not only calls into question progressive narratives about social justice, it also lampoons the Catholic Church, one of his preferred targets throughout his career.

There is little denying that Monzó constructs his own version of the legend to suit his purpose, particularly regarding the depiction of Robin Hood as a distressed, resentful aristocrat and the poor family as lazy and unproductive. His version strongly relies on the views expressed by *Atlas Shrugged*'s character Ragnar Danneskjöld, with the difference that, in contrast to Monzó's Robin Hood, Ragnar acknowledges that the portrayal of the legendary outlaw in the original ballads is completely different from the better-known contemporary versions:

> It is said that he [Robin Hood] fought against the looting rulers and returned the loot to those who had been robbed, but that is not the meaning of the legend which has survived. He is remembered, not as a champion of *property*, but as a champion of *need*, not as a defender of the *robbed*, but as a provider of the *poor*. He is held to be the first man who assumed a halo of virtue by practicing charity with wealth which he did not own, by giving away goods which he had not produced, by making others pay for the luxury of his pity. (Rand 2007: 577. Italics in original)

Unquestionably reminiscent of Rand's portrayal of the character in this excerpt, Monzó's Robin Hood also touches upon the theme of private property, one of the cornerstones of libertarian philosophy. After pointing out that Robin Hood steals from the rich, the narrator adds that this is clearly a crime, because 'el fet que algú sigui ric no dóna a ningú carta blanca per atemptar contra el dret inalienable a la propietat privada, com a mínim en una economia de mercat' [the fact that someone was rich doesn't give anyone *carte blanche* to attack their inalienable right to private ownership, at least not in a market economy] (Monzó 1999: 530). Both Monzó's short story and Rand's *Atlas Shrugged*, therefore, place emphasis on the fact that Robin Hood is altruistic with stolen goods, thus shifting the focus from the allegedly high moral ground of his actions to his attack on the right to private property.

It can be argued that my reading of 'Fam i set de justícia' should consider more closely the implications of the overarching ironic perspective in Monzó's postmodern parodies, as Lunati's analysis does (1999). By their nature, however, postmodern parodies are politically contradictory, as Hutcheon has shown. In her own words, the authorized transgression at their core makes them 'a ready vehicle for the political contradictions of postmodernism at large' (2002: 97). As a result of its double-codedness, a postmodern parody 'may indeed be complicitous with the values it inscribes as well as subverts' (Hutcheon 2002: 102). Their polyvalent and contradictory nature is further illustrated by Fredric Jameson's analysis of postmodern parodies as texts that do not have a transgressive power because they promote political relativism (1991: 412). Accordingly, while most analyses of Monzó's work have focused on the ironic reading, my interpretations in this chapter also discuss more literal, less transgressive readings, given that, due to their fluidity and ambivalence, Monzó's ironic strategies can be seen as both subverting and legitimizing the discourses that they parody. For this reason, Monzó's 'Fam i set de justícia' can be read as a libertarian critique of the myth of Robin Hood, as well as a parody of such critiques. In either instance, the text manifestly engages with libertarian philosophy.

The circular ending of Monzó's 'Fam i set de justícia' faultlessly illustrates postmodern parodies' double-codedness vis-à-vis their fluidity and relativism. Towards the end of the story, Robin Hood realizes that the wealthy family from whom he has been repeatedly stealing have become destitute. The family on whom he had bestowed the stolen goods, for their part, are now able to enjoy a life of luxury thanks to the help they received. This, again, is represented in a highly sarcastic way. Robin Hood is back to rob the rich family and, dressed in rags, the aristocrats tell him that, while they understand his desire to 'fer justícia entre els homes i compensar les desigualtats socials que el dret successori perpetua' [bring justice to mankind and compensate for the social inequalities perpetuated by the right to inherit] (Monzó 1999: 533), he has made them destitute. Robin Hood then realizes that the initially poor family, by contrast, have managed to become extremely rich after learning the skills to navigate the capitalist economy; as the narrator tells us, their capital has exponentially increased thanks to their 'hàbil política d'inversions' [skilful investment policies] (1999: 534). All put together, the rich now live in abject poverty and the poor enjoy a life of luxury. The contrasting and defamiliarizing combination of medieval vocabularies such as 'dret successori' together with late-capitalist financial terms suggests that the narrative of Robin Hood is démodé and out of touch with reality, which in itself can be linked to the libertarian representation of progressive discourses as a remnant of the past. The tale finishes with an enraged Robin Hood heading, on his horse, to steal from the formerly impoverished family in order to redistribute their wealth, the problem of social injustice as yet unresolved. As a matter of fact, the narrative voice describes this event by repeating the short story's opening sentence. In light of this, it can be argued that Monzó's 'Fam i set de justícia' implies that, by not going to the root of the problem, Robin Hood's actions contribute to perpetuating the (unfair) system in an endless cycle. At the same time, however, it can be argued that Monzó's relativistic and libertarian-inspired critique of Robin Hood contributes to reinscribing the status quo regarding socioeconomic inequalities.

4.2 *Esplendor i glòria de la Internacional Papanates*: Opinion Pieces Criticizing the Legacy of Counterculture

The first years of the twenty-first century were times of pivotal change not only in Catalan and Spanish politics but also internationally. In 2000, José María Aznar gained an absolute majority for his second term of office in the Spanish government, which came to an end in 2004. His legislature was marked by a neoconservative agenda and a radically Spanish nationalist programme, as well as by his developments of closer ties with the US and the Bush administration, which led to Spain's support of the invasions of Afghanistan and Iraq. The last days of Aznar's government were particularly tragic and convoluted: on 11 March 2004, the Madrid terrorist bombings took place, killing 193 people and injuring almost 2,000, and only three days later the PP lost the General Election. José Luís Rodríguez Zapatero, leader of the PSOE, would soon become the new Prime Minister with a radically different political programme and public discourses. Only four months earlier, Catalonia had seen the formation of the first Tripartite coalition government, presided by Pasqual Maragall (2003–2006), putting an end to CiU's twenty-three-year domination of the Generalitat and heralding a new era in Catalan politics. The newly formed Catalan and Spanish governments aimed to develop left-reformist policies and embraced progressive discourses of equality, diversity and inclusivity. Quim Monzó's opinion articles in *La Vanguardia* during this shifting and unstable period would be compiled in *Esplendor i glòria de la Internacional Papanates* (2010), which included a selection of his pieces published between 2001 and 2004. As I show, a number of Monzó's articles debunk and criticize the progressive discourses, vocabularies and policies of the period, in particular the grassroots movement against the 2003 invasion of Iraq, the general strikes organized in Spain to protest against Aznar's economic reforms, campaigns by the PSOE to denounce sexist advertising campaigns, movements for pedagogical renovation and proposals by Catalan local councils to tackle the housing problem.

  Esplendor i glòria de la Internacional Papanates was published in March 2010, a completely different moment from that of the early years of the decade, when the articles therein were originally published. The PSOE and its Catalan instance, the Partit dels Socialistes de Catalunya (PSC), were still leading the Spanish and Catalan governments, even though both administrations were undergoing particularly difficult moments after the 2008 global financial crisis and ensuing economic recession. In Catalonia, the Tripartite government had also faced internal division due to the different and often opposed political projects of PSC and ERC regarding Catalonia's relationship to Spain. In this context, Monzó launched *Esplendor i glòria* in a well-attended press conference, with most journalists welcoming the author's attack on progressive politics. The Spanish *ABC*'s headline was 'Quim Monzó: "Los progres la cagan una y otra vez"' [Quim Monzó: 'liberals fuck it up again and again'] (Morán 2010), while the online Catalan *Vilaweb* pointed out his criticism of the *Tripartit*: 'Monzó: "Amb el Tripartit va arribar la Internacional Papanates"' [Monzó: 'with the Tripartite government arrived the "Fools Internationale"'] (*Vilaweb* 2010). *La Vanguardia* highlighted a specific phrase coined by Monzó to discredit progressive policies and discourses: 'Monzó revisa la llegada al poder del "imperio de la plastilina"' [Monzó analyses the rise to power of the 'plasticine empire'] (Piñol 2010b: 42). In spite of this, at the press conference Monzó himself argued that *Esplendor i glòria* was far from being political (Piñol 2010b: 42) and, according to Ada Castells's chronicle of the event, he declared that 'no he tingut mai una ideologia que m'hagi servit per guiar-me a la vida. Intento aplicar el sentit comú i res més' [I've never had a guiding ideology in my life. I just try to apply common sense and that's it] (2010: 36). Monzó's unsympathetic view of progressive politics as expressed in *Esplendor i glòria* can be read both in the context of the early and late years of the decade, that is, in the past moment in which the articles were first published and in the present moment in which the book came out. This illustrates how Monzó's articles move beyond the presentism of party-political discussions to engage with the broader cultural clashes that defined the decade.

Weeks after the book launch, most reviews of the book embraced Monzó's perspective, praising the articles' display of common sense, intelligence and logical thinking. In the cultural section of *Avui*, Xavier Pla celebrated the intelligent humour at the core of Monzó's articles, which 'es valen d'un innegable sentit comú i ús higiènic de la lògica per desemmascarar la farsa quotidiana de la vida política i els mitjans de comunicació' [make use of common sense and a hygienic use of logic to expose the daily hypocrisy of politics and the media] (Pla 2010: 12). In a similar vein, Lluís Muntada argued in *El País* that Monzó's book stood out for its intelligent common sense, which threw light on commonplaces and clichés (2010: 5). Jordi Barbeta, political editor of *La Vanguardia*, also stressed 'la defensa y la exigencia que hace del sentido común' [Monzó's defence and demand of common sense], and seized the opportunity to publicly thank Monzó for using the expression 'Internacional Papanates' in the title, inspired on the term 'Internacional Progresista Papanatas' coined by Barbeta (2010: 20). An evidently satirical rewording of Communist terminology, in his regular opinion pieces Barbeta used the expression to parody contemporary progressive discourses. As he puts it, the term 'Internacional Progresista Papanatas' describes:

> la actitud mitad hooligan mitad borrega que se ha extendido como una pandemia entre gentes que se proclaman de izquierdas, que han perdido la razón como instrumento para interpretar la realidad, y que lo han sustituido por la estulticia. (Barbeta 2010: 20)

> [the combination of hooliganism and foolishness that has spread as a pandemic among people who claim to be on the left and who have substituted reason by stupidity as a tool to interpret reality]

In *The Field of Cultural Production* (1993), Pierre Bourdieu has studied how authors and critics share the 'space of the judgments they apply' and, for this reason, their analyses tend to coincide. According to Bourdieu, these analytical agreements are key to maintaining the status quo within the field of literary production (1993: 87). The reception of *Esplendor i glòria* exemplifies Bourdieu's point; the reviews coincide with Monzó's viewpoints insofar as they describe him as a neutral commentator and as a free intellectual who dares to openly say what he thinks. In so doing, they portray Monzó as an independent voice in an otherwise subservient cultural milieu. This representation also fosters the narrative that Monzó's provocative, fluid and sometimes contradictory ideas cannot be politically pinpointed with ease, as if they emerged in a vacuum. However, the viewpoints expressed in *Esplendor i glória* manifestly interact with certain trends of the neoconservative backlash gaining momentum in early twenty-first century Spain. In *Spanish Neocon: La revuelta neoconservadora en la derecha española* (2012), Pablo Carmona, Beatriz García and Almudena Sánchez analyse how, in the early 2000s, relevant sections of the Partido Popular embraced and fostered the neoconservative ideas which were gaining influence in the US during the administration of George W. Bush. While liberals had dominated the PP from the mid-1980s, during José María Aznar's second term of office, 'la influencia de la renovada corriente neoconservadora que provenía de Estados Unidos fue ganando presencia' [a renewed neoconservative trend coming from the US was gaining influence] (Carmona, García and Sánchez 2012: 26). From their point of view, while the Spanish neoconservative right remains understudied, it has had a significant impact on Spanish political life (2012: 13).

In their book, Carmona, García and Sánchez argue that the ideas of the neoconservative intellectual Jeanne Kirkpatrick were particularly influential in Spain (2012: 30–36). Harshly critical of countercultural principles and values, Kirkpatrick asserts that neoconservatism emerged in the 1980s primarily as a reaction to defend America's values from 'counter-cultural liberalism' (2004: 40). From her point of view, while the countercultural movement had almost disappeared by the mid-1970s, its cultural legacy was much broader, to the point that she speaks of an ongoing 'cultural revolution' which constituted 'a sweeping rejection of traditional American attitudes, values, and goals' (2004: 233–34). The neoconservative project, therefore, aimed to discredit the still-operative values championed by the anti-war movement, feminist and environmentalist groups, movements for pedagogical renovation and the sexual revolution (Carmona, García and Sánchez 2012: 31). For Kirkpatrick, the American movement against the Vietnam War faultlessly exemplifies such countercultural principles, since its main argument was 'that the United States was immoral -- a "sick" society guilty of racism, materialism, imperialism, and murder of Third World people in Vietnam' (2004: 239). Taking their cue from American neoconservatism, conservative sectors in early twenty-first-century Spain waged a war against the cultural hegemony represented by 'los valores de los Mayos del '68 y sus formas de acción -- movilizaciones callejeras, desobediencia civil, desórdenes, etc' [the principles of the global May 68 and its forms of political action -- street demonstrations, civil disobedience, public disorders, etc] (Carmona, García and Sánchez 2012: 27).

The rising impact of American neoconservatism in Spain is encapsulated in José María Aznar's support of the 2003 invasion of Iraq, which the Spanish Prime Minister saw as an excellent opportunity for Spain to gain global influence and support (Kassam 2015). Tellingly, the narratives circulated by neoconservative American intellectuals were pivotal in promoting and planning the invasion of Iraq in 2003 (Record 2010: 47–50). Aznar's decision, however, was met with a huge opposition from the Spanish population, who took to the streets en masse to reject Spain's participation in the war. As a poll by the Centro de Investigaciones Sociológicas showed, 91% of Spanish citizens were against the intervention (Marcos 2003). In 2002 and 2003, Monzó published a number of pieces on the topic and none of those included in *Esplendor i glòria* is directly critical of Aznar's decision. By contrast, his pieces tend to ridicule protesters against the war and expose their contradictions. The article 'Grans esperances', for instance, talks about Bernat Carreras, a nineteen-year old anti-war activist from Barcelona. Monzó opens his article listing Carreras's impressive activist curriculum in spite of his youth, which includes voluntary activities at the Red Cross, support to the elderly at a Barcelona hospital and a stay in Galicia to help clean the coastline after the Prestige oil spill. However, he quickly adds how, at a bar, he overheard people criticizing Carreras for such 'tonterías' or for just being 'an exhibicionista que quiere batir el récord de bondad y solidaridad' [an exhibitionist who wants to break the record of goodness and solidarity] (Monzó 2010b: 131). Monzó's use of the word 'bondad' is revealing, as it echoes the term 'buenismo', coined by Spanish neoconservatives and which encapsulates their critique of progressive politics and discourses at the turn of the twenty-first century (Carmona, García and Sánchez 2012: 36). Subsequently, Monzó discusses Carreras's decision to start a hunger strike if the coalition declared war on Iraq and jeeringly points out that starting a hunger strike does not necessarily imply taking it to the ultimate consequences. On this point, Monzó's article elaborates on Félix Arroyo's experience. A Boston City councillor, Arroyo started a hunger strike against the Iraq War, but he soon 'se dio cuenta de que el hambre azuza' [realized that hunger is irritating] and limited the strike to the daylight hours, which moves Monzó to remark that Arroyo 'almuerza copiosamente' [has a plentiful morning meal] and, having eaten nothing during the daytime, 'cena como un señor' [dines like a lord] after sunset (2010b: 132). The article continues to poke fun at Arroyo, highlighting how this too ended up being a difficult and thus, he limited the strike to two Fridays per month (132). The article concludes by discussing how the American conservative press mocked Arroyo's decision and paralleled it to the hunger strike carried out by the American civil rights activist Jesse Jackson, who, as Monzó observes 'va deixar de menjar, durant dues hores senceres!' [fasted for two full hours!] (2010b: 132). In his well-known facetious style, Monzó's piece is anticipating that Carreras's hunger strike, if it takes place, will be more symbolic than real, as were Arroyo's and Jackson's (two examples that further illustrate Monzó's continuous interplay with discourses and narratives extracted from the American press). Therefore, Monzó's piece points to the alleged lack of bravery and coherence of these activists, while also hinting at the futility of their methods. In so doing, the piece shifts the focus from the widespread critique of the Spanish and US administrations to the debunking of the tactics and discourses of activists against the Iraq War.

Aznar's second term of office was controversial not only due to his support for the Iraq War, but also his social and economic reforms. His policy to overhaul unemployment benefits was met by a general strike called by the major trade unions

on 20 June 2002. The following day, Monzó published a surrealist chronicle of
the strike in *La Vanguardia*. Entitled 'Paisatge en vaga', it describes striking trade
unionists as having a leisurely drink at a pub and later being joined by the pub
landlord, in a scene that exposes all of them as strike-breakers for engaging in
consumerism on a day when you are not supposed to. Monzó's parodic stance is
further exemplified by the bizarre event he claims to have seen. When a security
guard stops a picket line from entering the shopping centre El Corte Inglés in order
to distribute political material, a protester complains that other people, most of them
seemingly tourists, are being allowed to enter the store. A group of demonstrators
thus argue that they must be allowed in, while one of them 'treu la seva targeta de
client d'El Corte Inglés i l'enarbora "Escolti, que sóc client, vull entrar"' [takes out
his Corte Inglés credit card and raises it on high. 'Look! I'm a customer, I want to
go in'] (Monzó 2010b: 56).[2] According to Monzó, although all the demonstrators
started chanting 'volem entrar',

> com sovint passa amb els crits repetits, al cap de poc les paraules evolucionen
> i, fingint un sobtat interès pel dispendi, n'hi ha que criden: 'Volem comprar!
> Volem comprar', mentre piquen als vidres de les portes amb les seves targetes
> d'El Corte Inglés. (2010b: 56)

> [as often happens when people chant, after a while the slogan evolves and,
> evincing a sudden interest in making a purchase, some begin to cry 'We want
> to shop! We want to shop!' all the while tapping on the glass doors with their
> Corte Inglés cards]

Satirical representations of strikers' dubious activities are pitted against descriptions
of how smaller businesses find a way around the restrictions imposed by the strike.
A deli shop, for instance, keeps its shutters half open to allow customers to enter
without attracting the attention of pickets. A bar owner tells a striker/customer that,
'nosaltres, si no treballem, no mengem' [if we don't work, we don't eat] (2010b:
55). The overall effect of this accumulation of vignettes is to 'other' strikers and
pickets, presenting trade unionists as a selfish collective which, in going on strike,
disturbs the lives of common people who cannot afford to do the same. The critical
perspective is again slightly skewed: while the strikers' opinions are not included
in the article and they are represented satirically through a narrator that focuses on
the group's contradictions, the small shop-owners are given a voice and represented
more sternly, without a hint of irony, as bona fide victims of the strike. Following a
similar perspective and rhetoric technique to the previous article about the anti-war
hunger strikes and protests, Monzó here focuses on parodying striking trade unions.

   In the context of early twenty-first-century Spain, Monzó's articles ridiculing
and debunking protests against the Iraq War and Aznar's economic reforms can be
seen as interrelating with certain ideological elements of the American-inspired
project to achieve a (neo-)conservative hegemony in Spain. As Carmona, García and
Sánchez discuss, neoconservatives aimed to 'socializar mecanismos de pensamiento
que arruinasen las bases del modelo social y político del centro-izquierda' [socialize
ideological frameworks to debunk the social and political model of the centre-
left] (Carmona, García and Sánchez 2012: 28). Furthermore, Monzó's critique of

trade unions also coincides with libertarian ideas. As Brian Doherty puts it in his history of twentieth-century libertarian thought in the US, 'antiunion sentiment is almost universal among libertarian intellectuals' (2007: 304). Monzó's focus on the economic impact of the strike on small businesses echoes the critique of trade unions as expressed by the libertarian thinker Rothbard: 'Unions have become a nuisance with power to cripple the economy, but only as a result of numerous special privileges afforded by the government' (2006: 93).

Feminist practices and discourses were another target of the Spanish neo-conservative agenda and, in *Esplendor i glòria*, Monzó continues the line of critique manifested in his reaction to politically correct discourses analysed in the previous chapter. The article 'Espanya deixa marca' not only offers a particularly relevant example of Monzó's aloof attitude towards the feminist movement, but also of his argumentative style and techniques. It discusses the request made in 2003 by the Institut Català de la Dona, the Observatori de les Dones dels Mitjans de Comunicació and the PSOE that a tourist campaign by the Institut de Turisme de Espanya and the Catalan Generalitat be cancelled owing to its sexist overtones. As Monzó describes in his article, one of the campaign's posters was the tanned back of a woman showing 'l'inici de la marca d'un tanga, aquella pell pàl·lida que queda a la zona que la peça cobreix quan fas bronze' [the beginning of a G-string tan line, that bit of white skin in the body part covered by the swimsuit] (2010b: 127). In his characteristic frivolous and disingenuous manner, Monzó elaborates on how he hung the poster in his office and looked at it 'de prop, de lluny, des de la dreta, des de l'esquerra i fent la vertical, a veure si potser cap per avall li veia el sexisme' [closely, from far away, from the right, from the left and doing a handstand, just to check if upside-down I could see the sexism] (2010: 127). Nevertheless, he did not identify any trace of sexism in the image. Monzó's text can be seen as operating on the basis of a series of fallacious arguments. To start with, the article does not mention any of the reasons put forward by the organizations demanding the withdrawal of the poster, thus invisibilizing their arguments. After adamantly claiming that the poster is by no means sexist, Monzó embarks on a sarcastic string of rhetorical questions in which he wonders whether a series of historically and culturally relevant images are also sexist. First, he ponders whether a billboard by the lingerie clothing label Intimissimi showing women in underwear should be removed too (2010b: 127). Next, he argues that, by the same token, a large number of canonical works of Western art such as the *Venus de Milo*, Rubens's *The Three Graces* and Goya's *La Maja Desnuda* would also have to be censored due to their sexism. Specifically, he speculates: '¿Haurien de tancar el museu del Prado per exhibir-hi un atemptat a la dignitat de la dona com *La maja desnuda*?' [Should the Prado Museum close for exhibiting an affront to women's dignity like 'The Nude Maja'?] (2010b: 128). Monzó also relativizes the political potential of female nudity as a form of feminist protest by posing the following question: 'aquestes dones que a la mínima es reuneixen i es treuen la roba en protesta per la guerra a l'Iraq o pels abrics fets amb pells d'animals, ¿aquestes no són sexistes?' [these women who at the slightest chance get together and undress to protest against the Iraq War or fur coats, are they not sexist?] (2010b: 128). He further contends that the male body is similarly objectified in contemporary advertising but that this is never denounced. Monzó's deliberately specious argument here negates the historical conditioning of women's oppression, of which the objectification of the female body has been a central pillar. From the 1950s onwards, criticism of the patriarchal representation of the female body has occupied a central position in feminist discourses (Gill 2007: 9; Shildrick and Price 1999: 4–14; Thornham 2000: 159–66). In spite of the advances achieved by feminism since the second wave, recent scholarship warns against the increasing re-sexualization and commodification of women's bodies in contemporary popular culture and, in particular, in the advertising world (Gill 2007: 73; Genz and Brabon 2009: 1). Monzó's reaction to the feminist critique of this promotion campaign should be read within the context of a cultural battle to (re-)define what is considered a patriarchal representation in the twenty-first century. This is further illustrated by Monzó's invective in this selection from the article:

> El que veig és que als paladins del neopuritanisme se'ls hi ha anat definitivament l'olla. Aquest talibanisme transvestit de progressisme el van inaugurar alguns grups americans fa més de dues dècades, però és evident que els nostres conciutadans estan avui decidits a batre els seus rècords de quadriculació mental. (2010b: 127)

> [What I see is that the champions of neopuritanism have definitely lost their minds. This Talibanism disguised as progressivism was initiated by some American groups more than two decades ago, though it is pretty obvious that our fellow citizens are today determined to break their records of mental inflexibility]

Crassly misrepresenting contemporary feminism through a hyperbolic and highly biased rhetoric, this excerpt shows Monzó's intention to lambaste the feminist critique of patriarchal representations of the female body. Monzó's effective rhetorical style combines formal terms like 'paladins' with contemporary informalities such as 'anar-se l'olla', typical of street jargon —— the combination of high and colloquial registers has precisely been received by Antoni Maestre as one of Monzó's key argumentative techniques (2006: 147). Biased and bombastic rhetoric like 'neopuritanisme' or 'talibanisme vestit de progressisme' is not exclusive to this article, as further exemplified by other expressions in *Esplendor i glòria* like 'catecisme papanates' [fools' catechism] or the denunciation that 'escamots de progressistes patrullaran nit i dia pels carrers' [progressive gangs will patrol the streets day and night] (2010b: 173). This fragment seems to suggest that the dystopia represented in James Finn Garner's *Politically Correct Bedtime Stories* has now become a reality. As a matter of fact, Monzó explicitly connected Garner's short stories to the 'Internacional Papanates' in the article 'Tantos patitos feos', published in 2005. Praising Garner's book for 'burlarse de la asfixiante corrección política en que vivimos' [mocking the stifling political correctness in which we're living], Monzó states that, in a large number of schools, fairy tales by authors such as Hans Christian Andersen, Charles Perrault and the Brothers Grimm 'están hoy en día prohibidos por la censura progre de la Internacional Papanatas' [are today forbidden by the progressive censorship of the Fools Internationale] (qtd. in Maestre 2007: 601). In view of Monzó's allusion to political correctness in school curricula, it is no coincidence that a few articles in *Esplendor i glòria* discuss the movements in favour of pedagogical renovation, another hot topic for neoconservatives.

Debates about student-oriented pedagogies are complex and multifaceted, as they are not only determined by the educational methods implemented but also by public policy and investment as well as by sociocultural change. From the 2000s, in their backlash against countercultural values, American and Spanish neoconservatives have criticized how student-oriented methodologies are at the core of the faults and problems experienced by the education system. For them, these teaching methods foster the rejection of fundamental values such as discipline and effort, as well as promoting a lack of respect towards authority (Berman 1992: 3; Feldstein 1997: 15–17). As Carmona, García and Sánchez argue, the controversy over pedagogical renovation offers an excellent example of the neoconservative uses of counterculture's legacy. Analysing the disputes over education in the early 2000s in the region of Madrid, one of the strongholds of Spanish neoconservatism, they discuss how student-oriented pedagogies have their origins in the countercultural critique to a school system which prioritized discipline, fear and punishment (2012: 34–40). Through a focus on persuasion and collaborative student-oriented teaching methods, the ultimate aim was an egalitarian society in which education was equal for everyone (Carmona, García and Sánchez 2012: 34). This project has obviously been unsuccessful for several reasons, not least the lack of political will to push for these transformations, the pervasive school bureaucracy and a disastrous work-life balance which impedes most parents from getting involved in their children's education. In spite of this, the Partido Popular in Madrid 'ha tomado las viejas críticas a la escuela como la realidad efectiva del actual sistema educativo, emprendiendo una quijotesca empresa a favor de los valores de la autoridad y la disciplina' [has taken the old critique to schools as the actual reality of the education system, thus initiating a quixotic quest in favour of the principles of authority and discipline] (Carmona, García and Sánchez 2012: 34). Madrid, however, is a region with very little public spending on education, and in which the PP-led regional government largely favoured private and *concertada* schools in the early years of the 2000s. Monzó's viewpoints on this debate follow similar lines of critique. The article 'Colorimetria', for instance, talks about an English primary school which has instructed its teachers to write corrections on assignments only in green-colour pen because red is deemed too harsh on the students. Monzó rejects the policy on the grounds that a low mark is the same regardless of the colour used to mark, highlighting that, 'que a algú se li hagi acudit dictar una ordre així indica fins a quin punt un cert vessant de la pedagogia fa aigües' [the fact that someone has come up with such a guideline illustrates how a certain branch of pedagogy is falling apart] (2010b: 125). Monzó's parodic vocabularies focus on the issue of discipline and effort: if in his article he talks about 'estovament educatiu' [educative softening], during the public launch of *Esplendor i glòria* he coined the expression 'imperi de la plastilina' (Piñol 2010b: 42). Similarly, in an interview he stated that 'la renúncia de pares i professors a educar els fills ha fet molt de mal' [parents and teachers' abdication of their responsibility to educate kids has been very harmful] and remarked how strongly he disagrees with the growing idea that 'el nen és un reietó a qui no s'ha de prohibir res per no traumatitzar-lo, i tampoc no se l'ha d'obligar a fer cap esforç. Res de memoritzar!' [kids are little kings and, in order to avoid traumatizing them, they should never be forbidden from doing as they please, neither should they be forced to work hard. No memorizing at all!] (Castillo 2010). Monzó's arguments echo features of the neoconservative stance, focusing as they do on discipline, authority and hierarchy and putting the onus solely on teachers and parents, therefore opting to ignore the wider issues affecting the education system, such as the lack of public investment, the impact of students' diverse socio-economic backgrounds and parents' work-life balance.

The difficulties of access to housing for young people was another key debate during the decade. Local elections across Spain were held on 25 May 2003 and the progressive parties Esquerra Republicana de Catalunya (ERC) and Iniciativa per Catalunya Verds-Esquerra Unida i Alternativa (ICV-EUiA) made significant gains in Catalan councils, with their manifestos including proposals to tackle the housing problem faced by young people. On 9 November, only six months after the elections, Monzó published an article in *Magazine*, *La Vanguardia*'s Sunday supplement, disparaging the proposal made by some local councils to increase the Council Tax for empty houses. Monzó's text, entitled '¿Habites o simules?', neither engages with the councils' reasons nor with the housing crisis, instead sarcastically discussing the complexity of discovering whether a house is inhabited or not. Presuming that the local councils would base this on gas, water and electricity consumption, the opinion piece lists potential ways to avoid the tax increase if one has an empty property: turning on the lights, heating and household appliances or leaving all house taps open so that litres and litres of water flow through the pipes (2010b: 179). Monzó rounds the article off arguing that, with the extra money collected with the Council Tax increase, 'l'ajuntament podrà pagar creatives campanyes publicitàries demanant-nos que no malbaratem tanta electricitat i tanta aigua' [the local council will have the money to fund creative advertising campaigns reminding us not to waste water and electricity] (2010b: 179). Combining the derision of housing and environmentalist policies as well as hinting to their alleged futility, this conclusion is an example of Monzó's misleading sarcasm, as are certain specious analogies displayed in the article. Monzó, for instance, elaborates on a law in 1950s India which, as he says, forbade one from keeping a non-inhabited palace or a palace with unoccupied rooms (2010b: 178). He hopes that his revealing this does not incite the 'edils manifletes' [meddling councillors] to penalize those who, in their own flat, 'cauen en l'egoisme de tenir una habitació desocupada, amb trastos i sense que ningú no hi dormi!' [are so selfish to have an empty room, full of junk and with no one sleeping in there!] (178). Monzó's argumentative tactics here are similar to those displayed in 'Espanya deixa marca'. First, by suggesting that tackling the housing problem would inevitably trigger a waste of water and energy resources, he takes the story to a *reductio ad absurdum* conclusion which mirrors the circular ending that, as we saw earlier, marked his adaption of Robin Hood. In so doing, both texts seem to suggest that social problems like wealth inequality and the housing crisis cannot be solved through public policies, thus somewhat debunking progressive discourses and policy-schemes. Second, by hinting at the possibility that, if this tax is eventually approved, the next step could be to tax unoccupied bedrooms, the article manipulates and magnifies the local councils' proposal, in what is an obvious instance of straw-manning. Perhaps more importantly, '¿Habites o simules?' takes a clear stance against tax increases to tackle social problems, a standpoint in line with libertarians' critique of taxes (Doherty 2007: 589–90; Rothbard 2006: 30) and 'the use of state power to lessen social inequality' (McGirr 2001: 154). Ultimately, Monzó's column can be seen as prioritizing the individual right to property over governmental action to lessen the housing problem, a viewpoint which reverberates with libertarian discourses against governmental encroachment on individual liberties (Boaz 1997: 15; Morgan 1998: 37).

At the core of much libertarian thought is also the rejection of society's interference in the activities and behaviour of individuals (Friedman 1962: 1–3; Nozick 1974: ix; Rand 1964: 93–97; Rothbard 2006: 45). As Claire Morgan puts it, 'individuals have to remain aware of the danger to their liberty from both the state and society' (1998: 39). If the previous article touched upon individuals' relationship to the state through a focus on taxes and public policies, a number of articles in *Esplendor i glòria* also deal with the conflict between the individual and society more broadly. Two opinion pieces, tellingly ordered consecutively in the book, epitomize Monzó's stance on the matter. In 'En aquesta vall de llàgrimes', Monzó talks about how most participants in the 2004 Goya Awards ceremony, including the hosts, cried when receiving their prizes. Monzó is critical of what he sees as the contemporary trend of crying in public as a way to express one's feelings and emotions. In his own words, in our day and age, 'qui no plora és un insensible i un cavernícola' [if you don't cry you are insensitive and barbarian] (2010b: 209). For this reason, if one wants to show their emotional intelligence, 'no hi ha res com deixar escapar unes llàgrimes' [there is nothing like shedding a few tears] (2010b: 209). Further, he whimsically points out how the ceremony showed how actors are maestros in the art of pretension (2010b: 209). Beyond his point on public crying and the growing need to express emotions in public, by sarcastically hinting at the potential performative element in the actors' reactions to their awards, Monzó is suggesting that they essentially feign crying to abide by society's tastes. Subsequently, Monzó states that he also cries at times, and succinctly mentions a couple of hilarious examples to mock the trend. One, however, clearly deals with the relationship between individuals and society: 'Des que era un noi, davant les grans concentracions de masses sento —— de manera indefectible —— una esgarrifança i una por difusa, i els ulls se m'inunden' [Ever since I was a little boy, when I see large concentrations of people I inevitably feel a shiver and vague fear, and my eyes fill with tears] (2010b: 209). In this sentence, Monzó is also building on his well-known solitary personality which he has carefully constructed in his public statements. Beyond this personal preference, the importance he grants to individual freedom is further discussed in the subsequent piece, entitled 'El dret de la diferència'. In the article, he tells how, while having breakfast at a bar in the

Empordà region one morning, he saw a young boy weeping uncontrollably because he had to dress up and face-paint himself for the school carnival party. The boy's grandmother, who was taking him to school, told the bar patrons that the kid 'no suporta que el pintin ni el disfressin i que, cada any, quan arriba aquesta època, s'ho passa fatal' [hates face painting and dressing up. Every year, when the carnival season starts, he goes through a hard time] (2010b: 210). Monzó contextualizes the young boy's experience in terms of the continuous clash between the individual and society, and resorts to vocabularies of individuality that echo libertarian discourses, such as 'violence against the individual', '(individual) freedom' and 'the right to dissent':

> L'únic bo d'aquest trauma infantil és que, així, els nens van aprenent que la majoria exerceix sempre violència contra l'individu i que la llibertat, el dret a dissentir, és una cosa que no es dóna per suposada ni s'aconsegueix fàcilment. (2010b: 211)

> [The only good aspect of this childhood trauma is that kids learn that the majority always exerts violence against the individual, and that freedom and the right to dissent are neither taken for granted nor easily achieved]

While the examples analysed in this section illustrate Monzó's interplay with certain aspects of the neoconservative critique of counterculture, his work and public statements are largely distanced from fundamental ideological positions of Spanish neoconservatism, in particular from their traditionalist, moralist, pro-religion and Spanish nationalist positions. The ideological lines of American libertarianism, by contrast, offer a suitable overall framework to explore the political subtext of Monzó's literary and journalistic outputs. The term libertarianism is used here in its broad cultural sense, thus referring to the frequent coincidences between Monzó's ideological framework and elements of libertarian philosophy, and not in the sense that he openly advocates the establishment of a libertarian government or that his work and public viewpoints always concur with libertarian proposals — libertarianism itself being a particularly heterogeneous ideology.

Monzó's criticism of progressive narratives and countercultural values with a libertarian bent in his work from the mid-1990s onwards may seem surprising to some, given his participation in Barcelona's counterculture and engagement with politically radical discourses in the 1970s. Such ideological evolutions, however, have not been uncommon amongst those who participated in alternative cultural and political movements in Europe and the US during the 1960s and 1970s. In *The Sixties* (2010), English writer Jenny Diski offers a critical assessment of counterculture from the perspective of the twenty-first century. Having experienced the sociocultural and political spirit of 1960s London, Diski argues that the cult of radical individualism and permissiveness of the time paved the way for the rise of neoliberalism, self-interest and greed in the 1980s under Thatcher and Reagan. In Diski's own words, Thatcher's 'founding statement that "there is no such thing as society" could easily be derived from the "self at the centre" that seemed to many of us in the Sixties so unproblematical' (2010: 89). For her, the more self-centred and individualistic versions of counterculture provided fertile soil for the libertarian seed: 'it ought to have been immediately obvious that liberation and libertarianism were not at all one and the same thing' (88). Accordingly, at the heart of the connections between libertarianism and counterculture is their emphasis on the primacy of individual choice, a perspective which emerges as paramount when considering Monzó's ideological trajectory. Diski concludes quoting English journalist Charles Shaar Murray, who, in 1988, famously stated that 'the line from hippie to yuppie is not nearly as convoluted as people like to believe and a lot of the old hippie rhetoric could well be co-opted now by the pseudo-libertarian Right —— which has in fact happened' (2010: 135). Monzó's ideological journey, from participant in the politically engaged counterculture of the 1970s to disaffected detractor of progressive politics à la libertarianism at the turn of the twenty-first century can be seen as exemplifying the links and interrelations between counterculture and cultural libertarianism. Remarkably, in his 'Grans esperances' article criticizing the protests against the Iraq War, Monzó seems to offer an explanation, even a justification, for similar ideological evolutions:

> L'escriptor René Avilés va dir en una ocasió: 'Qui als vint anys no és comunista és un idiota, però qui als trenta anys continua sent-ho és un idiota rematat.' Canviïn 'comunista' per 'idealista', 'antiglobalitzador' o qualsevol altra paraula d'aquestes [...] i el sentit de la frase s'entén a la perfecció. (Monzó 2010b: 131–32)

> [The writer René Avilés once said: 'If you are not a communist at the age of twenty, you are an idiot, but if you are still a communist at the age of thirty, you are an utter idiot.' Swap 'communist' for 'idealist', 'antiglobalist' or any of these words [...] and the meaning of the sentence becomes pretty clear]

Despite the numerous links between Monzó's texts and cultural libertarianism, most reviewers continue to profile his texts as neutral, as if distanced from ideological positions. One explanation for this critical trend lies in the difficulty of connecting Monzó's viewpoints to conventional positions of the right and left in Catalonia and Spain. The peculiarity of libertarianism accounts for this difficulty, sharing as it does ideological elements not only with (neo-)conservatism but also with liberalism, such as the non-interference of religious or moral matters in the political sphere and the support of drug legalization (Boaz 1997: 109, 237). For this reason, libertarians claim that their ideology is neither rightist nor leftist, insofar as they are distanced from the former's intervention in the moral life of citizens and the latter's emphasis on the redistribution of wealth through public policy and taxes (Machan 2001: 95). A similarly middle-of-the-ground position is adopted by Monzó when, in an interview on *Esplendor i glòria*, he declares that, 'les actituds papanates de la dreta en el poder ja les coneixia. Ara he conegut les actituds papanates de l'esquerra un cop en el poder' [I was already familiar with the foolish attitudes of the right when in government. Now I have become familiar with the foolish attitudes of the left when in government] (Castillo 2010). Monzó's ideological (self-)positioning in this interview as a (purportedly) neutral and non-partisan commentator who monitors and criticizes the policies and discourses of both the right and the left offers yet another example of the recurrent interplay between his work and libertarian philosophy.

Notes to Chapter 4

1. All translations of 'Fam i set de justícia' are taken from Peter Bush's translation, *Guadalajara* (Monzó 2011a).
2. All translations of 'Paisatge en vaga' are taken from Mary Ann Newman's translation, published in *Words without Borders*: https://www.wordswithoutborders.org/article/landscape-with-strikers

CHAPTER 5

❖

Pornographic Imagery and Hegemonic Masculinity in Crisis

'Pornogràfic ho he estat tota la vida'
[I've been pornographic all my life]
Interview in *El Bloc dels 365*, 30 September 2012
(Rodríguez 2012)

In spite of Quim Monzó's strong disagreement with contemporary feminism, critical analyses of his work from the perspective of gender and sexuality studies have tended to skirt the topic. Extending the line of analysis initiated in the previous chapter, here I am going to explore how the presence of pornographic imagery in Monzó's fiction helps us better understand two facets of his work. First, how notions of masculinity vis-à-vis power relations between men and women play an essential role in understanding his fiction — and, in turn, his public statements on feminism. Second, how the study of pornography provides us with a prism through which to examine the tensions between high and mass forms of culture in Monzó's narrative in the context of early 1980s Catalan culture. My main aim in this chapter is to demonstrate that the hardly deniable influence of pornography on Monzó's fiction is intimately related to one of its central tensions, namely, the representation of Western hegemonic masculinity in crisis. Drawing on Gramsci's theories of hegemony in class relations, R. W. Connell formalized the concept of hegemonic masculinity to refer to 'the configuration of gender practice [...] which guarantees (or is taken to guarantee) the dominant position of men and the subordination of women' (2005: 77). Her objective was to analyse the dominant model of heterosexual masculinity, seen as authoritarian and built in opposition to women, as well as to other forms of masculinity subordinate to the hegemonic archetype. In agreement with Connell, Harry Christian stated that the dominant model of masculinity is mainly based on the following assumptions: first, that men are innately superior to women; secondly, that men are by nature competitive, tough, unemotional and prone to use violence if necessary; and finally, that men conceive sex not only as pleasure but also as a way to show and exert power (1994: 9–10). Although the notion of hegemonic masculinity has already been challenged (Connell 2005: xviii), the term remains useful for an understanding of the sense of inadequacy that characterizes Monzó's male characters, who repeatedly fail to meet the demands of hegemonic masculinity. Analysing the challenges, weaknesses and power inequalities that define Monzó's male characters will also throw light upon his stiff views on feminist politics in post-Francoist Spain.

Since the introduction of affordable photography printing in the mid-nineteenth century, the pornographic genre has kept growing constantly vis-à-vis technological developments (Slayden 2010: 54–57). Pornography was therefore part of the catalogue of (private) silent films in the late nineteenth century and sound films from the 1920s onwards. In the 1960s, with the advent of commercial films and discourses that normalized public discussions and representations of sexuality, pornography could reach a much broader audience, gradually but steadily becoming a product of mass culture. Since then, feminism has responded to and interacted with pornography in different and sometimes opposed ways. In the 1960s and 1970s, feminist circles welcomed pornography on the grounds that it promoted sexual liberation, since women's sexual desire was acknowledged and represented for the first time in mainstream cultural products (Clover 1993: 7). Feminist reactions to early pornographic products that reproduced patriarchal conceptions of sexuality did not bring about immediate campaigning for their prohibition, but were rather bent on denouncing their misogyny while at the same time promoting alternative non-sexist representations (Wilson 2001: 39–40). In Spain, pornography was officially banned during Franco's dictatorship, when its mere possession was considered an offence. This explains why in the 1970s, when pornography started to circulate, some young aspiring writers such as Quim Monzó were quick to explore its transgressive potential. As Monzó himself has stated: 'En pleno franquismo la pornografía era subversiva' [During Francoism, pornography was subversive] (González 2012). The audacious interplay between Monzó's work and pornographic imagery is at the heart of the transgressive and iconoclastic ethos of his trajectory, in what is another example of the pivotal impact of the 1960s and 1970s cultural trends in his oeuvre. During the 1980s, however, feminist opposition to pornography diversified into new positions, on the grounds that the genre seemed to be premised on pervasive representations of violence and abuse towards women. In this renewed critical context, activists in Great Britain and the US lobbied for laws to censor violent pornography and ban soft-porn magazines from newsagents (Rodgerson and Wilson 1991: 9–15; Norden 1990: 1–4). Nevertheless, differently positioned feminist activists rejected this line of action by highlighting pornography's role in the path towards the normalization of sex and of women's sexuality, while also deploring the presence of sexual violence against women in a significant percentage of pornographic products. Feminist debates on pornography were often cut across by other political and religious susceptibilities, with pro-censorship groups usually being criticized for their connivance with conservative and fundamentalist Christian groups (Clover 1993: 8; Wilson 2001: 41). These bitter disputes, known as the pornography wars, contributed extensively to the politicization of the field of pornography (Kimmel 2005: 75–83; Wilson 2001: 38–40). During the first decades of the twenty-first century, with the consolidation of an internet-led information economy, pornography has grown exponentially, and thanks to the all-round openness and availability provided by the Internet it 'is more accessible and mainstream than ever' (Attwood 2010: 2). In light of this, Linda Williams declares that 'pornographies', the term she uses to illustrate the genre's vast diversity and variety, 'have become fully recognizable fixtures of popular culture' (2004: 1).

Monzó's narrative production is imbued with the tensions and concerns of the above debates. An overview of his fiction through the prism of pornography reveals, first and foremost, that the recurrence of this imagery is too noticeable to be ignored from a critical perspective. Secondly, where pornographic imagery appears, it often depicts a pornographic utopia, or to use Steven Marcus's influential term, a pornotopia (Marcus 1970). In other words, these descriptions are used to create the idea of a fully sexualized world where men are always satisfied because women conform to, participate in and enjoy playing a part in men's sexual fantasies. Finally, Monzó's recourse to pornographic imagery does not skirt the depiction of male sexual violence against women, although typically these passages are used to point to a juncture of crisis in the characters' masculinity, occurring when they experience forms of loss of control in the face of women's agency. To illustrate this, I shall analyse Monzó's second novel *Benzina* (1983), and five of his short stories, namely: 'El regne vegetal' (*Olivetti, Moulinex, Chaffoteaux et Maury*, 1980), 'Pigmalió' (*El perquè de tot plegat*, 1993), 'La mamà' and 'Dos rams de roses' (*El millor dels mons*, 2001) and 'Una nit' (*Mil cretins*, 2007).

5.1. Men in Crisis: Porn and Cultural Hierarchies

As we saw in Chapter 3, the first section of the novel *Benzina* represents the creative crisis of Heribert, a crisis that, as I show, also manifests itself in relation to Heribert's hegemonic masculinity. Having lost his creative motivation, Heribert, whose wife is having an affair with Humbert, wanders aimlessly around New York and ends up in a sex shop, where he enters a cabin and watches a film scene featuring group sex between two women and a man. Although in the novel Heribert describes a recognizable pornographic scene, he does so in a seemingly detached manner and with a lack of any arousal, as the following example illustrates:

> El noi penetrava una de les noies mentre l'altra passava de besar la noia penetrada a besar el noi, i a besar els genitals de tots dos. [...] Ara, la càmera s'ocupava, en primer pla, de les activitats de la rossa, fins que el noi descarregà sobre el nas, els ulls i els llavis d'aquesta, que somreia feliç. També somreien feliços el noi i la noia castanya. (Monzó 1983a: 51–52)

> [The boy is penetrating one of the girls, while the other goes from kissing the girl being penetrated, to kissing the boy, to kissing both of their genitals. [...] Now the camera focuses, close up, on the activities of the blond girl, until the boy discharges all over her eyes, nose, and lips; she smiles contentedly. The boy and the brown-haired girl are also smiling contentedly]

The scene ends but Heribert stays in the cabin to watch the beginning, which he had missed on entering the cabin. Now 'apareixien les mateixes noies, però assegudes, vestides i totes finetes, bevent en gots llargs' [the same girls appear, now sitting down, all dressed and demure, drinking from tall glasses] (Monzó 1983a: 52). This image stands in contrast with the previous description, where the women were only wearing high heels and stockings. This scene hints at the typical pornographic theme of two bored girls waiting for their pizza delivery, who swiftly persuade the pizza delivery man to stay with them. In an interview, Monzó has remarked the comic potential of this prototypical sequence of pornographic films: 'Hay momentos buenísimos. Hablando de lugares comunes... A mí el rollo del pizzero me descojona' [There are great moments. Speaking of commonplaces... I find the idea of the pizza delivery man hilarious] (González 2012). But beyond the comedy of reproducing in the literary text, and without a shadow of irony or allegory, an archetypical pornographic scene, this passage in *Benzina* engages with one of the constitutive characteristics of pornography as a genre, namely that it seeks to perform the promise of cyclical sexual pleasure, which can be related to Fredric Jameson's idea of postmodern culture's 'perpetual present' (2001: 36). As Marcus has aptly put it: 'A typical piece of pornographic fiction [...] goes on and on and ends nowhere' (1970: 279). By staying in the cabin to (re-)watch the (beginning of the) scene, this excerpt alludes to the infinite, never-ending essence of pornography.

Threesome scenes consisting of two women and one man are part of the stock inventory of pornographic genres (Maina 2009: 131), a fact that lends itself to considerations from the perspective of hegemonic masculinity and its association with the value of male sexual potency, insofar as a *real* male cannot reject intercourse with two attractive young women. Furthermore, readiness to have sex is one of the key factors of dominant masculinity: as Victor Seidler puts it, 'sex is the way we prove our masculinity' (1989: 23). Constant sexual availability is therefore central to the values of hegemonic masculinity, this being the reason why it would be absurd within the pornographic frame for the pizza man to choose to continue with his work shift over the possibility of having a sexual experience. This narrative of endless sexual accessibility tends to involve the separation of sex and emotions, which according to Michael Kimmel is one of the markers of hegemonic masculinity, as is also the high status attached to non-relational sex (2005: 15). The pornographic genre is one of the best examples of this, because sexual encounters are nearly always casual and involve non-emotionally attached agents.

While the pizza delivery man in the pornographic scene throws himself eagerly into the experience of having unexpected sex with two strangers, Monzó's character Heribert does not show the slightest interest, let alone arousal, while watching the film. In his analysis of *Benzina*, Fernàndez observes how the novel depicts Heribert's inadequacies as the crisis of a male subject who has lost control of his sexual and professional skills, conspicuously manifested, for instance, in his erectility problems and difficulties in relating to women (1998: 263–68). Heribert's attitude when watching the film certainly reinforces this point: at several moments he seems more focused on describing the sex shop cabin than the activities on the screen. When he realizes that the cabin is equipped to facilitate masturbation, he starts frantically to look everywhere for stains, until he realizes that in doing so he is missing the film. Later on, after leaving the sex shop, he wonders 'perquè no havia experimentat cap erecció en tota l'estona, ni fullejant les revistes ni a la cabina' [why he hasn't had an erection the whole time, neither leafing through the magazines nor in the booth] (Monzó 1983a: 53). Heribert's lack of enthusiasm denotes the failure of his sexual drive, which calls into question his manhood. This might explain his rather odd behaviour afterwards, when he buys a women's magazine, walks into a bar's toilet, and starts masturbating while looking at the photos of female models, only to get bored soon afterwards and see his erection disappear. This can be read as a desperate attempt to reassert his normative masculinity, although he fails once again. Heribert's dysfunctionality is amplified by the fact that he is not aroused by a mainstream heterosexual pornographic representation, but by a women's magazine, with their characteristic focus on articles on make-up and weight-loss techniques. Through this description of women's magazines as fulfilling a pornographic function, the narrative not only exposes the former as a product that is determined by the male gaze, but also points to the subjective element in any attempt to define what constitutes pornographic material. As a matter of fact, Rick Poynor's study of pornotopic representations in contemporary visual culture asserts that most women's magazines, in constantly talking about and representing women's bodies, are part of contemporary pornotopias (2006: 31–38). Heribert's use of such magazines as masturbatory material could be said to exemplify Poynor's point and reinforces Heribert's dysfunctionality, inasmuch as he is not aroused in two archetypically pornotopic situations: the sex shop cabin and when masturbating to a women's magazine.

The presence of pornography in Monzó's narratives from the 1980s onwards can be read as part of the wider debate about popular and high culture in the Catalan context. In the 1970s, Monzó and other up-and-coming writers considered Catalan literature to be elitist and slow to adapt to the changing social and cultural trends. One of their main targets of criticism was the traditional division between high and mass culture, which they aimed to problematize (Crameri 2008: 75). Considerations about the division between high and mass forms of culture have also pervaded the debate on pornography (Clover 1993: 3), with most analyses focusing on just what differentiates pornography from erotica precisely in these terms, with pornography usually falling into the less respected (i.e. non-artistic) category. According to Lynda Nead, in modern cultural discourses a number of dichotomies have pushed pornography to a place outside the artistic milieu, typically through the instatement of cultural divisions between pornography and art, or between the aesthetic and the obscene (1993: 145). However, Bill Thompson has commented on how clear-cut divisions have gradually given way to more blurred categories, whereby 'in less than thirty years pornography has lost the pejorative inference given to it by the British literary establishment in an attempt to distance their "erotica" from the more popular fare' (1994: 1–2). Considering the strong link between Catalan literature and high cultural production (Crameri 2008: 73–75; Fernàndez 2008: 138, 173), Monzó's interrelation with unmistakable pornographic imagery in narrative texts from the early 1980s such as *Benzina* can be interpreted as a challenge to both the Catalan literary establishment and Western literary norms, which goes hand in hand with his well-known provocative public stance, constructed during the 1970s and which would continue to be a key element of his work throughout his career. Therefore, pornographic imagery in Monzó's fiction can be read as part of a strategy to insert popular themes in Catalan literary works and thus, make them attractive for a wider public at a time in which the Catalan literary system was being (re-)defined vis-à-vis the discourses and practices of cultural normalization in the early democratic period. Monzó's iconoclastic work ought to be read in relation to his working-class sociocultural background, alien to the Catalan literary tradition. As Josep Maria Ripoll puts it, 'Monzó té uns orígens professionals i culturals aliens a la tradició literària catalana i, fins i tot, a aquells aspectes més prototípics de la cultura catalana mateixa', further adding that 'per dir-ho més de pressa, Monzó no és llicenciat en filologia ni professor ni prové de la universitat' [Monzó's professional and cultural background is alien to the Catalan literary tradition and, what is more, to the most quintessential aspects of Catalan culture [...] to put it shortly, Monzó is neither a graduate in philology nor a teacher nor a university lecturer] (2010: 47). Taking Monzó's personal background into consideration offers another perspective to understand and historicize the constituent anti-bourgeois elements of his modernizing literary and cultural project. In fact, discussions about the artistic nature of pornography are pervaded by bourgeois notions of artistic and cultural creation. In her analysis of pornography, Kipnis states that the genre has been denied the category of art because its main intention is to trigger a physical response in the consumer (1993: 136). Drawing upon Bourdieu, she further notes that the division between mind and body is 'crucial for the bourgeois project of producing distance from the body, the unconscious and the materiality of everyday life (1993: 137). Accordingly, pornographic imagery in Monzó's fiction can also be linked to his working-class and anti-bourgeois attitude, which was perceived as transgressive and innovative in the Catalan literary system of the early 1980s.

Benzina not only illustrates the key role of pornography in Monzó's fiction, but also its problematization of the hierarchical cultural divisions that define literary genres. Wandering around New York, Heribert enters a bookshop and expresses his irritation about the way books have been arranged, and this leads him to wonder whether these categorizations are logical or illogical, needed or unnecessary:

> No havia entès mai per quins set sous hom decidia quina era la ratlla divisòria d'aquests els llibres *per a nens*, d'aquells els llibres *per a adults*, d'aquells altres els *llibres eròtics*, d'aquells altres encara de més enllà els llibres *porno*, i d'aquells altres encara més enllà *novel·les d'amor*. (Monzó 1983a: 30. Italics in original)

> [He has never understood by what right someone decides there is a dividing line that makes some books for *children*, some for *adults*, others *erotic*, still others *porno*, and, finally, those even farther beyond *romance*]

Heribert finds it difficult to understand the divisions between children's and adult literature, erotica, pornography and romantic novels, thus problematizing the hierarchy of genres. His vision illustrates three main points concerning some of the main tenets of cultural modernity. First, it shows the constructed nature of genre differentiations by ridiculing the moralizing tone that such clear-cut divisions once had. Second, it renders problematic the division between children/adult or erotic/pornographic material, which is at the core of Western cultural morality, based on the supremacy of rational judgement over emotions and the body (Kipnis 1993: 136–38). And third, in not being able to understand or abide by these boundaries, Heribert's masculinity comes across as even more maladaptive.

Masculine values, however, seem to be more resilient, and this leads Heribert to reassert his faith in binary oppositions: 'el que era de criatura era negar-se a acceptar que era bo que les cosses estiguessin classificades: tot i les imperfeccions de les etiquetes, aquella era l'única forma de delimitar-les, capir-les, controlar-les, copsar-les' [the really childish thing is to refuse to admit that it is good for things to be classified; despite the imperfections of the labels, this is the only way to delimit them, understand them, control them, grasp them] (Monzó 1983a: 30). It is not surprising that Heribert resorts to rationalization and the notion of some source of authoritative meaning when feeling doubtful, since the need for rationality and control is at the base of the values and principles of hegemonic masculinity (Seidler 1989: 2). We see, then, how the pornographic element in Monzó's narrative serves as a platform from which to enact a series of different crises and thus open them up for discussion: the problem of hierarchical generic classifications in the arts and the traditional patriarchal view of sex as a symbol of manhood.

5.2. Pornographic and Capitalist Utopias

If the first part of *Benzina* presents Heribert's downfall, the second focuses on Humbert's rapid rise to global artistic stardom. A consideration of Humbert's particular relation to sex will help introduce the second point I want to discuss with regard to the use of pornographic imagery in Monzó's narrative, namely the theme of pornographic utopia. Marcus coined the term 'pornotopia' to refer to 'that vision which regards all of human experiences as a series of exclusively sexual events or conveniences' (1970: 216), while Kimmel uses the term 'pornographic utopia' to refer to the world of fantasy created by pornography, and its influence on those who consume it (2005: 91). In the novel's second part, Humbert, now married to Helena, his agent, who used to be Heribert's wife and agent, enjoys a phase of extreme and excessive creativity, which is presented in the narrative as going hand in hand with a phase of heightened sexual drive and activity. At some point in the novel, Helena tells him that Heribert has had an affair with a woman called Hildegarda and, although this is the first time that he hears about this woman, Humbert becomes fixated with the idea of having sexual intercourse with her, and tries to arrange an encounter as a matter of urgency.

In the subsequent pages, the plot strongly evokes the notion of pornotopia or pornographic utopia, since Humbert experiences numerous sexual encounters, sporadic or not. He meets a woman he thinks is Hildegarda and, once in his car, without any preliminary introduction, he kisses and undresses her. In spite of her beauty, however, he loses his sexual appetite on realizing that her name is in reality Alexandra, a name which, not beginning with an 'h', sets her apart conspicuously from the rest of the novel's characters. He is still capable of consummating the encounter, but has to do so with his eyes closed and as quickly as he can. A couple of days later, he is finally able to meet Hildegarda. He kisses her immediately and the affair develops quickly, as that very evening they decide to travel to Chicago together, where he is launching a new exhibition. Humbert then plunges into a downward spiral. He has a sexual encounter with two twin sisters at a party, continues having sex with his wife and has intercourse on repeated occasions with Hildegarda during their trip. Most of the sexual descriptions in this part of the narrative are strongly influenced by erotic imagery. On one occasion, for example, Hildegarda is depicted stepping out of the shower enfolded in a towel, while Humbert 'li treia la tovallola i la deixava caure a terra, sense accedir a esperar que s'eixugués' [takes off her towel and lets it fall to the floor, without waiting for her to dry off] (Monzó 1983a: 170), thus echoing the ideal of immediacy and constant availability enacted in pornographic cinema.

The events in this part of the novel have an oneiric, and even surreal quality, as they contain strange conversations between Humbert and Hildegarda, the description of his bouts of insomnia and his obsession with work and sex. This material is interwoven with the description of numerous sexual encounters, which again are reminiscent of Scott Beattie's description of pornotopia as 'utopias of free excess or dystopic states of anomie' (2009: 5). Marcus had already described utopias as the space 'where time as we know it and some other kind of time intersect' (1970: 269). In the case of pornotopia, time is to be understood as sexual time: 'its real unit of measurement is an internal one — the time it takes either for a sexual act to be represented or for an autoerotic act to be completed' (Marcus 1970: 270). The passages from *Benzina* described above seem aptly to exemplify this facet of pornotopia, since Humbert engages in a relentless sexual spree, during which he is either engaging in sexual acts, masturbating or fantasizing about it. The fact that many of these intercourses are casual encounters with strangers builds into the indulging and fantasizing world of pornographic utopias. In view of this, the amalgamation of reality and dream analysed in Chapter 3 in relation to Jorge Luis Borges' fiction and Monzó's texts turns out to be a fundamental technique for the narration of Humbert's pornographic utopia. Humbert's unremitting sexual activities can also be read as symbolic of the association between sexual potency and social/professional success embedded in dominant masculinity: if Heribert is undergoing a creative crisis that undermines his sexuality, Humbert finds himself in exactly the opposite situation.

By contrast to Heribert's disorientation, which is also manifested in how he fails to seduce an admirer, Humbert knows how to keep in control during his sexual encounters with women and, following the narratives of hegemonic masculinity, he always makes the first move. As Seidler puts it: 'As boys, sex is often an issue of seeing how far we can get. [...] sex as achievement replaces any notion of sex as a pleasure' (1989: 39). Humbert's actions clearly embody Seidler's ideas: he wants to have casual sex with Hildegarda just because she had slept with Heribert. It will be the second time he has intercourse with a woman whom Heribert had previously dated. In fact, this is the driving force behind his sexual arousal: when he follows her, 'La mirava caminar davant d'ell. Li agradava. Se la imaginava en braços de l'Heribert, suau i càlida. Tingué una erecció' [He watches her walk in front of him. He finds her attractive. He imagines her in Heribert's arms, soft and warm. He gets an erection] (Monzó 1983a: 150). Heribert's loss of sexual appetite when realizing that he has mistaken Alexandra for Hildegarda shows that he is not having sex for pleasure, but for the sake of experiencing a sense of achievement. The whole novel can be interpreted as the story of Humbert's replacement of Heribert; having sex with Hildegarda is another step in this process. Despite this contrasting depiction, the circular structure of the novel also suggests that Humbert will eventually follow Heribert's path and lose his artistic inspiration. However, this doubling identification of both protagonists seems to rest on the outright commodification of women: Heribert's/Humbert's wife and Hildegarda are both useful tools in enhancing their career success and are also something to be possessed or acquired by them as symbols of success.

The short story 'Dos rams de roses' also has the concept of pornographic utopia at its core (*El millor dels mons*, 2001). The story tells of an unusual weekend in the life of a middle-aged man, whose boss gives him permission to leave his office early on a Friday afternoon and go home. This unnamed male protagonist seems to enjoy a perfect family life: he has a lovely wife, with whom he still enjoys a more than fulfilling sexual relationship, and two perfect children, who behave in an untypically mature manner. After arriving home, the family spends part of the weekend together in what seems the description of marital bliss, but by Saturday evening the husband feels the need to go out by himself. His wife, far from showing any opposition to the idea, vividly encourages him to do so. Once out, the man meets with the two young sisters who run the local florist and they end up sleeping together and smoking marijuana, in a pornotopian sequence where characters seem to lose the notion of time. When engaging in group sex, for instance, the protagonist describes how 'cada tantes hores miro el rellotge que duc al canell i les busques amb prou feines han avançat cinc minuts' [every few hours I look at the watch and its hands have hardly advanced five minutes] (Monzó 2001: 105), which alludes to the sense of never-ending pleasure that he is experiencing. This allusion to the disrupted subjective experience of time also taps into the dreamlike elements at the core of Monzó's pornographic utopia in this short story, characterized, just like *Benzina*, by the contamination of reality by dream. After this fulfilling individual experience, on Sunday afternoon the protagonist returns home and is welcomed with joy by his wife and children.

The events of this unnamed man's *perfect* weekend seem to represent the quintessential male fantasy, according to the ideals of hegemonic bourgeois masculinity: to have a quiet and fulfilling family life after being married for nine years, whilst simultaneously being able to have sexual encounters with other women and enjoy entire nights out without fear of reprisal from a partner. This can be read as the representation of absolute individual fulfilment from three different, yet interrelated, perspectives: bourgeois property, capitalist individuality and dominant masculinity. Furthermore, if this were not enough, the connection and sexual life of the couple is completely satisfying even when they have been together for nine years, as the protagonist/narrator tells us: 'Nou anys junts, amb dues criatures, i encara sentim el desig' [Nine years together, with two children, and we still desire each other] (Monzó 2001: 94). Subsequently, the short story narrates with vivid descriptions the quality time that the couple enjoys together. After spending the evening with their kids, they go out to a club and dance as they used to do in their youth. Back home, they copulate and then fall asleep. Their sexual relationship is described as fiery and imaginative. They have sex again in the middle of the night, and, in the morning, she wakes him up by giving him oral pleasure. In the scene, they both in sexual games, including anal explorations and sperm swapping, which adds to the narrator's portrayal of the protagonist as an accomplished example of modern masculinity: 'descarrego dins la boca [...]. Se m'acosta als llavis i me'n passa just la meitat, sense jo mostrar cap rebuig, com acostumen a fer alguns homes, ans al contrari' [I discharge in her mouth [...] She comes towards my lips and shares half of it with me. I don't reject it, as some men do: just the opposite] (2001: 98–99).

In spite of this satisfying married sex life, however, the main character feels the need to look for new experiences and to have sex outside marriage, as we have seen. While this is a clear vindication of casual and non-relational sex, the short story seems also to transmit the idea that married sex can still be adventurous. The text suggests that the male protagonist needs *carte blanche* to seek individual pleasure and that he will only encounter obliging women on his way, thus depicting 'a world in which we, and our partners, are always sexually satisfied. The pornographic utopia is a world of abundance, abandon and autonomy — a world, in short, utterly unlike the one we inhabit' (Kimmel 2005: 91). In this realm, women always seem to respond to men's advances: 'Pornography often represents women as inviting, apparently desiring intimacy and physical closeness' (Barker 1992: 134). It is not by chance, therefore, that 'Dos rams de roses' contains another threesome scene, the third mentioned in this chapter, which is a reworking of the man-with-two-sisters structure already seen in *Benzina* (Monzó 1983a: 164). These passages, which do not provide a detailed description of the group sex scenes, seem to suggest that the women engage in lesbian practices. In any case, as the patriarchal pornographic ideal dictates, the narrative focuses on two women devoted exclusively to pleasuring the male character. While the whole episode lacks descriptive detail, the reader is compelled to interpret it as a typical patriarchal sexual encounter, since the sexual group scene between a man and two women evokes the characteristically male-centred perspective of mainstream heterosexual pornography.

In addition to these pornographic fantasies, 'Dos rams de roses' also depicts a capitalist utopia. The main character's materialistic volitions are invariably satisfied and everything works perfectly according to the ideal of accomplished liberal individuality. He has a family, a job, a house and a car. The middle class married couple also owns a second residence in the coastal resort of Salou, where they spend some weekends. The male protagonist is constantly looking for pleasurable activities and is never disappointed: the water gets warm very quickly when he showers; at the night club, which has several areas to suit everyone's musical preferences, waiters are efficient and kind; when the whole family visit the circus they find a parking space right in front of the main entrance; when they are watching TV, the programmes are both entertaining and intellectually stimulating; when he feels overwhelmed by family life and wants to go out alone, his wife encourages him to sleep overnight at their house in Salou. If this level of perfection were not enough, on their way home from their night out, the couple give generous amounts of money to several mime-artists populating La Rambla, causing other citizens to imitate them in an apotheosis of charity. The couple even withdraws money from a cash point in order to continue their good deeds, as they want to share their happiness with 'tots els miserables que ens troben pel camí' [all the miserable people we find along our way] (Monzó 2001: 97), thus echoing the parody of philanthropy analysed in 'Fam i set de justícia' in the previous chapter. This situation is not only ironic because of its extravagant display of social harmony and solidarity, but also because in one of his opinion pieces Monzó has vociferously criticized the growing number of street artists in Barcelona's city centre, which, for him, 'es uno de los causantes de la harapienta imagen actual del centro de nuestra ciudad' [is one of the causes of the decrepit state of our city centre] (2010d: 20).

Unsurprisingly, 'Dos rams de roses' interlinks the pornographic and capitalist utopia. The gender and sexuality theorist Paul B. Preciado has studied the historical alliance between both utopias in the construction of contemporary masculinity, through his analysis of how the magazine *Playboy* came to symbolize the transformation of masculine values in the second half of the twentieth century, from the traditional model of the family breadwinner to the forever-youthful man who revels in consumerism, urban life and in the maximization of sexual encounters (Preciado 2010: 62). In his study, Preciado establishes a dichotomy between the post-war American nuclear family and the 'capitalismo farmacopornográfico' [pharmapornographic capitalism] promoted by *Playboy*, which counterposed sexual freedom and juvenile pleasure to the tedious monogamy of married life (2010: 52). According to Preciado, the magazine helped men escape from the confined spaces of marital domesticity by activating metaphors against traditional family life and monogamy, which is precisely what we see in the case of the protagonist of 'Dos rams de roses'. However, while Preciado points out that the model promoted by *Playboy* was 'la del joven soltero, urbanita y casero' [the urban and home-loving young bachelor] (2010: 34), Monzó's pornotopia seems to be even more complete, since the protagonist enjoys both a satisfying family life and casual sexual encounters. In consequence, the pornographic utopia depicted in Monzó's story blends married and single life into a never-ending state of masculine pleasure.

The theme of pursuit of total pleasure is so stretched in Monzó's story that the text acquires a powerful ironic meaning. Since the plot mixes real and plausible situations with hyper-real and oneiric elements provoked by drug consumption, the whole story could be interpreted as a parody of the sexual and capitalist utopia. Accordingly, 'Dos rams de roses' can also be read as a negation of what it seems to affirm, since the description of the marital relation experienced by the protagonist causes a sense of estrangement that hints at the fallacy of the ideology of matrimonial life and middle class domesticity. It is important to remember that the story begins with the main character bored in his office on a Friday afternoon, just before the weekend. His happiness starts when he decides to break his routine by asking for permission to leave work early, but this is only possible because the story is placed at the start of the weekend, the quintessential moment of regulated release and promise in contemporary capitalist lifestyles. This sense of harmony is slightly disturbed for the first time at the end of the short story, when the protagonist's wife is suspicious of him coming back home with a bucket of roses (she is unaware that this is a present from his two lovers). Her first doubts regarding her husband's sexual fidelity therefore coincide with the final hours of the weekend, which can be read as signalling a closure of the strongly linked pornographic and capitalist utopia.

5.3. Hegemonic Masculinity in Crisis and Sexual Violence

Hegemonic masculinity is a historically constructed set of values, and power is one of its main constituents (Beynon 2002: 16). As John MacInnes points out, terms such as 'hard, aggressive, strong, dominant, remote, powerful, fearful of intimacy, rational, unemotional, competitive, sexist and their synonyms' still define its essence (MacInnes 1998: 14). This aggressive and dominant type of masculinity is paramount in Monzó's texts, which include descriptions of rape and male sexual violence against women. A surreal autobiographical parody told in the first person, the short story 'El regne vegetal' (*Olivetti, Moulinex, Chaffoteaux et Maury*, 1980) revolves around a man who has done and seen it all in Barcelona from the 1960s up to the early 1980s: from the prostitutes and the American marines of the Sixth Fleet through the countercultural hippies of the 1970s and right up to the drug-addicts and small crime of the late 1970s, in a clear reference to the beginnings of the economic recession in Spain. As the narrator tells us, he was not impressed with the hippies because, already during the 1960s, 'vam aprendre a fer-nos cínics i aprofitats' [we learned to be cynical and opportunists], and further asserts that time has proved him right: 'avui, dels hippies ja no se'n canta ni gall ni gallina, i els aprofitats són els amos del món' [today, hippies have fallen into oblivion, and opportunists rule the world] (1999: 184). Julià Guillamon's reading of the story focuses on how this male protagonist's amorality and cynicism epitomize the end of the utopias associated with the convoluted period of the late 1970s in Catalonia (2001: 57–60). In my analysis, I wish to illustrate how the crisis of hegemonic masculinity and its relation to male sexual violence is fundamental to the configuration of the protagonist's cynicism and opportunism. The point of rupture takes place the day in which he rapes his girlfriend and, as the protagonist himself tells us, enjoys it to the degree that he resolves to 'convertir-me en un llibertí clàssic' [become a classic libertine] and, from then onwards, 'només tastaria els fruits prohibits' [only taste forbidden fruits] (Monzó 1999: 185). Initially, he becomes a rapist, and later engages in legal and illegal sexual practices, including being an 'exhibicionista, voyeur, pervertidor de menors, gigoló, sàdic, amant de la zoofília, masoquista, sodomita' [an exhibitionist, a voyeur, a pervert of minors, a gigolo, a sadist, a bestialist, a masochist, a sodomite] (Monzó 1999: 186). This short story, in the same way as 'Dos rams de roses', is focalized through a first-person male narrator, which arguably has the effect of increasing readers' identification with the narrative voice. This is achieved partly as the protagonist's conduct seems to be excused because forbidden actions are used to mount an attack on conventional morals, as the narrator himself acknowledges: 'terreny que m'era prohibit, terreny que prenia per assalt' [territory that was forbidden to me, territory that I took by assault] (Monzó 1999: 125). The text, therefore, relies strongly on the trivialization of male sexual violence and, by conflating unconventional sexual practices, both legal and illegal, also on the apparent attack to traditional sexual morals.

The main character's behaviour, however, changes when he meets a lovely and innocent young woman who is drinking orange juice in a bar. By contrast to his previous sexual drives, he enjoys engaging in slightly outdated courting practices with her: walking together along Barcelona's Passeig del Born and Les Rambles, drinking hot chocolate and talking about banalities. Back home, he seems troubled by his conduct and feelings for this woman. As he reflects: 'Em va fer por pensar que podia arribar a sentir-m'hi bé, fent aquell paper de bon minyó' [It was scary to realize that I could feel good being a nice boy] (1999: 187–88). To feel better, he masturbates watching porn: 'em vaig haver de masturbar mirant fotos de bèsties (porcs, gossos i asses) que penetraven bocabadades damisel·les de cabells rossos tenyits: bé havia de mantenir la integritat' [I had to masturbate looking at photos of beasts (pigs, dogs, donkeys) penetrating bewildered damsels with dyed blonde hair: I had to maintain my integrity!] (188). Once again, the text problematizes conventional morals through an upsetting image suggesting sexual violence against women. The role of pornography consumption in this scene is to enable the protagonist to revert to his old habits and reassure himself that his hegemonic masculine identity is restored.

On the following day, they meet at his house, where he takes the initiative and promptly kisses her. If he follows the values of hegemonic masculinity, she follows traditional feminine decorum, and therefore tries to resist his advances. To borrow Kimmel's words, this passage reminds us that, 'men still stand to gain status and women to lose it from sexual experience [...]. Boys are taught to try to get sex; girls are taught strategies to foil the boy's attempt' (2005: 5). The young woman's resistance alarms the protagonist, because 'potser de debò que ahir m'havia pres per un figaflor' [perhaps she had really taken me for a dopey] (Monzó 1999: 188). The term 'figaflor' is a condensation of myriad stereotypes related to flawed masculinity and sexual power. If she considers him a 'figaflor', this implies that his behaviour on their first date sent her the wrong message, confirming his worries about having been kind-hearted, when he wants to continue engaging in unusual intimate relations. Nevertheless, he finds some enjoyment in her refusal, as he points out that 'aquests adolescents d'ara, que no se't resisteixen, et fan perdre l'al·licient per les petites coses de la vida' [by not showing any resistance, these teenagers of our day and age kill the charm of the little things in life] (Monzó 1999: 189). This sentence can be seen as parody of one of the fundamental tenets of feminist sexual politics, that of women's sexual consent. The male protagonist then attempts to rape her, in a fragment replete with disturbing images of male sexual violence. At this moment, the narrative turns, once again, to a surrealistic mode which combines reality and fantasy. As an excuse not to have sex with him, for instance, the girl mentions being a convinced vegetarian, which means that she only allows herself to be penetrated by vegetables, an argument that he seemingly abides by. This grotesque element, together with the eccentricity of his previous comments, allows the narrative to dodge the obvious patriarchal violence and focus on the protagonist's internal struggle between a violent masculinity and the possibility of having a non-aggressive relationship with a woman.

In the end, he decides to instruct her sexually, only to find himself to be more terrified by her rapid progress, which is another example of the inherent contradictions of hegemonic masculinity. In effect, Tim Edwards has established a direct link between masculine anxieties and women's empowerment, because 'the prevailing order of patriarchy is seen as being undermined by –– if not necessarily under threat from — the emancipation of women' (2006: 15). Similarly, MacInnes links male restlessness to the liberation of women because 'the prevailing order of patriarchy is seen as being undermined by –– if not necessarily under threat from –– the emancipation of women' (1998: 18). The male character's unease increases at her delight in the Marquis de Sade's books, a series of texts interpreted by the feminist writer Angela Carter as 'unusual in his period for claiming the rights of free sexuality for women, and in installing women as beings of power in his imaginary worlds' (1984: 36). In view of this, the protagonist's reaction illustrates masculine anxieties surrounding women's sexual empowerment: he feels in control if both participants limit themselves to their historically assigned roles (he acts as an instructor, she acts as a learner), but is frightened by her sexual progression, which undermines his sense of control and virility. 'El regne vegetal', therefore, illustrates the paradoxes of dominant masculinity in the face of recent sociological changes in interpersonal relationships: feeling restless or inadequate, men resort to sexual violence in order to reassert their masculinity, since as Kimmel notes 'violence is often the single most evident marker of manhood' (Kimmel 2005: 36).

The plot has an open ending and the reader is left unsure as to whether the main character will be able to change or whether he will become even more violent. In contrast to this, 'Una nit' (*Mil cretins*, 2007) illustrates the total failure of hegemonic masculinity when facing recent transformations in interpersonal relations. The plot retells a classic fairy tale of Western culture, 'Sleeping Beauty'. A prince finds an unconscious princess in a room and quickly kisses her in order to wake her up. However, hard as he tries, she does not react. Anxious and disoriented, he undresses her and penetrates her several times, but this does not have any effect on her. Exhausted, he falls asleep next to her. A moment later the princess wakes up confused, stares at him and quickly leaves the room. This text epitomizes the failure of the fairy-tale narrative, in what is another example of how Monzó's postmodern parodic rewritings problematize the values of Western classical texts. Although the prince repeats the same action as other princes have done for centuries, the princess no longer wakes up. In fact, the prince goes much further than other princes, given that not only does he kiss the princess over and over again, but he also rapes her, which in itself encapsulates his failure and, in turn, the collapse of the master narrative. The message seems to be that the context has dramatically changed and the princess is no longer a passive being waiting for a man to save her. While she has been able to adapt to the new situation, he has not. His failure results from his lack of adaptation to the changing sociocultural reality, as he cleaves to his historical role and accordingly, does not make progress. The woman, on the contrary, modifies her actions and is therefore able to escape from the prince, who seemingly represents the oppression of women by hegemonic masculinity.

At the beginning of the text, unaware of what is to come, the prince kisses the princess thinking that that is 'el petó que la princesa ha esperat' [the kiss the princess has been waiting for forever][1] (Monzó 2007b: 137). After trying several times and missing the mark, he feels inadequate, and becomes worried about his masculine self:

> ¿Quina mena de príncep blau és, que els seus petons no són capaços de despertar l'adormida? Tots els príceps blaus se'n vanten, sempre, de despertar les princeses amb un únic petó, senzill però inapel·lable. Se sent inútil, i agraeix que, com a mínim, a la sala no hi hagi ningú que l'observi. (2007b: 138)

> [What kind of prince in blue is he, if his kisses aren't able to wake up the sleeping maiden? Princes in blue always boast about waking up princesses with a single but irresistible kiss. He feels useless, and is thankful that at least no one else is in the room watching him]

The romantic plot is thwarted the moment the prince begins to doubt his masculinity and compare himself to other princes. His last sentence shows that men are also objects of the patriarchal gaze, as he feels relieved because no one observes him: should this have happened, his failure would have been greater. As Kimmel explains, the fear of not being a *real* man is central to patriarchy and, accordingly, an individual's masculinity is kept in check by other men (2005: 36). From a hegemonic masculine perspective, the interpretation is clear: while past princes have always succeeded, he does not, which makes him anxious because, in a patriarchal system, 'you could never rest easy with your masculine identity, but always had to be ready to prove it' (Seidler 1989: 30). However, despite the fact that masculinity is controlled by other men, it is validated by women, which is why the prince feels humiliated when she does not engage with him. As Barker puts it, 'in order for men to experience themselves as masculine — as being real men — women are required to play their prescribed role of doing the things that make men feel masculine and therefore all right about themselves' (1992: 132). In Monzó's 'Una nit', however, the princess does not play her prescribed role. The narrative does not clarify whether this is a conscious or unconscious decision, which, as in other short stories analysed in this chapter, allows the plot to focus on the male character and his inner conflicts. The tension and anxiety experienced by the male protagonist is the prelude to further sexual violence: the princess's immobility moves him to undress and lick her, which triggers the appearance of pornographic imagery. The prince, however, is portrayed as naive: on thinking that no princess has ever been kissed in such a passionate way before, he displays his lack of awareness of recent changes in women's sexuality. Through this description, the narrative contrasts how women's sexuality was regarded in the past — as associated with romantic love and virginity — against present times — where sexual relations before marriage are common. In a last desperate attempt to wake her up, he penetrates her repeatedly, but she remains motionless. Soon he will fall asleep and she will wake up and leave the room, and him.

Episodes of men resorting to sexual violence against women are also found in *Benzina*, where Heribert does not know how to seduce a young admirer and considers the option of sexually abusing her: 'No sabia com actuar. ¿Havia de començar a besar-la tot d'una i, si es resistia, violar-la allà mateix? Li semblava recordar que no, que les coses no anaven ben bé així' [He doesn't know how to behave. Should he start kissing her right off and, if she resists, force her right then and there? He seems to remember it doesn't quite go like that] (Monzó 1983a: 66). Humbert's character also engages in a kind of imaginative rape in which he visualizes images of sexual violence that are very much influenced by pornography. While Humbert is sleeping next to Helena, for example, he starts developing an idea for a painting: 'Hi entraven dos homes per la porta i, tal com estava, bocaterrosa, la utilitzaven sexualment [...] com bèsties. No, no eren dos homes: eren tres' [Two men burst through the door and, just as she is lying, face down, they use her sexually [...] like animals. Not two men, three] (Monzó 1983a: 130). Interestingly, right after his vision Humbert jots down in his notebook: '*Reflexionar sobre la pornografia en vídeo*' [Reflect on video pornography] (Monzó 1983a: 130. Italics in original), in what is another example of how sexual violence appears in the intersection between pornography and hegemonic masculinity, as well as an instance of how high art and mass culture merge together in Monzó's narrative.

In the same vein as 'El regne vegetal', other short stories also centre upon the archetypical plot of the experienced male figure who shapes and instructs a young girl, which harks back to the myth of Pygmalion. Precisely, *El perquè de tot plegat* contains a literary adaptation of this myth, entitled 'Pigmalió', which Lunati has interpreted as a feminist representation of the crisis of hegemonic masculinity (1999). As in 'El regne vegetal', the female character in 'Pigmalió' enjoys being submissive and performing her lover's desires to perfection. Lunati argues that her enjoyment of sex both emancipates her and precipitates the downfall of the male protagonist, who reveals himself unable to adapt to her progression from passive recipient to active sexual agent. However, as Lunati also points out, this underscores her dependence on the expectations of her male sexual partner (1999). This is a convincing interpretation of the text: although the short story is ambiguous, sexual enjoyment allows the female character to subvert the patriarchal construction of women as passive sexual beings. Monzó's 'Pigmalió' also integrates pornographic imagery, which Lunati has commented on, observing that, 'tot i que Monzó explora un espai tradicionalment reservat a la pornografia, no es decanta pel voyeurisme

ni per imatges que explotin els cossos dels protagonistes o la seva relació sexual'
[although Monzo explores a space traditionally reserved for pornography, he does
not resort to voyeurism, nor to images that exploit the protagonists' bodies or their
sexual relationship] (Lunati 1999). I would argue, however, that the pornographic
imagery used to describe the young woman's acquired sexual taste is particularly
detailed and, furthermore, coincides with the archetypal representations of male-
centred pornography, as the following excerpt shows:

> Ara la noia és als seus peus, amb la boca oberta i els ulls encesos. Amb una
> cullera, Pigmalió recull la barreja de semen i llàgrimes que regalima per la cara
> de la noia i l'hi dóna a la boca, peixant-la com un bebè. Pigmalió mira, encisat i
> neguitós, com la noia llepa la cullera. ¿Què més pot fer-li? (Monzó 1999: 37–38)
>
> [Now the girl is at his feet, mouth open, eyes on fire. Holding a spoon,
> Pygmalion collects the mixture of semen and tears streaming down the girl's
> face and puts it in her mouth, feeding her like a baby. Pygmalion looks on,
> enraptured and anxious, as the girl licks the spoon. What else can he do?][2]

As we see above, the female character adopts a well-known posture in pornographic
settings when he ejaculates on her face, itself an emblematic pornographic ritual.
The narrative insinuates that they have performed deep-throating and describes
how he spoon-feeds his own semen to the woman. Kimmel highlights the centrality
and visibility of semen in pornography, and the fact that 'male ejaculation almost
invariably occurs outside the woman, and often on her' (2005: 90). This practice,
which focuses on the man's orgasmic pleasure, transmits the idea that this is not fake
sex, but real and visually exciting. Although the description is certainly succinct,
Monzó does not need to describe the sexual activities of the characters extensively,
because of the obvious allusions to pornographic imagery, which, on condensing
a series of clichés, the reader is meant to quickly recognize. Therefore Monzó's
'Pigmalió', already a highly intertextual text, relies for its full impact on the reader's
recognition of its dense pornographic imagery. The narrator's last question —— 'Què
més pot fer-li?' —— reinforces this interpretation, as it takes us back to Marcus's
point about pornography's inherently never-ending nature. In the same vein as
my analysis in the previous chapter, it can be argued that the recurrent presence
of irony in Monzó's stories also needs to be taken into consideration, as Lunati
herself does (1999). It is certainly important to take into account the transgressive
power of irony and the ambiguity of pornographic imagery in Monzó's fiction, as
my readings in this chapter do. However, as in the previous chapter, here I also put
forward more literal readings of Monzó's postmodern short stories, since by virtue
of their ambiguity, his ironic strategies neither affirm nor reject patriarchal values.

The practice of ejaculating on a woman's face is mentioned in another story
written by Monzó, 'La mamà' (*El millor dels mons*, 2001), which revolves around the
influence of pornography on young boys. The plot describes the trauma suffered by
a ten-year-old boy insulted by a school friend, who calls him 'fill de puta'. Unaware
of the figurative meaning of the expression, the boy takes the insult in its literal
sense and starts investigating his mother's life. Eventually, he warns his dad, who,
out of jealousy, believes the young boy and divorces his mother. Pornography is

also present in this text. The young boy's first introduction to sex had been through pornographic magazines, where he had learned that intercourse happens mainly in beds, cars, offices and garages. He further explains his view of male ejaculation, which shows the influence of pornographic imagery on children:

> al final, els homes se'ls escorren a la cara: no havia vist cap història fotogràfica on, al final, els homes s'escorreguessin en cap altre lloc que no fos la cara de les dones. Tirant lluny, s'escorrien als pits perquè no l'encertaven: això és el que pensava aleshores. Fins a tal punt n'estava convençut que creia que el final obligat de qualsevol acte sexual era que l'home s'escorregués a la cara de la dones i, si no era així, la cosa no havia anat bé. (Monzó 2001: 25)

> [in the end, men come on their faces: he had never seen any photo sequence in which, in the end, men would come anywhere else but a woman's face. At most, they would come on their breasts because they missed the face: this is what he thought at the time. He was so convinced that any sexual intercourse must end with a man coming on a woman's face that, if this didn't happen, he thought that something had gone wrong]

Peter Barker has asserted that the use of pornography plays a vital role in the early stages of men's sexuality: 'Men usually first see pornography when they are quite young: it is clandestinely circulated on the way home from school or, increasingly, watched on parent's videocassette players' (Barker 1992: 125). Nowadays, as a result of Internet, the exposure of young people to porn has greatly increased. The story 'La mamà' highlights both the centrality of pornographic material in adolescents' sexual education and the defining role that the visual representation of semen plays in this genre: the boy suspects that his neighbour ejaculates on his mother's face, and this leads him to 'començar a sentir una mena de fàstic cada cop que tornava de l'escola i la mamà m'acostava la cara per fer-me un petó' [start to feel a kind of repulsion every time he came back from school and his mum approached him to kiss his face] (Monzó 2001: 25–26), to the point that he finally rejects any physical contact with his mother's face.

Monzó's representation of pornographic imagery in 'La mamà' reflects contemporary debates about the relation between representation and reality, since, for the young boy, the representation of sex takes precedence over the real. In their award-winning essay on pornography, Andrés Barba and Javier Montes claim that pornography does not have a subversive power, since it tends to reaffirm the social order (2007: 73). In this they coincide with the feminist writer Angela Carter, who stated that most of pornography serves 'to reinforce the prevailing system of values and ideas' (Carter 1984: 18). Nevertheless, Barba and Montes are also of the opinion that, taken as a form of representation, pornography holds a transgressive value, this being the reason why it has been kept at the margins of the public sphere. In their own words, pornography problematizes 'la norma que rige el espacio común y las imágenes que resultan aceptables en él. En tanto que representación, el porno es siempre transgresor' [the norms that regulate the public space and the images that are considered acceptable. As a representation, pornography is always transgressive] (2007: 63). Accordingly, these critics establish a difference between the formal aspects of pornography — the type of pornography that is produced and consumed

–– and the social influence of the genre as a representation, tragicomically represented in Monzó's short story 'La mamà' by the distancing relation between the young boy and his mother. The debate about the potential transgressive role of pornography is linked to the relation between aesthetics and politics in Monzó's oeuvre: even though the role of pornography in his texts is ambivalent, in several public statements he has tried to reduce pornography to an aesthetic practice, thus rejecting the importance of the power relations upon which it rests. When asked why he likes porn, he replied that 'hostia, que es bella. Es bella y es excitante. [...] Porque es bello, porque ver a la gente tocándose es bello' [come on, because it's beautiful. It's beautiful and arousing. [...] Seeing people touching one another is beautiful] (González 2012). Monzó has also paralleled pornography and art, describing some of Poussin's and Picasso's paintings as pornographic: 'Una buena película porno es tan bella y respetable como un poussin o un picasso pornos' [A porn film is as beautiful and respectable as a porn Poussin or Picasso] (González 2012). By stating that pornography is not only a product of mass culture but also an artistic manifestation, Monzó takes a clear stance in a fundamental debate about the genre and further plays up his provocative public persona.

Taken together, Monzó's fiction represents pornographic imagery in complex, contradictory and critical manners, problematizing its impact on society. His texts allow for ironic readings which disrupt literal interpretations, productive as they are, as shown in this chapter. Furthermore, the characters influenced by pornography and the value-system of hegemonic masculinity are portrayed in a parodic, even grotesque manner, in these fictional narratives. They are depicted simply as archetypes: they are always men, and appear either unnamed or named just by a letter. More importantly, whether read ironically or otherwise, Monzó's texts vividly portray patriarchal oppression. Kimmel underlines the importance of examining the role of pornography in men's sexuality because 'although most pornographic images are of women, pornography is, at its heart, about men. It is about men's relationships with sexuality, with women, and with each other' (2005: 67). Monzó's texts certainly place the emphasis on the interplay and relations between pornography and men. The interactions between pornographic material and literary narrative used to explore the dark angles of masculinity do not say much about female characters, who are rather flat in comparison to male protagonists. Monzó's models of masculinity are almost invariably inadequate, anxious as they are about their own status in relation to women.

By contrast to his nuanced literary representation of hegemonic masculinity in crisis, Monzó's public statements on feminism tend to be unequivocally harsh, lacking the subtlety that characterizes his fiction. To a certain extent, Monzó's distaste for feminist politics may be linked to the crisis experienced by some of his characters in the face of the transformations in gender relations in post-Francoist Spain. Although the redefinition of sexual relations and subjectivities had a belated start as a result of Francoism, between 1975 and the last years of the twentieth century the situation changed considerably; as a result, the transformations did not appear gradual but drastic (Montero 1995: 382). Anny Brooksbank Jones remarks that, alongside socioeconomic factors, these shifts were no doubt prompted by the impact of the Spanish feminist movement: the explosion of activism in the 1970s, the politico-judicial institutionalization of a series of feminist demands during the 1980s, the creation of the Instituto de la Mujer in 1983 and the development of academic feminism from the 1980s onwards, among others (1995: 390–91; 1997: 1–18, 78). In the Catalan context, Josep-Anton Fernàndez and Adrià Chavarría assert that, from the late 1970s onwards, the region has seen a deep sociocultural transformation of gender roles which has, in turn, triggered a crisis of hegemonic masculinity (2003: 9–10). Furthermore, from the 1980s, sections of the feminist movement have significantly departed from the cult of casual sex at the core of the countercultural movement, as discussed by Jenny Diski in *The Sixties*, to give just one example (2010). Monzó's sidestepping the topic of the power relations at the core of sexual interactions between men and women can also be linked to the transformations in the contemporary feminist agenda from the 1980s onwards, which has tended to concentrate on and disrupt those power relations. The porn wars, in fact, took place during the 1980s, when the feminist movement problematized certain aspects of the sexual liberation unfolding in previous decades. In light of this, Monzó's male characters in crisis can be seen as the literary depiction of the tensions and anxieties which his articles deploy vis-à-vis feminist politics and discourses.

Notes to Chapter 5

1. All translations of 'Una nit' are taken from Peter Bush's translation in *A Thousand Morons* (Monzó 2012).
2. All translations of 'Pigmalió' are taken from Peter Bush's translation in *Why, Why, Why?* (Monzó 2019).

CHAPTER 6

❖

A Postmodern Intellectual
and a Celebrity Author

'Jo no sabria renunciar a fer ràdio, ni a fer televisió, si un dia en torno a tenir
ganes, que potser começo a tenir-ne. Crec que formen part d'un mateix *pack*.
Els relats, les novel·les, els articles de premsa i les intervencions radiofòniques
o televisives formen un tot, no sabria per on he de tallar. ¿He d'amputar una
part d'aquest tot per una certa idea decimonònica segons la qual la literatura és
allò escrit?'

[I wouldn't be able not to do radio or television if someday I feel like it again;
and perhaps I'm starting to feel like doing it again. I think they're all part of
the same pack. Short-stories, novels, press articles and contributions to radio
and TV all form a whole: I wouldn't know where to cut. Should I amputate
a part of this whole because of a nineteenth-century idea according to which
literature is only written text?]

Interview in *Avui Cultura*, 4 December 2003 (Piquer 2003: ii)

Two years after Quim Monzo's opening speech at the 2007 Frankfurt Book Fair,
a retrospective on his life and work was organized by the Institució de les Lletres
Catalanes, the Departament de Cultura i Mitjans de Comunicació of the Catalan
Generalitat and the Centre d'Arts Santa Mònica. The exhibition, which ran between
19 December 2009 and 11 April 2010, represented a definite step in the process of
canonization of Quim Monzó's literary and cultural project. Starting with Monzó
as a young and unknown artist in the early 1970s, the retrospective placed particular
emphasis on the author's life and on how his authorial persona related and adapted
to the changing socio-political and cultural conditions. As in previous narratives
of his career, Monzó was presented as a man in tune with his times. At the time
of this retrospective, he went through a period of extensive media exposure and
his image appeared in the front pages of Catalonia's foremost cultural magazines
L'Avenç (February 2010), *Caràcters* (February 2010) and *Serra d'Or* (May 2010). The
exhibition was complemented by the publication of a book/catalogue entitled *Quim
Monzó: Com triomfar a la vida*, which covered all aspects of the author's life and work.
On 4 February 2010, *La Vanguardia* announced that the book, which costs a good
twenty-five euros, had been among the bestselling non-fiction books in Catalan
for five weeks and, more importantly, that the number of visitors to the exhibition
surpassed those achieved by similar retrospectives on prominent authors like Mercè

Rodoreda, Josep Palau i Fabre and Joan Perucho (Piñol 2010a: 28–29).[1] In the late 2000s, not only was Quim Monzó's career recognized by the literary, cultural and political institutions of Catalonia, but he was probably the most popular living Catalan author. In this chapter, I wish to suggest that Quim Monzó's trajectory and public authorial persona can be studied as a case of celebrity authorship.

Celebrity authors are a manifestation of recent shifts in the literary milieu, namely the expansion of the cultural industry, the absorption of the publishing sector by large companies dedicated to entertainment and the increasing centrality of mass media and consumer culture. However, the rising importance granted to celebrity authors has triggered anxieties within the literary field. According to Wenche Ommundsen, celebrity writers encapsulate tensions between 'high cultural capital, the marketplace and the popular public sphere' (2007: 244). In his study of literary celebrity in the US, Joe Moran observes how these tensions point to a struggle for cultural authority between the advocates of the radical separation of art and commerce and those who insist that these are commensurable (2000: 7). The anxieties boil down to the growing commodification of literature, the blurring of the boundaries between high and low culture and the loss of cultural distinction traditionally associated with literary consumption and production. The economic success and particularly the media exposure enjoyed by celebrity authors has prompted concerns among participants in Western cultural systems because such values have traditionally been seen as extraneous to the literary world.

The Catalan literary field has been no exception to these dynamics. In his book *El descrèdit de la literatura* (1999) Xavier Bru de Sala contends that the conception of culture as a business has had a detrimental effect on Catalan literature because, on the one hand, Catalan texts have not attracted the attention of a wide readership and, on the other, such a commercial conception has negatively influenced the quality of Catalan literary texts, which in turn has alienated the educated minority (1999: 81–93). Explicitly critical of the commodification of literature, Bru de Sala rejects what he perceives as the current tendency whereby 'el nom de l'autor és una marca i els seus llibres, productes seriats d'una factoria anomenada editorial' [the name of the author is a brand and their books are serial products made by a factory called a publishing house] (1999: 22). Bru de Sala's critique is a fine example of the 'crítica culturalista' of the politics of cultural normalization, a stance that continued to be present in Catalan literature throughout the 2000s. In May 2004, eight Catalan authors (Alfred Bosch, Gemma Lienas, Baltasar Porcel, Carme Riera, Robert Saladrigas, Isabel-Clara Simó, Emili Teixidor and Ferran Torrent) presented the manifesto 'El Drac es menja Sant Jordi', in which they rejected the commercialization of Catalan literature and the growing relevance of what they called as the 'escriptors mediàtics' [media authors] (Capdevila 2004: 53). In their quest to distance themselves from such authors, the manifesto signatories demanded that established authors be separated from *mediàtics* at the Sant Jordi book fair. The authors concluded that the rising prominence of market values and mass media influence resulted in the banalization of literature. Bru de Sala's book and this manifesto illustrate concerns about the impact of market principles on Catalan literature, with specific emphasis on the importance granted to new indicators of literary merit, such as media appearances and popularity with readers, both of which have traditionally fallen outside of the prescribed pathways to literary canonization. Monzó's celebrity status provides an excellent platform from which to examine the tensions triggered in Catalan culture as a result of these sociocultural shifts as well as the dynamic relationship between popular success and recognition by the literary field in autonomous Catalonia.

The emergence of celebrity authorship is inextricably linked to contemporary changes in the model of the public intellectual in Western societies. In Zygmunt Bauman's influential theorization, models for public intellectual engagement today fall into two main categories: that of the modern thinker or 'legislator', who makes authoritative statements from a universal viewpoint, and that of the postmodern 'interpreter', who participates in a discursive dialogue instead of arbitrating on the value of such discourses from a position of authority (1987: 4–5). In the 1970s, Michel Foucault declared that the 'universal' intellectual acting as representative of the proletariat was undergoing a period of crisis and was being gradually replaced by the 'specific' intellectual, a figure who did not necessarily strive towards universalism, but was linked to a particular area of specialism (1980: 126–27). The French thinker also remarked that the perception that the role of the universal intellectual involved a 'moral, theoretical and political choice' that entailed personal sacrifices had been undermined by new social and cultural trends (1980: 126). Similarly, Edward Said argues that 'the old somewhat romantic-heroic notion of the solitary writer-intellectual' has faded away owing to the commercialization of culture in the newly globalized economy (2002: 20). These thinkers point to a transformation in the discourses on how public intellectuals participate in the public arena and, more specifically, to their displacement as the only voices of ethical and moral authority.

According to Josep-Anton Fernàndez, contemporary Catalan culture is confronted by the clash of two cultural models: 'el modern (jeràrquic, elitista i normatiu, centrat en el creador o l'artista) i el postmodern (diferencial, autoorganitzat, mercantilitzat, centrat en el consum)' [the modern (hierarchical, elitist and normative, centred in the creator or the artist) and the postmodern (differential, self-organized, marketized, centred in consumption)] (2008: 98). Fernàndez further adds that the politics of Catalan cultural normalization intend to combine elements, discourses and practices from both cultural paradigms, even though they are mutually contradictory and exclusive. If Bru de Sala and the signatories of the manifesto 'El Drac es menja Sant Jordi' seem to advocate the modern model, Fernàndez contends that the Catalan literary system needs to embrace the postmodern paradigm further, thus celebrating the consideration of literature as a commodity for entertainment and the blending of high and mass culture (2008: 89–90). In contrast to Bru de Sala and the signatories, Quim Monzó's literary and cultural project coincides with the postmodern model suggested by Fernàndez. In so doing, Monzó's work and public authorial persona has transcended the ideological boundaries established by the discourses and politics of cultural normalization, therefore bringing to the fore its founding contradictions. Monzó's success and popularity owes much to how his cultural project and interdisciplinary media persona is in tune with the recent transformations in the model for the literary author and public intellectual in postmodern societies. In this chapter, I examine how Monzó's work has sarcastically represented the modern model of the public intellectual at the core of the politics of cultural normalization. After this, I historicize four decades of Monzó's appearances in and interaction with mass and social media in order to explore the main features of his complex authorial persona. Monzó's media participation from the 1980s onwards goes against the grain of *resistencialisme* (an elitist mode centring on the creative artist and the rejection of mass culture and media) and transcends the limits of cultural normalization by parodying Catalan national symbols, the traditional model of authorship and the privileged position of literature within the cultural framework of Catalan nationalism.

6.1. The Intellectuals of Catalan Cultural Normalization

As early as 1985, Quim Monzó addressed the role of public intellectuals in auto-nomous Catalonia in his opinion piece 'L'intel·lectual', later included in *Zzzzzzzz* (1987). The piece revolves around a Catalan intellectual who, contrasted with a German thinker strongly critical of their own state, contributes to building the state's institutions. While Monzó initially uses the term 'estat' to refer to autonomous Catalonia, the piece quickly clarifies that such state, 'per particularismes que no duen enlloc —— mai no ha acabat de ser-ho del tot' [due to small and irrelevant details, has never really been a fully-fledged nation state] (1987: 101). Clearly alluding to Catalan intellectuals' involvement in the nation building policies of the Catalan government in the 1980s, the piece can be read as an early criticism of the politics of cultural normalization, at a time in which normalizing discourses intensified after the creation of Catalunya Ràdio and TV3 in 1983 and the consolidation of Convergència i Unió's (CiU) cultural programme after their landslide victory in the 1984 Catalan elections.

In 1992, Oriol Izquierdo elaborated on the detrimental influence of this cultural paradigm on Catalan literature, arguing that cultural normalization had become a metadiscourse that permeated all areas of the literary system and a guiding principle by which, at the end of the process, Catalan culture will allegedly achieve 'l'estadi de *normalitat*, que es defineix perquè tot hi serà més normal' [the stage of *normality*, in which everything will be more normal] (1992: 93–94. Italics in original). The notion of normality —— that is, the final stage of the processes that would lead to Catalan culture being *normal* —— has never been defined. Owing to the project's lack of clear and tangible aims, Izquierdo sees normalization as an endlessly redundant cycle, 'que si du enlloc deu ser a un enquistament de la situació o de les conductes de la suposada anormalitat' [which, if it takes us somewhere, it seems to be to a deadlock in which the allegedly abnormal attitudes are reproduced] (1992: 94).

Monzó's piece also emphasizes the lack of concrete objectives and the circularity at the core of cultural normalization. Through the parodic repetition of the imprecise and formulaic vocabularies of normalization, the text portrays the Catalan thinker as enthusiastic about his collaboration with political institutions, but oblivious to the final purpose of such contributions: 'Sap que només amb l'esforç de tots tindrem un estat prou sòlid, prou massís, prou fort per... ¿Per què? És igual' [They know that only with everyone's efforts will we have a solid enough, and robust enough, state for... For what? It doesn't matter] (1987: 101). The article also emphasizes that the participation of intellectuals in the process of nation-building fails to solve the situation but rather helps towards its reproduction, thus characterizing cultural normalization of a vicious circle:

> [The Catalan intellectual] Potser no sap — o potser sí, i fa veure que no — que arribat aquell moment [when the intellectual will have to struggle against the state structures that they have helped to build] no podrà fer gaire res, perquè no veurà per enlloc el monòlit, a no ser que es miri els peus i el vegi, a sota, gegantesc i inamovible davant els embats d'un intel·lectual [...] que malda per desemmascarar-lo. (1987: 102)

> [Perhaps they don't know — or maybe they do, but pretend not to — that, when the moment arrives, they won't be able to do much, because they won't see the monolith unless they look down to their feet; then they would see it, below them, a gigantic and immovable monolith, which an intellectual is striving to debunk]

In his characteristic biting tone, Monzó indicates that Catalan intellectuals may themselves be aware of the contradictory nature of normalization but nevertheless opt to ignore it. In so doing, Monzó's piece implies that intellectuals might be endorsing normalization for their own benefit, a possibility that has also been noted by Izquierdo, who observes that advocates of cultural normalization end up becoming 'imprescindibles' due to its circular nature (1992: 95). In consequence, 'L'intel·lectual' can be seen as a critique of how the politics and discourses of cultural normalization tend to be ineffective although infinitely reproducible, whilst simultaneously providing a context for authors interested in them to derive symbolic or material capital.

Monzó's article goes further in its criticism and suggests a link between the endeavours of Catalan intellectuals under Francoism and in post-Francoist times. In order to strengthen their institutions, the Catalan intellectual also 'tracta de netejar aquella pàtina de color ala de mosca que la dictadura hi havia deixat' [tries to remove that brown patina that the dictatorship had left on it] (1987: 101). Accordingly, the piece hints at the connections between *resistencialisme* and certain aspects of cultural normalization, a link that has already been identified by certain scholars. Izquierdo, for instance, indicates that normalization can be regarded as a reconversion of *resistentialist* attitudes of the Francoist era (1992: 95), while Kathryn Crameri and Fernàndez remark that the link between cultural production and national identity is at the core of both cultural models (Crameri 2008: 3–15; Fernàndez 2008: 42). In light of this, it could be suggested that Monzó's article rejects the instrumentalist view of cultural creation shared by the politics of *resistencialisme* and cultural normalization. 'L'intel·lectual' also mocks the role of the resistant and committed intellectual at the core of normalization owing to the association of Catalan culture with the mission of national building. As such, the piece illustrates Monzó's critique of the elements of cultural normalization that prevent Catalan culture from embracing the postmodernist paradigm.

The negative impact of the resistant and committed public intellectual in auto-nomous Catalonia is satirically portrayed in Monzó's novella 'Davant del rei de Suècia' (*El millor dels mons*, 2001). The plot zooms in on the life of Amargós, a Catalan poet who compulsively fantasizes about winning the Nobel Prize for Literature, an obsession that 'dóna sentit a la vida d'un escriptor' [gives meaning to a writer's life], as the narrator tells us (2001: 145). Monzó's characterization of this writer is highly undignified. Amargós leads an austere and self-disciplined lifestyle but is nevertheless troubled by fixations and compulsions. Obsessed with his own literary posterity and always referring to himself in the third person as 'el poeta', Amargós religiously devotes himself to his oeuvre while avoiding any distractions of the flesh. Through this characterization, Monzó mocks the model of the intellectual as self-sacrificing recluse: 'Haver-se lliurat en cos i ànima a la poesia li ha fet postergar sempre les possibilitats amoroses. [...] Ha après a viure sol, a controlar les pulsions lúbriques i a evitar les situacions que poden fer que aquest control falli' [Since he has devoted himself in body and soul to poetry, he has always had to postpone the affairs of love. He has learned to live solitarily, to control his lubricious desires and to avoid those situations in which these regulatory measures may fail] (2001: 201).

Amargós's fixation with the Nobel Prize serves as a platform from which to criticize the founding fallacies of cultural normalization. If 'L'intel·lectual' exclu-sively focused on the function of intellectuals in the never-ending reproduction of the discourses of normalization, 'Davant del rei de Suècia' revolves around the necessary involvement of the cultural field in this process. One day Amargós receives a letter from one of the nation's most important literary institutions announcing that its board, in agreement with other cultural institutions of the country, has elected him as the Catalan candidate for the Nobel Prize. Despite being the seventh time that Amargós has been nominated for the prize, he cannot help crying, just as he has done on the six previous occasions. The narrator describes how Amargós, although feeling extremely satisfied, is perfectly aware of the minute possibility of his winning the award: 'Tant li fa que, objectivament, les possibilitats reals d'aconseguir el premi siguin minses. La possibilitat, escassa o no, hi és, i amb ella l'opció de somiar' [He doesn't care that, objectively, the possibilities of being awarded the prize are very scarce. Scarce or not, the possibility is there and thus, alive is his dream] (2001: 135). The negligible probability of Amargós's success can be connected to Fernàndez's analysis of cultural normalization as also a fantasy (2008: 355–58). According to Fernàndez, normalization is an impossible dream that has been active since the late 1970s, 'modelant les consciències, estructurant els desitjos i promovent el malestar' [structuring subjectivities, shaping desires and promoting malaise] (2008: 357). The *fantasia de la normalització* is constituted by two unachievable premises: the fantasy of plenitude that intends Catalan culture to be the main vehicle for the expression of a harmonious society in which there are no identity conflicts, and the fantasy of becoming a dominant culture equivalent to that of other European nation states (2008: 358). For Fernàndez, both objectives are impossible to achieve because of the subordination of Catalan culture to the Spanish state, a status quo which the model of cultural normalization does not aim to confront. This national dependence is, in fact, the main reason put forward by Amargós for his reduced hopes. As the narrator recounts, the poet:

> per tranquil·litzar-se, cavil·lava que no era pas culpa seva sinó dels interessos d'uns acadèmics sempre amatents als condicionants polítics. Un condicionants polítics que ja havien barrat el pas a Guimerà. I a Carner. Per aquella catèrvola de robots escandinaus políticament condicionats, el cas de Mistral era tan excepcional com irrepetible. A un Mistral d'ara no li donarien el premi! Sempre n'havia estat conscient. (2001: 143)

> [to calm down, deliberated over the fact that it wasn't his fault, since the decision depended on the interests of a cohort of academics influenced by political factors. Such political factors had already blocked Guimerà's candidature, and Carner's. For that bunch of politically influenced Scandinavian robots, Mistral's prize was an exceptional and one-of-a-kind event. A Mistral of today would not be awarded the prize! He had always known that]

Amargós mentions Catalan authors Angel Guimerà and Josep Carner, both nominated to the Nobel Prize on several occasions, as well as Frédéric Mistral, the Occitan writer who won the Nobel Prize for Literature in 1904. The reference to these three authors and to the political motivations behind the decisions of the Nobel committee are obvious allusions to the train of thought present in Catalan culture which maintains that no Catalan author has ever been awarded the prize because Catalonia is not an independent state (Aliaga 2017; Andreu 2015; Gallén and Nosell 2011; Vilallonga 2017). The emphasis on Amargós's reduced chances of receiving the Nobel Prize seems to be Monzó's way of poking fun at the constant attempts by participants in Catalan culture to promote a Catalan candidate for the Nobel Prize. Such endeavours are typical manifestations of the practices and vocabularies of cultural normalization, as shown in an article in *El País Catalunya* where journalist Marc Andreu relates that ex-President Jordi Pujol 'admets la seva dèria pel Nobel com una fita més de "la construcció d'una Catalunya amb ambició cultural"' [admits his obsession for the Nobel Prize as another milestone in the 'building of a culturally ambitious Catalonia'] (2015). Considering that the Nobel Prize becomes an obsession for Amargós, it could be suggested that the desires, foibles and constant discontent experienced by the Catalan poet epitomize the *malestar en la cultura catalana* resulting from the unsuccessful policies of cultural normalization.

'Davant del rei de Suècia' further develops Monzó's critique of the model of modern intellectual in post-Francoist Catalonia by exposing the constructed nature of their public image, with a particular focus on authorial posterity and disinterestedness. Troubled by the idea that he might die without being awarded the Nobel Prize, Amargós's quest for posterity is also exemplified by his self-positioning in relation to the previous tradition: for instance, he revisits 'els poetes de referència, els que li permeten ressituar-se en la cadena infinita que arrenca dels primers bards' [the canonical poets in order to re-situate himself within the infinite chain which starts with the first bards] (2001: 206). In like manner, he meticulously re-reads the collected letters of two fictitious authors, Berelli and Vilaclara, hinting at the self-constructed image of writers through personal letters. These passages also ridicule the prestige granted to the national canon in the model of cultural normalization. Possibly with a view to being included in the national canon, Amargós writes a personal diary, a genre derided by Monzó in his opinion piece 'Qui dia passa, dietari empeny' (1989), wherein he parodically analyses his own intention to start a diary and wonders what to write: '¿El que he fet *de debò*? ¿El que *de debò* he pensat? ¿O el que m'interessa que la gent cregui que he fet o he pensat? I ¿què m'interessa que cregui la gent que he fet o pensat?' [What I've *really* done? What I've *really* thought? Or what I want people to think I've done or thought? And what do I want people to think I've done or thought?] (1990: 111. Italics in original) Monzó's article constructs a critique of journals, portraying them as carefully designed artefacts disseminated by authors in a clear attempt to intervene in their posterity. The tension between truth and fiction is at the core of the genre, according to Rachel Langford and Russell West, who observe that literary diaries can be considered 'as a mode of production of subjectivity' (1999: 8). Moreover, the apparent spontaneity of literary journals can be seen as increasing the portrayal of writers as geniuses, in line with Pierre Bourdieu's theories on how the literary field operates a series of strategies to maintain an ideology of artistic creation that profiles authors as charismatic figures (1993: 76). By contrast, Monzó's text satirically depicts how the cultural field embraces and promotes authorial strategies of self-aggrandisement, as well as poking fun at writers' quest for posterity.

Journal-writing is not the only literary activity exposed as self-interested in 'Davant del rei de Suècia'. Monzó's novella also reflects on the particular status of poetry in the literary field. Amargós's appreciation of high culture incorporates a regret about the current popularity enjoyed by prose narrative, surpassing that of poetry: 'es preguntava si no s'hauria d'haver dedicat a la novel·la. La poesia era un art que interessava a ben pocs' [he was wondering if he should have dedicated himself to write novels. Poetry was an art that interested only a few readers] (2001: 143). As Bourdieu stresses, poetry is the most elitist written genre and therefore, is not prevalent because it is not addressed to a wider public but confines itself to a small audience, mainly other poets (1993: 47–48). For this reason, however, poetry is at the top of the hierarchy of the arts, whereas the novel occupies a central place in the hierarchy in terms of both its symbolic and economic capital (Bourdieu 1993: 51). By focusing on Amargós's solipsistic rancour, Monzó, who publishes narrative works that have the potential to reach a wider audience, mockingly portrays poetry as an art form detached from society. The text even dwells upon the small number of words required in the art of poetry and the great time and effort that composing a poem takes, thus parodying the pretentiousness and insularity of a literary genre that is far removed from the narrative content of popular cultural products: 'Sovint, però, no hi havia res més que aquell vers durant setmanes i mesos. I, de cop, un segon vers que encaixava perfectament amb l'anterior. Quina alegria aleshores! De vegades Amargós ha trigat anys a confeccionar un únic poema' [Often, however, for weeks and months there was nothing else than that verse. And then, all of a sudden, a second verse which linked perfectly with the first one. What a joy! Sometimes, Amargós has needed several years to write just one poem] (2001: 144). Bourdieu's point that poets form a kind of *'caste'* that registers 'an assurance of an essential superiority over all other writers' (1993: 62. Italics in original) is echoed in Amargós' proclamation that, 'la narrativa no feia per ell, no li permetia enlairar-se tan fàcilment' [narrative wasn't for him, it didn't allow him to fly high] (2001: 144). Through the representation of the dichotomy between poetry and prose narrative, the text satirically points out poetry's marginal position within a market-led literary field, problematizing the division between poetry as pure and disinterested art and prose narrative as commercial and corrupted commodity.

Bourdieu remarks that the values of purity and commitment traditionally associated with public intellectuals are a construction spread by the participants in the field because all cultural practices ultimately seek to acquire authority (1991: 656–58). In Bourdieu's own words, 'the underlying law of this paradoxical game is that it is to one's interest to be disinterested' (1993: 154). Monzó's Amargós precisely exemplifies how authors present their task as based on virtue and compromise, whereas their actual objective is to gain symbolic and material capital. For this reason, the poet reads the cultural supplements of newspapers not to expand his knowledge or simply for enjoyment, but to be informed of how the situation of the field might affect him professionally (2001: 128). The narrator also describes how Amargós, in his quest for the Nobel Prize, 's'ha anat treballant tota una xarxa de coneguts en diverses institucions culturals europees' [has been building a network of contacts in several European institutions] (2001: 135), in what is a clear reference to the central role played by social connections in the field of literary production, however much this is concealed by participants in the field. Similarly, when Amargós reflects on how to review a book published by a colleague, there is not a single mention of the book's merits or weaknesses, only of the different exchanges of symbolic capital between the two authors. The poet aims to write 'una reflexió sincera però no comprometedora sobre un llibre de poemes d'un conegut de l'època llunyana en què havia fet d'editor i a qui no acaba de saber si considerar amic, ni si mai necessitarà estar-hi en bones relacions' [a sincere but non-committal review of a poetry book published by an acquaintance from the old days when Amargós was a publisher; he didn't know whether to consider him a friend, or if he would ever need to be in good relations with him] (2001: 131). Monzó's novella exposes and mocks, in his well-known pungent style, the construction of the 'value of disinterestedness' by writers in an overly self-aware manner. By revealing Amargós's hypocrisy, the text also displays how the construction of an implied authorial identity vis-à-vis the rules of the cultural field rests on a series of performative fallacies, including the feigning of disinterestedness. Additionally, given that Bourdieu describes the rules of the field of literary production as largely implicit or unstated (1993: 72–73), 'Davant del rei de Suècia' can be read as a critical disclosure of the internal rules of the field, a creative stance which could in turn be said to promote an understanding of Monzó's own work and authorial identity as consciously detached from the tacit protocols of the literary field.

6.2. The First Steps of a Celebrity Author: A Postmodern Authorial Persona

Owing to the industrialization of culture, the growth of mass media and the rising influence of consumer culture, 'the celebrity system has now become an integral part of literary culture' (Franssen 2010: 94). One of the key characteristics promoted by the celebrity model lies in the direct relationship between the author's public persona and the audience. For this reason, just as in the case of the new model of public intellectual, celebrity authorship has been connected to the expansion of democratic standards and the pluralism of cultural voices in Western societies (Bauman 1987: 134–38; Cawelti 2004: 50–51). The new situation allows audiences to have a greater control over cultural products by allowing citizens to express their views publicly in a variety of ways, such as mass media consumption, as well as through the more participatory means of social media and blogs. As P. David Marshall puts it, 'the celebrity embodies the empowerment of the people to shape the public sphere' (1997: 7). Despite the fact that the isolation of Franco's Spain delayed the development of such shifts in Catalan culture, the growth of mass cultural products and the expansion of the book industry from the 1970s onwards granted Catalan readers a greater role in shaping the cultural field. Catalonia being a non-state culture, other conditions must be taken into account, such as the perception of culture and the vernacular language as repositories of national identity present both in the politics of *resistencialisme* and cultural normalization. Since the early 1980s, Monzó engaged with the public through innovative means. During this period, he was already publishing regular opinion pieces in daily Barcelona newspapers, as well as taking part in Catalan radio programmes, transcending the borders of written culture. These media collaborations revealed Monzó as a literary author keen to respond to the shifting norms of the cultural paradigm, primarily by crafting an image of his figure and written texts as accessible, open and mundane. Quim Monzó's interdisciplinary authorial persona was a novelty in the Catalan literary system of the early 1980s, still dominated by resistentialist discourses and attitudes.

Monzó began making radio appearances on the newly established Catalunya Ràdio in 1983. Alongside Ramon Barnils and Jordi Vendrell, he presented the late-night programme *El lloro, el moro, el mico i el senyor de Puerto Rico. El lloro* deliberately avoided seriousness, consisting of light-hearted interviews with a wide range of Catalan public figures, such as the author Pere Calders, the journalists Xavier Domingo and Manuel Ibáñez Escofet, the historian Josep Termes, the religious personalities Miquel Batllori and Maur M. Boix and the actor Albert Boadella, among others. The programme also contained a series of comical sketches combining politics, humour and sex, a selection of modern music and the section 'Anotícies de la una', where the three hosts discussed the main news from a humorous, yet critical, angle. The talk show was mainly addressed to a nocturnal audience who appreciated its combination of 'una desinhibida i àgil ironia amb una intel·ligència lúcida i punyent' [a lively and uninhibited irony with a sharp and lucid intelligence] (Filella 2002: xiv). The characteristics that were to define Monzó's authorial persona were already in place: the ironic take on social, political and cultural realities; surrealism and linguistic playfulness; a recourse to the vocabularies of nightlife, alcohol, drugs and sexual freedom; and, finally, an irreverent critique of the cultural and political tenets of Catalan nationalism (the language, the literary canon and the milestones of national history). The programme helped modernize the discourses of Catalan nationalism through self-referential parody and satirical commentary. Journalist Vicent Partal has recently stated that he admired programmes like *El lloro* or *El mínim esforç*, also hosted by Monzó, Barnils and Vendrell, and broadcast by Catalunya Ràdio, because 'ens va permetre descobrir que era possible ser nacionalista sense ser carrincló, i que era possible ser culturalment brillant sense ser espanyolista' [it allowed us to discover that we could be nationalists without being tacky and culturally brilliant without being pro-Spanish] (2013: 152). Partal's words illustrate how Monzó's media participation in the early 1980s was key to transforming Catalan nationalism by adapting it to the postmodernist shift in Catalan society and culture. Furthermore, they illustrate how Monzó's work and public profile were key in problematizing the relatively widespread representation of Catalan nationalism in the 1980s as insularist and parochial (Amat 2015: 329–45; Dowling 2013: 131). Relatedly, Monzó's role as a mediator of Anglo-American culture has been pinpointed as a key element in this process. Radio journalist Jordi Beltran, who worked in Catalunya Ràdio at the time, remarks that Monzó drew upon Monty Python's surrealist humour when creating *El lloro* (2013: 106). As one of the first radio programmes in the Catalan language in the autonomous period, *El lloro* was therefore instrumental in offering a radically new image of Catalan culture, with up-to-date foreign influences adapted to the sociocultural transformations developing in Catalonia. Although Monzó continues to contribute to Catalan radio programmes, *El lloro* has remained his most popular radio contribution to date, acquiring an almost mythical status in the history of Catalan media.

In spite of *El lloro*'s popularity, what launched Quim Monzó into stardom was *Persones humanes*, a late night television show broadcast by the Catalan public television channel TV3 from 1993 until 1996. Monzó contributed to the programme during its first season, which ended just before the summer of 1994. Broadcast in front of a live studio audience, the show was hosted by the journalist Mikimoto, the artistic name of journalist Miquel Calçada, and included humorous round table debates on current affairs and public figures, comical sketches and live music, all conveyed in a markedly irreverent, critical and mundane mode. *Persones humanes* became a cult programme from the very first season, with a young and dedicated audience who stayed up late at night to enjoy the innovative content. At the end of the first season, Oleguer Sarsanedas, Head of Programmes for TV3, remarked that 'el lèxic i les claus del programa s'han incorporat a una franja important de la població catalana' [the programme's vocabularies and perspective have been welcomed and embraced by significant sections of the Catalan population] (M. M. 1994: 51). Monzó contributed a weekly monologue on a variety of topics in his characteristically pungent, defamiliarizing and highly comical style. His carefully crafted, yet seemingly spontaneous speeches, gained him wide public acclaim and facilitated his growing profile as a public intellectual capable of engaging with popular themes (football, sexuality, celebrities) through accessible, non-erudite language. The fact that he was introduced to the audience through a series of deliberately non-distinct labels ('persona física', 'Quim Monzó. Fill únic', 'aficionat al calçots' or 'especialista en el tema' [physical person; Quim Monzó. Only child; lover of *calçots*; specialist on the topic]) detaches his public images from that of the highly specialized intellectual who enlightens the population from a superior stance; in fact, Monzó's section in the programme was sarcastically named 'L'especialista'. Once again, the influence of Anglo-American humour was fundamental to Monzó's public persona, as Monzó himself recognized in an interview: 'la idea de la parodia televisiva, del experto a *máster* en nada no es mía. Es de algún anglosajón' [the idea of the parody TV section, of the expert and master of nothing, is not mine. It was created by some Anglo-Saxon person] (San Agustín 1996: 7. Italics in original). In the 1980s and 1990s, Anglo-American influences came to symbolize and signal the modernizing ethos of Monzó's cultural and intellectual programme.

Monzó's televised monologues endeared him to the audience as an exceptional comic wit. From family relationships and the Egyptian pyramids to education, the colour green and armies and wars, his speeches reinterpreted clichés and shared social understandings from a surreal ironic perspective. Monzó's speech on 23 September 1993 centred on national symbols and provides a suitable case study to explore how his TV participation also boosted the process of modernization of the discourses of Catalan nationalism. In his idiosyncratic deadpan expression, Monzó dissects the lyrics of the Catalan anthem, 'Els segadors', and those of the anthem of the region of Extremadura. He starts with a definition of national anthems as musical pieces upon which a given symbolic function is conferred, normally through means of state reinforcement. He then proceeds to ludicrously suggest that, if a government decided to choose Manolo Escobar's popular and lowbrow song 'El porompompero' as its national anthem and 'posés un regiment d'infanteria formal al costat en senyal de respecte, doncs la gent ja no se'n riuria mai més del porompompero' [put an infantry regiment in formation as a sign of respect, then people would never again make fun of the porompompero] (*Persones humanes* 1993). In so doing, Monzó's monologue hints at the essential constructed nature of all national symbols. Continuing with a close textual reading of both anthems, Monzó observes how the Extremaduran song glorifies the region's lack of industrialization in a way that illustrates how narratives of nation building 'appeal to myth, tradition and nature' (Day and Thompson 2004: 149). In fact, Monzó clearly states that the Extremaduran hymn 'intenta viure del record, d'un passat així mitificat' [tries to live in the memories of days gone by, in a kind of mythicized past] (*Persones humanes* 1993). Subsequently, Monzó pokes fun at the Catalan anthem's image of the 'defensors de la terra' [defenders of the land] cutting off their chains with a sickle and farcically points out the practical difficulty, if not impossibility, of such an endeavour. In his typically preposterous way, Monzó also ridicules the lines 'per quan vingui un altre juny | esmolem ben bé les eines' [let us sharpen our tools well

| for when another June comes] (*Persones humanes* 1993). The sentence here invokes the riot that took place in Barcelona on 7 June 1640, known as Corpus de Sang, an uprising which marked the starting point of the *Guerra dels Segadors* [Reapers' War]. Also known as the Catalan Revolt, it is considered a war of liberation by Catalan nationalists and, for this reason, the lyrics of the modern national anthem written by Emili Guanyavents in 1899 are based on the revolt of 1640. Monzó, however, takes the reference to the month of June in a slightly different manner, to literally mean that Catalans experience adversity annually in the month of June perhaps because that is when the whole of Spain's working population is required to submit the arduous and much feared tax declaration. In this way, Monzó's speech rests on the parodic reappropriation of the stereotype of Catalan thriftiness as well as on the debunking of a highly symbolic image for Catalan nationalism.

In the monologue, Quim Monzó ridicules the symbols and historical mytho-logizations at the core of Romantic grand narratives of nation building. Through the problematization of traditional nationalism, Monzó embraces the mainstream view among scholars that nations, together with their myths and symbols, are socio-historical constructions and are therefore not immutable (Billig 1995; Gellner 1983; Hobsbawm 1991; Smith 1991). The monologue exposes not only the arbitrary nature of national symbols, but also the fact that they are meant to be perceived by national communities as indicators of historical continuity and cohesion, when in fact they are 'spurious and artificial' (Day and Thompson 2004: 89). As Monzó himself sarcastically notes, 'totes les lletres d'himnes, si te les mires fredament doncs són, jo no diria ridícules, sinó una mica pretensioses' [if you read them coldly, all anthems' lyrics are perhaps not ridiculous but a bit pretentious] (*Persones humanes* 1993). Monzó's post-nationalist, anti-Romantic interpretation of Catalan national symbols in prime time on TV3 can be interpreted as a critique of the nationalistic excesses of *resistencialisme* and cultural normalization, as well as a deliberate strategy to modernize Catalan nationalism in general. It is not by chance that *Persones humanes* was welcomed by a young audience eager to forget the oppositional discourses of the past and enjoy a completely different sociocultural and political reality. Perhaps more importantly, however, in paralleling the Catalan and the Extremaduran anthem, the monologue betrays the fact that Catalonia is not recognized as a nation by the Spanish current legal framework, but as a region of the country. Given that 'Els segadors' is generally referred to as the 'Himne nacional de Catalunya' by nationalist politicians, the monologue can also be read as a derision of the unattainable fantasies of the plenitude at the core of Catalan cultural normalization. After all, the Catalan government does not have an infantry regiment and thus lacks a significant symbolic and material structure of power that defines nation states.

The impact achieved by *Persones humanes* in its first year was pivotal in making Monzó a household name in Catalonia. In February 1993, he published the immensely popular and widely acclaimed short story collection *El perquè de tot plegat* and then, from April onwards, he featured weekly in *Persones humanes*. Quim Monzó's books were a massive success in the Sant Jordi book fair of 1994, occurring in the midst of his TV appearances. On April 24, an item in *El Punt* indicated that 'les obres de Quim Monzó van ser les més venudes en un Sant Jordi multitudinari' [Monzó's books were the best-sellers on a massive Sant Jordi's Day] (Riera 1994: 20). The journalist further pointed out that Monzó's literary triumph had occurred despite the fact that the author had not released a new book in 1994, thereby suggesting that the author's media popularity was crucial in effectively sustaining his success with the public. To illustrate this the article recounted an episode in Figueres where 'una ciutadana va demanar tranquil·lament "un llibre d'aquell escriptor que surt a la televisió i que fa riure tant"' [a lady calmly asked for 'a book by that amusing writer who appears on the telly'] (1994: 20). While Monzó's literary activity was the basis of his success as a writer, there is little denying that his contribution to *Persones Humanes* boosted his popularity with the public and, in so doing, helped him sell more books, promoting his oeuvre and Catalan literature in general. This is one of the reasons why Monzó's literature was received by the cultural field as a key normalizing agent. However, this public acclaim rested on a cultural project that moved beyond and openly criticized the discourses of Catalan cultural normalization. The specific characteristics of Monzó's successful literary and cultural project reveal the inherent contradictions of this cultural model.

Monzó's participation in television and his increasing celebrity status activated a debate within the Catalan literary field about the very notion of literary authorship. As Gaston Franssen observes, literary authorship and popular celebrity bring together two 'seemingly incompatible socio-aesthetic configurations' (2010: 92). Franssen indicates that celebrity authors are perceived as detaching literature from long-established notions of distinction and remarks that the division between traditional and celebrity authorship rests on two main dichotomies. First is the long-established perception of artistic creators as disinterested persons, which collides with the logic of profitability at the core of celebrity authorship. Secondly, while old-style authorship capitalized on a dissociation from fame, celebrity authors benefit from media exposure (2010: 92–94). Monzó's particular kind of authorial popularity fits within the characteristics of celebrity authorship and, for this reason, became a cause of concern for his contemporaries in the Catalan literary field, as illustrated by the manifesto 'El Drac es menja Sant Jordi', in which the signatories clearly expressed their disapproval of mass media exposure as a way of propping up literary success. The signatories' misgivings can be explained in that print culture 'has predominantly been regarded as the domain of the educated middle classes, associated with regimes of taste and modes of consumption equated with "quality" cultural experiences' (Turner 2004: 45). There is little doubt that the lady who requested Monzó's book at the Sant Jordi book fair in Figueres does not fulfil such a mode of consumption, thus entailing a loss of distinction that troubles certain authors and critics. The day after the Sant Jordi book fair in 1994, Jordi Ibàñez, lecturer at the Universitat Pompeu Fabra and literary critic of *El País Catalunya* at the time, published an article strongly critical of Monzó's interdisciplinary authorial persona which throws light on the tensions provoked by Monzó's cultural project.

Entitled 'El preu del riure', Ibàñez's article disapproves of Monzó's excessive presence in mass media and blames the Catalan literary system for allegedly being unable to facilitate the professionalization of literary writers, without these authors needing to pursue extra income through activities like journalism and translation (1994: xi). Ibàñez's representation of Catalan culture as defective is indicative of the anxieties provoked by the ideology of cultural normalization. At the same time, the literary critic rejects Monzó's decision to 'fer-se un sobresou com a còmic a la televisió' [get extra dividends as a TV comedian] when he is precisely 'un escriptor de talent positivament reconegut' [a widely recognized author] and 'un dels pocs, per no dir l'únic, escriptor professional de la seva generació' [if not the only then one of the few professional writers of his generation] (1994: xi). Ibàñez attributes Monzó's media appearances to a desire for further income, rather than recognizing them as intrinsic features of his cultural project. Ibàñez's viewpoint reveals the concerns that Monzó's celebrity status triggered among certain participants in the Catalan literary field, where the view that a writer must dissociate their public persona from commercialized culture reigned supreme until Quim Monzó broke this tacit rule in the 1980s and 1990s.

Ibàñez's article explicitly rejects the main features of Monzó's authorial persona, illustrating how this was perceived by some critics as sitting uneasily with the author's literary activity. The criticism rests on a series of dichotomies: seriousness versus comicality; authenticity in art versus banality; intellectualism versus anti-intellectualism. For the literary critic, Monzó's work reveals how 'l'humor fàcil i xaró ha esborrat la via subtil de treball i rigor que conduïa a l'autenticitat en literatura i en art' [simple and tacky humour has come to substitute the subtle and rigorous work which leads to literary and artistic authenticity] (1994: xi). Critical interpretations of celebrity authorship generally link this alleged artistic inauthenticity to a loss of cultural value that defines postmodernist culture (Marshall 1997: xi, 11; Moran 2000: 2–3; Ommundsen 2007: 249; Turner 2004: 5). Accordingly, Ibàñez's dichotomies illustrate the tension between the modern and postmodern model of authorial persona and associated concerns about the loss of distinction. In this new cultural model, the audience feels empowered to shape the public scene and, consequently, celebrities generally 'provide a sense and coherence to a culture' (Marshall 1997: x) or even help construct a community's cultural identity (Turner 2004: 103). For this reason, Ibàñez's article portrays Monzó's literature and public persona as signifiers of the status of Catalan culture ('la imatge de Quim Monzó [...] és una de les postals que reprodueixen més fidelment el paisatge de la cultura catalana actual') and Catalan people ('no hi ha dubte que és un tipus fet a la mida de l'estat anímic del país') [Quim Monzó's image is a perfect postcard to represent the true state of present day Catalan culture [...] there is little doubt that the man fits perfectly with the country's state of mind] (1994: xi). Overall, the article reveals a struggle to impose a cultural dominant in the Catalan literary field of the autonomous period; the anxieties experienced by certain authors and literary critics were based on their realization that what they considered non-literary activities were key in this struggle. For this reason, this negative appraisal of Monzó's media participation should be read in conjunction with the critical trend that presents Monzó's work as banal, which increased during the 1990s (Malé 1997: 162; Ollé 1998: 53; Pladevall i Arumí 1993: 121), coinciding with the growing

impact of Monzó's literary and cultural project. Monzó's critics were concerned
about the transformations that Catalan society and culture were undergoing in the
1980s and 1990s, a series of shifts that they saw as epitomized by Quim Monzó's
cultural project.

The article also criticizes Monzó's media appearances for not incorporating any
socio-political critique, a function traditionally associated with the modern public
intellectual. However, only three months before Ibàñez's piece came out, one of
Monzó's monologues had stirred controversy not just in Catalonia but also across
Spain. Aired on 20 January 1994, the monologue was an ironic account of the
supposed trials and tribulations experienced by European royal families on a daily
basis. In opposition to what the 'gent perversa i antimonàrquica' [perverse and
antimonarchic people] believe, Monzó argues that the Royals, 'no paren en tot el
dia' [don't stop all day long], constantly participating in activities such as 'hípica,
esquí, obres de beneficència, inauguracions' [horse riding, skiing, charitable and
philanthropic work, inauguration of events] (*Persones humanes* 1994). As if this was
not enough, Monzó adds that they are also burdened with the task of delivering a
Christmas message every year, which he describes as 'una feinada que la gent no
valora' [a lot of work which people don't value] (*Persones humanes* 1994). The ironic
intent of the monologue is obvious and needs no further explanation. However,
what made this monologue the subject of a public controversy in the Catalan and
Spanish context was that Monzó was indirectly referring to the Spanish Royal
Family at a time when the Spanish media treatment of the Royals was very cautious.
For instance, Monzó clearly refers to the members of the Spanish Royal Family
when he mentions that 'es veuen obligats a agafar el iot i passar-se tot l'estiu prenent
el sol' [they're forced to spend all summer sunbathing in their yachts] or that they
have to mingle with the common people in the mandatory visit to the winter ski
resort Baqueira Beret (*Persones humanes* 1994). Monzó's monologue uses language
in a very elaborate manner to reinforce the socio-political function of irony: he
deploys the colloquial verb 'pringar' (to get one's hands dirty) to refer to activities
like sailing and skiing and resorts to outmoded class terminology by referring to
the viewers as 'teleespectadors plebeus', to the Royals as people with 'sang blava'
and to the rest of the population as 'obrers' or 'súbdits'. The speech was so badly
received by the Spanish Royal Family that Catalonia's President, Jordi Pujol, had to
publicly apologize on behalf of the public television channel. The episode featured
on the front pages of Catalan newspapers *Avui* and *El Punt* (22 January 1994), and it
was widely commented on in opinion articles and editorials in Catalonia and also
across Spain; it received even more attention when, a few weeks later, Televisión
Española banned the emission of El Gran Wyoming's programme *El peor programa de
la semana* simply because Monzó had been invited on set. This controversy should
also be read vis-à-vis the political and media offensive launched in mid-1993 by
the Partido Popular (PP) to weaken the Partido Socialista Obrero Español (PSOE)
owing to its post-electoral pact with Pujol's CiU. In Paola Lo Cascio's words,
between 1993 and 1995, 'el nacionalisme català havia estat el blanc d'una campanya
anticatalana de desgast en contra del govern socialista' [Catalan nationalism had

been the target of an anti-Catalan campaign to erode the socialist government] (2008: 305).

Needless to say, this controversy boosted Monzó's profile and popularity with both Catalan and Spanish audiences. Monzó's handling of this case of censorship reveals his adept exploitation of a potentially damning situation for greater public visibility. On 1 March 1994, Quim Monzó and El Gran Wyoming featured in a two-page joint interview in *La Vanguardia*. Instead of questioning TVE's decision, Monzó purported to welcome it wholeheartedly, on the grounds that it helped him gain more public notoriety and enhance his sales (Amela 1994: 2–3). Jorge Herralde, founder and director of Anagrama, Monzó's publishing house in Spanish, described the event similarly in a related press conference as a 'descomunal promoción' (Moret 1994). Neither Monzó nor Herralde indulge in what Bourdieu has termed the anti-economic logic of cultural production, instead accepting the reality of the author as an economic product and thus identifying the logic of profitability as an intrinsic part of the literary field. Furthermore, in no instance did Monzó show anger or outrage. Rather, he responded in a flippant and tongue-in-cheek manner, proclaiming that he 'iba a levantarme en medio del programa, iba a sacar una bomba del sobaco (sudada, claro) y hacer volar Prado del Rey [TVE studios]' [was going to stand up in the middle of the programme, take out a bomb from my sweaty armpit and blow up Prado del Rey], as well as playing down the case of censorship by saying 'esto ya dura semanas. Deberíamos darlo por clausurado o empezará a oler [...] Hay que tomarse más gin-tonics y a otra cosa, mariposa' [this has been going on for weeks. We should move forward or otherwise it will start to stink. Let's drink more gin and tonics and Bob's your uncle] (Amela 1994: 2–3). Through such public statements, Monzó appeared as an iconoclastic public intellectual with a mundane authorial image, apparently indifferent to the suppression of his public voice on the Spanish state television channel. Writing about this controversy for *El Punt*, Josep Maria Pasqual stated that, 'Persones humanes sempre ha fet l'efecte de ser el model de programa que un país lliure deu poder permetre's el luxe de fer' [Persones humanes has always seemed to be the type of programme that a free country can afford the luxury of doing] (1994: 12). Pasqual's statement demonstrates that the TV programme, and in particular Monzó's monologues, were perceived as pushing the discursive limits of the main politico-cultural model for an autonomous Catalonia, that is, *la normalització*; once again, his work was received as challenging the consensual normality of post-Francoist democracy in Catalonia. Furthermore, Monzó's reaction to the ban not only illustrates the futility of censorship in the age of mass media, but also how artists can capitalize on such events to increase their fame and public visibility. The outcome of this episode exemplifies how celebrity authors profit from the complex interactions between literature, commerce and the public. As we have seen, Monzó gradually acquired celebrity status over the course of the 1980s and 1990s by engaging with mass media, mass culture and market values through a reflexive strategy of self-representation. In the 2000s, his success and fame only continued to rise.

6.3. Quim Monzó in the Twenty-First Century: A Canonical Celebrity Author

Quim Monzó's work and continued visibility in the Catalan media in the twenty-first century has consolidated his status as the foremost author of his generation as well as the most prominent celebrity writer in the Catalan cultural field. In 2001, Monzó featured on television again when he played himself in the successful TV3 sitcom *Plats Bruts*. In contrast with his monologues in *Persones humanes*, Monzó's performance in *Plats bruts* takes place in the fictional space, in what is an example of the blending of the literary writer and the public persona at the heart of the model of celebrity authorship; in John Cawelti's words, this is 'perhaps the most interesting twentieth-century development in the relationship between celebrity and literature' (2004: 56). Entitled 'Tinc talent', the episode starts with one of the protagonists, Lopes, being asked by Monzó himself to become his ghost writer for a sum of twenty thousand pesetas. Lopes accepts the job and the book he writes for Monzó eventually achieves great success. Later, the episode displays the front covers of *La Vanguardia*, *Avui* and *El Periódico de Catalunya* reporting the triumph of a new book by the famous author Quim Monzó entitled *Quinze contes*, with a cover that follows the famous house style of Quaderns Crema, Monzó's mainstay publisher since 1978. Some days later, Monzó is interviewed on the radio station where Lopes works and the presenter, to whom Lopes has confessed the truth, confronts Monzó and demands that he admit to not having written the text, an accusation which Monzó denies. At this point, the plot enters the realm of the surreal. Author Sergi Pàmies bursts into the studio claiming that he is the real author of the book, only for the novelist Maria de la Pau Janer to follow suit. The presence of these other authors notwithstanding, it is clear that this episode of *Plats bruts* revolves around the literary persona of Quim Monzó, who is repeatedly referred to in the script as 'un dels millors escriptors de la literatura catalana' [one of the best writers of Catalan literature] or with a sense of familiarity as 'el Monzó' (*Plats bruts* 2001). Broadcast in prime time, this TV show illustrates that, at the turn of the century, Quim Monzó had become a cultural brand clearly recognizable for the Catalan audience. In fact, while in *Persones humanes* he performed as the individual Quim Monzó, here he was impersonating a fictional representation of his literary persona.

If the questions of indirect promotion and book sales were considered in relation to the controversy surrounding the Spanish Royal Family, the *Plats bruts* episode confronts the audience with the question of plagiarism, an issue which intersects the debate over authority and authenticity. Similarly, the episode's comical effect rests on the sustained demythologizing of literary creation. For example, after receiving the manuscript written by Lopes, Monzó ludicrously describes the writing process to his editor as 'dues setmanes molt intenses' [two very intense weeks] (*Plats bruts* 2001), mocking conventional representations of literary writing as painful and strenuous, a narrative in which Amargós constantly indulged in 'Davant del rei de Suècia'. The show also ridicules the notion that a literary author has a uniquely distinctive literary voice by having a character deny that Monzó had plagiarized the text because, 'només ell podria haver escrit una cosa així' [only he could have written something like this], while reading aloud some lines from the book (*Plats bruts* 2001). This sentence, together with the title of the chapter, 'Tinc talent', can be read as a parody of the figure of the literary writer as genius.

The episode's final plot twist reveals a case of multiple plagiarisms. Lopes's text, it appears, was in fact an amalgamation of various different sources, including a text that Maria de la Pau Janer confesses to have copied from the writer of popular medicine, Doctor Corbella, who had, in turn, copied it from the author and scriptwriter Maria Jaén, who had based her text on a stolen manuscript by the popular priest and essayist Mossen Ballarín. This spiralling sequence of literary adaptations (and outright forgery) can be seen as a parody of the eminently postmodernist concept of intertextuality and the demise of the notion of the 'original author' (Barthes 1981: 208–13; Foucault 1977: 113–38). There is also an obvious reference to the intermingling of high and mass culture, as the contested authorship of Monzó's *Quinze contes* encompasses a range of different types of writers from the author of bestsellers to that of self-help books. The unassuming conception of literary creation displayed by this episode of *Plats bruts* conforms to the current social perception that the excessive valorization of literary activity 'is seen primarily as a tool for conservative, elitist cultural hegemony' (DeKoven 2002: 105). Accordingly, Monzó's performance seems to oppose the traditional view of literary creation and consumption associated with elitism and distinction, thereby portraying him once again as an outsider in a literary field strongly linked with high cultural production (Crameri 2008: 73–75; Fernàndez 2008: 138, 173). This idea is further reinforced in the final scene: Monzó, Pàmies and de la Pau Janer are reading the cultural section of *Avui*, which presents the event of the radio show as 'una divertidíssima paròdia' [a hilarious parody] masterminded by the three writers (*Plats bruts* 2001). Subsequently, Monzó insists that he dislikes writing enormously and proclaims that he started doing so because it helped him to 'lligar' [hook up] (*Plats bruts* 2001). This conclusion further problematizes elevated interpretations of literary creation and authorship, as well as representing Monzó as a common and unpretentious man interested in the pleasures of the flesh. By doing so, Monzó's public persona challenges the mind/body divide at the core of the Western intellectual tradition.

In spite of his success, in turn-of-the-century Catalan culture Quim Monzó's cultural project continued to have its critics. 2003 saw the advent of the literary group *Els Imparables*, formed by Sebastià Alzamora, Hèctor Bofill and Manuel Forcano, who mounted a merciless attack on the post-Francoist Catalan literary system and advocated a model for Catalan literature based on high European culture and an elitist view of literary creation, as well as on the rejection of mass culture and the rising influence of market values in the Catalan literary field (Alzamora, Bofill and Forcano 2005). Given such a literary programme, it is not surprising that they criticized Quim Monzó's work. After being awarded the *Premi Josep Pla* in 2003 for his novel *L'últim evangeli*, Bofill stated that the literary and cultural project of some of the main Catalan authors in the post-Francoist period was defined by banality and by a 'cultura de la superficialitat' [culture of superficiality] (qtd. in Vila 2003: 56). When asked to name such authors, Bofill mentions Jordi Puntí, Sergi Pàmies and

Quim Monzó. Shortly thereafter, Bofill delivered a talk in Badalona in 2004 and, according to a text published in *Vilaweb*, the author described the Catalan literary fiction of the 1980s and 1990s as 'poc combativa — parapetada molt sovint rera [*sic*] un còmode vel d'ironia, a la manera d'un Quim Monzó' [not very combative — often sheltered behind a veil of irony, à la Quim Monzó] (*Vilaweb* 2004).

Els Imparables's criticisms of Monzó can be analysed from two interrelated perspectives. Firstly, its authors reject the postmodern cultural paradigm embodied by Monzó's work and authorial persona. They are concerned by how it blurs the boundaries between high and mass culture, challenges the traditional representation of the intellectual as a committed public individual, celebrates the marketization of Catalan culture, advocates the gradual distancing of Catalan literature from the realm of the symbolic and engages in mass media participation from a (self-) parodic perspective. Secondly, this younger generation tries to gain power through aesthetic conflicts. Bourdieu argues that aesthetic conflicts are political conflicts for the power to impose a cultural dominant in the field (1993: 101). This is the reason why in the above-mentioned interview, Bofill states that 'aquesta generació dels 50–60 [...] és hora que faci un discurs més elaborat o deixi pas als que venim darrere' [it is about time that this generation of the 1950s and 1960s generates better and more elaborated discourses or makes way for the next generation] (qtd. in Vila 2003: 56). Bofill's words clearly illustrate that these three authors 'cannot make their own mark without pushing into the past those who have an interest in eternalizing the present state of affairs' (Bourdieu 1993: 187). While these authors managed to occupy a position in the literary and cultural system, they did not push Monzó into the past, given that his recognition within the Catalan cultural field continued to rise after these attacks, in particular after delivering the opening speech at the Frankfurt Book Fair in 2007.

Monzó's successful lecture at Frankfurt was not only celebrated by the Catalan cultural system but also by Catalan audiences, who shared and circulated it on social media. In an era dominated by visual culture, his performance on stage was as fundamental as the content of his speech. Monzó's peculiar looks and gestures as well as recognizable voice have proved key to his success: his vocal and physical tics (Monzó was diagnosed with Tourette's syndrome in his late twenties), deadpan tone and fake seriousness have been identified by journalist and TV producer Toni Soler as crucial elements of what he has termed the 'personaje Monzó' (2009: 4). It is not by chance that Monzó's impersonation in the popular TV3 comedy show *Polònia* since 2007 exploits his singular aspect, physique, demeanour and performativity. Monzó's public authorial persona is successful not only because of what he says, but also because of how he says it and how he physically performs it. Admittedly, the fact that he appears in *Polònia* is further proof of his celebrity status in the Catalan cultural system.

Another of the dichotomies problematized by celebrity authorship is the divide between the public and private lives of authors (Cawelti 2004: 48; Moran 2000: 62). In her study of literary celebrity in Canada, Lorraine York observes that this gives way to a blurring of the boundaries 'between privacy or intimacy and publicity'

(2007: 12). Readers' interest in authors' private lives were already a feature of Victorian Britain, when authors began to be interviewed in their own homes by cultural magazines and newspapers. The advent of photography was key to this transformation. Richard Salmon indicates that photographs reproduced the authors, their home, working space and material possessions, thus forging a 'still more radical apprehension of intimacy between literary celebrities and their readers' (1997: 169). If home photos provided a means of enhancing the relation between writers and their readers in the late nineteenth century, their contemporary parallel can be found in television programmes that revolve around a public figure's home. A prominent example of this in Catalonia was the TV3 programme *El convidat* (2010–2015), presented by the journalist Albert Om. In each episode, Om is invited to spend a weekend at the house of a famous person, adopting the role of a guest who accompanies the celebrity on their usual routine in order to show, as the programme website points out, 'l'univers més íntim' [the most intimate universe] of the host (Om 2013).

Following an exceptionally successful first season, *El convidat* visited Monzó in his own home in the opening episode of the second season on 19 September 2011. From the outset, Monzó is described as a distinguished writer, 'un referent del país' and 'un geni del present' [a model and inspiration for the country [...] a genius of today] (*El convidat* 2011). The camera films inside Monzó's flat while Om talks to the author's wife about their life as a couple and the author's personality. The camera reveals shelves full of books and TV series such as *Little Britain* and *The Sopranos*. Towards the end of the programme, as Om is packing to leave, Monzó is filmed reading the English language short story collection *Up in the Old Hotel* (1992), written by *The New Yorker*'s regular contributor Joseph Mitchell. These tokens of Anglo-American cultural influences, together with the fact that Monzó is shown reading a book in English, seem to represent again that Monzó's modernizing project for Catalan culture owes much to the cosmopolitan and worldly cultural influences embraced by his cultural project in post-Francoist Catalonia. Quim Monzó's career is therefore depicted in opposition to a parochial, oppositional conception of Catalan literature which tends to emphasize the local literary tradition in order to highlight the long history and resilience of the vernacular literature. As in other public appearances, Monzó declares his pride in his working class origins, which can be read as another example of his own self-positioning: by so saying, he intends to be perceived as an author who does not entirely belong to a literary system dominated by middle class discourses and participants (Crameri 2008: 23, 30). Monzó's class background and practices are further emphasized by the programme's depiction of his penchant for unpretentious gastronomy, as they are shown having lunch in a popular bar in L'Eixample, Monzó's own neighbourhood, and dinner at a Chinese restaurant. Intentionally funny moments arise when the literary author and TV presenter are seen buying a mattress in a shop: both lying on the mattress, Monzó refers to Om as 'carinyo' in a performative twinkle of homosocial bonding (*El convidat* 2011). In conversation with Om, Monzó confides that he enjoys lying for the sake of lying and that he used to steal novels from bookshops when he was young.

Taken together, Monzó's appearance in the high-profile television programme *El convidat* depicts an image of the author that is far from the old-style intellectual who functions in an elitist and socially segregated cultural field. On the contrary, Monzó visibly capitalizes on his spontaneity and unpretentiousness, his laid-back manners and his ability to enjoy mundane tasks. When asked about his biggest dream, Monzó initially begs Om to avoid that question, before finally answering that, 'la cosa que més s'acosta al benestar és poder escriure, passar-me la vida escrivint' [writing is what makes me more content in life; I'd be happy to spend my life writing], thus conveying a deep love of and dedication to literature (*El convidat* 2011). However, this valorization of writing is overshadowed by his anti-sentimental and anti-utopian nature; by the end of the programme Om defines Monzó as a 'militant de l'escepticisme que no té il·lusions' [militant sceptic with no hopes or dreams] (*El convidat* 2011). Monzó takes this image of a serious writer who is devoted to his work and combines it with that of a sceptical individual who detaches himself from weighty issues through irony and an enjoyment of bodily experiences. Hence, Monzó benefits from a privileged position as a public intellectual while, at the same time, appearing to be the common man, thereby exemplifying how the complex nature of postmodern intellectuals and celebrity culture allows for the combination of diverse authorial images.

Several Catalan newspapers highlighted the programme's all-round success. Watched by an average of 820,000 viewers, it was the second most viewed TV show during the prime time hours that day, with audience ratings surpassing that of the first season (of 722,000 viewers) (*La Vanguardia* 2011). The programme also shone bright on the social network Twitter: the hashtag #ElConvidat and the names Quim Monzó and Albert Om became Trending Topics in Spain (*Ara* 2011a; *La Vanguardia* 2011). Quim Monzó's profile on Twitter displayed a cheeky and playful attitude. Before the show started, Monzó replaced his Twitter profile picture with one of Albert Om and announced that he was going to bed, only to continue to tweet about matters that were entirely unrelated to the programme. After the broadcast ended, Monzó interacted with Om on Twitter and reminded him to give back the books and shaver he had taken. During the programme, Om and Monzó discussed the expression 'fer sexe', vehemently rejected by Monzó on the grounds that it is an unnecessary calque from English — a topic which was also widely debated on social media. Three days later the online newspaper *Vilaweb* contributed to this linguistic debate by publishing the views of authors Joan Olivares, Marta Rojals and Màrius Serra on the suitability of the expression (Cassany 2011). Again, Monzó's public persona is combining different authorial images: on the one hand, he comes across as a Catalan intellectual concerned about the vernacular language; on the other hand, the expression referred to the sexual act, again a bodily experience and a topic traditionally not discussed by foremost intellectuals. Monzó is therefore projecting the image of a modern and up-to-date Catalan public intellectual, who is concerned about the language spoken by the population in their real-life experiences rather than about elevated and formal terms. At the time, Quim Monzó was relatively new to Twitter (he had opened his profile in February

2011) and during the programme he gained one thousand five hundred followers (Gordillo 2011). This string of examples reveals Monzó as a writer who uses mass and social media to raise his public profile, whilst also illustrating that celebrity authors challenge the division between promotion and self-promotion.

Monzó's public momentum after *El convidat* can undoubtedly be connected to his presence on Twitter, possibly the most influential social network nowadays. Thanks to its combination of interpersonal and mass communication, Twitter has become a powerful instrument for the configuration of virtual communities and, for this reason, it is used by myriad personalities as a form of contact with the public. Nevertheless, the use of Twitter by literary writers has also brought about tensions in Western cultural fields. In 2013, the multi-award-winning American novelist and essayist Jonathan Franzen published *The Kraus Project*, in which he strongly rejects the growing presence of technology in human life. Discussing the impact of social media on the literary world, Franzen is critical of the writers who have joined Twitter. Franzen establishes a division between a generation of young authors who, from his point of view, unapologetically use Twitter to promote their work instead of focusing on writing, whom he scornfully refers to as 'yakkers and tweeters and braggers' (2013: 273), and established authors like Salman Rushdie, who have, in his own words, 'succum[bed]' to Twitter (12). It is interesting that he mentions Rushdie, given that the author's use of Twitter has been considered as an example of ineffective literary promotion on social media. As discussed by journalist Nesrine Malik, Rushdie 'frequently tweets cringeworthy and self-promoting material' and 'unblushingly retweeted a link that called him "the most important writer of our time"' (2013). From her point of view, this is not the right attitude for literary authors on Twitter, who should refrain from self-aggrandizement, pomposity and constant self-promotion, and instead develop 'a character and a Twitter profile that is not merely a bludgeon wrought of [their] own brilliance' (2013). Relatedly, in her study of Twitter and social media, Michele Zapaviggna observes the central role played by humour and frivolity in social media interactions (2012: 152). In the case of authors and public intellectuals, where a modicum of inaccessibility and mystique would have been promoted in the not so distant past, the values of exposure, charisma and down-to-earthiness seem to be essential to create a successful social media public profile. These values have been at the core of Monzó's public authorial persona since the early 1980s and, for this reason, his Twitter profile is in accordance with mainstream practices and discourses within this social media network.

Monzó's use of Twitter can be seen as partly re-enacting a postmodernist model of celebrity authorship, in which, paradoxically, the use of anti-authorial forms of public engagement and promotion has captivated most users of this social networking site. Seldom engaging in any form of literary commentary or interaction with other participants in the cultural field, Monzó's tweets are playful and mischievous. This style was visible from the very moment Monzó joined the network, when he engaged in a comical interaction with the Spanish talent-show judge Risto Mejide and repeatedly insulted a more anonymous user (*Ara* 2011c). A week later, he took to retweeting other users' tweets en masse, to the degree that some of his followers complained because the author had annoyingly filled their timeline with random and uninteresting tweets (*Ara* 2011b). Over the years, Monzó's iconoclastic use of Twitter has consolidated a public image that strays significantly from the modern etiquette of literary (self-)promotion. Avoiding self-important solemnity and gravity, Monzó relishes engaging with B-list celebrities and Twitter trolls. The author regularly retweets students in Catalonia who curse at him and his texts, a compulsory element of the high school curriculum. He has tweeted photos of a *caganer* figurine of himself and even links to bizarre pornographic webpages (Marrugat 2014a: 71; Monzó 2013a, 2013b). Despite the fact that he generally tweets his daily opinion piece in *La Vanguardia*, this literary self-promotion is lost in a myriad of random, grotesque and absurd tweets, as well as others discussing regional, national and international politics. Occasionally, too, he has parodied the associated practices of literary promotion in his tweets. In response to a user who interacted with him on Twitter to say that he enjoyed reading one of his books, Monzó wryly replied: '¡Muy bien! (¿Cómo te pasó los 50 euros que te prometí si hacías ese tuit recomendándolo?)' [Excellent! (How do I transfer the 50 euros I promised you if you recommended my book on Twitter?)] (Monzó 2013c). More recently, Quim Monzó has been very active tweeting in favour of the Catalan pro-independence movement and against the imprisonment of its leaders. There is little doubt that Quim Monzó has cultivated an apparently real and genuine personality on Twitter, distanced from traditional images of literary authorship and instead featuring as an approachable author who wears his literary triumph lightly. Thanks to these Twitter practices, Monzó's public image reveals itself again to be in tune with the changing relationship between authors and the public.

In recent years, Monzó's media profile has been further developed through a range of multi-faceted activities. In December 2009, he participated in the eighteenth edition of *La Marató* on TV3, a charity event dedicated to lesser known illnesses, in which he talked about his Tourette's syndrome. In April 2010, he wrote a micro story for the cultural and electronic product retail chain FNAC, which was inscribed on a badge and offered to customers. Since 2012, he has played an active part in the promotion of the Sant Jordi book fair in collaboration with *La Vanguardia* by writing a yearly short story in collaboration with Facebook and Twitter users — the final texts are published in eBook format (*La Vanguardia* 2012, 2013, 2014, 2015). In October 2012, he appeared in a TV commercial for *Banc Sabadell*, where he debunked the commonplaces associated with the notion of 'seny', one of the fundamental discourses of the Catalan national imaginary. In May 2013, he collaborated with the Museu de les Aigües in Cornellà by writing a short story about water scarcity. In September 2013, he played the leading role together with actor Juanjo Puigcorbé in the promotional video of the Via Catalana, a 480 kilometre human chain in support of Catalan independence from Spain, held on 11 September 2013. This short selection of Monzó's media interventions shows that the rules of the contemporary cultural field include the increasing commodification of authorship, a commodification that is textual and visual, as well as digital. Monzó has acutely understood the gradual shift towards the commodification of authorship, while at the same time remaining an anti-establishment figure owing to his detachment from the more conventional rules of the cultural field (i.e. distinction, the anti-economic logic) and his deployment of a public authorial persona adapted to the recent sociocultural transformations in media and communication.

Notes to Chapter 6

1. The retrospective on Joan Perucho, entitled 'El món de Joan Perucho. L'art de tancar els ulls', ran between 23 November 1998 and 6 January 1999 at the Arts Santa Mònica. The enhibition on Josep Palau i Fabre, entitled 'Josep Palau i Fabre, l'alquimista', was also held at the Arts Santa Mònica between 27 November 2000 and 24 January 2001. 'Mercè Rodoreda: La mort de la innocència' took place over the centenary of her birth, between 26 March 2008 and 15 June 2008, at the Palau Robert in Barcelona.

AFTERWORD

❖

2010–2020:
Ten Years that Shook Catalonia

'––Enric González: Si la setmana que ve hi hagués un referèndum sobre la independència, tu què votaries?
––Quim Monzó: Votaria que sí! Claríssimament. El que passa és que amb el cul petit, calculant quins serien els ineptes que ens caurien al damunt aleshores.'

[––Enric González: If there was a referendum on independence next week, how would you vote?
––Quim Monzó: I would vote yes! Without a single doubt. Though without excessive conviction, as I would be thinking about the incompetents we would have to suffer from then on]

Interview in *Jot Down*, 30 August 2012 (González 2012).

This book has offered a genealogy of the tensions and anxieties that have characterized Quim Monzó's interdisciplinary trajectory from a fringe, countercultural artist in the mid-1970s to a canonical literary author with celebrity status in the 2010s. Two interrelated aims have determined my analysis: to put forward a new understanding of Monzó's multifaceted work and contribution to modernizing Catalan culture, and to trace some of the key clashes and contradictions that have defined the interactions between *resistencialisme*, cultural normalization and postmodernist cultural discourses in Catalonia from the late Francoist period up to the present day. Specifically, I have argued that Quim Monzó's literary and cultural programme has been successful and remarkably popular thanks to his destabilization of the nationalist limits and contradictions of cultural normalization from a postmodernist cultural angle. Monzó's work has been characterized by his challenge to the intrinsic link between language, identity and literary production in Catalonia, by a tense and demythologizing relationship with the previous literary tradition from a (self-)parodic stance and by his disruption of the historically established association of Catalan literature with high cultural production. In so doing, Monzó's fluid and ambivalent cultural programme has both subverted and legitimized the previous Catalan literary tradition in line with the parodic postmodern zeitgeist unfolding in the West from the mid-1960s onwards. Paradoxically, Monzó's achievements and popular acclaim have turned him into the main literary success story of Catalan cultural normalization in the democratic period despite his work's tense interplay with normalizing discourses. As in previous times, Catalan culture in the post-Francoist period has been defined by the interrelations and clashes between Catalonia and Spain and, in this sense, I have tried to identify the seldom acknowledged thread that runs through Monzó's disruption of the politics of *resistencialisme*, Catalan cultural normalization and the *Cultura de la Transición*: his critique of their consensual nature from a radically pro-independence stance characterized by iconoclastic and (self-)ironic discourses.

My analyses in this monograph have been based on four key interrelated premises. First, while scholarship on Monzó's work has tended to focus on his post-1978 outputs, I have argued that the specific sociocultural trends of the late 1960s and early 1970s are pivotal to understanding Monzó's literary and cultural production throughout his career. The sociocultural spirit experienced by Monzó in his formative years, reflected in *L'udol del griso al caire de les clavegueres* and in his political cartoons and collages, emerges as key to historicizing the provocative and transgressive nature of his modernizing cultural programme. His parody of Salvador Espriu as early as 1976 and the subsequent clash with Montserrat Roig encapsulates Monzó's tense relation with the Catalan literary tradition, while his political cartooning brings into focus his disagreement with the consensual discourses regarding Catalonia's status within Spain and the subordinate relationship of Catalan culture to the Spanish state. Secondly, I have tried to establish that the interrelations with American cultural trends and political ideologies have been pivotal to the configuration and development of Monzó's intellectual project and its impact on Catalan cultural and political debates. By focusing on the American transnational framework, my book has departed from and challenged the tendency to locate Monzó's influences within the exclusive network of the Catalan literary tradition. As I have shown, the impact of American trends on Monzó's work is overarching and goes beyond the sometimes-mentioned connections between American postmodern authors and his fiction. His work's interrelation with American culture and countercultural discourses, the (re-)location of *Benzina*'s plot to New York, the interplay between his textual production and cultural libertarianism, and his translation of John Barth's essays and James Finn Garner's parody of political correctness all illustrate Monzó's role as an authoritative mediator of American literary and politico-cultural ideas. The relevance of studying Monzó's pre-1978 output and considering the American transnational framework comes into focus when historicizing Monzó's ideological transition from counterculture to cultural libertarianism. Third, by contrast to most scholarship, I have tackled the long-ignored question of the political subtext of Monzó's cultural production. Monzó has generally been received as an author detached from political ideologies and debates because his work and public profile depart from the traditional notion of intellectual engagement. I have contended, on the one hand, that Monzó's trajectory and oeuvre is imbued with political tensions and anxieties and, on the other, that his engagement therewith is characterized by a postmodernist, ironic perspective, highly fluid and polyvalent yet also political. To this end, I have explored the interplay between Monzó's work and national politics (his life-long support for Catalonia's independence from Spain, his caricature of the vocabularies of cultural normalization, his (self-)parodic integration of Catalan nationalism as identity politics in *Contes per a nens i nenes políticament correctes*, his destabilization of Catalan national(ist) myths, his satire of the Spanish Royal Family), socio-political theories (the impact of cultural libertarianism, his unsympathetic view of political correctness) and debates about gender and sexuality. By analysing Monzó's harsh public statements about contemporary feminism vis-à-vis his fictional portrayal of hegemonic masculinities in crisis my book has thrown light upon a complex and often sidelined aspect of Monzó's work and trajectory. As I have argued, the crisis of masculinity experienced by his male characters can be read as the fictional representation of Monzó's disorientation with the changing feminist agenda in post-Francoist Spain. Finally, while studies on Monzó's work have generally focused on his textual production (his fictional texts and opinion articles), I have put forward the idea that his interdisciplinary work in a variety of mediums and mass and social media platforms (his political cartooning, translations, participation in radio and TV and Twitter profile) are key constituents of Monzó's cultural programme and, as such, analysing them is fundamental to gaining a deeper understanding of his intellectual project and the ways in which it modernized Catalan culture. Through this varied body of work, Monzó has disrupted a series of cultural hierarchies, namely, high and mass culture, novels and short stories, fiction and journalism, the textual and the visual, promotion and (self-)promotion, whilst also adroitly fostering the image of an outsider to the Catalan cultural field. Relatedly, I have approached Quim Monzó as a postmodern intellectual and a celebrity author who has deftly navigated the complex interactions between high cultural capital and the popular public sphere in post-Francoist Catalonia to become a thriving, popular cultural brand.

Through each of these lines of inquiry, I have analysed Quim Monzó's work from an innovative critical perspective while also throwing light upon the tensions and contradictions that his trajectory reveals vis-à-vis Catalan cultural normalization. The critical manoeuvres that disregard Monzó's work prior to 1978 or read it as a young and radical stage can be connected to the consensual project of cultural normalization, which aimed to leave behind the politically radical elements of the late Francoist and Transition periods. The incessant description of Monzó's literary and cultural production as neutral and non-ideological is also located within this narrative of cultural and political normality in democratic Catalonia. The cultural discourses emphasizing the sequential connections between Monzó's fiction and that of previous Catalan authors reveal the tendency to construct a continuous, linear literary tradition with a view to promoting a sense of historical and communal Catalan literary identification. The definition of Monzó's fiction and participation in mass media as 'banal' by some critics encapsulates the anxieties regarding the postmodernization of Catalan culture from the 1980s and the associated loss of symbolic capital of literary production in particular and high culture in general. Overall, Monzó's oeuvre brings to the fore the contradictory combination of *resistentialist* and postmodernist elements that has defined Catalan cultural normalization in the post-Francoist period.

In this afterword, I would like to analyse how Quim Monzó's work has responded to the profound political transformations unfolding in Catalonia since 2010, with a focus on his role as a national public intellectual. On 23 May 2020, in the midst of the COVID-19 global pandemic, Monzó published an opinion piece in *La Vanguardia* with the enigmatic title 'Aquest ja no és el meu món', in which the author talked about the cliché press articles about how the pandemic would transform our lives. Specifically, Monzó discussed and made fun of a piece published in the celebrity news Spanish magazine *¡Hola!* on house interior design in the post-COVID-19 world. After this text, Monzó stopped publishing his regular articles in *La Vanguardia*. He had begun contributing six opinion pieces per week to *La Vanguardia* after the 2007 Frankfurt Book Fair but, in 2019, he reduced his contribution to three per week (on Tuesday, Thursday and Saturday). The relevance and central role of his opinion column in Catalonia's most influential paper is demonstrated by its location next to the newspaper's editorial. Monzó's opinion pieces had become a feature of Catalonia's cultural life and the fact that he halted his regular contributions was widely discussed on Twitter as well as in articles by critics and authors, with Mercè Ibarz and Miquel Bonet interpreting it as the end of Monzó's career and by Joan Safont as a well deserved pause (Bonet 2020; Ibarz 2020; Safont 2020). Monzó's pause, however, was temporary, and he resumed his regular columns in *La Vanguardia* from 1 September 2020 –– as he confessed in an interview, he suffered a severe depression during the COVID-19 lockdown period (Camps 2020). Albeit short-lived, the discontinuation of Monzó's articles in May 2020 after more than thirty years of periodic contributions to the press becomes particularly symbolic not only because he did so in the middle of a global pandemic, but more importantly because 2020 marked the tenth anniversary of the landmark ruling on Catalonia's Statute of Autonomy by Spain's Constitutional Court. The tribunal's decision sparked the modern Catalan independence movement, triggering a process which has shaken the foundations of Catalonia's society, politics and culture.

On 28 June 2010, after four long years of deliberations, Spain's Constitutional Court issued a 881-page-long document on Catalonia's *Estatut*, approved in the region by referendum in 2006. Of the Statute's 223 articles, the Court suspended fourteen and curtailed another twenty-seven, including the *Estatut*'s definition of Catalonia's as a nation and the distinctive status of Catalan language above Spanish in the autonomous community. The ruling sparked outrage in the region, where pro-independence feeling had been steadily on the rise since the early 2000s owing to José María Aznar's unionist discourses and policies, the ensuing Catalan Tripartite government with Esquerra Republicana de Catalunya and its pro-independence project and the economic recession which hit Spain heavily from 2008 onwards. On 10 July 2010, a demonstration against the Constitutional Court's ruling took place in Barcelona under the slogan 'Som una nació. Nosaltres decidim' [We are a nation. We decide]. Possibly the biggest march in the history of Catalonia up to that date, the protest was led by the presidents of the Catalan Generalitat and the Catalan Parliament since the recuperation of the autonomy in 1980; this included José Montilla, Pasqual Maragall, Jordi Pujol, Ernest Benach,

Joan Rigol and Heribert Barrera. On the following day, Quim Monzó published a chronicle of the demonstration in *La Vanguardia* entitled 'Indignación y crema solar'. The full-page piece appears next to a photo of an enormous *estelada* hanging from a balcony and, in his distinctive style, Monzó offers a very personal chronicle of what he saw, from the banners reading 'Espanya no vol els teus drets. Treu-te la bena! Digues prou!' and 'Adéu, Espanya!' [Spain doesn't want you to have rights. Open your eyes! Enough is enough! [...] Goodbye Spain] to the teenager who is playing table football with an *estelada*-flag cape in the Passeig de Gràcia's iconic furniture store Vinçon —— 'No es una imagen habitual' [It's not a common image], Monzó adds laconically (2010c: 21). According to Monzó, the court ruling illustrates 'la aversión a la democracia en la que se cimienta España' [the aversion to democracy on which Spain is founded] (2010: 21). Monzó, however, strongly disapproves of the Catalan political leaders' lack of unity and, in another instance of his tense relation with Catalan nationalism, also derides the banal folklore of some demonstrators wearing a *barretina* hat: 'tipos con barretina que degradan a base de folklorismo lo que supuestamente quieren ensalzar' [chaps with *barretina* who discredit with their folklorism the ideas they allegedly want to promote] (2010: 21). With his typically sharp eye, Monzó remarks that the demonstrators' widespread appetite for independence reveals how deeply damaged the links between Catalonia and Spain are. As he puts it,

> Los gritos de "In-de-pen-dènci-a!" son constantes, y al acabar la tarde sólo un sordo podría negar que ha sido el más coreado. Nunca en mi vida había visto tanto hartazgo, tanta convicción de que los lazos con España se han podrido. Nada que ver con el espíritu de la mani de 1977, que visto desde este 2010 parece medio cándido. (2010c: 21)

> [The chanting of "Independence" is constant, and only a deaf person could deny it has been the most popular slogan to shout. Never in my life had I seen such enervation, such a strong conviction that the ties with Spain are strained. It's so different from the spirit of the 1977 demonstration, which from today's perspective seems rather naïve]

Monzó connects the demonstration to the historic, and equally massive, rally in favour of the Catalan Statute of Autonomy under the slogan 'Llibertat, Amnistia, Estatut d'Autonomia' in 1977, during the Transition to democracy. By doing so, his article brings to the fore the long grassroots demand for greater autonomy in Catalonia. Perhaps more importantly, however, by pointing out how the momentum for separation from Spain has substantially increased, Monzó brings into focus the transformations that have taken place in Catalonia between the two historical landmark marches. For many in Catalonia, the Constitutional Court ruling was viewed as an attack against the will of the Catalan people as expressed by its Parliament and later in a referendum. Beyond this, the Court's decision seemed to rule out proposals for further devolution to Catalonia or a federal territorial model within the legal framework of the Constitution. As Andrew Dowling puts it, the Tribunal's 'judgement seemed to close off further opportunities for federalism unless the 1978 Constitution was amended' (2018: 4). However, a scenario in which the Constitution could be amended seems quite improbable given the current balance of party power in the Spanish Parliament. If the Constitutional Court's ruling shut down the chances to develop a federal system in Spain, the massive demonstration on 10 July can be seen as the turning point marking the start of the modern Catalan independence moment (Bambery and Kerevan 2018: 163–66; De Toro 2017: 31–33; Dowling 2018: 5; Marí 2018: 7–11; Partal 2018: 118–24; Vargas 2018: 174–77). From then onwards, as Monzó anticipated in his article, the discourses arguing that independence is the only solution to Spain's lack of democratic credentials boomed in the region.

Less than a year after, on 15 May 2011, anti-austerity protests erupted across Spain, with activists occupying squares and camping out in cities throughout the country; the 15-M Movement, also known as *Indignados*, was born. A reaction to the consequences of the economic crisis in Spain, the *Indignados* protested against high unemployment rates, welfare cuts, political and economic corruption, the rigid two party political system characteristic of the post-Francoist period and the lack of opportunities for young graduates. After three years of economic recession, the 15-M was given generous media coverage in its initial stages and was welcomed with excitement by the majority of the population. This was due, in no small measure, to the movement's heterogeneous and rather general complaints, non-party alignment and lack of hierarchies or clear leadership. During the first days, for instance, the PSOE-led administration and the PP avoided criticizing the protesters and declared that the 15-M demands should be considered by the political institutions (Montesinos 2011; Ruiz Sierra 2011). Izquierda Unida, for their part, stated that the demonstrators 'Son los nuestros' (Anguita 2011), while Unión, Progreso y Democracia pointed to the convergences between the grassroots movement and the party's manifesto (*Europa Press*). The biggest and most influential camps were Madrid's Plaza del Sol and Barcelona's Plaça de Catalunya, known as Acampada Sol and Acampada Barcelona respectively. As happened the previous year with the first Arab Spring revolts, social media outlets, in particular Twitter, were key in stimulating the protests. On 16 May, the tags #15M, #AcampadaBCN and #AcampadaSol became global trending topics. Due to the climate of interconnected worldwide unrest, in no small measure linked to the global effects of the financial crisis and the transnational nature of social media, #SpanishRevolution became the most-widely circulated tag and also one of the movement's recognizable names outside Spain (Varsavsky 2011).

On 19 May 2011, only four days after the protests began, Monzó's opinion article in *La Vanguardia*, entitled 'He aquí la Spanish Revolution', revolved around the *Indignados*. In contrast to his understanding and sympathetic view of the demonstration against the Constitutional Court's watering down of the *Estatut*, Monzó's article criticizes and parodies the 15-M, turning out to be one of the first commentators to publicly condemn the Spanish anti-austerity movement. The article first challenges the expression 'Spanish Revolution', pointing out that the protests are far from being a revolution: 'la Spanish Revolution no va a ningún sitio convincente. Para empezar, porque, más que una revolución, de momento es una acampada' [the Spanish Revolution is not going anywhere. To start with, because right now it's an occupation rather than a revolution] (2011b: 22). Monzó declares that defending politicians is far from his intention and, after this, he raises a number of objections to the 15-M demands, discourses and modes of political organization. On the one hand, he whimsically defines as 'lindo' [cute] their aim to put an end to *bipartidismo* but observes that, 'para eso están las urnas: para votar a otros partidos que no sean los que cortan el bacalao' [this is what elections are for: to vote for political parties other than those in power] (2011b: 22). On the other, he takes aim at their lack of clear demands or proposals, declaring that 'la empanada mental que los campistas exhiben es tan grande que resulta difícil saber qué quieren' [the mental confusion displayed by the occupiers is so great that it's difficult to know what they want] (2011b: 22). From here onwards, Monzó's text deploys argumentative techniques similar to the ones analysed in previous chapters. First, he puts forward a string of rhetorical questions about the protesters' objectives following the *reductio ad absurdum* technique and, ultimately, parallels their critique of partitocracy to a dictatorial system: '¿qué piden exactamente? ¿Qué no haya partidos? Miau, porque cuando no hay partidos es que hay partido único?' [what exactly are they demanding? A system without political parties? Eek, because no parties means a one-party system] (2011b: 22). The article reveals Monzó's distrust of the movement's challenge to established political parties and parliamentary forms of political participation, a stance which can be connected to his critique of grassroots movements and trade unions, as analysed in Chapter 4. Monzó also derides a proposal by one of the political organizations supporting the protest which demanded the nationalization of banks and Spain's withdrawal of the European Union. Subsequently, Monzó focuses on parodying the catchy slogans (banal and naive for some) that characterized the Spanish occupy movement, such as 'Falta pan para tanto chorizo'. The piece ends by reproducing a pair of tweets mocking the *Indignados* which caught Monzó's attention, one poking fun at their apparent over-reliance on the Internet and the other at their immaturity: 'Poco después decía @200bares: "Mamá, ¿me das dinero para la acampada?"' [Shortly after @200bares said: Mum, can you give me some money for the occupation?] (2011b: 22). Taken as whole, Monzó's article combines a critique of the movement's heterogeneity and indefinability as well as a rebuttal of some of its proposals together with a parody of its apparently shallow discourses and ineffective modes of political organization.

Monzó's aloof view of Spanish anti-austerity protests can be read from two different angles. Luis Moreno Caballud views the 15-M as a democratizing movement emerging in relation to new forms of social and digital communication, and which has triggered a 'crisis generalizada de modelos de autoridad basados en el individualismo' [widespread crisis of the models of authority based on individualism] (2013: 106). According to him, the 'politics of the commons' at the heart of the *Indignados* partly explain why established cultural and journalistic figures lambasted the protesters so aggressively, in particular their use of social media as a channel for protest and communication (2003: 109–10). An established author himself, Monzó's line of critique can be interpreted within this frame, focusing as he does on the movement's lack of clear demands, horizontal modes of organization, alleged excessive reliance on social media and disruption of the institutional channels for political participation. Monzó's unsympathetic stance, however, seems to betray a deeper anxiety: the fact that the 15-M was destabilising, even challenging, the agenda of the burgeoning Catalan independence movement by either ignoring the question of the relation between Catalonia and Spain or by depicting Spain's regional nationalisms as ideologies which fostered divisions among the protesters. A movement articulated all over Spain, in its early stages the *Indignados* exclusively focused on anti-austerity protests and aimed to push national tensions aside. Discussions about the use of the Catalan language at the Acampada Barcelona's mass meetings soon appeared and pro-independence activists denounced that it took months of debates to approve a document supporting people's right to self-determination. On 17 June 2011, for instance, *El Punt Avui*'s article on the topic was entitled 'Catalunya, vetada en el dret a l'autodeterminació a l'acampada de Barcelona' (*El Punt Avui* 2011). Josep-Lluís Carod-Rovira, the former vice-president of the Catalan Generalitat for ERC from 2006 to 2010, published a particularly critical piece denouncing the *Indignados*' Spanish nationalist stance which, from his point of view, represented Catalan nationalism as divisive, disregarded the Catalan language in their slogans and did not accept Catalonia's right to self-determination (2011). As Gonzalo Torné sums up, 'que en el 15-M no hubiese banderas desorientó a columnistas veteranos como Quim Monzó, quien, pese a los recortes sociales, solo ha visto en las manifestaciones a estudiantes aburridos y acomodados' [the fact that there were no flags in the 15-M disoriented established columnists like Quim Monzó, who, despite the welfare cuts, only saw bored, well-off students in the demonstrations] (2012: 58).

These two articles by Monzó in the early years of the decade emerge as highly relevant, insofar as they can be seen as anticipating the political clashes and cultural wars between independentism and the Comuns which have defined the 2010s in Catalonia. In the early years of the decade, anti-austerity protests across Spain and the growing demands for independence in Catalonia triggered what came to be known as the 'crisis del Régimen del 78'. This crisis was particularly felt in Catalonia owing to the combination of the Generalitat's demands for further devolution, massive grassroots pro-independence rallies and growing anti-austerity protests (Dowling 2018: 91, 138; Bambery and Kerevan 2018: 174–91). The Catalan independence movement, articulated both institutionally and as a popular movement, was able to capitalize on societal discontent, quickly becoming 'a popular vehicle for anti-system mobilization that went beyond electoralism' (Bambery and Kerevan 2018: 191). From 2015, however, the coalitions set up by the political space of the Comuns in Catalonia (Catalunya Sí que es Pot and Barcelona en Comú) gained institutional power and social influence with a political programme that focused on anti-austerity and which did not give priority to the question of the national relation between Catalonia and Spain. In general, the Comuns proposed a 'federalist' or 'confederalist' solution which aimed to increase the degree of Catalonia's sovereignty without necessarily seceding from Spain. This triggered a deepening division between the Catalan independence movement and the Comuns, given how both aimed to represent the notion of 'rupture' at a time in which the Spanish state was suffering a profound crisis of legitimacy in Catalonia. As Andrew Dowling and Jordi Amat have observed, the rise of the Comuns and Ada Colau was in direct competition with Catalan independentism's monopoly of societal discontent. According to Dowling, Catalan separatism 'faced direct challenge from a movement that sought to embody the new politics. The ending of the monopoly of societal grievance with the emergence of the Comuns resulted in fierce political competition' (2018: 119). Amat, for his part, emphasizes the relevance of Colau's election as Mayor of Barcelona in June 2015, which revealed that 'el independentismo no era la única propuesta política que impugnaba con fuerza el *statu quo* y lo hacía con una agenda que trascendía el pleito territorial' [separatism was not the only political movement which seriously challenged the status quo, and Colau did so with a programme which went beyond the territorial conflict] (2017: 83. Italics in original). At stake was whether Catalonia's independence was a necessary condition for the rupture with the Regime of 1978. In light of this, it does not come as a surprise that, since the mid-2010s, Monzó has aimed to debunk the Comuns.

In the Catalan regional elections of 27 September 2015, the left-wing coalition Catalunya Sí que es Pot (CSQP) gained eleven seats. One of CSQP's MPs was the author and feminist activist Gemma Lienas, who submitted a number of questions to the Catalan Government about the Llei d'Igualtat Efectiva de Dones i Homes in late 2015. The Generalitat answered in mid-March 2016 and one of Lienas's questions about the presence of women in children's fairy tales and textbooks came to public attention after it was picked up by a journalist. On 24 March 2016, Monzó tweeted, 'els contes infantils políticament correctes que demanen @GemmaLienas i @BCNenComu ja són aquí!' [the politically correct bedtime stories demanded by @GemmaLienas and @BCNenComu are already here!], alongside the front cover of *Contes per a nens i nenes políticament correctes* (2016a). His article in *La Vanguardia* on 29 March, entitled 'Els nous contes doctrinals', also dealt with the topic. Monzó discusses how, in the US, the gun rights advocacy group National Rifle Association (NRA) had also published their own rewritings of children tales, in their case, as Monzó tells us, with characters such as Hansel and Gretel and Little Red Riding Hood using fire arms to defend themselves from potential perils (2016b: 22). Monzó closes his article with his characteristic sarcasm, remarking that 'pagaria el que fos per veure al CCCB una lectura pública paral·lela dels contistes de l'ANR i de CSQP, seguida d'un debat entre tots dos grups literaris' [I would pay anything to see a simultaneous public reading of the NRA and CSQP children tales at the CCCB, followed by a debate between both literary groups] (2016b: 22). To express his disagreement with Lienas, Monzó resorts to his translation of Garner's parodic short stories, published more than twenty years earlier and now turned into a symbol of his distaste for the feminist agenda and its attention to representation and language. Furthermore, by mentioning the American NRA, he continues to bring into the debate examples and trends from the US. On the day after Monzó's piece came out, Gemma Lienas published the article 'Contes i nenes' in the magazine *Treball*, associated with the PSUC, in which she discusses the controversy in detail and without any trace of irony, criticising the 'micromasclismes' at the core of the discussion and mentioning Monzó's tweet. Defining him as 'un excel·lent escriptor i un notori antifeminista' [an excellent writer and a notorious anti-feminist], Lienas remarks how Monzó's tweet inspired a large number of Twitter users to ridicule 'la idea de voler que hi hagi no només homes i nens sinó també dones i nenes als llibres que fan servir les nostres criatures' [the desire for our children's books not only to talk about men and boys but also about women and girls] (2016). Joan Coscubiela, who strongly opposed Catalan separatism in his role as speaker of CSQP in the regional Parliament, tweeted in support of Lienas: 'Genial resposta als micromasclismes, camuflats de frivolitat @QuimMonzo' [Excellent answer to gender microaggressions, disguised as frivolity @QuimMonzo] (2016). Lienas and Coscubiela, therefore, denounce Monzó's public stance on feminism and the latter accuses Monzó of being frivolous, which illustrates how certain progressive political sectors receive his overarching ironic perspective in public debates.

If there is one politician who embodies the Comuns's challenge to the Catalan independence project through a federalist/confederalist position regarding Catalonia's status within Spain, it is Ada Colau. In 2015, she asserted that 'no soy independentista. Ni catalana ni española. Estoy por superar las fronteras porque sólo existen para la gente pobre' [I am not independentist, neither Catalan nor Spanish. I am in favour of moving beyond borders, which only exist for poor people] (Landaluce 2015). Monzó's aversion towards such a political stance is illustrated by his public attack on Ada Colau in the summer of 2018. The second half of 2017 was perhaps the most fraught and controversial period of Catalonia's recent history, defined not only by the 1 October referendum and the Unilateral Declaration of Independence of 27 October, but also by the Barcelona terrorist attacks of 17 August 2017. A year later, on 12 August 2018, *El País* published an interview with Ada Colau about how she experienced the attack and its aftermath. The article's heading was Colau's declaration that, 'el silencio era atronador. Lloré muchas veces' [the silence was deafening. I cried several times], with the following subheading: 'Ada Colau, alcaldesa de Barcelona, relata en una entrevista con este diario cómo vivió las primeras horas y días después del atentado' [Ada Colau, Mayor of Barcelona, recounts in an interview how she experienced the first hours and days after the attack] (Piñol 2018). On the day after, Monzó tweeted the text of the heading and subheading alongside three images from the massive demonstration against the attacks which took place in Barcelona on 26 August 2017. The three pictures showed Ada Colau alongside King Felipe VI and Queen Letizia of Spain and Catalan President Carles Puigdemont. Colau appeared smiling in all three images, while King Felipe, Queen Letizia and President Puigdemont were shown with grave, serious faces (2018a). Monzó's tweet had more than six thousand retweets and likes and quickly made it into the news. The controversy became so big that, on the day after, Colau replied to Monzó on Twitter, which, predictably, amplified the controversy further. In her response, Colau contended that it had been an incredibly complex and difficult day, and that those three pictures had been taken at a moment in which 'alguna gent cridava "visca el president" i altra "viva el rey". Una senyora al costat va dir "viva todos pq todos sentimos el mismo dolor" i em va arrencar un somriure' [some people were shouting 'hurrah for the President' and others 'hurrah for the King'. A lady next to me said 'hurrah for everyone because we all feel the same pain' and she made me crack a smile] (2018). Colau concluded her tweet saying 'quina tristor aquest us difamatori @quimMonzo' [your slander makes me sad @quimMonzo] (2018). While Colau had taken twenty-four hours to reply, Monzó answered in a mere nine minutes, tweeting another image from a different moment of the demonstration in which Colau was also smiling, alongside a text that read: 'I aquest altre somriure ¿qui l'hi va arrencar? El càmera? Quants motius per somriure en un moment tràgic...' [And who made you crack a smile here? The camera operator? So many reasons to smile at a tragic moment...] (2018b). Colau did not reply to Monzó's second tweet. Much like during the controversy with Gemma Lienas, two high-profile members of the Comuns expressed their support for Colau on Twitter. David Cid, member of Iniciativa per Catalunya Verds and MP for Catalunya en Comú in the Spanish Parliament, criticized Monzó's tweet, noting that one of the issues which has always provoked contradictory feelings in him 'és veure gent intel·lectualment potentíssima, brillant en el seu camp, dient autèntiques barbaritats' [is seeing incredibly talented people, brilliant in their fields, speaking utter nonsense] (2018). The former CSQP MP Lluís Rabell replied to Cid's tweet saying that this was part of the grandeur and misery of human nature, adding that 'es pot escriure com els àngels... i, alhora, ser un perfecte canalla. La història està plena d'exemples que superen @QuimMonzo en ambdós pols de la contradicció' [one can write like an angel... and at the same time be a real scoundrel. History is packed with examples that surpass @QuimMonzo in both poles of the contradiction] (2018). Beyond Monzó's obvious disagreement with the Comuns, the controversies with Lienas and Colau illustrate, on the one hand, how Twitter has become a key space for Monzó's cultural and political intervention in the 2010s and, on the other, his consolidated status as one of Catalonia's major authors, given how Lienas, Cid and Rabell, though critical of his politics, vehemently praise and commend his writing and career.

Monzó's attack on Colau presents different layers of meaning. By pointing out Colau's alleged deceptiveness, Monzó seems to be critical of her capitalization on emotions in politics and well-known savviness with the press, even to the point of suggesting that her grief is just a performance — a critique of Colau which is not new and which interrelates with myriad discourses about new politics and feminism in 2010s Spain. Beyond this, the war of tweets between Monzó and Colau can be seen as encapsulating the political clashes and cultural wars between independentism and the Comuns during the 2010s. The first three images tweeted by Monzó portray Ada Colau, King Felipe VI and Carles Puigdemont, three personalities who can be seen as embodying three radically different positions vis-à-vis the Catalan pro-independence push. If Puigdemont represents separatism, King Felipe VI embodies the Spanish State. Ada Colau, for her part, claims to hold a middle-of-the-road position, detached from both Catalan and Spanish nationalism. In fact, in her reply to Monzó's tweet, Ada Colau continued to (self-)position herself in the middle of the conflict between Puigdemont/Catalan–separatism and King Felipe/Spanish–unionism, as if she represented a neutral, non-aligned position, more emotionally intelligent and less passionate regarding national(ist) claims, which recognizes the plurinational and plurilinguistic reality of Spain but does not concur with Catalonia's unilateral secession; in relation to his, is not by chance that, in her response to Monzó, Colau pointed out the grief shared by everyone after the attacks regardless of their position in the national conflict, thus hinting at a sense of unity beyond political differences. However, in August 2018, when the controversy took place, the images tweeted by Monzó had an uncanny feeling, completely different from the moment when they were taken. Carles Puigdemont was in exile along with some members of his government, while the remaining *consellers* who did not leave Spain had been imprisoned since early November 2017, joining the Catalan separatist leaders Jordi Cuixart and Jordi Sànchez, who had been jailed in mid-October. Puigdemont had left Spain the last weekend of October, after the Catalan Parliament declared independence from Spain in a largely un-solemn manner on the afternoon of Friday 27 October. A mere two hours later, the Spanish Senate approved Article 155 of the Constitution, granting the Spanish government powers to impose direct rule over the Catalan autonomy. Directly afterwards, Mariano Rajoy's government dissolved the regional parliament and called elections for 21 December 2017. King Felipe VI, for his part, had played a key role in the events of October 2017. His emergency speech on 3 October, two days after the banned referendum which left hundreds of people injured as riot police stormed polling stations, took an uncompromising line against Catalan separatism, notably departing from the neutrality that had characterized the Spanish crown vis-à-vis the relations between Catalonia and Spain in the democratic period. As a result, King Felipe VI was seen under a completely different light by Catalan pro-independence supporters, who interpreted his public address as 'a green light to the Spanish right and far right to mobilize on the streets in opposition to Catalan calls for independence' (Bambery and Kerevan 2018: 213–14). Ada Colau's situation had not changed: in October 2017, she was the Mayor of Barcelona and continued as such in the summer of 2018. In light of this, Monzó's tweeted images seem to become a representation of what he and many supporters of Catalonia's independence disapprove of the Comuns: their apparent middle-ground stance in the national conflict while the Spanish government violently cracked down on the Catalan referendum and dissolved Catalonia's autonomy, with pro-independence leaders either jailed or fleeing into exile, Catalonia's political subordination to the Spanish state emerging clearer than ever. Seen in this light, Monzó's tweet betrays his view that the Comuns's position does not appropriately consider Catalonia's subordination to the Spanish state structures and, ultimately, favours Spain's unity and integrity, which explains why his work and public statements throughout the 2010s have aimed to discredit the political space of the Comuns.

In the 2010s, Monzó has also frequently expressed his support for the Catalan independence movement and, from late September 2017, he has also denounced political repression in Catalonia. He has done so through his regular opinion articles in the press, participation in mass media and also by signing manifestos and contributing to grassroots campaigns. In 2013, for instance, together with actor (and later Esquerra Republicana de Catalunya councillor for Barcelona) Juanjo Puigcorbé, Monzó starred in the Assemblea Nacional Catalana commercial 'L'11 de Setembre tenim una cosa en comú: Fem Via!', which advertised the Via Catalana 400 kilometre human chain for the Catalan *Diada* of 11 September 2013. In the commercial, Monzó and Puigcorbé are depicted as two neighbours who hate each other but by chance come together to join hands in the Catalan Way. They do so unwillingly, though Puigcorbé eventually cracks a smile while Monzó does not. A few years later, in mid-2017, the socio-political situation was completely different. On 20 September, Barcelona saw mass demonstrations after the first police raid against the planned referendum vote. On the day after, a manifesto of around 650 Catalan authors in favour of the referendum of self-determination was presented, with Monzó amongst the signatories, alongside names such as Jaume Cabré, Marta Rojals and Albert Sánchez Piñol. In its headline, *El País* highlighted Monzó's and Cabré's support of the text: 'Cabré y Monzó califican la acción del Estado de "supremacismo apolillado"' [Cabré and Monzó define the State's action as 'outdated supremacism'] (Geli 2017). Entitled 'L'1 d'octubre els escriptors també votarem', the manifesto defended the democratic nature of the Catalan referendum for self-determination and denounced what they considered as the Spanish government's attacks 'contra la llibertat d'expressió i altres drets fonamentals' [against freedom of expression and other fundamental rights] (Juanico 2017). The text closed by calling on Catalan citizens to vote regardless of their preference because 'ara mateix el que hi ha en joc no és només el futur del país. Ens hi juguem també la llibertat d'expressió, la dignitat de ser ciutadans de ple dret' [at stake now is not only the future of the country, but also the right to freedom of expression and our dignity as citizens] (Juanico 2017). The Via Catalana commercial and this manifesto exemplify the modern Catalan independence movement's growing detachment from linguistic and cultural nationalism to favour, instead, notions of democracy, self-determination, diversity in difference and people's right to decide.

As we saw in the introductory chapter, in March 2018, Monzó was informed of the jury decision for the *Premi d'Honor de les Lletres Catalanes* by a hand-written letter by Òmnium Cultural's President, Jordi Cuixart, delivered by the association's vice-President Marcel Mauri. Cuixart was in jail and could not communicate the decision to Monzó by phone call, as had been customary up to 2018. In the press conference, Monzó denounced the imprisonment of Catalan separatist leaders, declaring that, 'és tan escandalós el que fa la injustícia espanyola amb la gent i tan sorprenent l'absoluta complaença amb què mitjans suposadament crítics haurien de respondre que a partir d'aquí no hi ha més coses per explicar' [it's so appalling what the Spanish injustice is doing to people and so surprising that allegedly critical media do not denounce it that there's nothing left to be said] (qtd in Mur 2018).

In spite of this string of examples, Monzó has never embraced the enthusiasm and cheerful energy that has defined the modern Catalan independence movement. Instead, he has shown his support for independence in a tense, demystifying manner, characterized by his down-to-earth pessimism. During the *Premi d'Honor* press conference, for instance, when asked about whether he desired Catalonia's independence, he laconically answered 'a mi em sembla perfecte i jo ho vull, on s'ha de firmar?' [I think that's a great idea and I am totally for it, where shall I sign?], only to then sternly denounce the situation of the Catalan language, which, from his point of view, is 'sota mínims acceptables', heading towards 'irlandització' [below acceptable levels [...] Irishization] (*La Vanguardia* 2018). Monzó's glass-half-empty style, his inability to become too excited about anything –– even his own successes — taps into his postmodernist public persona, detached from passionate national(ist) feelings and emotions. Similarly, he warned that the events of 1 October 2017 would be quickly forgotten:

> Quedarà en la història però passarà un temps i... que la gent no es pensi que això no ha passat mai. Coses així han passat sempre, estem així de tota la vida. Ja eren això els merders dels anys trenta, que no els he viscut. Jo els he après de la gent gran, dels meus pares que m'ho explicaven. Amb això passarà igual. (Serra 2018)

> [It'll be part of our history but time will pass and... people shouldn't think that this has never happened. Things like this have always happened, this has been our historical experience. The troubles of the 1930s, which I didn't experience myself, were already like this. I learned about them from older people, from my parents. This will be the same]

Monzó's reference to the 1930s and politico-cultural interventions in the 2010s illustrate how the interrelations, alliances and clashes between the national and the social question have been strongly intermingled in Catalonia's convoluted history since the early twentieth-century (Amat 2015: 295–300; Dowling 2013: 8–9). Quim Monzó's work and career has offered an excellent case study for some of the tensions and anxieties that have defined Catalan nationalism from the 1970s up to the present day. As a matter of fact, Monzó's discourses in the mid-2010s, during the Catalan push for independence, echo his political cartoons and collages during the Spanish Transition in the mid-1970s. In the 1970s, Monzó denounced political repression and debunked the leftwing parties and organizations that did not support Catalonia's right to independence (the PSUC, the PCE, the CNT); in the 2010s, he has denounced political repression and debunked the Comuns for exactly the same reasons. There are, however, two historical differences between both periods. In the 1970s, Monzó's work came out in the marginal, politically radical magazine *Canigó*, while, in the 2010s, his articles have been published in Catalonia's most influential newspaper and his declarations made in prime time, during the ceremony of Catalan literature's most important award. If Monzó's position within the Catalan cultural system has gone from the margins to the mainstream, so it has the impact and relevance of pro-independence discourses in Catalonia.

WORKS CITED

❖

ABRIL, ALBERT. 1976. 'Quim Monzó, escriptor català', *Canigó*, 17 July, 458: 26

ADELLI, JOAN-ELIES. 2007. 'Transvestisme literari.' *Avui*, 10 December, p. 24

AGUILAR, PALOMA. 2002. *Memory and Amnesia: The Role of the Spanish Civil War in the Transition to Democracy* (New York and Oxford: Berghahn)

——2008. *Políticas de la memoria y memorias de la política* (Madrid: Alianza Editorial)

ALIAGA, XAVIER. 2017. 'El Nobel, un anhel amb lletra petita', *El Temps*, 25 April, pp. 60–64

ALONSO, VICENT. 2003. '*Uf, va dir ell*: d'heures sifilítiques i multicolors', in *Actes del dotzèc Col·loqui internacional de llengua i literatura catalanes*, 3 vols, ed. by Anne Charlon and Marie-Claire Zimmermann, I (Barcelona: Abadia de Montserrat), pp. 409–22

ALZAMORA, SEBASTIÀ, HÈCTOR BOFILL, and MANUEL FORCANO. 2005. *Dogmàtica imparable: Abandoneu tota esperança* (Barcelona: L'esfera dels llibres)

AMARGANT, JOSEP. 1991. 'Sergi Pàmies: *La primera pedra*', *Revista de Catalunya*, 50: 207

AMAT, JORDI. 2015. *El llarg procés: Cultura i política a la Catalunya contemporània (1937–2014)* (Barcelona: Tusquets)

——2017. *La conjura de los irresponsables* (Barcelona: Anagrama)

AMELA, VICTOR. 1994. 'Quim Monzó y El Gran Wyoming: La verdad al desnudo. La entrevista que prohibió TVE', *Revista La Vanguardia*, 1 March, pp. 2–3

ANDREU, MARC. 2015. 'Una literatura sense Nobel', *El País Catalunya*, 22 April, <http://cat.elpais.com/cat/2015/04/22/cultura/1429734129_161843.html> [accessed 15 July 2020]

ÀNGELS, JUAN, ANTONÍ MARTÍ, ALBERT ABRIL, RAMON SERRA, ANTONI REIG, RICARD BALLESTER, DOLORS FUSTER and QUIM MONZÓ. 1976. 'Els botiflers de la Universitat Catalana', *Canigó*, 480: 4

ANGUITA, JULIO. 2011. 'Son los nuestros', *El Mundo*, 20 May, <http://www.elmundo.es/elmundo/2011/05/20/espana/1305911111.html> [accessed 15 July 2020]

Ara. 2011a. '#elconvidat arrenca amb força', *Ara*, 19 September, <http://www.ara.cat/media/convidat-reaccio-twitter-Monzo_0_557344412.html> [accessed 15 July 2020]

——2011B. 'La misteriosa desaparició de Quim Monzó de Twitter', *Ara*, 9 February, <http://www.ara.cat/media/misteriosa-desaparicio-Quim-Monzo-Twitter_0_424157761.html> [accessed 15 July 2020]

——2011C. 'Quim Monzó sacseja Twitter', *Ara*, 1 February, <http://www.ara.cat/media/Quim-Monzo-entra-sacseja-Twitter_0_419358249.html> [accessed 15 July 2020]

ARCHILÉS, FERRAN. 1997. '"... O no serà": 20 anys de nacionalisme polític al País Valencià', *L'Avenç*, 214, pp. 26–31

——2009. 'El "olvido" de España: Izquierda y nacionalismo español en la transición democrática: el caso del PCE', *Historia del Presente*, 14, pp. 103–22

ARÓSTEGUI, JULIO. 2000. *La Transición (1975–1982)* (Madrid: Acento)

ATTWOOD, FEONA. 2010. 'Porn Studies: From Social Problem to Cultural Practice', in *Porn. com: Making Sense of Online Pornography*, ed. by Feona Attwood (New York: Peter Lang) pp. 1–13

Avui. 1996a. 'Els llibres més venuts', *Avui*, 8 February, pp. xiv.

——1996B. 'Sant Jordi 96', *Avui*, 23 April 23, pp. i–xxxii.

AYMERICH, MARTA. 2009. 'Vet aquí...', *Diari de Girona*, 8 January, pp. 2.

BALAGUER, ENRIC. 1997. 'Quim Monzó i la societat postmoderna. *El perquè de tot plegat*, un comentari de text', *Caplletra, revista internacional de filologia*, 22, pp. 81–89

BALCELLS, ALBERT. 1996. *Catalan Nationalism: Past and Present* (Basingstoke: Palgrave Macmillan)

BALIBREA, MARI PAZ. 1999. *En la tierra baldía: Manuel Vázquez Montalbán y la izquierda española en la postmodernidad* (Barcelona: El Viejo Topo)

BALLART, PERE. 2008. 'Diàleg. El vigor d'un sistema literari desvertebrat', in *La literatura catalana en la cruïlla (1975–2008)*, ed. by Isabel Graña and Teresa Iribarren (Vilanova i la Geltrú: El Cep i la Nansa), pp. 213–30

BAMBERY, CHRIS, and GEORGE KEREVAN. 2018. *Catalonia Reborn: How Catalonia Took on the Corrupt Spanish State and the Legacy of Franco* (Edinburgh: Luath Press)

BARBA, ANDRÉS, and JAVIER MONTES. 2007. *La ceremonia del porno* (Barcelona: Anagrama)

BARBETA, JORDI. 2010. 'Papanatas', *La Vanguardia*, 7 March, pp. 20

BARGALLÓ VALLS, JOSEP. 2008. 'Frankfurter Buchmesse 2007: Un balanç literari' in *La literatura catalana després de Frankfurt*, ed. by Jordi Coca, Albert Mas-Griera, Biel Mesquida, Josep Piera, Isabel-Clara Simó, Josep Bargalló Valls, and Jordi Galves (Vilafranca del Penedès: Andana) pp. 47–68

BARKER, PETER. 1992. 'Maintaining Male Power: Why Heterosexual Men Use Pornography', in *Pornography: Women, Violence and Civil Liberties*, ed. by Catherine Itzin (Oxford: Oxford University Press) pp. 124–44

BARRENECHEA, ANA MARÍA. 1965. *Borges: The Labyrinth Maker* (New York: New York University Press)

BARTH, JOHN. 1984. *The Friday Book: Essays and Other Nonfiction* (London: The Johns Hopkins University Press)

BARTHES, ROLAND. 1981. 'The Death of the Author', in *Theories of Authorship: A Reader*, ed. by John Caughie (Oxford and New York: Routledge), pp. 208–13

BASSNETT, SUSAN. 2002. *Translation Studies* (London: Routledge)

BATISTA, ANTONI, and GREGORIO LÓPEZ RAIMUNDO. 1976. *PSUC: Per Catalunya, la democracia i el socialisme* (Barcelona: L'Avenç)

BAUMAN, ZYGMUNT. 1987. *Legislators and Interpreters: On Modernity, Post-Modernity and Intellectuals* (Cambridge: Polity)

BILLIG, MICHAEL. 1995. *Banal Nationalism* (London: SAGE)

BEATTIE, SCOTT. 2009. *Community, Space and Online Censorship: Regulating Pornotopia* (Burlington: Ashgate)

BECKWITH, FRANCIS J. 1994. 'The Epistemology of Political Correctness', *Affairs Quarterly*, 8(4): 331–40

BELTRAN, JORDI. 2013. 'Quan feien *El lloro* notaves que no hi havia un control per part de l'emissora, sinó que era tal com rajava', in *Vint i Ramon Barnils*, ed. by Laia Altarriba (Barcelona: Edicions DAU), pp. 103–09.

BERMAN, PAUL. 1992. 'Introduction: The Debate and Its Origins', in *Debating P.C. The Controversy over Political Correctness on College Campuses*, ed. by Paul Berman (New York: Dell), pp. 1–26

BEYNON, JOHN. 2002. *Masculinities and Culture* (Buckingham: Open University Press)

BIEL, RICARD. 2011. 'Monzó: el que li devem i el que no', *Benzina: Revista d'excepcions culturals*, 54: 5

BLACK, STANLEY. 2001. *Juan Goytisolo and the Poetics of Contagion: The Evolution of a Radical Aesthetic in the Later Novels* (Liverpool: Liverpool University Press)

BLAKE, JIM. 1997. 'Entrevista amb Quim Monzó', *BarcelonaReview.com*, May, <http://www.barcelonareview.com/arc/inter/eqm_int.htm> [accessed 15 July 2020]

BOAZ, DAVID. 1997. *Libertarianism: A Primer* (New York: The Free Press)

BOFILL, HÈCTOR. 2009. 'Literatura sense política', *Avui*, 23 February, pp. 20

BONET, MIQUEL. 2020. 'Després del Monzó', *TarragonaDigital*, 22 June, <https://tarragonadigital.com/el-forum/despres-del-monzo> [accessed 15 July 2020]

BOU, ENRIC. 1988. 'La literatura actual', in *Història de la literatura catalana*, vol. 11, ed. by Martí de Riquer, Antoni Comas, and Joaquim Molas (Barcelona: Ariel), pp. 355–419

——2009. 'Revulsió cosmopolita', in *Panorama crític de la literatura catalana: Segle XX. De la postguerra a l'actualitat*, vol. 6, ed. by Enric Bou (Barcelona: Vicens Vives), pp. 540–601

BOURDIEU, PIERRE. 1993. *The Field of Cultural Production* (New York: Columbia University Press)

BROCH, ÀLEX. 1980. *Literatura catalana dels anys setanta* (Barcelona: Edicions 62)

BROOKSBANK JONES, ANNY. 1995. 'Work, Women, and the Family: A Critical Perspective', in *Spanish Cultural Studies: An Introduction*, ed. by Helen Graham and Jo Labanyi (Oxford: Oxford University Press), pp. 386–93

——1997. *Women in Contemporary Spain* (Manchester: Manchester University Press)

BROWNE, ANTHONY. 2006. *The Retreat of Reason: Political Correctness and the Corruption of Public Debate in Modern Britain* (London: Civitas. The Institute for the Study of Civil Society)

BRU DE SALA, XAVIER. 1987. 'Literatura i literatures', in *Segones reflexions crítiques sobre la cultura catalana*, ed. by Josep Guifreu and others (Barcelona: Departament de Cultura de la Generalitat de Catalunya), pp. 95–116

——1999. *El descrèdit de la literatura* (Barcelona: Quaderns Crema)

BUCH, ROGER. 2012. *L'herència del PSAN* (Barcelona: Editorial Base)

BUFFERY, HELENA, and ELISENDA MARCER. 2011. *Historical Dictionary of the Catalans* (Lanham: Scarecrow Press)

BUSH JR., HAROLD K. 1995. 'A Brief History of PC, with Annotated Bibliography', *American Studies International*, 33(1): 42–64.

CALAFAT, FRANCESC. 1992. 'Tribulacions d'una literatura en expansió', in *70–80–90 Literatura (Dues dècades des de la tercera i última)*, ed. by Àlex Broch and others (València: Edicions 3 i 4), pp. 63–89

CAMERON, DEBORAH. 1994. '"Words, Words, Words": The Power of Language', in *The War of the Words: The Political Correctness Debate*, ed. by Sarah Dunant (London: Virago), pp. 15–34

CAMPBELL, NEIL, JUDE DAVIES and GEORGE McKAY. 2010. 'Introduction', in *Issues in Americanisation and Culture*, ed. by Neil Campbell, Jude Davies, and George McKay (Edinburgh: Edinburgh University Press), pp. 1–38

CAMPILLO, MARIA. 1983. 'Benzina', *Serra d'Or*, 286–87: 57

CAMPS, CHRISTIAN, and JORDI GÀLVEZ. 1998. 'Limiar/Préambule', *Revue d'Études Catalanes*, 1: 6–8

CAMPS, JOSEP. 2008. 'D'Ítaca al Congo: la novel·la catalana dels anys de la democràcia', in *La literatura catalana en la cruïlla (1975–2008)*, ed. by Isabel Graña, and Teresa Iribarren (Vilanova i la Geltrú: El Cep i la Nansa), pp. 93–119

CAMPS, MAGÍ. 2018. 'Quim Monzó, un Premi d'Honor de les Lletres Catalanes en el bibliobús', *La Vanguardia*, 5 June, <https://www.lavanguardia.com/cultura/20180605/444096205098/quim-monzo-premi-honor-de-les-lletres-catalanes-bibliobus.html> [accessed 15 July 2020]

——2020. 'Quim Monzó: "El meu somni és aconseguir fer columnes d'opinió sense opinió"', La Vanguardia, 30 August, <https://www.lavanguardia.com/encatala/20200830/483167638411/quim-monzo-retorn-entrevista.html> [accessed 31 August 2020]

CANALS, ENRIC. 1997. 'Cien mil personas, en el parque de Montjuich', *El País*, 3 July,

<https://elpais.com/diario/1977/07/03/portada/236728802_850215.html> [accessed 15 July 2020]

'Exhort a Canigó'. 1976. *Canigó*, 27 November, 477:11

CAPDEVILA, JORDI. 2004. 'Vuit escriptors denuncien la banalització del Dia del Llibre', *Avui*, 8 May, p. 53.

DE CARA I CASALEIZ, HILARI. 1989. 'La postmodernitat literària: L'obra de Quim Monzó', (unpublished doctoral thesis, Universitat de les Illes Balears, Volume 2)

CAROD-ROVIRA, JOSEP-LLUIS. 2011. 'Indignació espanyola', *Nació Digital*, 16 June, <https://www.naciodigital.cat/opinio/1964/indignacio/espanyola> [accessed 15 July 2020]

CARBÓ, FERRAN, DOLORES JIMÉNEZ, ELENA REAL, and RAMON X. ROSSELLÓ. 2000. 'Pròleg', in *Les literatures catalana i francesa: postguerra i engagement*, ed. by Ferran Carbó and others (Barcelona: Abadia de Montserrat), pp. 5–6

CARDÚS I ROS, SALVADOR. 2007. 'De lo correcto a lo biempensante', *La Vanguardia*, 16 May, pp. 29

CARMONA, PABLO, BEATRIZ GARCÍA, and ALMUDENA SÁNCHEZ. 2012. *Spanish Neocon: La revuelta neoconservadora en la derecha española* (Madrid: Traficantes de Sueños)

CARTER, ANGELA. 1984 [1979]. *The Sadeian Woman* (London: Virago)

CASALS, PAU. 1971. 'Entrega de la Medalla de la Pau de l'ONU a Pau Casals', online video recording, *YouTube*, 6:37, 25 October, 2011, <https://www.youtube.com/watch?v=CMWZEjERlwQ> [accessed 15 July 2020]

CASSANY, ROGER. 2011. 'Tothom a cardar', *Vilaweb.cat*, September 21, <http://www.vilaweb.cat/noticia/3930213/20110921/tothom-cardar.html> [accessed 15 July 2020]

CASTELLS, ADA. 2001. 'Quim Monzó: "M'he adonat que la vida és més amarga" ', *Avui*, 9 February, pp. 38

——2007. 'L'horror nostre de cada dia', *Avui*, 26 October, pp. 45

——2010. 'Monzó es carrega la progressia hipòcrita', *Avui*, 4 March, pp. 36

CASTILLO, DAVID. 1989. 'Gloria in excelsis deo', *El Temps*, 10 April, pp. 68–71

——2010. 'La renúncia a educar ha fet molt de mal', *Avui*, 23 April, <http://www.elpuntavui.cat/noticia/article/5-cultura/19-cultura/161139-la-renuncia-a-educar-ha-fet-molt-de-mal.html?cca=1> [accessed 15 July 2020]

CASTILLÓN, XAVIER. 1996. 'Aglomeracions a la UdG per escoltar els nous contes de l'escriptor Quim Monzó', *Avui*, 10 May, p. 19

CAWELTI, JOHN G. 2004. *Mystery, Violence, and Popular Culture* (Madison: University of Wisconsin Press)

CHRISTIAN, HARRY. 1994. *The Making of Anti-Sexist Men* (London: Routledge)

CID, DAVID (@ciddavid). 2018. Twitter post, 14 August, 'Una de les coses que sempre m'ha generat més contradiccions és veure gent intel·lectualment potentíssima, brillant en el seu camp, dient autèntiques barbaritats. Especialment em passa amb escriptors i escriptores. Aquests dies en xoc seguint el discurs de @QuimMonzo'

CLAVIER, BRENDT. 2007. *John Barth and Postmodernism* (New York: Peter Lang)

CLOUET, RICHARD. 2002. 'The Robin Hood Legend and its Cultural Adaptation for the Film Industry: Comparing Literary Sources with Filmic Representations', *Journal of English Studies*, 3: 37–46

CLOVER, CAROL J. 1993. 'Introduction', in *Dirty Looks: Women, Pornography, Power*, ed. by Pamela Church Gibson, and Roma Gibson (London: BFI), pp. 1–4

COLAU, ADA (@AdaColau). 2018. Twitter post, August 14, 'Va ser 1dia trist i difícil x molts motius. En aquest moment tens alguna gent cridava "visca el president" i altra "viva el rey". Una senyora al costat va dir "viva todos pq todos sentimos el mismo dolor" i em va arrencar un somriure. Quina tristor aquest us difamatori @quimMonzo'

CONNELL, R.W. 2005. *Masculinities* (Cambridge: Polity)

CÒNSUL, ISIDOR. 1989A. 'Ditirambe i elegia d'una erecció', *Avui*, 23 April, p. 59

——1989B. 'Quim Monzó: *La magnitud de la tragèdia*', *Revista de Catalunya*, 32: 153–54

——1995. *Llegir i escriure. Papers de crítica literària* (Barcelona: La Magrana)

——1997. 'Vint-i-cinc anys de novel·la: 1975–1995 (una aproximació)', *Caplletra, revista internacional de filologia*, 22: 11–25

——2008. 'Treure pit', in *La literatura catalana després de Frankfurt*, ed. by Jordi Coca, Albert Mas-Griera, Biel Mesquida, Josep Piera, Isabel-Clara Simó, Josep Bargalló Valls, and Jordi Galves (Vilafranca del Penedès: Andana), pp. 129–42

CORNELLÀ-DETRELL, JORDI. 2011. *Literature as a Response to Cultural and Political Repression in Franco's Catalonia* (Woodbridge: Tamesis)

CORTADELLAS, XAVIER. 2007. 'Ascensors que no funcionen', *Presència*, 2–8 November, p. 26

COSCUBIELA, JOAN (@jcoscu). (2016). Twitter post, March 30, 'Genial resposta als micromasclismes, camuflats de frivolitat @QuimMonzo'

CRAMERI, KATHRYN. 2000A. *Language, the Novelist and National Identity in Post-Franco Catalonia* (Oxford: Legenda)

——2000B. 'The Role of Translation in Contemporary Catalan Culture', *Hispanic Research Journal*, 1(2): 171–83

——2008. *Catalonia: National Identity and Cultural Policy: 1980–2003* (Cardiff: University of Wales Press)

CREIXELLS, EUGÈNIA. 1987. 'Pròleg', in *El lloro, el moro, el mico i el senyor de Puerto Rico*, ed. by Ramon Barnils, Quim Monzó, and Jordi Vendrell (Barcelona: Empúries), pp. 7–8

CRUMBAUGH, JUSTIN. 2009. *Destination Dictatorship: The Spectacle of Spain's Tourist Boom and the Reinvention of Difference* (Albany: State University of New York)

CUCÓ, ALFONS. 2002. *Roig i blau: La transició democràtica valenciana* (València: Tàndem)

CURRAN, JAMES. 2005. 'A New Political Generation', in *Culture Wars. The Media and the British Left*, ed. by James Curran, Ivor Gaber, and Julian Petley (Edinburgh: Edinburgh University Press), pp. 3–36

DASCA, MARIA. 2008. 'La invenció del relat', in *La literatura catalana en la cruïlla (1975–2008)*, ed. by Isabel Graña, and Teresa Iribarren (Vilanova i la Geltrú: El Cep i la Nansa), pp. 121–47

DAVIS, ANDREA. 2015. 'Enforcing the Transition: The Demobilization of Collective Memory in Spain, 1979–1982', *Bulletin of Hispanic Studies*, 92 (6): 667–89

DAVIS, HOWARD. 2009. 'Revisiting the Concept of the Public Intellectual', in *Intellectuals and Their Publics: Perspectives from the Social Sciences*, ed. by Christian Fleck, Andreas Hess and E. Stina Lyon (Farham: Ashgate), pp. 261–69.

DAY, GRAHAM, and ANDREW THOMPSON. 2004. *Theorizing Nationalism* (New York: Palgrave Macmillan)

DEKOVEN, MARIANNE. 2002. 'The Literary as Activity in Postmodernity', in *The Question of Literature: The Place of the Literary in Contemporary Theory*, ed. by Elizabeth Beaumont Bissell (Manchester: Manchester University Press), pp. 105–25

DELGADO, LUISA ELENA. 2014. *La nación singular: Fantasías de la normalidad democrática española (1996–2011)* (Madrid: Siglo XXI)

DÍAZ, ELÍAS. 1995. 'The Left and the Legacy of Francoism: Political Culture in Opposition and Transition', in *Spanish Cultural Studies: An Introduction*, ed. by Helen Graham, and Jo Labanyi (Oxford: Oxford University Press), pp. 283–91

DISKI, JENNY. 2010. *The Sixties* (London: Profile)

DIXON-KENNEDY, MIKE. 2006. *The Robin Hood Handbook: The Outlaw in History, Myth and Legend* (Thrupp: Sutton Publishing).

DOBSON, R. B., and JOHN TAYLOR. 1976. *Rymes of Robin Hood: An Introduction to the English Outlaw* (London: Heinemann)

DOHERTY, BRIAN. 2007. *Radicals for Capitalism: A Freewhelming History of the Modern American Libertarian Movement* (New York: Public Affairs)

DORCA, JORDI. 2013. 'Antoni Martí, la tenacitat d'un cineasta', *Revista de Girona*, 277: 48–50

DOWLING, ANDREW. 2013. *Catalonia since the Spanish Civil War: Reconstructing the Nation* (Eastbourne: Susses University Press)

——2015. 'Political Cultures, Ruptures and Continuity in Catalonia Under the Franco Regime', in *Funcions del passat en la cultura catalana contemporània: Institucionalització, representacions i identitat*, ed. by Josep-Anton Fernàndez, and Jaume Subirana (Lleida: Punctum), pp. 221–39

——2018. *The Rise of Catalan Independence: Spain's Territorial Crisis* (London: Routledge)

DRIEVER, STEVEN L. 1997. 'The Signification of Sorian Landscapes in Antonio Machado's *Campos de Castilla*', *ISLE: Interdisciplinary Studies in Literature and Environment*, 4 (1): 43–70

DUIGNAN, PETER, and LEWIS H. GANN. 1992. *The Rebirth of the West: The Americanization of the Democratic World, 1945–1958* (Maryland: Rowman & Littlefield)

DUNANT, SARAH. 1994. 'Introduction: What's in a Word?', in *The War of the Words: The Political Correctness Debate*, ed. by Sarah Dunant (London: Virago), pp. vii–xv

DUSTER, DAVID. 1996. 'La dictadura del PC', *Revista La Vanguardia*, 23 February, pp. 2–3.

EDWARDS, JANIS L. 1997. *Political Cartoons in the 1988 Presidential Campaign: Image, Metaphor, and Narrative* (New York: Routledge)

EDWARDS, TIM. 2006. *Cultures of Masculinity* (London: Routledge)

EISNER, WILL. 1985. *Comics and Sequential Art* (Florida: Poorhouse)

El convidat. 2011. 'Quim Monzó', online video recording, TV3–Televisió de Catalunya. 18 September, <http://www.ccma.cat/tv3/alacarta/programa/titol-video/video/3687891/> [accessed 15 July 2010]

ENSENYAT, XISCA. 1984. '"Ningú no necessita guanyar-se la vida escrivint"', *Los Cuadernos de Baleares*, 15 July, pp. 11

EPITROPOULOS, MIKE-FRANK G., and VICTOR ROUDEMETOF. 1998. 'Introduction: America and Europe, Fragile Objects of Discourse', in *American Culture in Europe: Interdisciplinary Perspectives*, ed. by Mike-Frank G. Epitropoulos and Victor Roudemetof (Westport: Praeger), pp. 1–14

Europa Press. 2011. 'Díez dice que UPyD coincide con alguna petición del 15M', *Europa Press*, 20 May 20, <http://www.europapress.es/videos/video-diez-dice-upyd-coincide-alguna-peticion-15m-20110520161551.html> [accessed 15 July 2020]

FALAKY NAGY, JOSEPH. 1980. 'The Paradoxes of Robin Hood', *Folklore*, 91(2): 198–210

FALCÓN, LIDIA. 1999. *Memorias políticas (1959–1999)* (Madrid: Vindicación Feminista)

FEATHERSTONE, MIKE. 1991. *Consumer Culture and Postmodernism* (London: SAGE)

FELDMAN, SHARON G. 2015. '"Next to Normal": Toward a Pathology of Public Theater in Contemporary Catalonia', in *Funcions del passat en la cultura catalana contemporània. Institucionalització, representacions i identitat*, ed. by Josep-Anton Fernàndez and Jaume Subirana (Lleida: Punctum), pp. 39–59

FELDSTEIN, RICHARD. 1997. *Political Correctness: A Response from the Cultural Left* (Minneapolis and London: University of Minnesota Press)

FERNÀNDEZ, JOSEP-ANTON. 1998. 'My Tragedy is Bigger than Yours: Masculinity in Trouble and the Crisis of Male Authorship in Quim Monzó's Novels', *Forum for Modern Language Studies*, 34(3): 262–73

——2008. *El malestar en la cultura catalana* (Barcelona: Empúries)

FERNÀNDEZ, JOSEP-ANTON and ADRIÀ CHAVARRIA. 2003. 'Introducció', in *Calçasses, gallines i maricons: Homes contra la masculinitat hegemònica*, ed. by Josep-Anton Fernàndez and Adrià Chavarría (Barcelona: Angle), pp. 9–21

FERNÀNDEZ, JOSEP-ANTON and JAUME SUBIRANA. 2015. *Funcions del passat en la cultura catalana contemporània: Institucionalització, representacions i identitat* (Lleida: Punctum)

FERNÁNDEZ-SAVATER, AMADOR. 2012. 'Emborronar la CT (del "No a la guerra" al 15-M)', in *CT o la Cultura de la Transición*, ed. by Guillem Martínez (Barcelona: Random House Mondadori), pp. 37–51

FIGUERES, JOSEP M. 1979. 'Quim Monsó [*sic*]: reflexions "marginals"', *Avui*, 15 April, p. 19

FILELLA, XAVIER. 2002. 'Uns senyors de Puerto Rico', *Avui*, 14 February, p. xiv

FOUCAULT, MICHEL. 1977. *Language, Counter-Memory, Practice: Selected Essays and Interviews* (New York: Cornell University Press)

——1980. *Power/Knowledge: Selected Interviews and Other Writings, 1972–1977*, ed. by Colin Gordon (New York: Pantheon)

FRANSSEN, GASTON. 2010. 'Literary Celebrity and the Discourse on Authorship in Dutch Literature', *Journal of Dutch Literature*, 1 (1): 91–113

FRANZEN, JONATHAN. 2013. *The Kraus Project* (London: Fourth State)

FRIEDMAN, MARILYN. 1995. 'Codes, Canons, Correctness, and Feminism', in *Political Correctness: For and Against*, ed. by Marilyn Friedman and Jan Narveson (Maryland: Rowman & Littlefield), pp. 1–45

FRIEDMAN, MILTON. 1962. *Capitalism and Freedom* (Chicago: University of Chicago Press)

GABILONDO, JOSEBA. 2002. 'State Melancholia: Spanish Nationalism, Specularity, and Performance: Notes on Antonio Muñoz Molina', in *From Stateless Nations to Postnational Spain/De naciones sin estado a la España postnacional*, ed. by Silvia Bermúdez, Antonio Cortijo Ocaña, and Timothy McGovern (Boulder, CO: Society of Spanish and Spanish American Studies), pp. 237–71

GALLÉN, ENRIC, and DAN NOSELL. 2011. *Guimerà i el Premi Nobel: Història d'una candidatura* (Lleida: Punctum)

GALVES, JORDI. 2008. 'Nous episodis de la mort-viva: Vilafranca 2008, unes setmanes després de la Fira de Frankfurt', in *La literatura catalana després de Frankfurt*, ed. by Jordi Coca and others (Vilafranca del Penedès: Andana), pp. 69–88

GÀLVEZ, JORDI. 1998. '*Guadalajara*: lecture de quatre contes', *Revue d'Études Catalanes*, 1: 107–56

——2001. 'En la flor de la vida', *Avui*, 8 February, p. 80

GARNER, JAMES FINN. 2011 [1994]. *Politically Correct Bedtime Stories* (London: Souvenir Press)

GELI, CARLES. 2017. 'Manifiesto de 600 escritores en catalán a favor del referéndum', *El País*, 21 September, <https://elpais.com/ccaa/2017/09/21/catalunya/1506018616_076203.html> [accessed 15 July 2020]

GELLNER, ERNEST. 1983. *Nations and Nationalism* (Malden, Oxford and Victoria: Blackwell)

GENTIC, TANIA. 2013. 'Between Language and Sound: Space and the Aural in Quim Monzó's *Uf, va dir ell*', *Catalan Review*, 27: 137–55

GENZ, STÉPHANIE, and BENJAMIN A. BRABON. 2009. *Postfeminism: Cultural Texts and Theories* (Edinburgh: Edinburgh University Press)

GILL, ROSALIND. 2007. *Gender and the Media* (Cambridge: Polity)

GIRONELL, MARTÍ. 1995. 'Hi havia una vegada...' *Diari de Girona*, 24 November, p. 36

GLICKMAN, LAWRENCE B. 1999. 'Introduction: Born to Shop? Consumer History and American History', in *Consumer Society in American History: A Reader*, ed. by Lawrence B. Glickman (New York: Cornell University Press), pp. 1–14

GONZÁLEZ, ENRIC. 2012. 'Quim Monzó y Enric González o cómo construir un idioma,' *Jot Down*, 30 August, <http://www.jotdown.es/2012/08/quim-monzo-catala/> [accessed 15 July 2020]

GORDILLO, SAÜL. 2011. '@QuimMonzo guanya 1.500 seguidors després d'El convidat de TV3', *Saul.cat*, 23 September 23, <http://www.saul.cat/article/3721/quimmonzo-guanya-1.500-seguidors-amb-el-convidat> [accessed 15 July 2020]

GRAELLS, GUILLEM-JORDI. 1996. 'La generació literària dels setanta', in *La generació dels setanta: 25 anys*, ed. by Guillem-Jordi Graells and others (Barcelona: Associació d'Escriptors en Llengua Catalana), pp. 11–23

GRAHAM, HELEN, and JO LABANYI. 1995. 'Glossary', in *Spanish Cultural Studies: An Introduction*, ed. by Helen Graham, and Jo Labanyi (Oxford: Oxford University Press), pp. 419–25

GRING-PEMBLE, LISA, and MARTHA SOLOMON WATSON. 2003. 'The Rhetorical Limits of Satire: An Analysis of James Finn Garner's Politically Correct Bedtime Stories', *Quarterly Journal of Speech*, 89 (2): 132–53

GUIBERNAU, MONTSERRAT. 2004. *Catalan Nationalism: Francoism, Transition and Democracy* (London: Routledge)

GUIFREU, JOSEP. 1987. 'Cultura, comunicació i dependència', in *Segones reflexions crítiques sobre la cultura catalana*, ed. by Josep Guifreu and others (Barcelona: Departament de Cultura de la Generalitat de Catalunya), pp. 7–30

GUILLAMON, JULIÀ. 1985. 'Quim Monzó contra el propi mite', *Avui*, 31 March, pp. 5–6

——1999. 'Vida metropolitana: De la contracultura a la Barcelona postolímpica', *Revista de Catalunya*, 141: 112–32

——2001. *La ciutat interrompuda* (Barcelona: La Magrana)

——2002. 'Jamones y escopetas Remington', *La Vanguardia Cultura/s*, 11 December, p. 16

——2004. 'De la contracultura al estupor', in *Splassshf*, by Quim Monzó (Barcelona: Círculo de Lectores), pp. 7–20

——2008. 'Uf, dijo él', *La Vanguardia Cultura/s*, 13 February, p. 5

——2009. *Monzó: Com triomfar a la vida* (Barcelona: Galaxia Gutenberg)

——2013. 'Espriu i Monzó', *La Vanguardia*, 11 April, p. 38

——2018. 'Convèncer per KO', *La Vanguardia*, 8 March, <https://www.lavanguardia.com/cultura/20180308/441345265145/convencer-per-ko.html> [accessed 15 July 2020]

PAU, SANTI and OTHERS. 1976. 'Editorial: "Tecstual". Realització i projecte en procés (i per tant contradictori)', *Tecstual*, 1: 5–10

HAC MOR, CARLES. 1977. 'El gañido de la narrativa al borde de las escrituras', *El Viejo Topo*, 5: 52

HALL, STUART. 1994. 'Some "Politically Incorrect" Pathways through PC', in *The War of the Words: The Political Correctness Debate*, ed. by Sarah Dunant (London: Virago), pp. 164–83

HARVEY, DAVID. 2005. *A Brief History of Neoliberalism* (New York: Oxford University Press)

HAWORTH, ALAN. 1994. *Anti-Libertarianism: Markets, Philosophy and Myth* (London: Routledge)

HERMANS, THEO. 1985. 'Introduction: Translation Studies as a New Paradigm', in *The Manipulation of Literature*, ed. by Theo Hermans (London: Croom Helm), pp. 7–15

HESS, STEPHEN, and SANDY NORTHROP. 2011. *American Political Cartoons: The Evolution of a National Identity, 1754–2010* (New Jersey: Transaction)

HOBEREK, ANDREW. 2007. 'Introduction: After Postmodernism', *Twentieth-Century Literature*, 53 (3): 233–47

HOBSBAWM, ERIC. 1991. *Nations and Nationalism Since 1780: Programme, Myth, Reality* (Cambridge: Cambridge University Press)

HUERTAS, JOSEP MARIA. 1987. 'Oriflama. Entre l'església i la política', in *Tele/Estel, Arreu, Oriflama, Canigó i Presència: Cinc Revistes Catalanes entre la dictadura i la transició*, ed. by Josep Faulí and others (Barcelona: Diputació de Barcelona i Col·legi de Periodistes de Barcelona), pp. 51–76

HUTCHEON, LINDA. 2002. *The Politics of Postmodernism* (London: Routledge)

IBÀÑEZ, JORDI. 1994. 'El preu del riure', *El País Catalunya, Extra Sant Jordi*, 23 April, p. xi

IBARZ, MERCÈ. 2020. 'Quim Monzó. Essencials (9)', *Vilaweb*, 5 June, <https://www.vilaweb.cat/noticies/quim-monzo-essencials-9/> [accessed 15 July 2020]

ILLAS, EDGAR. 2007. 'Short Stories against Barcelona's Urban Transformation.' *Transtext(e)s Transcultures: Journal of Global Cultural Studies*, 3, pp. 84–97

—— 2013. 'Política monzoniana', *El Punt Avui*, 14 October, p. 19

IZQUIERDO, ORIOL. 1992. 'Una autocrítica', in *70–80–90 Literatura (Dues dècades des de la tercera i última)*, ed. by Àlex Broch and others (Valencia: Edicions 3 i 4), pp. 91–112

—— 1996. 'Quantes generacions perdudes...', in *La generació dels setanta: 25 anys*, ed. by Guillem-Jordi Graells and othersf (Barcelona: Associació d'Escriptors en Llengua Catalana), pp. 31–43

JAMESON, FREDRIC. 1991. *Postmodernism, or, the Cultural Logic of Late Capitalism* (London: Verso)

JANICK, VICKY K. 1998. 'Introduction', in *Fools and Jesters in Literature, Arts and History: A Bio-Bibliographical Sourcebook*, ed. by Vicky K. Janick (Westport: Greenwood), pp. 1–25

JARNÉ, ANTONIETA. 2006. 'Del Tardofranquisme (1973) a la victòria socialista (1982)', in *De l'esperança al desencís: La transició als Països Catalans*, ed. by Josep Fontana and others (Lleida: El Jonc), pp. 9–21

JIMÉNEZ LOSANTOS, FEDERICO. 2007. *La ciudad que fue: Barcelona, años 70* (Barcelona: Temas de Hoy)

JUANICO, NÚRIA. 2017. 'Més de 640 escriptors firmen un manifest a favor del referèndum', *Ara*, 21 September <https://www.ara.cat/cultura/Mes-escriptors-firmen-manifest-referendum_0_1873612802.html> [accessed 15 July 2020]

JULIANA, ENRIC. 2014. 'El día que el Partido Comunista dijo sí a la Monarquía', *La Vanguardia*, 9 June, <http://www.lavanguardia.com/politica/20140608/54408780625/dia-partido-comunista-dijo-si-monarquia-enric-juliana.html> [accessed 15 July 2020]

KAGAN, ROBERT. 2008. 'Neocon Nation: Neoconservatism, c. 1776', *World Affairs*, 170 (4): 13–35

KASSAM, ASHIFA. 2015. 'Spanish Ex-Prime Minister Defends Decision to Back Iraq War', *The Guardian*, 2 November, <https://www.theguardian.com/world/2015/nov/02/spain-ex-premier-jose-maria-aznar-iraq-war> [accessed 15 July 2020]

KELLER, LAWRENCE F. 1993. 'The Roots of Political Correctness: Puritanism Revisited, Pluralism Experienced', *Administrative Theory & Praxis*, 15(1): 36–45.

KIMMEL, MICHAEL S. 2005. *The Gender of Desire: Essays on Male Sexuality* (New York: State University of New York Press)

KIPNIS, LAURA. 1993. 'She-Male Fantasies and the Aesthetics of Pornography', in *Dirty Looks. Women, Pornography, Power*, ed. by Pamela Church Gibson, and Roma Gibson (London: BFI), pp. 124–43

KIRKPATRICK, JEANE. 2004. 'Neoconservatism as a Response to the Counter-Culture', in *The Neocon Reader*, ed. by Irwin Stelzer (New York: Atlantic), pp. 233–40

KLEIN, NAOMI. 2007. *The Shock Doctrine* (London: Penguin)

KNIGHT, STEPHEN. 1994. *Robin Hood: A Complete Study of the English Outlaw* (Oxford and Cambridge: Blackwell)

—— 2003. *Robin Hood: A Mythic Biography* (Ithaca, NY: Cornell University Press)

KREHAN, KATE. 2016. *Gramsci's Common Sense: Inequality and Its Narratives* (Durham: Duke University Press)

KROES, ROB. 1996. *If You've Seen One, You've Seen the Mall: Europeans and American Mass Culture* (Urbana: University of Illinois Press)

LABANYI, JO. 1994. 'Nation, Narration, Naturalization: A Barthesian Critique of the 1898 Generation', in *New Hispanisms: Literature, Culture, Theory*, ed. by Mark I. Millington and Paul Julian Smith (Ottawa: Dovehouse), pp. 127–49

LANDALUCE, EMILIA. 2015. 'Ada Colau: "El palacete de los Urdangarin también se debería okupar"', *El Mundo*, 9 May, <https://www.elmundo.es/cataluna/2015/05/09/554d1cf1ca4741c4508b4575.html> [accessed 15 July 2020]

LANGFORD, RACHEL, and RUSSELL WEST. 1999. 'Introduction: Diaries and Margins', in *Marginal Voices, Marginal Forms: Diaries in European Literature and History*, ed. by Rachel Langford, and Russell West (Amsterdam: Rodopi), pp. 6–21

La Vanguardia. 2011. 'Éxito en el arranque de temporada de "El convidat", con Quim Monzó', *La Vanguardia*, 20 September, <http://www.lavanguardia.com/television/20110920/54218728293/exito-en-el-arranque-de-temporada-de-el-convidat-con-quim-monzo.html> [accessed 15 July 2020]

——2012. 'Los seguidores de *La Vanguardia* en Facebook firman un Ebook con Quim Monzó', *La Vanguardia*, 6 June, <http://www.lavanguardia.com/participacion/20120607/54306963103/seguidores-facebook-ebook-quim-monzo.html> [accessed 15 July 2020]

——2013. 'Los lectores de LaVanguardia.com escriben un relato junto a Quim Monzó en Twitter', *La Vanguardia*, 23 April, <http://www.lavanguardia.com/concursos/20130423/54372747384/lectores-lavanguardia-com-escriben-relato-quim-monzo.html> [accessed 15 July 2020]

——2014. 'Los usuarios de LaVanguardia.com escriben junto a Quim Monzó una historia por Sant Jordi', *La Vanguardia*, 22 April, <http://www.lavanguardia.com/concursos/20140422/54406036707/usuarios-lavanguardia-com-escriben-quim-monzo-historia-sant-jordi.html> [accessed 15 July 2020]

——2015. 'La web de *La Vanguardia* se vuelca con Sant Jordi 2015', *La Vanguardia*, 22 April, <http://www.lavanguardia.com/libros/sant-jordi/20150422/54430089153/web-la-vanguardia-sant-jordi-2015.html> [accessed 15 July 2020]

——2018. 'L'escriptor Quim Monzó rep el 50è Premi d'Honor de les Lletres Catalanes', *La Vanguardia*, 7 March, <https://www.lavanguardia.com/vida/20180307/441333758585/lescriptor-quim-monzo-rep-el-50e-premi-dhonor-de-les-lletres-catalanes.html> [accessed 20 July 2020]

LIENAS, GEMMA. 2016. 'De contes i nenes', *Treball, revista de reflexió i crítica política d'esquerres, ecologista i feminista*, 30 March <http://revistatreball.cat/de-contes-i-de-nenes/> [accessed 15 July 2020]

LLADONOSA, MANEL. 2006. 'Cultura, història i antifranquisme', in *De l'esperança al desencís: La transició als Països Catalans*, ed. by Josep Fontana and others (Lleida: El Jonc), pp. 23–48

LO CASCIO, PAOLA. 2008. *Nacionalisme i autogovern: Catalunya, 1980–2003* (Catarroja: Afers)

LODGE, DAVID. 1992. *The Art of Fiction* (London: Penguin)

LÓPEZ CRESPÍ, MIQUEL. 2001. *No era això: Memòria política de la Transició* (Lleida: El Jonc)

LUNATI, MONTSERRAT. 1999. 'Quim Monzó i el cànon occidental: una lectura de "Pigmalió"', *Journal of Catalan Studies*, 2 <http://www.uoc.edu/jocs/2/articles/lunati/> [accessed 15 July 2020]

——2008. 'Collage o trencadís: Quim Monzó, un flâneur a Barcelona', in *Poètiques de Ruptura*, ed. by Maria Muntaner, Mercè Picornell, Margalida Pons, and Josep Antoni Reynés (Palma: Lleonard Muntaner), pp. 217–39

M. M. 1994. 'Mikimoto participa com a "megahereu" en l'última edició de *Persones Humanes*', *Avui*, 14 April, p. 51

McGIRR, LISA. 2001. *Suburban Warriors: The Origins of the New American Right* (Princeton: Princeton University Press)

MACHADO, ANTONIO. 1997 [1912]. *Poesías completas* (Madrid: Espasa Calpe)

MACHAN, TIBOR R. 2001. 'Libertarian Justice', in *Social and Political Philosophy: Contemporary Perspectives*, ed. by James P. Sterba (London: Routledge), pp. 93–114

MacINNES, JOHN. 1998. *The End of Masculinity* (Buckingham: Open University Press)

MAINA, GIOVANNA. 2009. 'Pornscapes: Re-Enacting Porn Film in the Landscapes of Contemporary Pornography', *Cinema&Cie, International Film Studies Journal*, 9 (12): pp. 127–32

MAESTRE BROTONS, ANTONI. 2006. *Humor i persuasió: L'obra periodística de Quim Monzó* (Alacant: Universitat d'Alacant)

——2007. 'Quim Monzó contra el tòpic', in *La projecció social de l'escriptor en la literatura catalana contemporània*, ed. by Ramon Panyella (Barcelona: Punctum and Grup d'Estudis de Literatura Catalana Contemporània), pp. 595–604

——2008. 'Cretins sense fronteres: paral·lelismes en l'articulisme de Monzó i Fruttero & Lucentini', in *Atti del IX Congresso internazionale della Associazione Italiana di Studi Catalani: La Catalogna in Europa, l'Europa in Catalogna. Transiti, passaggi, traduzioni*, <http://www.filmod.unina.it/aisc/attive/Maestre.pdf> [accessed 15 July 2020]

——2010. 'Experimentalisme i contracultura en *L'udol del griso al caire de les clavegueres* de Quim Monzó', in *Transformacions: Llenguatges teòrics i relacions interartístiques* (1975–2000), ed. by Maria Muntaner and others (Barcelona: Abadia de Montserrat), pp. 235–61

——2011. 'Zombie Language: The Parody of Newspaper Columns in Quim Monzó's Radio Commentaries', *Catalan Journal of Communication and Cultural Studies*, 3 (1): 63–78

——2012A. *Essències d'estil: Aproximació a la narrativa breu de Sergi Pàmies* (Alacant: Publicacions de la Universitat d'Alacant)

——2012B. 'La narrativa experimental de Quim Monzó', in *Literatura catalana del segle XX i de l'actualitat*, ed. by Eberhard Geisler (Frankfurt: Peter Lang), pp. 99–116

——2012C. 'Splassshf: còmic i experimentació narrativa', *Ítaca, Revista de Filologia*, 3: 149–77

——2015. 'Els residus de la Transició: abjecció, trauma i adaptació', *Journal of Iberian and Latin American Studies*, 21 (1): 39–54

MALIK, NESRINE. 2013. 'Twitter and the (Not So) Subtle Art of Literary Self-Promotion', *The Guardian*, 12 March, <http://www.theguardian.com/commentisfree/2013/mar/12/mohsin-hamid-twitter-self-promotion> [accessed 15 July 2020]

MALÉ, JORDI. 1997. 'Quim Monzó: Guadalajara', *Revista de Catalunya*, 115: 159–62

MARCO, JOSÉ MARÍA. 2005. 'Conservadoras, liberales y neoconservadoras: Fundamentos morales de una sociedad libre', *Cuadernos de pensamiento político*, 8: 129–40

MARCOS, PILAR. 2003. 'El 91% de los españoles rechaza la intervención militar en Irak, según el CIS' *El País*, 28 March, <http://elpais.com/diario/2003/03/28/espana/1048806001_850215.html> [accessed 15 July 2020]

MARCUS, STEVEN. 1970 [1964]. *The Other Victorians: A Study of Sexuality and Pornography in Mid-Nineteenth Century England* (London: Book Club Associates)

Els Marges. 1983. 'Presentació', *Els Marges*, 27/28/29: 3–4

MARÍ, ISIDOR. 2018. 'Pròleg', in *El procés català amb ulls mallorquins*, by Pere Sampol Mas (Palma: Lleonard Editor), pp. 7–11

MARRUGAT, JORDI. 2008. 'Armand Obiols i la configuració del Grup de Sabadell (1918–1928)', *Els Marges*, 85: 17–51

——2014A. 'L'escriptor català: de la televisió al Twitter (passant per l'hipertext, l'SMS, Bluetooth i Facebook)', in *Les tecnologies digitals en la producció literària*, ed. by Germà Colón Domènech, and Santiago Fortuny Llorens (Castelló: Publicacions de la Universitat Jaume I), pp. 37–74

——2014B. *Narrativa catalana de la postmodernitat: Històries, formes i motius* (Barcelona: Publicacions de la Universitat de Barcelona)

MARSHALL, P. DAVID. 1997. *Celebrity and Power: Fame in Contemporary Culture* (Minnesota: University of Minnesota Press)

MARTÍNEZ, GUILLEM. 2012. 'El concepto CT', in *CT o la Cultura de la Transición*, ed. by Guillem Martínez (Barcelona: Random House Mondadori), pp. 13–23

MARTÍ-OLIVELLA, JAUME. 1982. 'Quim Monzó o la contraescriptura generacional', in *Actes del Tercer Col·loqui d'Estudis Catalans a Nord-Amèrica* (Barcelona: Abadia de Montserrat), pp. 249–60

MARTÍN GARCÍA, OSCAR J., and FRANCISCO J. MARTÍN RODRÍGUEZ. 2013. '¿Seducidos por el inglés? Diplomacia pública angloamericana y difusión de la lengua inglesa en España, 1959–1975', *Historia y Política*, 29: 301–30

MASANÉS, CRISTINA. 2001. 'Qui és l'amo de les paraules?', *El Punt*, 21 December, pp. 27

MAURICI I FRADES, MAGDALENA. 1977. 'Quim Monzó: *L'udol del griso al caire de les clavegueres*', *Canigó*, 512: 35.

MCCAFFERY, LARRY. 1982. *The Metafictional Muse: The Works of Robert Coover, Donald Barthelme and William H. Gass* (Pittsburgh: University of Pittsburgh Press).

MCGLADE, RHIANNON. 2016. *Catalan Cartoons: A Cultural and Political History* (Cardiff: University of Wales Press)

MEDHURST, MARTIN J., and MICHAEL A. DESOUSA. 1981. 'Political Cartoons as Rhetorical Form: A Taxonomy of Graphic Discourse', *Communication Monographs*, 48: 197–236

MERINO, IMMA. 1989. 'Quim Monzó és el triomfador en les vendes del primer dia del llibre', *El Punt*, 23 April, p. 3.

MEROÑO I CADENA, PERE. 2011. *Canigó: Setmanari independent dels Països Catalans* (Barcelona: Abadia de Montserrat)

MILLAS, JAIME. 1976. 'Multa a una librería valenciana', *El País*, 6 November, <https://elpais.com/diario/1976/11/05/cultura/215996403_850215.html> [accessed 15 July 2020]

MINCHINELA, RAÚL. 2012. 'La CT y la cultura digital: cómo dar la espalda a internet', in *CT o la Cultura de la Transición*, ed. by Guillem Martínez (Barcelona: Random House Mondadori), pp. 151–60

MIRALLES, GUILLEM. 2004. 'No he escrit mai perquè somiés ser un escriptor', *Paper de Vidre*, 27, <http://www.traces.uab.es/tracesbd/pdv/2004/pdv_a2004m9d23n27p5.pdf> [accessed 15 July 2020]

MOLAS, JOAQUIM. 1983. 'La cultura catalana i la seva estratificació', in *Reflexions crítiques sobre la cultura catalana*, ed. by Pierre Vilar and others (Barcelona: Departament de Cultura de la Generalitat de Catalunya), pp. 131–55

MOLINER, EMPAR. 2008. 'Las y los ratas y ratos', *El País*, 7 April, <http://elpais.com/diario/2008/04/07/catalunya/1207530442_850215.html> [accessed 15 July 2020]

MOLINERO, CARME, and PERE YSÀS. 2014. *La cuestión catalana: Cataluña en la transición española* (Barcelona: Crítica)

MONZÓ, QUIM. 1974. 'Un domingo por la mañana', translated from the Catalan by Toni Puig, *Ajoblanco*, 2, pp. 24–25

—— 1976A. 'A Madrid fan dissabte', *Canigó*, 468: n.p.

—— 1976B. 'A propòsit d'"Espriu, vexat"', *Arreu, setmanari d'informació general de Catalunya*, 6, November 29–December 5: 34

—— 1976C. 'Capítol de novel·la', *Tecstual*, 1: 80–94

—— 1976D. *L'udol del griso al caire de les clavegueres* (Barcelona: Edicions 62)

—— 1976E. 'Prohibit el Dia del País Valencià', *Canigó*, 471: 9

—— 1976F. 'Setè atemptat a "Tres i Quatre"', *Canigó*, 475: 6

—— 1976G. 'Us treiem en Villa', *Canigó*, 479: 7

—— 1976–1977. 'Lorem Ipsum Dolor Sit Amet', *Qwert Poiuy: Revista de Literatura*, 10–11: 135–36

—— 1977A. 'Amor quotidià', *Pol·len d'Entrecuix*, 2: n.p.

—— 1977B. 'Don José Peirats, anarcolerrouxista i de les J.O.N.S', *Canigó*, 509: 17

—— 1977C. 'Madrid la nuit', *Canigó*, 485: 14

—— 1977D. 'Zaaaaaass', *Pol·len d'Entrecuix*, 1: n.p.

—— 1978. 'Escenes de plaça', *Canigó*, 541: 35

—— 1983A. *Benzina* (Barcelona: Quaderns Crema)

—— 1983B. 'La literatura de l'exhauriment', *Els Marges*, 27/28/29: 269–78

—— 1983C. 'La literatura del reompliment (Narrativa postmoderna)', *Els Marges*, 27/28/29: 279–89

—— 1987. *Zzzzzzzz* (Barcelona: Quaderns Crema)

—— 1990. *La maleta turca* (Barcelona: Quaderns Crema)

—— 1991. *Hotel Intercontinental* (Barcelona: Quaderns Crema)

—— 1995. 'La blancaneu', *Avui*, 9 November, pp. viii–ix

—— 1999. *Vuitanta-sis contes* (Barcelona: Quaderns Crema)

—— 2000. *Tot és mentida* (Barcelona: Quaderns Crema)

—— 2001. *El millor dels mons* (Barcelona: Quaderns Crema)

—— 2002. 'La primera vez y dos retornos', *La Vanguardia Cultura/s*, 11 December, pp. 10

—— 2007A. 'Quim Monzó: Discurs Inaugural', *Institut Ramon Llull*, October 9, <http://www.frankfurt2007.cat/arxius/discursinaugural.pdf> [accessed 15 July 2020]

—— 2007B. *Mil cretins* (Barcelona: Quaderns Crema)

—— 2010A. *Gasoline*, translated by Mary Ann Newman (Rochester: Open Letter).

—— 2010B *Esplendor i glòria de la Internacional Papanates* (Barcelona: Quaderns Crema)

—— 2010C. 'Indignación y crema solar', *La Vanguardia*, 11 July, pp. 21

—— 2010D. '¿Por qué perder más tiempo?', *La Vanguardia*, 6 October, pp. 20

—— 2011A. *Guadalajara*, translated by Peter Bush (Rochester: Open Letter)

—— 2011B. 'He aquí la Spanish Revolution', *La Vanguardia*, 19 May, pp. 22

—— 2012. *A Thousand Morons*, translated by Peter Bush (Rochester: Open Letter)

—— (@quimmonzo). 2013a. Twitter post, 23 December, '@estefaldina @lafeadelbaile Et voilà!'

—— (@quimmonzo). 2013b. Twitter post, 11 February, '@Grassonet_Bord http://xvideos.com/tags/pissing'

—— (@quimmonzo). 2013c. Twitter post, 21 December, '@Rafadepaco ¡Muy bien! (¿Cómo te paso los 50 euros que te prometí si hacías ese tuit recomendándolo?)'

—— (@quimmonzo). 2016a. Twitter post, 24 March, 'Els contes infantils políticament correctes que demanen @GemmaLienas i @BCNenComu ja són aquí!'

—— 2016B. 'Els nous contes doctrinals', *La Vanguardia*, 29 March, pp. 22

—— (@quimmonzo). 2018a. Twitter post, 13 August, '"El silencio era atronador. Lloré muchas veces" Ada Colau, alcaldesa de Barcelona, relata cómo vivió las primeras horas y días después del atentado'

—— (@quimmonzo). 2018b. Twitter post, 14 August, 'I aquest altre somriure ¿qui l'hi va arrencar? El càmera? Quants motius per somriure en un moment tràgic...'

—— 2019. *Why, Why, Why?*, translated by Peter Bush (Rochester: Open Books)

—— 2020. 'Aquest món ja no és el meu', *La Vanguardia*, 23 May, p. 20

Monzó, Quim and Biel Mesquida. 1977. *Self-service* (Barcelona: Iniciativas Editoriales)

Monzó, Quim and Maria Roura. 1995. *Contes per a nens i nenes políticament correctes* (Barcelona: Quaderns Crema)

Montero, Rosa. 1995. 'The Silent Revolution: The Social and Cultural Advances of Women in Democratic Spain', in *Spanish Cultural Studies: An Introduction*, ed. by Helen Graham, and Jo Labanyi (Oxford: Oxford University Press), pp. 381–85

Montesinos, Pablo. 2011. 'González Pons llama a que "no se apague el espíritu del 15-M"', *LibertadDigital.com*, 19 May, <http://www.libertaddigital.com/nacional/2011–05–19/gonzalez-pons-llama-a-que-no-se-apague-el-espiritu-del-15-m-1276423921/> [accessed 20 July 2020]

Moran, Joe. 2000. *Star Authors: Literary Celebrity in America* (London: Pluto)

Moreno-Caballud, Luis. 2013. 'Desbordamientos culturales en torno al 15-M', *Teknocultura*, 10 (1): 101–30

Moret, Xavier. 1994. 'La productora de "El peor programa de la semana" estudia si demanda a TVE por la suspensión', *El País*, 2 March, <http://elpais.com/diario/1994/03/02/radiotv/762562828_850215.html> [accessed 20 July 2020]

——2004. 'Crítica y público, a favor', *El País Babelia*, 27 November, p. 8

MORGAN, CLAIRE. 1998. 'Liberty for Individuality', *The Good Society*, 8 (2): 37–43

MORIMURA, SUSUMU. 2007. 'The Libertarian View of Human Nature', *Hitotsubashi Journal of Law and Politics*, 35: 1–6

MUNIESA, BERNAT. 2006. 'La transició: la legitimació de la dictadura franquista', in *De l'esperança al desencís: La transició als Països Catalans*, ed. by Josep Fontana and others (Lleida: El Jonc), pp. 67–82

MUNTADA, LLUÍS. 2010. 'L'expansió de l'univers', *Els País Quadern*, 29 April, p. 5

MUR, GERARD E. 2018. 'Quim Monzó: "La llengua està sota mínims"', *Núvol: El digital de cultura*, 7 March, <https://www.nuvol.com/llibres/quim-monzo-la-llengua-esta-sota-minims-51376> [accessed 20 July 2020]

NADAL, MARTA. 1990. 'Quim Monzó: Contra la hipocresia de la falsa normalitat', *Serra d'Or*, 372: 11–15

NEAD, LYNDA. 1993. '"Above the Pulp-line". The Cultural Significance of Erotic Art', in *Dirty Looks: Women, Pornography, Power*, ed. by Pamela Church Gibson and Roma Gibson (London: BFI), pp. 144–55

NICOL, BRAN. 2009. *The Cambridge Introduction to Postmodern Fiction* (Cambridge: Cambridge University Press)

NIÑO, ANTONIO. 2012. *La americanización de España* (Madrid: Libros de la Catarata)

NOGUÉS, JOAN. 1998. 'Llengua, comunicació i postmodernitat en Quim Monzó', *Revue d'Études Catalanes*, 1: 35–46

NORDEN, BARBARA. 1990. 'Campaign against Pornography', *Feminist Review*, 35: 1–8

NOYES, DOROTHY. 2006. 'Waiting for Mr. Marshall: Spanish American Dreams', in *The Americanization of Europe: Culture, Diplomacy, and Anti-Americanism after 1945*, ed. by Alexander Stephan (New York: Berghahn), pp. 307–34

NOZICK, ROBERT. 1974. *Anarchy, State, and Utopia* (New York: Basic)

NÚÑEZ-SEIXAS, XOSÉ MANUEL. 2000. 'The Reawakening of Peripheral Nationalisms and the State of the Autonomous Communities', in *Spanish History Since 1808*, ed. by José Alvarez Junco, and Adrian Shubert (London: Arnold), pp. 315–30

ÑÍGUEZ BERNAL, ANTONIO. 1987. 'Las relaciones políticas, económicas y culturales entre España y los Estados Unidos en los siglos XIX y XX', *Quinto Centenario*, 12: 71–134

OLLÉ, MANEL. 1998. 'Quim Monzó, l'escriptor de més?', *Revue d'Études Catalanes*, 1: 47–55

——2007. 'Quim Monzó: ¿Hi ha tanta diferència entre l'Starbucks i el Guggenheim?', *L'Avenç*, 325: 18–25

OLLER, DOLORS. 1979. 'El somni i l'embriaguesa: les dues representacions de Quim Monzó', *Revista Quaderns Crema*, 1: 91–97

OM, ALBERT. 2013. 'El final', *Blogs.ccma.cat*, 27 December 27, <https://www.ccma.cat/tv3/el-convidat/> [accessed 20 July 2020]

OMMUNDSEN, WENCHE. 2007. 'From the Altar to the Market-Place and Back Again: Understanding Literary Celebrity', in *Stardom and Celebrity: A Reader*, ed. by Sean Redmon, and Sue Holmes (London: SAGE Publications), pp. 234–55

ORJA, JOAN. 1989. *Fahrenheit 212: Una aproximació a la literatura catalana recent* (Barcelona: La Magrana)

DE PALOL, MIQUEL. 2007. 'El tret per la culata', *Avui*, 30 October, p. 24

PALUMBO, GIUSEPPE. 2009. *Key Terms in Translation Studies* (London: Continuum)

PARTAL, VICENT. 2013. 'Amb aquells programes de ràdio molta gent va descobrir que es podia ser nacionalista sense ser carrincló, i que era possible ser culturalment brillant sense ser espanyolista', in *Vint i Ramon Barnils*, ed. by Laia Altarriba (Barcelona: Edicions DAU), pp. 146–55

——2018. *Nou homenatge a Catalunya* (Barcelona: Ara Llibres)

PASQUAL, JOSEP MARIA. 1994. 'La "megadisculpa"', *Avui*, 22 January, p. 12

PELLS, RICHARD. 1997. *Not like Us: How Europeans Have Loved, Hated, and Transformed American Culture since World War II* (New York: Basic)

Persones humanes. 1993. 'Monologue by Quim Monzó', Season 2, Episode 3, online video recording, TV3–Televisió de Catalunya, 23 September, <https://www.youtube.com/watch?v=kEB6cRT4RUc> [assessed 20 July 2020]

PICORNELL, MERCÈ. 2013. *Continuïtats i desviacions: Debats crítics sobre la cultura catalana en el vèrtex 1960/1970* (Palma: Lleonard Muntaner)

——2007. 'Trencavel, Ignasi Ubac i la (re)construcció de la literatura catalana', in *Textualisme i subversió: Formes i condicions de la narrativa experimental catalana (1970–1985)*, ed. by Margalida Pons (Barcelona: Abadia de Montserrat), pp. 81–126

PINEDA CACHERO, ANTONIO, AURORA LABIO BERNAL, and LORENA R. ROMERO DOMÍNGUEZ. 2009. 'Comunicación política, ideología y nuevas tecnologías en el contexto ibérico: Un estudio del diario *Libertad Digital*', Paper presented at 6º Congresso SOPCOM, 14–18 Abril, pp. 2966–80, <http://conferencias.ulusofona.pt/index.php/sopcom_iberico/sopcom_iberico09/paper/viewFile/232/203> [accessed 20 July 2020]

PIÑOL, ÀNGELS. 2018. '"El silencio era atronador: Lloré muchas veces"', *El País*, 12 August, <https://elpais.com/ccaa/2018/08/08/catalunya/1533746023_975641.html> [accessed 20 July 2020]

PIÑOL, ROSA MARIA. 2004. 'Un grupo de escritores dejará de participar en el día del Libro por su "banalización"', *La Vanguardia*, 8 May, p. 43

——2010A. 'Fiebre Monzó', *La Vanguardia*, 4 February, pp. 28–29

——2010B. 'Monzó revisa la llegada al poder del "imperio de la plastilina"', *La Vanguardia*, 4 March, p. 42

——1995. 'Caperucita, los tres cerditos y el "pc"', *La Vanguardia*, 3 November, pp. 47–48

PIQUER, EVA. 1995. 'Una paròdia de l'obsessió', *Avui*, 9 November, p. ix

——1998. 'Quim Monzó, periodista', *Revue d'Études Catalanes*, 1: 167–74

——2003. 'Quim Monzó: "El borreguisme cultural d'aquest país m'ha atribuït molts fills que no reconec"', *Avui Cultura*, 4 December, pp. i–iii

PLA, XAVIER. 2010. 'Frenar l'entusiasme', *Avui*, 1 April, pp. 12–13

PLADEVALL I ARUMÍ, ANTONI. 1990. 'Montserrat Roig: *El cant de la joventut.*' *Revista de Catalunya*, 42: 145–46

——1993. 'Narrativa', *Revista de Catalunya*, 73, pp. 119–23

Plats bruts. 2001. 'Tinc Talent', Season 5, Episode 3, May 14, online video recording, TV3–Televisió de Catalunya <https://www.youtube.com/watch?v=odO5chtxIi4> [accessed 20 July 2020]

PLEGUEZUELOS, RAFAEL R. 2009. 'Garner, James Finn (1960–)', in *Encyclopedia of American Popular Fiction*, ed. by Geoff Hamilton, and Brian Jones (New York: Facts on File), p. 130

POYNOR, RICK. 2006. *Designing Pornotopia: Travels in Visual Culture* (New York: Princeton Architectural Press)

PONS, AGUSTÍ. 2013. *Espriu, transparent* (Barcelona: Proa)

PONS, DAMIÀ. 2008. 'El maig francès del 68: Un altre episodi d'una dècada intensa', *Revista del Centre d'Estudis Jordi Pujol*, 6: 165–75

PONS, MARGALIDA. 2007. 'Formes i condicions de la narrativa experimental (1970–1985)', in *Textualisme i subversió: Formes i condicions de la narrativa experimental catalana (1970–1985)*, ed. by Margalida Pons (Barcelona: Abadia de Montserrat), pp. 7–79

——2011. 'El primer Monzó i l'*altre*: Lectures lineals i lectures tabulars', *Els Marges*, 95: 50–69

PRECIADO, BEATRIZ. 2010. *Pornotopía: Arquitectura y sexualidad en "Playboy" durante la guerra fría* (Barcelona: Anagrama)

Premi d'Honor de les Lletres Catalanes. 2018. 'Acte de lliurament del Premi d'Honor de les Lletres Catalanes 2018 a Quim Monzó', online video recording, TV3–Televisió de Catalunya, 9 June, <https://www.ccma.cat/tv3/alacarta/programa/premi-dhonor-de-les-lletres-catalanes-2018/video/5816069/> [accessed 20 July 2020]

PRESTON, PAUL. 1987. *The Triumph of Democracy in Spain* (London: Routledge)

PRIETO, JOAQUÍN. 1977. 'La bandera nacional ondeará en los actos del Partido Comunista de España', *El País*, 16 April, <http://elpais.com/diario/1977/04/16/espana/229989610_850215.html> [accessed 20 July 2020]

PSHENITSYN, SERGEI. 2011. 'Political Correctness in Translation: Cultural and Linguistic Problems', in *Translation and Interpretation in a Multilingual Context*, ed. by Thanomnuan O'Charoen, and Tongtip Poonlarp (Bangkok: Chulalongkorn University Printing House), pp. 242–55

Público. 2012. 'La RAE cree que con el lenguaje no sexista "no se podría hablar"', *Público*, 4 March, <http://www.publico.es/culturas/424807/la-rae-cree-que-con-el-lenguaje-no-sexista-no-se-podria-hablar> [accessed 15 July 2020]

PUJOL I COLL, JOSEP. 1989. 'Uf!', *El Punt*, 19 May, p. 24

PUJOLS, ADRIÀ. 2018. 'Quim Monzó, el gegant', *La Llança*, 13 March, <https://www.elnacional.cat/lallanca/ca/actualitat/quim-monzo-gegant_246600_102.html> [accessed 20 July 2020]

PUIGDEVALL, PONÇ. 1999. 'Crònica d'un temps difícil', *Presència*, 23–29 May, p. 30

—— 2003. 'Contra l'instit gregari', *El País Quadern*, 27 March, p. 4

—— 2008. 'Veus contemporànies', in *La literatura catalana després de Frankfurt*, ed. by Jordi Coca and others (Vilafranca del Penedès: Andana), pp. 99–107

El Punt Avui. 2011. 'Catalunya, vetada en el dret a l'autodeterminació a l'acampada de Barcelona.' *El Punt Avui*, 17 June, <http://www.elpuntavui.cat/politica/article/17-politica/425196-catalunya-vetada-en-el-dret-a-l-autodeterminacio-a-l-acampada-de-barcelona.html> [accessed 20 July 2020]

PUNTÍ, JORDI. 2010. 'La benzina de Monzó', *L'Avenç*, 354, p. 72

PYM, ANTHONY. 1998. *Method in Translation History* (Manchester: St Jerome)

QUIROGA, ALEJANDRO. 2009. 'Coyunturas críticas: La izquierda y la idea de España durante la Transición', *Historia del Presente*, 13: 21–40

RABELL, LLUÍS (@LluisRabell). 2018. Twitter post, 14 August, 'Això forma part de les grandeses i misèries de la condició humana, @Ciddavid: es pot escriure com els àngels... i, alhora, ser un perfecte canalla. La història està plena d'exemples que superen @QuimMonzo en ambdós pols de la contradicció'

RAGUÉ ARIAS, MARIA JOSÉ. 1971. *California Trip* (Barcelona: Kairós)

RAND, AYN. 1964. *The Virtue of Selfishness: A New Conception of Egoism* (New York: Penguin)

—— 2007. *Atlas Shrugged* (London: Penguin)

RECORD, JEFFREY. 2010. *Wanting War: Why the Bush Administration Invaded Iraq* (Washington, DC: Potomac Books)

REIXACH, JAUME. 1990. 'Monzó: com s'ho fa?', *El Punt*, 11 May, p. 24

RESINA, JOAN RAMON. 2011. 'A Spectre is Haunting Spain: The Spirit of the Land in the Wake of the Disaster', *Journal of Spanish Cultural Studies*, 2 (2), pp. 169–86

RIBAS, JOSÉ. 2007. *Los 70 a destajo: Ajoblanco y libertad* (Barcelona: RBA Libros)

RIBBANS, GEOFFREY. 2009. 'Introduction', in *Campos de Castilla*, by Antonio Machado (Madrid: Cátedra), pp. 11–98

RIERA, MIQUEL. 1994. 'Les obres de Quim Monzó van ser les més venudes en un Sant Jordi multitudinari', *El Punt*, 24 April, p. 20

—— 2007. 'Els explicaré un conte', *Presència*, 2–8 November, pp. 2–7

RIPOLL, JOSEP-MARIA. 2010. 'L'exposició i el catàleg Monzó: La magnitud de tot plegat i el perquè de la tragèdia', *Serra d'Or*, 605: 46–51

Ritzer, George, and Michael Ryan. 2010. 'Americanisation, McDonaldisation and Globalisation', in *Issues in Americanisation and Culture*, ed. by Neil Campbell, Jude Davies, and George McKay (Edinburgh: Edinburgh University Press), pp. 41–60

Robertson, David. 1993. *A Dictionary of Modern Politics* (London: Europa)

——2004. *The Routledge Dictionary of Politics* (London: Routledge)

Rockwell Jr., Llewellyn H. 2006. 'Introduction', in *For a New Liberty: The Libertarian Manifesto*, ed. by Murray N. Rothbard (Alabama: Ludwig von Misses Institute), pp. ix–xii

Rodgerson, Gillian, and Elizabeth Wilson. 1991. *Pornography and Feminism: The Case against Censorship* (London: Lawrence & Wishart)

Rodríguez, Oriol. 2012. 'Quim Monzó', *El Bloc dels 365*, 30 September, <https://elblocdels365.wordpress.com/2012/09/30/quim-monzo/> [accessed 20 July 2020]

Rodríguez Jiménez, Francisco J. 2010. 'Controversias de la Guerra Fría cultural: Una reflexión desde los American Studies, 1945–1975', *Revista Complutense de Historia de América*, 36: 79–102

Roeder, Katherine. 2008. 'Looking High and Low at Comic Art', *American Art*, 22 (1): 2–9

Roig, Montserrat. 1976. 'Salvador Espriu, vexat', *Arreu, setmanari d'informació general de Catalunya*, 4, 15–21 November, p. 25

Roig, Sebastià. 2001. 'Mons', *Diari de Girona*, 14 February, p. 2

Romero-Salvadó, Francisco J. 1999. *Twentieth-Century Spain: Politics and Society in Spain 1898–1998* (Basingtoke: Palgrave Macmillan)

Rothbard, Murray N. 2006 [1973]. *For a New Liberty: The Libertarian Manifesto* (Alabama: Ludwig von Misses Institute)

Rubert de Ventós, Xavier. 1983. 'Cultura i política', in *Reflexions crítiques sobre la cultura catalana*, ed. by Pierre Vilar, Joan Triadú, Josep Ferrater i Mora, Josep Maria Castellet, Joaquim Molas, Xavier Rupert de Ventós, Miquel Tarradell, Josep Termes, and Joan Fuster (Barcelona: Departament de Cultura de la Generalitat de Catalunya), pp. 157–57

——2002. 'La excepción americana', *La Vanguardia Cultura/s*, 11 December, p. 12

Said, Edward. 2002. 'The Public Role of Writers and Intellectuals', in *The Public Intellectual*, ed. by Helen Small (Oxford: Blackwell), pp. 19–39

Safont Plumed, Joan. 2020. 'Monzó en pausa i l'oportunitat de rellegir-lo', *La Llança*, 18 June, <https://www.elnacional.cat/lallanca/ca/profunditat/monzo-quim-plega-pausa-articulisme-rellegir_514296_102.html> [accessed 20 July 2020]

Salmon, Richard. 1997. 'Signs of Intimacy: The Literary Celebrity in the "Age of Interviewing"', *Victorian Literature and Culture*, 25 (1): 159–77

Sámano, José. 1994. 'TVE vetó anoche el programa de El Gran Wyoming por invitar al escritor que ridiculizó a la infanta Elena en TV3', *El País*, 16 February, <http://elpais.com/diario/1994/02/16/radiotv/761353201_850215.html> [accessed 20 July 2020]

San Agustín, Arturo. 1996. 'Quim Monzó: "Yo nunca he sido feliz"', *El Periódico de Catalunya*, 24 October, p. 7

Sarret, Josep. 2008. 'Quim Monzó: "Supermán sólo hay uno"', *Quimera 292*, March, pp. 36–42

Sauder, Andrea. 2009. 'Politically Correct Bedtime Stories', in *Encyclopedia of American Popular Fiction*, ed. by Geoff Hamilton, and Brian Jones (New York: Facts on File), pp. 273–74

Seidler, Victor J. 1989. *Rediscovering Masculinity: Reason, Language and Sexuality* (London: Routledge)

Serra, Montserrat. 2018. 'Quim Monzó: "L'estat espanyol està molt desesperat"', *Vilaweb*, 18 March, <https://www.vilaweb.cat/noticies/quim-monzo-lhumor-ens-ha-salvat/?f=rel> [accessed 20 July 2020]

SMETHURST, PAUL. 2000. *The Postmodern Chronotope* (Amsterdam: Rodopi)

SHILDRICK, MARGRIT, and JANET PRICE. 1999. 'Openings on the Body: A Critical Introduction', in *Feminist Theory and the Body: A Reader*, ed. by Janet Price and Margrit Shildrick (Edinburgh: Edinburgh University Press), pp. 1–14

SIMBOR, VICENT. 2005. *El realisme compromès en la narrativa catalana de postguerra* (Valencia: Abadia de Montserrat)

SLAYDEN, DAVID. 2010. 'Debbie Does Dallas Again and Again: Pornography, Technology, and Market Innovation', in *Porn.com: Making Sense of Online Pornography*, ed. by Feona Attwood (New York: Peter Lang), pp. 54–68

SMITH, ANTHONY D. 1991. *National Identity* (Nevada: University of Nevada Press)

SOLER, TONI. 2009. '¿Nuestro gran escritor mediático?', *La Vanguardia Cultura/s*, 9 December, p. 4

SOTO, ÁLVARO. 1998. *La transición a la democracia: España, 1975–1982* (Madrid: Alianza)

SOTO, FERNANDO. 1996. *Por el sendero de la izquierda* (Sevilla: Universidad de Sevilla)

STEPHAN, ALEXANDER. 2006. 'Cold War Alliances and the Emergence of Transatlantic Competition: An Introduction', in *The Americanization of Europe: Culture, Diplomacy, and Anti-Americanism after 1945*, ed. by Alexander Stephan (New York: Berghahn), pp. 1–20

SUBIRANA, JAUME. 2018. *Construir con palabras: Escritores, literatura e identidad en Cataluña (1859–2019)* (Madrid: Cátedra)

SULLÀ, ENRIC. 1977. 'L'udol del griso al caire de les clavegueres', *Els Marges*, 10, pp. 127–29

TAMAMES, RAMÓN. 2013. *Más que unas memorias* (Barcelona: RBA Libros)

THOMPSON, BILL. 1994. *Soft Core* (London: Cassell)

THORNHAM, SUE. 2000. *Feminist Theory and Cultural Studies: Stories of Unsettled Relations* (London: Arnold)

TORNÉ, GONZALO. 2012. 'Un mes en el que la CT enfermó', in *CT o la Cultura de la Transición: Crítica a 35 años de cultura española*, ed. by Guillem Martínez (Barcelona: Random House Mondadori), pp. 53–64

DE TORO, ALFONSO. 2018. 'Pluralidad de mundos y hoyos negros: Líneas y bandas infinitas o la superación del pensamiento binario en la obra de J. L. Borges', in *La paradoja como forma literaria de la innovación: Jorge Luis Borges entre la tradición judía y el hipertexto*, ed. by Corinna Deppner (Hildesheim: Georg Ols Verlag), pp. 31–70

DE TORO, SUSO. 2017. *La llicó catalana* (Barcelona: Gregal)

TURNER, GRAEME. 2004. *Understanding Celebrity* (London: SAGE)

TUSELL, JAVIER. 2007. *La transición a la democracia (España, 1975–1982)* (Madrid: Espasa Calpe)

——— 2011. *Spain: From Dictatorship to Democracy: 1939 to the Present* (Oxford: Blackwell)

TYMOCZKO MARIA. 2007. *Enlarging Translation, Empowering Translators* (Manchester: St. Jerome)

UCELAY-DA CAL, ENRIC. 2009. 'José Peirats, el autodidacta como intelectual orgánico', in *Josep Peirats Valls, De mi paso por la vida: Memorias*, ed. by Susana Tavera García and Gerard Pedret Otero (Barcelona: Flor del Viento), pp. 21–112

USALL, RAMON. 2006. 'L'esquerra independentista catalana i la Transició espanyola', in *De l'esperança al desencís: La transició als Països Catalans*, ed. by Josep Fontana and others (Lleida: El Jonc), pp. 163–93

RECORD, JEFFREY. 2010. *Wanting War: Why the Bush Administration Invaded Iraq* (Dulles: Potomac Books)

RUIZ SIERRA, JUAN. 2011. 'Zapatero, sobre las movilizaciones de jóvenes: "Hay que escucharles"', *El Periódico de Catalunya*, 16 May, <http://www.elperiodico.com/es/noticias/politica/zapatero-sobre-las-movilizaciones-jovenes-hay-que-escucharles-1008037> [accessed 20 July 2020]

TOWNSON, NIGEL. 2009. 'Introducción', in *España en cambio: El segundo franquismo, 1959–1975*, ed. by Nigel Townson (Madrid: Siglo XXI), pp. xi–xlvi

VAÏSSE, JUSTIN. 2010. *Neoconservatism: The Biography of a Movement* (Cambridge, MA: Harvard University Press)

VALLVERDÚ, FRANCESC. 1976. 'Una plaga que cal aïllar: el "terrorisme intel·lectual"', *Arreu, setmanari d'informació general de Catalunya*, 6, 29 November–5 December, pp. 34–35

VARGAS, MICHAEL. 2018. *Constructing Catalan Identity: Memory, Imagination, and the Medieval* (Basingstoke: Palgrave Macmillan)

VARSAVSKY, MARTIN. 2011. '"Spanish Revolution" of 2011 Explained', *HuffPost.com*, 25 May, <https://www.huffpost.com/entry/spanish-revolution-of-201_b_867156> [accessed 20 July 2020]

VIADEL, FRANCESC. 2009. *"No mos fareu catalans" Historia inacabada del blaverisme* (València: Publicacions de la Universitat de València)

VILA I DELCLÓS, ENRIC. 1999. 'Sant Jordi, Sant Jordi', *Avui*, 23 April, pp. xviii

—— 2003. 'La moderació ha portat la cultura catalana a l'agonia', *Avui*, 8 September, p. 56

VILAREGUT, RICARD. 2004. *Terra Lliure. La temptació armada a Catalunya* (Barcelona: Columna)

VILARÓS, TERESA M. 1998. *El mono del desencanto: Una crítica cultural de la transición española* (Madrid: Siglo XXI)

Vilaweb. 2004. 'Hèctor Bofill fa un apassionat i crític repàs sobre la literatura catalana recent', *Vilaweb.cat*, 22 November, <http://www.vilaweb.cat/noticia/923643/20041122/hector-bofill-apassionat-critic-repas-literatura-catalana-recent.html> [accessed 20 July 2020]

—— 2010. 'Monzó: "Amb el Tripartit va arribar la Internacional Papanates"', *Vilaweb.cat*, 4 March, <http://www.vilaweb.cat/noticia/3697669/20100304/monzo-tripartit-arribar-internacional-papanates.html> [accessed 20 July 2020]

—— 2018. '[VÍDEO] El discurs de Quim Monzó quan ha rebut el Premi d'Honor de les Lletres Catalanes', online video recording, *Vilaweb.cat*, 4 June, <https://www.vilaweb.cat/noticies/video-el-discurs-de-quim-monzo-en-rebre-el-premi-dhonor-de-les-lletres-catalanes/> [accessed 20 July 2020]

VILALLONGA, BORJA. 2017. 'La importància de tenir un Estat', *El Temps*, 25 April, p. 4

VILA-SANJUÁN, SERGIO. 2008. 'La americanización de la cultura española', *La Vanguardia Cultura/s*, 15 October, pp. 14–15

VINCENT, ANDREW. 2009. *Modern Political Ideologies* (Hoboken, NJ: Wiley-Blackwell)

VOLONTE, LLORENÇ. 1977. 'L'"obra" de "Quim Monzó"', *Canigó*, 5 February, 487: 2

WEIGEL, MOIRA. 2016. 'Political Correctness: How the Right Invented a Phantom Enemy', *The Guardian*, 30 November, <https://www.theguardian.com/us-news/2016/nov/30/political-correctness-how-the-right-invented-phantom-enemy-donald-trump> [accessed 15 July 2020]

WELLS, CARAGH. 2008. 'The Poetics of the "gest inútil" in Quim Monzó's *Benzina*', *Bulletin of Spanish Studies*, 85 (3): 307–24

WILSON, ELIZABETH. 2001. *The Contradictions of Culture: Cities, Culture, Women* (London: SAGE)

WILSON, JOHN K. 1995. *The Myth of Political Correctness: The Conservative Attack on Higher Education* (Durham: Duke University Press)

WOLFSON, ADAM. 2004. 'Conservatives and Neoconservatives', in *The Neocon Reader*, ed. by Irwin Stelzer (New York: Atlantic), pp. 215–31

YORK, LORRAINE. 2007. *Literary Celebrity in Canada* (Toronto: University of Toronto Press)

YSÀS I SOLANES, PERE. 1997. 'Introducció', in *La transició a Catalunya i Espanya*, ed. by Carme Molinero, and Pere Ysàs i Solanes (Barcelona: Fundació Doctor Lluís Vila D'Abadal), pp. 9–13

ZABALLA, BEL. 2013. 'Carme Junyent: "Que s'acabi aquesta comèdia de desdoblar en masculí i femení"', *Vilaweb*, 31 October 31, <http://www.vilaweb.cat/noticia/4153027/20131031/carme-junyent-sacabi-comedia-desdoblar-masculi-femeni.html> [accessed 15 July 2020]

ZAPATA, GUILLERMO. 2012. 'La CT como marco: un caso de éxito no CT: el 15-M. O de cómo puede suceder un éxito no previsto en una cultura, como la CT, que controla los accesos al éxito y al fracaso', in *CT o la Cultura de la Transición*, ed. by Guillem Martínez (Barcelona: Random House Mondadori), pp. 141–50

ZAPPAVIGNA, MICHELE. 2012. *Discourse of Twitter and Social Media* (London: Continuum)

ZIEGLER, HEIDE. 1987. *John Barth* (London: Routledge)

INDEX

❖

pornography 25, 126–32, 135, 138, 141–44
    pornographic utopia 128, 132–36
postmodernism 3, 11, 26, 82, 86, 88–89, 92, 112
Prat de la Riba, Enric 57
Preciado, Paul B. 136
Pueblo 77
Puigcorbé, Juanjo 169, 183
Puigdemont, Carles 180–82
Puigdevall, Ponç 17
Pujol, Adrià 21
Pujol, Jordi 7, 68–69, 71–73, 152, 161, 174
Puntí, Jordi 8, 20, 88–89, 94, 164

Quaderns Crema 21, 94, 96, 163
Queneau, Raymond 9
Quert Poiuy: Revista de Literatura 5, 32, 34

Rabasa, Rosa M. 34
Rabell, Lluís 181
Racionero, Luis 5, 31, 44
Ragué, María José 5, 31, 40, 44
Rajoy, Mariano 182
Rand, Ayn 25, 107, 109
rape 137, 139–41
    see also sexual violence
Reagan, Ronald 105, 123
realism 5, 32, 41, 88, 93–94
referendum of self-determination (1 October 2017)
    3–4, 79, 174, 180, 182–83
Régimen del 78: 24, 54–55, 58, 178
resistencialisme 4–5, 8, 13, 23, 29–52, 57, 90, 150, 155,
    158, 171–72
    oppositional cultural model 34, 46, 49–51, 72, 90
Riba, Carles 84
Ribas, Pepe 31, 33, 40–41, 44
right:
    far right 67, 182
    New Right 19, 95
Ripoll, Josep Maria 131
Robertson, David 105–06
Robin Hood 13, 18, 25, 107–12, 121
Rockwell, Llewellyn H. 105
Rodoreda, Mercè 2, 20, 147, 170 n. 1
Rodríguez Zapatero, José Luis 18, 25, 103, 113
Roig Montserrat 47, 49–51
Rojals, Marta 167, 183
Rothbard, Murray 110, 118
Roura, Maria 10, 24–25, 83, 94, 96–103
Royal Family (Spanish) 18, 161, 163, 173
Rubert de Ventós, Xavier 81
ruptura 58, 60, 66
    ruptura pactada 54, 68, 70, 77
Rushdie, Salman 168
Rusiñol, Santiago 84

Said, Edward 148

Salinger, J. D. 9, 83
Salmon, Richard 166
Sánchez, Almudena 115–17, 120
Sánchez Piñol, Albert 183
Sant Jordi's Day 11, 102, 147, 158–59, 169
Saura, Antonio 31
Seidler, Victor 129, 133, 140
self-determination 3, 77, 79–80, 178, 183
separatism 27, 66, 179–82
    see also independentism
    Catalan separatist leaders 23
    Catalan separatist movement 182–83
Serra, Màrius 14, 20, 167
Serrat, Joan Manuel 62, 74
sexuality 4, 19, 25, 126–27, 133, 136, 144, 157, 173
    free sexuality 5, 41
    men's sexuality 143–44
    sexual liberation 31, 127, 145
    sexual politics 19, 139
    women's sexuality 127, 141
sexual violence 19, 127–28, 137–41
Sió, Enric 57
Simó, Isabel-Clara 56, 60–61, 147
Solé i Tura, Jordi 57
Soler, Toni 165
Solidaridad Obrera 77
Spanish Constitution 6, 68, 77–79, 175–76, 182
    Spanish Constitutional Court 55, 174–76
Statute of Autonomy (Catalonia) 55, 61, 78–79, 174–75
Stephan, Alexander 29, 41
Suárez, Adolfo 47, 58, 60–61, 63, 68, 70, 72–73
Subirana, Jaume 23, 27 n. 3

Tamames, Ramon 58
Tàpies, Antoni 31, 46
Tarradellas, Josep 73
Tecstual 5, 32, 34
Teixidor, Emili 57
Tele/eXprés 5, 32, 51
Terribas, Mònica 22
textualisme 4–6, 32, 36, 45, 93–94
    experimentalism 6, 9, 24, 36, 45, 93–94
Thatcher, Margaret 104, 123
Tierno Galván, Enrique 71–72
Torné, Gonzalo 178
Trabal, Francesc 2, 10, 27 n. 2
Transition 6–9, 24, 27 n. 1, 41, 44–47, 49–80, 104, 173,
    175, 184
    consensus 9, 52, 54–56, 58, 60–61, 63, 68, 72–73, 77
    Cultura de la Transición 13, 54, 73, 172
translation 10, 24–25, 35, 82–88, 94–103, 106, 160, 172,
    179
transnational 4, 10, 19, 24, 35, 83, 88, 103, 105, 172,
    176
Treball 180
Tripartite (Catalan government) 18, 25, 103, 113, 174

www.ingramcontent.com/pod-product-compliance
Lightning Source LLC
Chambersburg PA
CBHW081417090426
42738CB00017B/3390